Harvard Studies in Comparative Literature
Founded by William Henry Schofield

24

THE SINGER OF TALES

THE SINGER
OF TALES

⇒Albert B. Lord⇐

SECOND EDITION

Stephen Mitchell and Gregory Nagy, Editors

HARVARD UNIVERSITY PRESS

Cambridge, Massachusetts   London, England

Second printing, 2001

Library of Congress Cataloging-in-Publication Data

Lord, Albert Bates.
The singer of tales / Albert B. Lord; Stephen Mitchell and
Gregory Nagy, editors—2nd ed.
    p. cm.
Previous ed.: Cambridge : Harvard University Press, 1960.
Includes bibliographical references and index.
ISBN 0-674-00283-0
1. Epic poetry—History and criticism. 2. Folk songs, Slavic—
History and criticism. 3. Poetry, Medieval—History and criticism.
4. Homer.   I. Mitchell, Stephen, 1943–   II. Nagy, Gregory. III. Title.

PN1303 .L62 2000
809.1'32—dc21   00-021247

CONTENTS

INTRODUCTION

TO THE SECOND EDITION

by Stephen Mitchell and Gregory Nagy

This new edition of *The Singer of Tales* marks the fortieth anniversary of the original publication of Albert B. Lord's book (1960). The words of Lord, as well as the original pagination, have been preserved unchanged. Important new features, however, have been added.

The first of these features involves the principal evidence that Lord had at his disposal, the audio recordings of South Slavic heroic songs made by his teacher, Milman Parry, in 1933–1935, and his own audio recordings, made in 1950–1951. This recorded treasury is housed in the Milman Parry Collection in Widener Library (Room C) at Harvard University. The editors of *The Singer of Tales* 2000, who are also the Curators of the Milman Parry Collection, are publishing all the recorded passages of heroic song—as well as the conversations—quoted at length by Lord in the ten chapters of his original 1960 book (pp. 17, 18, 26–27, 39–42, 46, 55, 58–63, 69–70, 72–77, 82–83, 109–110, 126, 286–288). This "audio publication" is featured in the compact disk (CD) that accompanies this new edition of *The Singer of Tales*.[1]

Second, the CD contains a unique video publication of what is referred to in Parry's fieldnotes (PN 12470) as a "kino" that, on August 10, 1935, recorded part of a song performance by the *guslar* (singer) Avdo Međedović, whom Parry and Lord valued as the most accomplished of all the South Slavic singers they encountered.[2]

Third, the CD contains selected photographs from the Collection, with Albert Lord's original typed captions; these photos were meant to accompany an essay Lord drafted in 1937 on their collecting project in the former Yugoslavia.[3]

---

1. Production of the accompanying CD was made possible by a generous grant from the Ilex Foundation. The editors also wish to thank Casey Dué, David Elmer, Thomas Jenkins, Matthew Kay, and especially Mary Louise Lord.

2. PN, "Parry Number," is used by The Milman Parry Collection of Oral Literature, Harvard University (hereafter abbreviated as MPCOL), to organize and archive the more than 12,500 texts Parry collected in the former Yugoslavia from 1933 to 1935. See Kay 1995 (new edition forthcoming), which contains complete contextual information (for example, dates, locations, singers, and type of record) about each of the epics in the collection.

3. This essay, "Across Montenegro Searching for Gusle Songs," was intended for a popular audience but was never published. The word *gusle* designates the string instrument of the *guslar* (see Chap. 2, p. 18, below).

Fourth, the CD contains facsimiles of Béla Bartók's handwritten transcriptions of selected songs quoted by Lord in *The Singer of Tales*.

Milman Parry had no preconceived plans for establishing one of the world's preeminent collections of oral tradition; that he did so was a by-product of his main purpose. By the early 1930s he was carefully planning, as he himself wrote, to set "lore against literature" in a rational and scientific analysis of the mechanisms and aesthetics of oral poetry.[4] For Parry, who was a Classics scholar by training, the backdrop for this project was the famous "Homeric Question": How had the poet or poets of the *Iliad* and the *Odyssey* composed those two great poems at the very beginning of European literary tradition? Before Parry, the competing theories about the genesis of Homeric poetry had been formulated primarily in terms of "unitarians" and "analysts," opponents and advocates of "Liedertheorie," and so on. Against this backdrop, Parry sought to immerse himself in the actual living oral traditions of epic songmaking, an idea that he developed in his days as a doctoral student in Paris (1925–1928).[5]

What distinguished Parry from most earlier Classicists who had posed the "Homeric Question" was not only his hypothesis that the *Iliad* and the *Odyssey* were originally the products of an oral tradition that was older than any written literature; it was also his formulation of a method for *testing* this hypothesis, a discovery procedure capable of moving the debate from the content of orally produced songs to the actual process through which such songs are produced in performance. Indeed, it is rare in humanistic endeavors to find instances in which the conception and execution of the work adhere so closely to the scientific method (observation of phenomena; hypothesis formulation; experimentation to test the hypothesis; and a conclusion that validates, or modifies, the hypothesis). This goal Parry and Lord pursued vigorously by examining a living tradition of oral poetry and learning how it worked. In Parry's own formulation, the overall problem is this:

> If we put lore against literature it follows that we should put oral poetry against written poetry, but the critics so far have rarely done this, chiefly because it happened that the same man rarely knew both kinds of poetry, and if he did he was rather looking for that in which they were alike. That is, the men who were likely to meet with the songs of an unlettered people were not ordinarily of the sort who could judge soundly how good or bad they were, while the men with a literary background who published oral poems wanted above all to show that they were good as literature. It was only the students of the "early" poems who were brought in touch at the same time with both lore and literature.[6]

---

4. From the 1935 typescript of Milman Parry's "The Singer of Tales" (on which more later) in the MPCOL, p. 3. The person closest to Parry in this project, Albert Lord, has on several occasions outlined its history—in greatest detail, for example, in his "General Introduction" to Parry |1954|:5–15, as well as in his retrospective and personal remarks, "The Legacy of Milman Parry," made at the centennial meeting of the American Folklore Society in Cambridge, Massachusetts, in 1988.

5. Antoine Meillet, with whom Parry associated closely in these years, had great influence on the young scholar's ideas. See Harry Levin's Preface to this volume.

6. Parry, "The Singer of Tales," MPCOL, p. 3. We see here the germ of a method that we associate today with the academic discipline of "ethnopoetics."

During his years in Paris (1925–1928), Parry had made contact with Matija Murko, who at that time was the most eminent ethnographer working on South Slavic (Serbo-Croatian) oral traditions in the former Yugoslavia.[7] Still, the South Slavic Balkans were not Parry's first choice for his scientific experiment. According to his student Albert Lord, Parry had hoped to conduct his project in the former Soviet Union (following up on ethnographic work that dated back to the late nineteenth century, especially Radloff's collection of Kara Kirghiz epics from Central Asia).[8] Political events in that part of the world made it difficult to obtain a visa, however, and Parry was in the end forced to look elsewhere. Once he had settled on the South Slavic area, he began to design a master plan for testing his hypotheses on the still-vibrant traditions of oral epic in the Balkans. Parry elegantly lays out his thoughts in his initial report on this work entitled "Project for a Study of Jugoslavian Popular Oral Poetry":[9]

My purpose in undertaking the study of this poetry was as follows. My Homeric studies[10] have from the beginning shown me that Homeric poetry, and indeed all early Greek poetry, is oral, and so can be properly understood, criticized, and edited only when we have a complete knowledge of the processes of oral poetry; this is also true for other early poetries such as Anglo-Saxon, French, or Norse, to the extent they are oral. This knowledge of the processes of an oral poetry can be had up to a certain point by the study of the character of a style, e.g., of the Homeric poems; but a full knowledge can be had only by the accumulation from a living poetry of a body of experimental texts sought after in accordance with a fixed plan to show, for example: (a) to what extent an oral poet who composes a new poem is dependent upon the traditional poetry as a whole for his phraseology, his scheme of composition, and the thought of his poem; (b) to what extent a poem, original or traditional, is stable in successive recitations of a given singer; (c) how a poem is changed in a given locality over a number of years; (d) how it is changed in the course of its travels from one region to another; (e) in what ways a given poem travels from one region to another, and the extent to which the poetry travels; (f) the different sources of the material from which a given heroic cycle is created; (g) the factors that determine the creation, growth, and decline of the heroic cycle; (h) the relation of the events of an historical cycle to the actual events; and so on and so on. I found the Jugoslavian poetry ideal for the collection of such experimental texts. In certain regions more open to occidental influences the poetry has been largely lost, e.g. in Dalmatia and in the northern regions about Belgrade and Zagreb; but in Hercegovina, Bosnia, Montenegro, southern Serbia, and particularly in the border region where the Serbo-Croatian dialects shade off into Bulgarian, the old ways of life and with it the poetry have been affected very little. [. . .] The greater number of older men do not read; the younger men have been taught the barest elements and read and write only by ear; there were no books sold in the three towns which I visited and few newspapers. The influence of the printed texts has been slight and sporadic, and it is easily recognized when there has been any.

---

7. See the bibliography on Murko provided by Lord in Chap. 1, pp. 280–281n1, and Chap. 3, p. 283n12, below.

8. See below at Chap. 2, p. 281n4, for a basic bibliography on Radloff; for the same on Žirmunskij see Chap. 2, p. 281n4 and Chap. 10, p. 296n1.

9. "Project for a Study of Jugoslavian Popular Oral Poetry" is one of three typewritten reports from Parry in the MPCOL detailing aspects of his project, as well as the budget issues connected with it.

10. Parry at this point lists his publications to date (see below at Chap. 1, p. 279nn3 and 4), along with references to reviews. The publications have been collected by his son, Adam Parry: see Parry 1971 in the Bibliography that immediately follows this Introduction; the reviews of Parry's work have been tracked and analyzed by Lamberterie 1997.

I was able to obtain in the few weeks of the summer a number of the sort of texts I sought, e.g. several recitations of the same poem by the same singer; recitation by a singer of a poem which he had just heard for the first time; recitations of the same poem from uncle and nephew; several recitations of the same poem from the same region and from neighboring regions; versions from uncontaminated traditions of certain of the more famous poems which have been printed in other versions over the period of a hundred years that the poetry has been noted; a poem composed immediately after the narration of an event; and so on. When I shall have enough suitable material of this sort I propose to make from [it] a book illustrating the process of traditional oral poetry. Such a book, I believe, will be indispensable to anyone who pretends to deal with any of the early literatures. [...] In my own field of Homeric study criticism can not go ahead until such a book is written; and I believe that this is more or less true of the other early literatures.[11]

As late as the mid-1930s, no one had collected songs of this sort in what might be regarded as a natural way, that is, without artificial breaks necessitated by the demands of the limited recording technology available. To this end, Parry commissioned Sound Specialties Company of Waterbury, Connecticut, to prepare a recording device for him consisting of two turntables connected by a toggle switch. The careful back-and-forth alternation of the turntables allowed the normal time limit of several minutes of recording on a twelve-inch disk to be expanded virtually infinitely. In an age when most fieldworkers—whether linguists, folklorists, anthropologists, or ethnomusicologists—employ various miniaturized recording devices, such as videocameras, a comment by Parry in one of his field reports is eye-opening: "I have already written to the purchasing agent at Harvard instructing him to order for me from the aluminum company *another half-ton of discs,* which will be approximately 3,000 discs" (emphasis added).[12] As awkward in design, although not in fidelity, as such a device may seem by contemporary standards, it quite remarkably allowed the singers Parry met to continue their songs as fit their designs as composers rather than the necessities of the sound-recording medium. Suddenly there was available something very close to epic in its natural environment with respect to such important facets of performance as length, rests, and the character of composition. Although it might be imagined that the equipment Parry and Lord were using was inferior, they took great care to procure the highest quality of materials. In annotating the detailed listings of his budget, for example, Parry notes that

... the sound apparatus which I am using, which was made by the Sound Specialties Company of Waterbury, Connecticut, was designed so that it obtained a plate voltage of 300 volts from a motor-generator operated by a six volt automobile battery. It was the designer's original plan to choke back the static of the motor-generator by means of condensers, but he by no means succeeded in doing so, and from the very beginning the noise from the motor-generator made its way into the loud-speaker and the cutting head. I was, however, able, by constant care of the condensers and the motor-generators and by a very particular use of the microphone, to obtain recordings free of motor disturbances. Of late, however, the motor disturbance had increased to such a point that it seemed altogether necessary, if we were to continue our recordings under conditions of sufficient freedom and were to obtain records of the highest quality, to make some

---

11. Parry, "Project for a Study of Jugoslavian Popular Oral Poetry," MPCOL, pp. 1–3.
12. Parry, "Report on Work in Jugoslavia, June 18–October 19 [1934]," MPCOL, p. 15.

radical change in the design of the apparatus. I accordingly took it to Zagreb, and consulted with the technician of the Bell Edison phonograph works in that place. The result was the elimination of the motor-generators, and the substitution of a 300 volt battery. I have now been working for some time with this new equipment, and I consider that while my previous discs were good, those which I am now making are even finer, and indeed are altogether as good a quality as can be obtained on aluminum.[13]

Although the equipment Parry used may have been cumbersome, that does not mean that it was inadequate to its important task, as those who listen to the accompanying CD will readily attest.

Following an initial study in the summer of 1933, Parry returned for a longer stay in the former Yugoslavia from June 1934 to September 1935. This time, he was assisted by Albert Lord, Nikola Vujnović (a *guslar* from Stolac, Hercegovina), Ibro Beča (also a *guslar* from Hercegovina), Hamdija Šaković and Ibrahim Hrustanović ("two young Moslems" who collected many of the women's songs), Ilija Kutuzov (a Russian émigré teaching in the gymnasium in Dubrovnik, who moved to Belgrade in September 1934), and a number of typists.[14] During their fifteen-month collecting trip, Parry and his team of assistants assembled more than 12,500 individual texts, mostly in written form, but also a great number through sound recordings on more than 3,500 individual twelve-inch aluminum disks.

The number of heroic songs (*junačke pjesme*), women's songs (*ženske pjesme*), conversations with singers, and instrumental pieces they recorded is itself quite astonishing, but the sheer magnitude of their work can sometimes mask more important elements of what they accomplished. In line with Parry's intention of not merely observing and recording oral tradition, he and his co-workers were rigorous about what they collected, as well as experimental in their approach to the materials. Indeed, Parry's notes and reports display great satisfaction with the materials he was encountering and recording, but it is from the draft of a text written in 1937 by Parry's assistant Albert Lord and intended for a popular audience that we form the liveliest impression of how events unfolded (the numbering of the figures cited here matches the photographs accompanying the essay; these are on the CD):

The best method of finding singers was to visit a Turkish coffee house, and make inquiries there. This is the center for the peasant on market day, and the scene of entertainment during the evening of the month of Ramazan. We found such a place on a side street, dropped in, and ordered coffee. Lying on the bench not far from us was a Turk smoking a cigarette in an antique silver "cigarluk" (cigarette holder). He was a tall, lean and impressive person (Fig. 27). At a break in our conversation he joined in. He knew of singers. The best, he said, was a certain Avdo Međedović, a peasant farmer who lived an hour away. How old is he? Sixty, sixty-five. Does he know how to read or write? *Ne zna, brate!* (No, brother!). And so we went for him and ordered coffee for our new friend, Began Ljuca Nikšić. Began was a find. The son of famous Captain Mehmed of Nikšić who had

---

13. Parry, "Report on Work in Yugoslavia, October 20, 1934–March 24, 1935," MPCOL, pp. 10–11.

14. Unquestionably, the most important figures among the assistants were Lord and Vujnović. It was Vujnović who transcribed the more than 3,500 phonograph recordings in Dubrovnik in 1934–1935 and the summer of 1937, and later at Harvard in 1938–1940.

led the Turks in the defense of that city, he had been chosen by King Nikola to be an adjutant in his court (Fig. 28). While we were waiting for Avdo to arrive Began told of his life.

Finally Avdo came (Fig. 29), and he sang for us old Salih's favorite of the taking of Bagdad in the days of Sultan Selim. We listened with increasing interest to this short homely farmer, whose throat was disfigured by a large goiter. He sat cross-legged on the bench, sawing the *gusle,* swaying in rhythm with the music. He sang very fast, sometimes deserting the melody, and while the bow went lightly back and forth over the string, he recited the verses at top speed. A crowd gathered. A card game, played by some of the modern young men of the town, noisily kept on, but was finally broken up.

The next few days were a revelation. Avdo's songs were longer and finer than any we had heard before. He could prolong one for days, and some of them reached fifteen or sixteen thousand lines. Other singers came, but none could equal Avdo, our Yugoslav Homer.[15]

The expression "our Yugoslav Homer" is telling: it encapsulates the Parry-Lord "theory," which has become the germ of an ongoing academic debate among Classicists concerning the definition of *their* Homer. Even in its ethnography, *The Singer of Tales* reveals its Classical roots: Lord's Foreword begins, "This book is about Homer. He is our Singer of Tales." At the end of his first paragraph, Avdo becomes the Yugoslav Homer: "He is our present-day Balkan Singer of Tales." What makes Avdo special is his Homeric aura, and the influence of Classicism is palpable.[16]

Further, the expression "our Yugoslav Homer" is relevant to the ongoing political debates and ideological struggles in the Balkans, despite the fact that both Parry and Lord studiously avoided politics or ideology in their ethnographic work. To understand this relevance, we may start with a political formulation by a Balkanist concerning the South Slavic oral traditions: "Both Muslims and Christians sing in the same language and according to the same metrical constraints, and they utilize the same formulaic and thematic material. The differences between them are in the ethnic identity of hero and villain and in the length of the songs."[17] It is important to add that the official designation of Muslim (regularly spelled Moslem by Parry and Lord) was initiated by the former Yugoslav government only in 1971.[18]

In the case of the Christian traditions of oral poetry, a preeminent figure is the Serbian ethnographer and cultural leader Vuk Stefanović Karadžić (1787–1864), who published a canonical four-volume collection, *Srpske narodne pjesme* (Serbian folksongs), that highlights the so-called Kosovo songs. The political significance of this publication may be conventionally formulated as follows:

Serbian Christian songs are seen by Serbs as a unique expression of Serbian national identity. This is especially true for Kosovo songs. These songs related events and emotions surrounding the Battle of Kosovo in 1389, which the Serbs lost to the Turks. According to the song texts, the Serbian Prince Lazar was offered a choice between victory on earth and loss on

---

15. Lord, "Across Montenegro Searching for Gusle Songs" (typewritten manuscript, March 1937), MPCOL.

16. Compare Hainsworth 1991 on Classical models of "epic."

17. Alexander 1998:274, with reference to Coote 1978.

18. Alexander 1998:273.

earth coupled with victory in heaven. The Serbian defeat is therefore glorified in these songs, and in the Serbian consciousness, as a moral victory.[19]

Another preeminent figure in the publication of Serbian oral traditions was Petar Petrović Njegoš (1813–1851). He, too, along with Vuk, is key to the formation of Serbian Christian national identity.[20]

In the case of the Muslim traditions of oral poetry, Lord himself observes evenhandedly in *The Singer of Tales:* "In Sarajevo, too, the Moslems were busy reproducing songs from the *Matica Hrvatska* collection and from [Kosta] Hörmann. Most of this activity has taken place since the turn of the century, particularly since 1918."[21] Lord's point about the Muslim oral traditions, however, is that they were relatively less influenced by the printed text of canonical publications than were the corresponding Christian traditions. Lord's main point remains that Parry concentrated on collecting songs from the Muslim tradition for precisely that reason. Like Parry, Lord makes no value judgment about the actual content of conflicting Christian and Muslim world-views or ideologies.[22] Rather, he is following Parry in developing scientific approaches to studying the effects of the printed word on oral traditions. For Parry and Lord, empirical evidence showed that the ideology of the printed word destabilized the oral traditions of the various South Slavic cultures that they were analyzing. When Lord speaks of this destabilization as a "disease" that afflicts oral tradition, he is referring to the ideology of the printed word, not to the printed word itself: "There are very few younger singers, particularly among the Christian population, who have not been infected by this disease. This is somewhat less true among the Moslems, because none of their collections has been given the almost sacred authority of Vuk's or Njegoš's." Commenting on later historical developments, this time in the Communist era of Yugoslavia, Lord observes: "Common fare in all school books have been the songs from Vuk's collection or, to a lesser extent, from Njegoš's work. School teachers played a large role in collecting and they and the younger generation have been the chief purveyors of the songs in their printed forms."[23]

---

19. Alexander 1998:274. See further Reðep 1991.

20. It is a Serbian convention to refer to Vuk Karadžić simply as Vuk: see Alexander 1998:277.

21. See below at Chap. 6, p. 291n32, where Lord explains that volumes III and IV of the Croatian *Matica* (edited by Luka Marjanović), published in 1898 and 1899, respectively, contain Muslim songs from northwest Bosnia; as Lord mentions, the collection by Kosta Hörmann of Muslim material from Bosnia and Hercegovina was first published in 1888 and 1889. Lord is here drawing attention to the new ideological frame of the Sarajevo second edition of 1933. Note too the important observations of Lord pp. 136–137 (and p. 290n13) on the Franciscan monk Andrija Kačić-Miošić (1704–1760) and the publication of his *Razgovor ugodni naroda slovinskoga* (first edition 1756). See also his remarks at p. 136 on the inclusion of some of the songs from the *Razgovor* in Johann Gottfried Herder's *Stimmen der Völker in Liedern* (Leipzig, 1778–1779). On the "romanticism" of Herder and his contemporaries, see in general Bausinger 1980.

22. The rubric Christian has to be subdivided further from the historical perspective of cultural and political antagonisms between Orthodox and Roman Catholic points of view, which shape respectively the various Serbian and Croatian models of ethnic and national identity.

23. See below at pp. 136–137.

In addition to the question of the influence of print culture on the actual form of a given oral tradition, Parry and Lord systematically and evenhandedly studied the more general question of the influence of ideology on the actual content of the oral traditions of Christian as well as Muslim communities in the Balkans. A salient case in point is their comparison of the Kosovo songs of the Christian Serbs with the corresponding Kosovo songs of the Muslim communities, including the versions sung in Albanian.[24]

In light of this historical background, we can better appreciate the perspective of Balkan specialists concerning the Parry-Lord approach to the South Slavic oral tradition:

> The perceived dichotomy between the work of Vuk and the Parry-Lord enterprise is due more to the reception of the work of each (both in the West and in the former Yugoslavia) than to the material itself. The songs collected by Vuk are viewed almost as literary, inviolate texts, certainly as part of a canon; they also are inextricably connected with the question of Serbian identity. The songs collected by Parry and Lord are viewed as the raw field data on which a theory was constructed, and some scholars (significantly, those lacking a knowledge of the original language) criticize the songs as falling short of the aesthetic standards associated with Western epic.[25]

Such criticism has proved to be a persistent obstacle to the Parry-Lord legacy. Moreover, it is actually an understatement to say that some Western scholars criticize the aesthetic standards of South Slavic oral songmaking traditions merely because they do not know the language. Much of this kind of criticism, as Lord documents in his later books, has also been shaped by an overall ignorance of the historical facts concerning literacy and its cultural implications in the Balkans.[26] Besides this additional obstacle, there is yet another, closely related one: many scholars romanticize literacy itself as if it were some kind of uniform and even universal phenomenon—exempt from the historical contingencies of cultural and even cognitive variations.[27] Such romanticism, combined with an ignorance of the ideological implications of literacy in the South Slavic world, has led to a variety of deadly prejudices against any and all kinds of oral traditions.[28] In some cases, these prejudices have gone hand in hand with a resolute blindness to the potential ideological agenda of literacy in its historical contexts. From the very beginning of their work on the South Slavic oral traditions, Parry and Lord had to contend with such obstacles.

---

24. See especially Lord 1984; also Lord 1991:108–109 and n. 12. Cf. Lord, Chap. 1, p. 10, below.

25. Alexander 1998:277. For an overview of ethnographic work on the South Slavic oral traditions before Parry and Lord, see Koljević 1980. This book, published by Oxford University Press, has been promoted by some Oxford scholars as an alternative to, or even a replacement for, Lord's *Singer of Tales*. As Koljević's introduction makes clear, however, his book is not about the ethnographic evidence and its theoretical ramifications, but about the history of the ethnography itself (pp. 7–8).

26. See Lord 1991 and 1995.

27. Conversely, others have romanticized oral tradition itself as if it, too, were some kind of universal phenomenon in and of itself: for further discussion, see Lord at pp. 8 and 136 below. See also in general Bausinger 1980.

28. Lord's 1995 book (especially chap. 8) confronts many of these prejudices.

After the unforeseen death of Milman Parry on December 5, 1935, soon after his return to the United States, the project of continuing his work suddenly fell on the shoulders of the young Albert Lord. Lord confronted his teacher's unfinished research agenda by conscientiously following through on Parry's own evolving priorities.[29]

As we have seen, one salient fact that had increasingly engaged the attention of Parry was that the most accomplished singing in the former Yugoslavia seemed to come mainly from the Muslim areas, and even there, some of the best singers— such as Salih Ugljanin—were bilingual speakers of Albanian and "Bosnian" (the term used by Parry's informants to designate their dialect of the language spoken throughout Croatia, Bosnia-Hercegovina, and Serbia). As Parry writes in his unpublished notes, "In Novi Pazar I found a Moslem who had been raised in the area of Southern Serbia which is largely bilingual, who could sing the same song either in Serbian or Albanian, and accordingly I hope to obtain some definite evidence on the passage of songs between peoples of different languages."[30]

In 1937, when Lord was a Junior Fellow in Harvard's Society of Fellows, he finally had the chance to return to the Balkans and pursue the implications of this seminal observation by Parry. He traveled through northern Albania and collected a corpus of recorded songs now housed in the Milman Parry Collection along with their South Slavic counterparts.[31] Then, on several occasions after the Second World War, he went back to Yugoslavia and made numerous further recordings there, supplementing Parry's original recordings from the 1930s. It was especially during his work there in 1950 and 1951 that Lord most successfully fulfilled Parry's overall research design. Despite the upheaval and disruption created by the war, Lord was able in a number of cases to return to the same areas of Yugoslavia that Parry's expedition had visited in the 1930s and even to record some of the same singers, including Avdo Međedović.[32]

In all his accomplishments during those years, Lord was following a blueprint implied by the book (also titled "The Singer of Tales") begun by Parry in 1935, only to be interrupted by his untimely death.[33] In an article published in 1948,

---

29. He outlines these priorities in an early article, Lord 1948 (see pp. 40–44); reprinted in Parry 1971:465–478 (see pp. 473–478).

30. Milman Parry, "Report on Work in Jugoslavia, June 18–October 19," MPCOL, p. 4. On the vital topic of bilingualism in Albanian and Serbo-Croatian oral traditions, the work of Parry and Lord has been continued by John Kolsti in his 1990 book, *The Bilingual Singer: A Study in Albanian and Serbo-Croatian Oral Epic Traditions.*

31. See Lord 1948, p. 43: "While in Dubrovnik in the summer of 1937 I had an opportunity to study Albanian and in September and October of that year I travelled through the mountains of northern Albania. [. . .] I collected about one hundred narrative songs, many of them short, but a few between five hundred and a thousand lines in length. We found out that there are some songs common to both Serbo-Croatian and Albanian tradition and that a number of the Moslem heroes of the Yugoslav poetry, such as Mujo and Halil Hrnjica and Đerđelez Alija, are found also in Albanian."

32. See Lord, Chap. 4, p. 94, below.

33. See Lord's description of this book at Chap. 1, p. 279n1.

Lord reprinted the seven typewritten pages that Parry had finished.[34] In 1949, Lord submitted his own "Singer of Tales" as a Ph.D. thesis for the Department of Comparative Literature at Harvard. The Foreword to his 1960 book sets the historical context for the evolution of that 1949 thesis into the finished book. In his Preface to this book, Harry Levin gives further context, especially in terms of three of the four Harvard departments that were to become integral parts of Lord's academic life: Classics, Slavic, and Comparative Literature (the fourth, Folklore, took shape later, in 1967). Meanwhile, beyond the 1948 article, Lord was systematically following through on further projects initiated by Parry.[35]

With the publication of *The Singer of Tales* in 1960, Lord's continuation of Parry's unfinished projects reached a milestone. *Singer* covers most of the agenda envisioned by Parry when he undertook to write his own "Singer." Meanwhile, the organization of what became the Milman Parry Collection at Harvard University in 1936 had in effect institutionalized Parry's legacy.[36] This legacy, it is important to note, represents the combined efforts of Parry and Lord, despite Lord's consistent self-effacement. The Parry-Lord legacy is self-evident in Lord's *The Singer of Tales*.

The clear picture of an integral Parry-Lord legacy became somewhat clouded with the publication, in 1971, of the writings of Milman Parry as collected by his son, Adam Parry, under the title *The Making of Homeric Verse*.[37] In his fifty-three-page Introduction to his father's collected writings, the son questions the links that connect the work of Parry and Lord. Lord's *The Singer of Tales* is pictured as something quite different from the book that Milman Parry had intended.[38] Adam Parry tends to detach his father's work from Lord's and to attach it instead to the work of Classicists who resist the comparison of South Slavic traditions with Homer.[39] According to Adam Parry, "not the slightest proof has yet appeared that the texts of the *Iliad* and *Odyssey* as we have them, or any substantial connected portion of these texts, were composed by oral improvisation of the kind observed and described by Parry and Lord and others in Jugoslavia and elsewhere."[40] He finds it "quite conceivable" that "Homer made use of writing to compose a poem in a style which had been developed by an oral tradition."

---

34. Lord 1948:37–40.

35. For a basic bibliography on Lord's work in these early years of his career, see below: Chap. 1, p. 279n2; Chap. 3, p. 284nn17 and 18; Chap. 4, p. 284n1; Chap. 7, p. 293nn4–6.

36. There is an informal accounting in Lord's unpublished 1988 essay, "The Legacy of Milman Parry." In 1936, following Parry's death and the subsequent donation to the university by Parry's widow, Mrs. Marion Parry, of his recordings, books, papers, and other materials, a faculty committee was formed to oversee the care and use of what became The Milman Parry Collection of Oral Literature.

37. Parry [1971]; hereafter abbreviated as *MHV*.

38. See Adam Parry in *MHV*, pp. xxxvii (n. 3), xlii (n. 1), xliii (n. 1), and xlviii. On Milman Parry's unfinished "Singer of Tales," see the comments of Adam Parry, *MHV* pp. xxxix, xli.

39. Adam Parry, *MHV*, p. xxxviii, citing (Adam) Parry 1966 and Kirk 1962.

40. Adam Parry, *MHV*, p. lxi, n. 1. On the dangers of using the word "improvisation" in reference to oral traditions, see Lord 1991:76–77.

Lord's subsequent work, especially his books of 1991 and 1995, has countered such claims by way of comparative research. As he announced already in his Foreword to *Singer* 1960, Lord's methodology is fundamentally comparative: "This book is about Homer. He is our Singer of tales. Yet, in a larger sense, he represents all singers of tales from time immemorial and unrecorded to the present." Lord's phrasing, "in a larger sense," refers to the comparative evidence, for the study of which he deploys comparative methodology.

The integral legacy of Parry and Lord emerges most clearly if we look more closely at their comparative methods, which typify the academic discipline of Comparative Literature.[41] This point is driven home by Harry Levin's Preface. Lord, during his years as a professor at Harvard University, was in fact an active member of the Comparative Literature Department as well as the Departments of Classics and Slavic Languages and Literatures. His thesis, as we have seen, was produced under the aegis of the Comparative Literature Department, and *The Singer of Tales* was originally published as volume 24 (1960) of that department's monograph series, Harvard Studies in Comparative Literature. Lord's methodology, like Parry's, is fundamentally comparative in nature. *The Singer of Tales* is a premier example.

The comparative methods of Parry and Lord are closely connected to the *méthode comparative* of historical linguistics, especially as exemplified by Antoine Meillet.[42] In the collected writings of Milman Parry, we can see explicit references to the decisive influence of Meillet. The most telling instance can be found in Parry's "Ćor Huso: A Study of Southslavic Song," an unfinished work dating from his final years, 1933 to 1935.[43] In his preliminary notes for the planned foreword to that work, Parry explicitly recognizes the importance of the living South Slavic oral traditions as a central comparandum for the study of Homer, and he attributes to Meillet the impetus for this recognition.[44] On the other hand, in his Introduction to his father's work, Adam Parry discounts the influence of Meillet.[45] Indeed, as we have seen, he generally discounts the comparative aspects of Milman Parry's methodology. By contrast, Lord's *The Singer of Tales* continues and extends Parry's comparative approaches, and his later books (Lord 1991 and 1995) extend

---

41. On this discipline, see Guillén 1993, especially pp. 173–179, with reference to Parry and Lord.

42. A fundamental work on the comparative method is Meillet 1925.

43. Fragments of this work of Milman Parry's have been published by Adam Parry in *MHV,* pp. 437–464, who describes these fragments as "extracts" (*MHV,* p. xxxix). Mary Louise Lord is planning a full edition of Milman Parry's "Ćor Huso," which will be published by MPCOL.

44. Milman Parry, *MHV,* p. 439. See also his remarks in *MHV,* pp. 8–9, 20–21, 244, and 326n3. Parry (*MHV,* p. 439) acknowledges that it was Meillet who introduced him to the works of Matija Murko (on whom see again Lord, Chap. 1, pp. 280–281n1, and Chap. 3, p. 283n12, below).

45. See especially *MHV,* p. xxiii. For extensive documentation of the undervaluing of Meillet's methodology in Adam Parry's Introduction, see Lamberterie 1997 (especially p. 15), whose work vindicates Levin's observation on Parry and Meillet in the Preface.

these approaches even further. In sum, the Parry legacy is in fact the Parry-Lord legacy not only in Classics and Slavic but also in Comparative Literature.

Since the publication of *The Singer of Tales* in 1960, the Parry-Lord legacy has extended well beyond the disciplines of Classics, Slavic Studies, and even Comparative Literature. The book has become relevant to the study of a wide variety of literatures for their own sake—written as well as "oral." Part II of *Singer* ("The Application"), for example, makes specific reference to the ancient Greek epic tradition and the medieval traditions in Old English, Old French, and so on.

The engagement of medievalists in the applications of the Parry-Lord approach is particularly fraught with controversy. The Parry-Lord demonstration of a popular or "democratic" aesthetic in oral traditions has met with some measure of hostility toward the extension of that model to medieval Europe, where it suggests the possibility of literature outside the domination of the church and court hierarchies, with their strangleholds on the presumed sine qua non for authorship, namely, literacy.[46] Nevertheless, the ongoing debates between these points of view have considerably expanded our understanding of the interplay that often existed between the vernacular oral traditions and the Latin and Latinate literatures of the élite.[47] In response to the vast variety of debates concerning the medieval applications of *The Singer of Tales,* Lord follows up with a spirited survey in *The Singer Resumes* (1995), notably in chapter 8 of that book. Of particular interest are his references to the work of Daniel Donoghue (1987), John Miles Foley (1985), Joseph Harris (1983), Lars Lönnroth (1971), Stephen Mitchell (1987), Jeff Opland (1980), Alain Renoir (1988), and Fred C. Robinson (1985).[48]

The exponential growth of comparative studies in oral "literature" and its relationship to written literature is conveyed in Lord's 1986 survey, "Perspectives on Recent Work," published in the influential journal *Oral Tradition.*[49] In this article, Lord singles out a wide variety of scholars who work in these fields: Karl Reichl (1985) on Central Asian epics, especially Uzbek; John D. Smith (1981) on the Pabuji epic of western India;[50] Joseph F. Nagy (1985) on medieval Irish traditions;[51] Daniel P. Biebuyck (1969), John William Johnson (1985), and Gordon Innes (1974) on "epic" in Africa;[52] James T. Monroe (1972) and Michael Zwettler (1978) on early Arabic traditions;[53] Leonard Muellner (1976), Gregory Nagy

---

46. See especially Lord 1986a.

47. On this important point, see, for example, Ziolkowski 1991. For a discussion of the debate among medievalists in northern Europe, see Mitchell 1991:1–6 et passim.

48. In other chapters of Lord 1995, he also surveys applications in other areas. Especially noteworthy is his discussion, in chap. 2, of oral lyric poetry, with specific reference to a comparison of Serbo-Croatian women's songs with Latvian *dainas* (on which see also Vikis-Freibergs 1984).

49. Lord 1986b. For further bibliography on theories and applications connected with the work of Parry and Lord, see Foley 1985; also Haymes 1973.

50. See also Blackburn 1989.

51. See also MacCana 1980.

52. See also Okpewho 1979; also Opland 1988 and 1989.

53. See also Slymovics 1987 and Reynolds 1995 on latter-day Arabic oral "epic."

(1979), and Richard Janko (1980) on ancient Greek epic;[54] Donald K. Fry (1967), Robert Creed (1982), John M. Foley (1981), John Niles (1983), and Alain Renoir (1981) on Old English epic and lyric;[55] Lars Lönnroth (1976), Peter Buchholz (1980), and Jesse Byock (1982) on Old Norse poetics;[56] Joseph Duggan (1981) on Old French *chansons de geste;* Ruth Webber on the Spanish ballad (1951);[57] Olga M. Davidson (1985) on classical Persian epic;[58] and Ching-Hsien Wang on Chinese lyric (1974).[59]

The Singer of Tales has not only become a classic for the general study of oral and written literatures but has also evolved into a standard textbook within folkloristics. In addition to his tight focus on discovering the process by which oral tradition is composed, Parry was intensely aware, as his reports make clear, of the important ethnological and folkloristic dimensions of his project (for example, the supernatural, belief systems, and so on).[60] Already in Parry's early writings we can sense the respect for, and the curiosity about, *both* the mechanism *and* the matter of oral traditional literature, and this unified, synergistic view of folklore is fully elaborated in Lord's continuation of Parry's work. The intellectual ramifications of this point, together with the fact that Parry and Lord were assiduous fieldworkers, are significant, even if they are occasionally lost on critics within the "literature versus anthropology" debate of American folklore studies who assume that Parry and Lord are "mere" literary scholars.[61]

---

54. See also Nagler 1974; Martin 1984 and 1989; Hainsworth 1991.

55. See also, for example, Krishna 1982 on Middle English traditions.

56. See also Mitchell 1991 and 1997.

57. See also Webber 1986 on Spanish epic.

58. Lord also cites Davidson 1988, then forthcoming (cf. Davidson 2000); now see also Skjærvø 1994 and 1998.

59. Lord's death in 1991 preceded the publication of important works-in-progress prominently mentioned by him in other similar contexts, including those of Margaret Beissinger (1991), David Bynum (1993), Matthew Kay (1995), and Susan Niditch (1996).

60. Parry, "Project for a Study of Jugoslavian Popular Oral Poetry," MPCOL, p. 6.

61. Zumwalt 1988:110–111 notes that it was Albert Lord, who in her dichotomy is conceived of solely as a literary scholar, who objected at the Midcentury International Folklore Congress held at Indiana University from July 21 to August 4, 1950, to interpretations and approaches that decontextualize texts and leave the folk out of folklore—yet surely Lord, who had already at that point spent a number of years collecting materials in the Balkans, had at least as much practical fieldwork experience as most of those approaching folklore from a more directly anthropological perspective. To the idea that one should focus on a search for archetypes, Lord objected, "I wonder whether it is possible to arrive at any archetype of a tale or a song or an epic, if we consider that in every performance of an art form in oral tradition, whether it be a tale or an epic, the individual singer introduces variations" (Thompson 1953:275). Lord presented a plenary paper at the Fourth Symposium (pp. 305–310), but it is perhaps especially in his remarks as a participant in the recorded sessions (pp. 13, 28, 62–63, 96, 103, 116, 137, 140, 169–170, 296, 313, 316, in addition to 275) that one sees his sophisticated sense of both ethnographic fieldwork and the folk who are the object of that work: "Everything in the poem belongs to the group, but the poem itself and the formula in which it happens in a particular performance is the singer's. Every item is the tradition. But when a great singer is sitting in front of an audience, his music, the expression of his face, and his particular version of the poem at the time is his" (p. 316).

Harvard University's long history of engagement with the study of folklore, exemplified by the fact that the American Folklore Society itself was founded at a meeting in Harvard's University Hall early in 1888,[62] provided a deeply supportive atmosphere for the kind of work *The Singer of Tales* represents, even in its first formulation as Lord's Ph.D. dissertation. The submission of this first version of *Singer* was itself a revolutionary event: "His thesis defense, which was a defense in the real sense of a new and controversial thesis, called on all of Lord's expertise and powers of persuasion, and many of the committee members— Maurice Bowra, John Finley, Roman Jakobson, Harry Levin, Francis Magoun, and Renato Poggioli—left the room with their points of view changed."[63] The completion and acceptance of Lord's dissertation, and his subsequent appointment to the faculty at Harvard, were to have a profound influence on folklore studies in the United States.

Indeed, according to a man who was considered the dean of American folklore studies during his lifetime, there exists a direct line of development from Parry and Lord's 1933–1935 expedition in Yugoslavia through *The Singer of Tales* to the formation of the first undergraduate major in folklore and mythology in the United States. Commenting on the founding of Harvard's Committee on Degrees in Folklore and Mythology in 1967, Richard Dorson notes: "The folklore program at Harvard University, making available the first undergraduate major in folklore and mythology in the United States, developed from the strong research interests in the Yugoslav oral epic of the Slavic department's Albert Lord. His well-known book, *The Singer of Tales,* followed the guidelines of Lord's colleague in classics, Milman Parry, who conceived the idea of illuminating the Homeric epics through the study of living folk epics."[64]

The publication in 1960 of *The Singer of Tales* coincided with an important cultural moment in Western folklore scholarship. In the immediately preceding years, such vital and durable landmarks in the field as the English translation of Vladimir Propp's *Morphology of the Folktale* (1958) and Richard Dorson's *American Folklore* (1959) appeared. Although these seminal folklore studies approach the topic from different formulations of the issues facing folkloristics, scholars were suddenly presented with multiple opportunities to revisit well-worked problems and see them from fresh new angles. Like these two earlier works, Lord's *The Singer of Tales* was adopted for use in a variety of introductory and

---

62. The American Folklore Society was organized in Cambridge, Mass., on January 4, 1888, and those present included Harvard professor Francis James Child (the society's first president), George Lyman Kittredge, recently appointed as lecturer in the College, and Cambridge resident and Harvard alumnus William Wells Newell (the organizer of the society and the first editor of *The Journal of American Folklore*).

63. "Albert Bates Lord, Memorial Minute," presented to the Faculty of Arts and Sciences, Harvard University, on February 14, 1995 (published in the *Harvard Gazette,* March 30, 1995) and written by a faculty committee consisting of Frank M. Cross, Jr., Joseph C. Harris, Harry T. Levin, John E. Malmstad, Stephen Mitchell, Gregory Nagy, and Rulan Pian.

64. Dorson 1972:5.

advanced classes, and the ideas developed by Parry and Lord were well represented in one of the most widely used folklore textbooks in the United States in the 1960s, 1970s, and 1980s.[65] The influence of what was being called the "oral formulaic theory"—although those well acquainted with the material understood that the empirical nature of the study had moved it well beyond the stage of mere theory—is notable in the variety of folklore materials besides the Balkan epic (for example, Anglo-American balladry, folk preaching in the American South, and Bantu oral poetry) that were now subjected to scrutiny through the ideas found in *The Singer of Tales*.[66]

In addition to the numerous folklore genres and traditions directly affected by the work of Parry and Lord, at least two prominent theoretical approaches to folklore—ethnopoetics, with its deep concern for the artistic performance in its cultural matrix, and performance theory, with its holistic view of the dynamic process of creation and its relation to both performer and audience—are anticipated in their writings. In fact, Richard Bauman's influential *Verbal Art as Performance* (1977) acknowledges that *The Singer of Tales* is one of the first works to conceive of folklore texts in terms of "emergent structures," and, he continues, "one of Lord's chief contributions is to demonstrate the unique and emergent quality of the oral text, composed in performance. His analysis of the dynamics of the epic tradition sets forth what amounts to a generative model of epic performance."[67]

As in any experiment looking to hew to the scientific principle, the quality of the results will vary greatly depending on the quality of the evidence and the manner in which it is collected. In modern terms, when such approaches as "participant observation" have become the hallmark of ethnographic fieldwork, the question arises: What were the effects of Parry's arranging the circumstances of the singing, of even paying singers for their work? In the first instance Parry, with his confidence in his knowledge of the culture and of fieldwork techniques growing daily, was well aware of what he was doing and why he was doing it. Moreover, he had the indispensable help of Nikola Vujnović, a man who was not only from the Balkans but was himself a singer. Indeed, it might be more accurate to say that Parry's insistence on collecting only certain kinds of songs from singers with certain local reputations and offering remuneration, often accompanied by food and drink, occasioned singing of exactly the sort he was looking for, that is, the sort of songs that had once been sung at the courts of the beys in the time of the Ottomans. Lord contemplates the lin-

---

65. Lord 1965, "Yugoslav Epic Folk Poetry," is included in *The Study of Folklore*. The article's own graceful introduction to the material, together with the editor's generous remarks in his headnote about the findings of Parry and Lord, gave assurance parallel to that of *The Singer of Tales* itself that the results of the Balkan expeditions would be introduced to generations of folklore students in English-speaking countries.

66. A review of the many areas influenced by Parry and Lord up to the mid-1980s is provided by Foley 1985.

67. Bauman 1977:38–39. For more on "generative" models, see Nagler 1974.

gering prestige of those glory days when he recalls the chapbooks that were cir-
culating at the same time Parry was recording such master singers as Avdo
Međedović:[68]

> Little paperbacks of Moslem epic songs appeared in Sarajevo in the 1920s published by a
> bookstore in Sarajevo. These included the *Smailagić Meho* that was read to Avdo Međedović,
> and many others.[69] [. . .] The little paperbacks had only a few songs, no commentary at all,
> and were cheap. [. . .] Since the songs themselves are from the world of orality, they were
> wholly accessible to its citizens, who indeed created them. In spite of the fact that they are
> written down and can be read, they belong to the world of orality. [. . .] *It is the accessibility of
> the projects of the world of orality to the world of literacy that is important.* The little books
> described above were intended for the businessmen in the Sarajevo shops to bolster their feel-
> ing of a heritage from a Moslem heroic age, for the former Moslem officials, aristocrats, the
> *potomci begovi* ("the once-upon-a-time beys") to remember the past glories that were once
> sung of in their courts, which were now relegated to, or remained only in, the coffeehouses.[70]

Parry is outspoken about his methods of dealing with the South Slavic song
culture as he analyzes the costs of entertaining and paying singers and of hiring
Vujnović as his assistant:

> Since the poetry in the mind of the people is associated with moments of relaxation, and
> since they easily become wearied by the fastidious details of recording—the reasons for which
> they naturally fail to understand (and when wearied they will give a shortened and worthless
> version of a poem),—it is necessary to keep them in spirits with wine, rakija, turkish coffee,
> and cigarettes. On a fairly lavish entertainment depends in no small measure the prestige of
> the recorder and the willingness of the singers to give their best efforts. The material for the
> entertainment is itself not costly, coffee, wine, or rakija costing only a few cents a glass; but it
> must be given to many in large quantities. Also the pay is small, varying from fifty cents to a
> dollar for a day's dictating or an evening's singing, but it must be paid to each singer [. . .]
> [Vujnović's] so to speak professional knowledge of the poetry (he gave me one of my finest
> texts), the fact that he was of the region and knew the people and their ways, and his unusu-
> ally ready understanding of what I wanted in the ways of particular kinds of texts, went a long
> way toward making the people accept me and believe they knew what I was doing. He was
> absolutely honest (to the point of insisting on losing his own money in the matter of cigarettes
> distributed); I placed him in charge of the expenditures (which added to my own prestige) and
> in this country where nothing has a fixed price he saw to it that I paid only the proper amount.
> He was particularly good at the ticklish business of paying the proportionate sum which the
> local reputation of each singer gave him a right to.[71]

Also relevant is Parry's ambitious coverage: had he, for example, stayed in
some single location on the Dalmatian coast throughout his time in Yugoslavia,
we would know far less about the complexities of epic singing generally in the
Balkans (though we might understand singing in that one spot at a very profound

---

68. Lord 1986a:50.

69. On the history of this particular chapbook, see Chap. 4, p. 79, below.

70. This last sentence, focusing on transitions in the Muslim South Slavic song culture from
the courts of the beys of yore to the coffeehouses frequented by Parry's *guslari* in the 1930s, is
a precious indication of Lord's fine-tuned diachronic sensibilities. For his understanding of
the term *diachronic,* see Lord 1995:196–197.

71. Parry, "Project for a Study of Jugoslavian Popular Oral Poetry," pp. 8–9.

level). And even if "salvage folklore" (a parallel drawn from the idea of "salvage archaeology") is not very highly regarded today, it retains a kernel of truth, and Parry was keenly aware of the need to collect as much material as he could in as little time as he had. In fact, as Parry expresses clearly in his application for supplementary funding of his research, he had exactly that purpose in mind:

> The old life and the old ways of song and speech are quickly going. I have found by experience that I risk obtaining poor material, both from a literary point of view and for my own purposes of study of oral processes, if I collect from anyone under fifty years of age. The old men are my best subjects, and four of those from whom I collected songs last year have already died. It is likely that the collection which I am making at present will remain as the one great collection of Southslavic oral material.[72]

Parry's sense of purpose in his collecting of songs from the South Slavic song culture centers on the collector's prioritizing of performance—authentic performance as authenticated by the audiences of the song culture. These research priorities are manifestly continued in Lord's *The Singer of Tales*. Even the title of this book, with its pointed use of the word "singer," conveys this essential aspect of performance (in English, "to sing" *is* to perform, making further qualification, such as "singing in performance," unnecessary).

Albert Lord's influence on the direction of studies in oral traditions began in 1934 when he was Milman Parry's assistant and his recently graduated student; nearly six decades later, when he died, Lord was the Arthur Kingsley Porter Professor of Slavic and Comparative Literature, emeritus, but he was still a student in the most profound sense. He never stopped learning about ever new parallels to be found for Homer, for Huso, and for all the other singers of tales. His range kept expanding, growing to include an enormous variety of oral epic and lyric poetry, as reflected in his 1991 book of essays, *Epic Singers and Oral Tradition,* and in his posthumously published *The Singer Resumes the Tale* (1995). Together with *The Singer of Tales,* these two books embody an idea that kept evolving over time, becoming ever more comprehensive without ever laying claim to universal applicability.[73]

But for all the many accolades Lord received in his lifetime, it is Parry's acknowledgment of the twenty-three-year-old Lord's contributions to their venture that should be the last word:

> . . . my assistant, Mr. Albert Lord, is shortly leaving for a month in Greece. His help has been altogether indispensable to me, and I may say that I have done twice as much work since I had his very able assistance. He has relieved me altogether of the very long labeling and cataloguing of the manuscripts and discs, has helped me with the keeping of accounts and the presentations of reports, has typed some 300 pages of my commentary on the collected texts,[74]

---

72. Parry, "Report on Work in Jugoslavia, June 18–October 19 [1934]," p. 14. For other models of folklore collection, we cite the exemplary work of Glassie 1982.

73. Both Parry and Lord studiously avoided making universalizing claims about oral traditions, despite the assumptions of some critics concerning "orality" (see Finnegan 1976).

74. Apparently a reference to Parry's manuscript of "Ćor Huso," to be published by MPCOL (M. L. Lord, editor).

and most particularly he has ably run the recording apparatus while we are working in the field, this for the first time leaving me free to be with the singer before the microphone, and to oversee and take part in the putting of questions to the singers. [. . .] I myself feel the greatest gratitude to him for the help which he has given me and the expedition is under the greatest obligation to him.[75]

BIBLIOGRAPHY

Acker, P. 1998. "Revising Oral Theory: Formulaic Composition in Old English and Old Icelandic Verse." *Garland Studies in Medieval Literature* 16. New York.

Alexander, R. 1998. "South Slavic Traditions." In *Teaching Oral Traditions,* ed. Foley, 273–279.

Andersson, T. M. 1964. "The Problem of Icelandic Saga Origins: A Historical Survey." *Yale Germanic Studies* 1. New Haven.

Bäuml, F. 1984. "Medieval Texts and the Two Theories of Oral-Formulaic Composition: A Proposal for a Third Theory." *New Literary History* 16:31–49.

Bakker, E. J. 1997. *Poetry in Speech: Orality and Homeric Discourse.* Ithaca.

Bartók, B., and A. B. Lord. 1951. *Serbo-Croatian Folk Songs: Texts and Transcriptions of Seventy-Five Folk Songs from the Milman Parry Collection and a Morphology of Serbo-Croatian Folk Melodies.* New York.

Başgöz, I. 1982. "Formula in Prose Narrative *Hikaye.*" In *Folklorica: Festschrift for Felix J. Oinas,* ed. E. Zygas and P. Voorheis, 27–57. Indiana University Uralic and Altaic Series. Bloomington.

Bauman, R. 1977. *Verbal Art as Performance.* Prospect Heights, Ill.

———. 1986. *Story, Performance, and Event: Contextual Studies of Oral Narrative.* Cambridge, England.

Bausinger, H. 1980. *Formen der "Volkspoesie."* 2nd ed. Berlin.

Beissinger, M. H. 1991. *The Art of the Lăutar: The Epic Tradition of Romania.* Harvard Dissertations in Oral Tradition. New York.

Ben-Amos, D. 1976. "Analytical Categories and Ethnic Genres." *Folklore Genres,* ed. D. Ben-Amos, 215–242. Austin.

Biebuyck, D. 1976. "The African Heroic Epic." *Journal of the Folklore Institute* 13:5–36.

———. 1978. *Hero and Chief: Epic Literature from the Banyanga, Zaïre Republic.* Berkeley and Los Angeles.

Biebuyck, D., and K. Mateene. 1969. *The Mwindo Epic from the Banyanga.* Berkeley and Los Angeles.

Bird, C. S. 1976. "Poetry in the Mande: Its Form and Meaning." *Poetics* 5:89–100.

Blackburn, S. H. 1989. "Patterns of Development for Indian Oral Epics." In *Oral Epics in India,* ed. Blackburn et al., 15–32.

Blackburn, S. H., P. J. Claus, J. B. Flueckiger, and S. S. Wadley, eds. 1989. *Oral Epics in India.* Berkeley and Los Angeles.

Buchholz, P. 1980. *Vorzeitkunde: Mündliches Erzählen und Überliefern im mittelalterlichen Skandinavien nach dem Zeugnis von Fornaldarsaga und eddischer Dichtung.* Skandinavistische Studien 13. Neumünster.

---

75. Parry, "Report on Work in Yugoslavia, October 20, 1934–March 24, 1935," MPCOL, p. 12. MPCOL, with the help of Casey Dué, Thomas Jenkins, and Matthew Kay, has produced a video record of the life and work of Albert B. Lord, "Albert B. Lord: A Multimedia Event."

Bynum, D. E., trans. 1993. *Serbo-Croatian Heroic Poems: Epics from Bihać, Cazin, and Kulen Vakuf.* Collected by Milman Parry, Albert B. Lord, and David E. Bynum. With additional translations by Mary P. Coote and John F. Loud. Milman Parry Studies in Oral Traditon. New York. See also Parry [1979].

Coote, M. P. 1978. "Serbocroatian Heroic Songs." *Heroic Epic and Saga,* ed. F. Oinas, 257–285. Bloomington, Ind.

Danek, G. 1998. "Mythologische Exempla bei Homer und im südslawischen Heldenlied." *Acta Antiqua et Archaeologica* 27 (Epik durch die Jahrhunderte: Internationale Konference Szeged 1997; ed. I. Tar), 82–91. Szeged.

Davidson, O. M. 1985. "The Crown-Bestower in the Iranian Book of Kings." *Acta Iranica, Hommages et Opera Minora* 10: *Papers in Honour of Professor Mary Boyce,* 61–148. Leiden.

———. 1988. "A Formulaic Analysis of Samples Taken from the *Shâhnâma* of Ferdowsi." *Oral Tradition* 3:88–105. Reworked as the Appendix of Davidson 1994.

———. 1994. *Poet and Hero in the Persian Book of Kings.* Ithaca.

———. 2000. *Comparative Literature and Classical Persian Poetry.* Bibliotheca Iranica: Intellectual Traditions Series, no. 4. Costa Mesa, Calif.

Dorson, R. M. 1959. *American Folklore.* Chicago.

———. 1972. *Folklore: Selected Essays.* Bloomington, Ind.

Erdely, S. 1995. *Music of Southslavic Epics from the Bihać Region of Bosnia.* Milman Parry Studies in Oral Tradition. New York.

Figueira, T. J., and G. Nagy, eds. 1985. *Theognis of Megara: Poetry and the Polis.* Baltimore.

Finnegan, R. 1970. *Oral Literature in Africa.* Oxford.

———. 1976. "What Is Oral Literature Anyway? Comments in the Light of Some African and Other Comparative Material." In *Oral Literature and the Formula,* ed. Stolz and Shannon, 127–166. Reprinted in Foley 1990:243–282.

Fisher, L. G. 1990. *Marko Songs from Hercegovina a Century after Karadžić.* Harvard Dissertations in Folklore and Oral Tradition. New York.

Foley, J. M. 1985. *Oral-Formulaic Theory and Research: An Introduction and Annotated Bibliography.* New York.

———, ed. 1981. *Oral Traditional Literature: A Festschrift for Albert Bates Lord.* Columbus, Ohio.

———, ed. 1986. *Oral Tradition in Literature: Interpretation in Context.* Columbia, Mo.

———, ed. 1987. *Comparative Research on Oral Traditions: A Memorial for Milman Parry.* Columbus, Ohio.

———, ed. 1990. *Oral-Formulaic Theory: A Folklore Casebook.* New York and London.

———, ed. 1998. *Teaching Oral Traditions.* New York.

Glassie, H. 1982. *Passing the Time in Ballymenone: Culture and History of an Ulster Community.* Publications of the American Folklore Society, no. 4. Philadelphia.

Goody, J. R. 1977. *The Domestication of the Savage Mind.* Cambridge, England.

Goody, J., and I. Watt. 1968. "The Consequences of Literacy." *Literacy in Traditional Societies,* ed. J. Goody, 27–68. Cambridge, England.

Guillén, C. 1985. *Entre lo uno y lo diverso: Introducción a la literatura comparada.* Barcelona.

———. 1993. *The Challenge of Comparative Literature.* Translation, by C. Franzen, of Guillén 1985. Harvard Studies in Comparative Literature 42. Cambridge, Mass.

Hainsworth, J. B. 1991. *The Idea of Epic.* Berkeley and Los Angeles.

Hainsworth, J. B., and A. T. Hatto, eds. 1989. *Traditions of Heroic and Epic Poetry II: Characteristics and Techniques.* London.

Harris, J. 1983. "Eddic Poetry as Oral Poetry: The Evidence of Parallel Passages in the Helgi Poems for Questions of Composition and Performance." In *Edda: A Collection of Essays,* ed. R. J. Glendinning and H. Bessason, 210–242. Manitoba Icelandic Series. Manitoba.

————. 1986. "Eddic Poetry." In *Old Norse-Icelandic Literature: A Critical Guide,* ed. C. Clover and J. Lindow, 68–156. Islandica 45. Ithaca.

————, ed. 1991. *The Ballad and Oral Literature.* Harvard English Studies 17. Cambridge, Mass.

Hatto, A. T. 1980. "Kirghiz: Mid-Nineteeth Century." *Traditions of Heroic and Epic Poetry,* ed. A. T. Hatto, 300–327. London.

Haymes, E. R. 1973. *A Bibliography of Studies Relating to Parry's and Lord's Oral Theory.* Publications of the Milman Parry Collection of Oral Literature. Cambridge, Mass.

Haymes, E. R., and S. T. Samples. 1996. *Heroic Legends of the North: An Introduction to the Nibelung and Dietrich Cycles.* New York.

Innes, G. 1974. *Sunjata: Three Mandinka Versions.* London.

Janko, R. 1982. *Homer, Hesiod and the Hymns: Diachronic Development in Epic Diction.* Cambridge, England.

————. 1992. *The Iliad: A Commentary,* general ed. G. S. Kirk. *Volume IV: Books 13–16.* Cambridge, England.

Johnson, J. W. 1980. "Yes, Virginia, There Is an Epic in Africa." *Research in African Literatures* 11:308–326.

Kay, M. W. 1995. *The Index of the Milman Parry Collection, 1933–1935: Heroic Songs, Conversations and Stories.* Milman Parry Studies in Oral Tradition.

Kirk, G. S. 1962. *The Songs of Homer.* Cambridge, England.

Koljević, S. 1980. *The Epic in the Making.* Oxford.

Kolsti, J. 1990. *The Bilingual Singer: A Study in Albanian and Serbo-Croatian Oral Epic Traditions.* Harvard Dissertations in Folklore and Oral Tradition. New York.

Krishna, V. 1982. "Parataxis, Formulaic Density, and Thrift in the *Alliterative Morte Arthure.*" *Speculum* 57:63–83.

Lamberterie, C. de. 1997. "Milman Parry et Antoine Meillet." In Létoublon 1997:9–22.

Létoublon, F., ed. 1997. *Hommage à Milman Parry: Le style formulaire de l'épopée homérique et la théorie de l'oralité poétique.* Amsterdam.

Lönnroth, L. 1971. "Hjálmar's Death-Song and the Delivery of Eddic Poetry." *Speculum* 46:1–20.

————. 1976. *Njáls Saga: A Critical Introduction.* Berkeley.

Lord, A. B. 1948. "Homer, Parry, and Huso." *American Journal of Archaeology* 52:34–44.

————. 1953. "Homer's Originality: Oral Dictated Texts." *Transactions of the American Philological Association* 94:124–134. Rewritten, with minimal changes, in Lord 1991:38–48 (with an "Addendum 1990" at pp. 47–48).

————. 1960. *The Singer of Tales.* Harvard Studies in Comparative Literature 24. Cambridge, Mass.

————. 1965. "Yugoslav Epic Folk Poetry." In *The Study of Folklore,* ed. A. Dundes (Englewood Cliffs, N.J., 1965), 265–268 [originally published in *Journal of the International Folk Music Council* 3 (1951), 57–61].

————. 1974. "Perspectives on Recent Work on Oral Literature." *Forum for Modern Language Studies* 10:1–21. Reprinted in Foley 1990:31–51.

————. 1984. "The Battle of Kosovo in Albanian and Serbocroatian Oral Epic Songs." In *Studies on Kosova, ed.* A. Pipa and S. Repishti, 65–83. East European Monographs 155. Boulder, Colo., and New York.

————. 1986a. "The Merging of Two Worlds: Oral and Written Poetry as Carriers of Ancient Values." In Foley 1986:19–64.

————. 1986b. "Perspectives on Recent Work on the Oral Traditional Formula." *Oral Tradition* 1:467–503. Reprinted (and abbreviated) in Foley 1990:379–405.

————. 1991. *Epic Singers and Oral Tradition.* Ithaca.

————. 1995. *The Singer Resumes the Tale,* ed. M. L. Lord. Ithaca.

Loud, J. F. *See* Bynum 1993.

MacCana, P. 1980. *The Learned Tales of Medieval Ireland.* Dublin.

Martin, R. P. 1984. "Hesiod, Odysseus, and the Instruction of Princes." *Transactions of the American Philological Association* 114:29–48.

————. 1989. *The Language of Heroes: Speech and Performance in the Iliad.* Ithaca.

Meillet, A. 1925. *La méthode comparative en linguistique historique.* Paris.

Mitchell, S. A. 1987. "The Sagaman and Oral Literature: The Icelandic Traditions of Hjör- leifr inn kvensami and Geirmundr heljarskinn." In Foley 1987:395–423.

————. 1991. *Heroic Sagas and Ballads.* Ithaca.

————. 1997. "Courts, Consorts and the Transformation of Medieval Scandinavian Litera- ture." *Germanic Studies in Honor of Anatoly Liberman,* ed. M. Berryman, K. G. Goblirsch, and M. Taylor, 229–242. *North-Western European Language Evolution,* 31–32.

Monroe, J. T. 1972. "Oral Composition in Pre-Islamic Poetry." *Journal of Arabic Literature* 3:1–53.

Muellner, L. 1976. *The Meaning of Homeric EYXOMAI through Its Formulas.* Innsbrucker Beiträge zur Sprachwissenschaft 13. Innsbruck.

Nagler, M. N. 1974. *Spontaneity and Tradition: A Study in the Oral Art of Homer.* Berkeley and Los Angeles.

Nagy, G. 1974. *Comparative Studies in Greek and Indic Meter.* Harvard Studies in Comparative Literature 33. Cambridge, Mass.

————. 1979. *The Best of the Achaeans: Concepts of the Hero in Archaic Greek Poetry.* 2nd ed. 1999, with new Introduction. Baltimore.

————. 1981. "An Evolutionary Model for the Text Fixation of Homeric Epos." In Foley 1981:390–393.

————. 1985. "Theognis and Megara: A Poet's Vision of His City." In Figueira and Nagy 1985:22–81.

————. 1986. "Ancient Greek Epic and Praise Poetry: Some Typological Considerations." In Foley 1986:89–102.

Nagy, J. F. 1985. *The Wisdom of the Outlaw: The Boyhood Deeds of Finn in Gaelic Narrative Tra- dition.* Berkeley and Los Angeles.

————. 1986. "Orality in Medieval Irish Narrative." *Oral Tradition* 1:272–301.

Niditch, S. 1996. *Oral World and Written Word: Ancient Israelite Literature.* Library of Ancient Israel. Louisville, Ky.

O'Keefe, K. O. 1990. *Visible Song: Transitional Literacy in Old English Verse.* Cambridge, Eng- land.

Okpewho, I. 1979. *The Epic in Africa: Toward a Poetics of the Oral Performance.* New York.

Ong, W. J. 1977. "African Talking Drums and Oral Noetics." *New Literary History* 8:411–429. Reprinted in Ong, 1977. *Interfaces of the Word: Studies in the Evolution of Consciousness and Culture,* 92–120. Ithaca.

————. 1982. *Orality and Literacy.* London.

————. 1986. "Text as Interpretation: Mark and After." In Foley 1986:147–169.

Opland, J. 1988. "Lord of the Singers." *Oral Tradition* 3:353–367.

Opland, J. 1989. "Xhosa: The Structure of Xhosa Eulogy and the Relation of Eulogy to Epic." In Hainsworth and Hatto 1989:121–143.

Parks, W. 1986. "The Oral Formulaic Theory in Middle English Studies." *Oral Tradition* 1:636–694.

Paroli, T. 1974. "Gli elementi formulari nelle introduzioni metriche a discorso diretto dell'-antica poesia germanica." *Ricerche linguistiche* 6:87–230.

Parry, A. 1966. "Have We Homer's *Iliad?*" *Yale Classical Studies* 20:177–216.

Parry, M. 1928a. *L'épithète traditionnelle dans Homère: Essai sur un problème de style homérique.* Paris. Translated in Parry 1971:1–190.

———. 1928b. *Les formules et la métrique d'Homère.* Paris. Translated in Parry [1971]:191–234.

———. 1930. "Studies in the Epic Technique of Oral Verse-Making. I. Homer and Homeric Style." *Harvard Studies in Classical Philology* 41:73–147. Reprinted in Parry [1971]:266–324.

———. 1932. "Studies in the Epic Technique of Oral Verse-Making. II. The Homeric Language as the Language of an Oral Poetry." *Harvard Studies in Classical Philology* 43:1–50. Reprinted in Parry [1971]:325–364.

———. [1953]. *Serbo-Croatian Heroic Songs. Novi Pazar: Serbocroatian Texts.* Belgrade and Cambridge, Mass.

———. [1954]. *Serbo-Croatian Heroic Songs. Novi Pazar: English Translations,* ed. and trans. A. B. Lord. Cambridge, Mass., and Belgrade.

———. [1971]. *The Making of Homeric Verse: The Collected Papers of Milman Parry,* ed. A. Parry. Oxford. Abbreviated as *MHV.*

———. [1974a]. *Serbo-Croatian Heroic Songs: The Wedding of Smailagić Meho,* trans. A. B. Lord. Publications of the Milman Parry Collection. Cambridge, Mass.

———. [1974b]. *Serbo-Croatian Heroic Songs. Ženidba Smailagina Sina,* ed. D. E. Bynum with A. B. Lord. Publications of the Milman Parry Collection. Cambridge, Mass.

———. [1979]. *Serbo-Croatian Heroic Songs. Bihaćka Krajina: Epics from Bihać, Cazin, and Kulen Vakuf,* ed. D. E. Bynum. Publications of the Milman Parry Collection. Cambridge, Mass.

———. [1980]. *Serbo-Croatian Heroic Songs. Ženidba Vlahinjić Alije, Osmanbeg Delibegović i Pavičević Luka,* ed. D. E. Bynum. Cambridge, Mass.

Peabody, B. 1975. *The Winged Word.* Albany.

Propp, V. I. 1958. *Morphology of the Folktale,* ed. and with an Introduction by S. Pirkova-Jakobson; trans. L. Scott. Bloomington, Ind.

Radloff, W. 1885. *Proben der Volksliteratur der nördlichen türkischen Stämme* V: *Der Dialekt der Kara-Kirgisen.* St. Petersburg.

———. [1990]. Preface from Radloff 1885. Translated by G. B. Sherman and A. B. Davis. *Oral Tradition* 5:73–90.

Redep, J. 1991. "The Legend of Kosovo." *Oral Tradition* 6:253–265.

Reichl, K. 1985. "Oral Tradition and Performance of the Uzbek and Karakalpak Epic Singers." *Fragen der mongolischen Heldendichtung* III, ed. W. Heissig, 613–643. Wiesbaden.

———. 1992. *Turkic Oral Epic Poetry: Traditions, Forms, Poetic Structure.* New York.

Renoir, A. 1986. "Oral-Formulaic Rhetoric and the Interpretation of Texts." In Foley 1986:103–135.

———. 1988. *A Key to Old Poems: The Oral-Formulaic Approach to the Interpretation of West-Germanic Verse.* University Park, Pa.

Reynolds, D. F. 1995. *Heroic Poets, Poetic Heroes: The Ethnography of Performance in an Arabic Oral Epic Tradition.* Ithaca.

Scholes, R., and R. Kellogg. 1966. *The Nature of Narrative.* Oxford and New York.

Skjærvø, O. 1994. "Hymnic Composition in the Avesta." *Die Sprache* 36:199–243.

———. 1998. "Eastern Iranian Epic Traditions II: Rostam and Bh¥ßma." *Acta Orientalia Academiae Scientiarum Hungaricae* 51:159–170.

Slymovics, S. 1987. *The Merchant of Art: An Egyptian Hilali Oral Epic Poet in Performance.* Berkeley and Los Angeles.

Smith, J. D. 1980. "Old Indian: The Two Sanskrit Epics." *Traditions of Heroic and Epic Poetry,* ed. A. T. Hatto, 48–78. London.

———. 1989. "Scapegoats of the Gods: The Ideology of the Indian Epics." In Blackburn et al. 1989, 176–194.

———. 1990. "Worlds Apart: Orality, Literacy, and the Rajasthani Folk-*Mahâbhârata.*" *Oral Tradition* 5:3–19.

Stolz, B. A., and R. S. Shannon, eds. 1976. *Oral Literature and the Formula.* Ann Arbor.

Thompson, S., ed. 1953. *Four Symposia on Folklore.* Indiana University Folklore Series 8. Bloomington.

Toelken, J. B. 1967. "An Oral Canon for the Child Ballads: Construction and Application." *Journal of the Folklore Institute* 5:75–101.

Vikis-Freibergs, V. 1984. "Creativity and Tradition in Oral Folklore, or the Balance of Innovation and Repetition in the Oral Poet's Art." *Cognitive Processes in the Perception of Art,* ed. W. R. Crozier and A. J. Chapman, 325–343. Amsterdam.

Webber, R. H. 1986. "The *Cantar de Mio Cid:* Problems of Interpretation." In Foley 1986:65–88.

Ziolkowski, J. 1991. "Cultural Diglossia and the Nature of Medieval Latin Literature." In Harris 1991:193–213.

Zumthor, P. 1972. *Essai de poétique médiévale.* Paris.

———. 1983. *Introduction à la poésie orale.* Paris.

———. 1984. *La Poésie de la Voix dans la civilisation médiévale.* Paris.

Zumwalt, R. 1988. *American Folklore Scholarship: A Dialogue of Dissent.* Bloomington, Ind.

Zwettler, M. J. 1978. *The Oral Tradition of Classical Arabic Poetry.* Columbus, Ohio.

PREFACE

The term "literature," presupposing the use of letters, assumes that verbal works of imagination are transmitted by means of writing and reading. The expression "oral literature" is obviously a contradiction in terms. Yet we live at a time when literacy itself has become so diluted that it can scarcely be invoked as an esthetic criterion. The Word as spoken or sung, together with a visual image of the speaker or singer, has meanwhile been regaining its hold through electrical engineering. A culture based upon the printed book, which has prevailed from the Renaissance until lately, has bequeathed to us — along with its immeasurable riches — snobberies which ought to be cast aside. We ought to take a fresh look at tradition, considered not as the inert acceptance of a fossilized corpus of themes and conventions, but as an organic habit of re-creating what has been received and is handed on. It may be that we ought to re-examine the concept of originality, which is relatively modern as a shibboleth of criticism; there may be other and better ways of being original than that concern for the writer's own individuality which characterizes so much of our self-conscious fiction. We may even come to believe that, great as some authors have been, their greatness is finally surpassed by that of the craft they have served; hence, whenever we reckon their contributions, we should also remember their obligations; no credit need be lost if some of it is shared anonymously with others trained in the same techniques and imparting the same mythology.

The present study sets forth the considered findings from twenty-five years of collection, transcription, and interpretation in the field of oral literature. These years have been strategic for applying scholarly methods to a subject which first developed amid the enthusiasms of the Romantic Movement; a systematic approach has been made feasible by the more recent development of facilities for intensive travel and phonographic reproduction; and literary history has been empowered to draw upon — and, reciprocally, to illustrate — folklore, anthropology, musicology, linguistics, and other related disciplines. The issue upon which such investigations still converge is all too well known, under its classical aspect, as the Homeric Problem. That problem may have remained unsolved for centuries because it was irrelevantly formulated: because, on the one hand, a single literate author was taken for granted and, on the other, the main alternative was a quasi-mystical belief in communal origins. Those presuppositions have been radically challenged by the sharp insight and the rich documentation to which this volume offers a key. Its authority rests on a monumental substructure, *Serbocroatian Heroic Songs,* the series of texts, translations, and commentaries now being published under the joint auspices of Harvard University Press and the Serbian Academy of Sciences. Here, by way of critical *prolegomenon* and editorial *parergon,* the editor sums up what he has learned in bringing together that unique body of epic material.

What is more, and what commands a special interest transcending that material, he concretely discerns and lucidly states the principles he has been watching at work. Moreover, in the second part of the book, he extends their application to the *Iliad* and the *Odyssey,* and demonstrates their relevance to *Beowulf,* the *Chanson de Roland,* and other epics previously conceived as "literary." Careful stylistic and thematic analysis of such works has raised questions, and stimulated certain conjectures, as to the form and function of heroic poetry. These hypotheses, through a happy conjunction of opportunity and ingenuity, have been fully tested in a "living laboratory": the school of nonliterate bards, surviving yet declining in Yugoslavia and other South Slavic regions, has been caught at perhaps the latest possible moment; and its recorded songs provide both a solid basis for comparative studies and a new comprehension of oral technique. Through a wealth of contextual testimony, we are permitted to witness the act of composition — which, as Professor Lord makes abundantly clear, is at once a transmission and a creation. Vividly he communicates to us his personal sense of contact with the singers, as he and his collaborator sought them out or listened to them in Turkish coffeehouses during the nights of the Ramazan. In the mind's ear, we too are enabled to hear them, improvising out of their fabulous memories, filling in with stock epithets and ornamental formulas, accompanying themselves on their one-stringed fiddle, the *gusle.* And we are led to realize, more acutely than we could have done before, that the epic is not merely a *genre* but a way of life.

Formally, it might be described as a dynamic structure. Indeed the whole undertaking might be viewed, from some degree of distance, as an inquiry into the dynamics of poetic construction. The poem is, by this definition, a song; its performer is, at the same time, its composer; whatever he performs, he re-creates; his art of improvisation is firmly grounded upon his control of traditional components; and the tales he tells bear a family resemblance to many sung in other countries under other circumstances. The canons of esthetics, and even those of epistemology, should be at least as well satisfied by that approximation to the artistic event, at the very instant it happens, as they are by the frequent distortions of print or of the personalities behind it. Our conception of Homer, in particular, has not been helped by reinterpretations which cast him in the mold of latter-day authorship. Yet it is greatly enhanced, not undermined, by being approached through a more precise understanding of those patterns which he supremely exemplifies and those standards which he establishes for others working in his medium. Professor Lord appreciates, as perceptively as any critic or commentator, the "subtlety and intricacy" of the Homeric poems. He never loses sight of the qualitative distinction between Homer and Petar Vidić. But since he has heard and talked with Petar Vidić, while Homer himself remains an opaque attribution, the humble *guslar* has light to throw upon the Ionian *epos*. More significant than our value-judgments, which we are always free to make as we like, is our knowledge of literature as a process, endlessly multiform and continuous.

Professor Lord's exposition speaks for itself, with an expert attention to detail which will meet both Hellenists and Slavicists upon their respective grounds. It is not because I would presume to mediate between specialists that I have set down these preliminary impressions, but because I am glad to attest *a fortiori* what *The Singer of Tales* can mean to a lay critic or common reader. It was my privilege to study with Milman Parry during the period, so prematurely cut short, when he was teaching Classics in Harvard College. Thus, by sheer good luck, I have been among those who watched his project from its inception, and who — after having feared that his accidental death would terminate it — have rejoiced to see it carried toward this completion. No one who knew Parry is likely to forget his incisive powers of formulation or to underrate the range and depth of his cosmopolitan mind. He has been appropriately hailed, by an eminent archeologist, as the Darwin of oral literature; for if the *évolution des genres* has been scientifically corroborated, it is largely owing to his discovery. Yet, as he himself would have been the first to admit, it was only a beginning; and he generously acknowledged the prescient counsel of his own teacher, Antoine Meillet. Albert Lord, in his turn, has become much more than the ablest of Parry's disciples. It should be recognized, in spite of his devoted modesty, that he too has pioneered; he has contributed many ideas and important modifications; his comprehensive mastery of the field has taken him far beyond any of his forerunners; it is he who has turned an exciting *aperçu* into a convincing argument. The Parry-Lord theory, like the epic itself, is the product of an imaginative collaboration.

HARRY LEVIN

Cambridge, Massachusetts
15 May 1959

FOREWORD

This book is about Homer. He is our Singer of Tales. Yet, in a larger sense, he represents all singers of tales from time immemorial and unrecorded to the present. Our book is about these other singers as well. Each of them, even the most mediocre, is as much a part of the tradition of oral epic singing as is Homer, its most talented representative. Among the singers of modern times there is none to equal Homer, but he who approaches the master most closely in our experience of epic song is Avdo Međedović of Bijelo Polje, Yugoslavia. He is our present-day Balkan Singer of Tales.

We believe that the epic singers from the dawn of human consciousness have been a deeply significant group and have contributed abundantly to the spiritual and intellectual growth of man. Although only two segments of the Indo-European peoples have been treated here in any detail, namely the Greeks and the Slavs (or more truly the speakers of Serbocroatian and of Bulgarian), it is my hope that the book is not parochial. Narrowness has never been excusable, whether it be ethnic, geographic, religious, social, or even academic, least of all in the space age. Of the epic songs of the past (or of the present for that matter) Homer's have always been recognized as supreme. When our collecting began in the nineteen-thirties the Yugoslav oral epic was accessible, alive, and distinguished. Russian and central Asiatic oral traditions might have done as well for purposes of comparative study, but for an American professor at that time they were not within easy reach.

This book concentrates on only one aspect of the singers' art. Our immediate purpose is to comprehend the manner in which they compose, learn, and transmit their epics. It is a study in the processes of composition of oral narrative poetry. Hence the reader must not seek here a survey of oral epics, or a history of oral epic in the Balkans or elsewhere.

This book is dedicated gratefully to my parents, who made it possible for me after my first academic degree to go to Yugoslavia with Milman Parry for fifteen months, and helped with my further education.

My debt to Milman Parry as master and friend can never adequately be expressed. He introduced me to a rich world of thought and fired me with an urge to explore it. But, as a true teacher, he left me free in my explorations and conclusions. Parry's genius as a scholar lay in a bold and imaginative rigorousness which insisted that a comprehension of oral poetry could come only from an intimate knowledge of the way in which it was produced; that a theory of composition must be based not on another theory but on the facts of the practice of the poetry.

The first form of this book served as a doctoral dissertation in the Department of Comparative Literature at Harvard in 1949. To its readers, Sir Cedric Maurice Bowra and Professor John H. Finley, Jr., I am deeply grateful for continued encouragement and most helpful exchange of ideas.

Professor H. T. Levin, who was at that time Chairman of the Department, a devoted admirer of Parry's achievements and like myself a pupil of Parry's at Harvard in the thirties, generously agreed to read the manuscript and to write a preface for the present book. I am happy to have this opportunity to express my deep gratitude to him for it and for years of inspiring association and never-failing help.

Thanks also are due to Roman Jakobson, Samuel Hazzard Cross Professor of Slavic Languages and Literatures at Harvard, who has always given unstintingly of his breadth of learning, particularly in the field of folklore and epic poetry. He also read the manuscript and suggested a number of criticisms. I was not able in every case to follow his suggestions, but I have noted them where I could.

Once again I wish to express my warm gratitude to the Department of Comparative Literature for its willingness to include this book in its series, Harvard Studies in Comparative Literature, and to the Chairman of that Department, Professor Renato Poggioli, for his kindness in reading the manuscript and encouraging me in its publication.

My wife, Dr. Mary Louise Carlson Lord, has been at my side constantly in the years of endeavor of preparing this book. Without her understanding care it would not have seen the light.

*   *   *

Some of the thoughts for this volume took shape during my years as a Junior Fellow in the Society of Fellows at Harvard from 1937 to 1940; a collecting trip to Albania in the fall of 1937 under the Society's auspices gave me experience in a part of the Balkans other than Yugoslavia. Further collecting in Yugoslavia was done in the spring of 1950 with a Guggenheim Fellowship, and with aid from the Ministry of Science and Culture of Yugoslavia, the Musicological Institute of the Serbian Academy of Sciences, and the Ministry of Science and Culture for the Republic of Macedonia, all of which also assisted us in the summer of 1951. More recent collecting (briefly in 1958 and more abundantly in 1959) in Bulgaria was made possible by the Inter-University Committee on Travel Grants in New York, the Committee for Friendship and Cultural Relations with Foreign Countries in Sofia, the Institute for Bulgarian Language and the Ethnographic Institute and Museum of the Bulgarian Academy of Sciences. To all these institutions as well as to their directors and staffs I am deeply indebted.

Fuller acknowledgment of assistance in collecting and publishing the materials of the Parry Collection, which form the basis for the research in this book, can be found in the Editor's Preface and Introduction to *Serbocroatian Heroic Songs,* Volume One, published by the Harvard University Press and the Serbian Academy of Sciences in 1954.

For technical assistance to assure the accuracy of the music illustrations I wish to thank Dr. Miloš M. Velimirović of the Music Department of Yale University. And I am grateful to Mrs. Patricia Arant of the Graduate School of Radcliffe College for compiling the index. Mrs. Eleanor Kewer of Harvard University Press has taken extraordinary care in the complex business of seeing this work through from manuscript to finished book. The designer and the printer, too, have met its linguistic challenges and the problems of composition and make-up with skill and imagination.

Cambridge, Mass.   A.B.L.
November, 1959

PART I. THE THEORY

CHAPTER ONE

INTRODUCTION

In the early thirties of this century, when Milman Parry began to write the book from which this one takes its name,[1] what was needed most in Homeric scholarship was a more exact knowledge of the way in which oral epic poets learn and compose their songs. Now in the late fifties of the same century the need is still great; in spite of the number of books about Homer and his poems, about epic poetry in general, and about specific epic traditions in various parts of the world, the student of epic still lacks a precise idea of the actual technique of *poiesis* in its literal meaning. Thanks to Parry, however, we have the material for the research necessary to determine what this technique is. He has left us his collection of South Slavic texts, which is the record on phonograph discs and in manuscripts of experiments in the laboratory of the living epic tradition of the Yugoslavs.[2]

In 1935 Milman Parry was Assistant Professor of Classics at Harvard University. He had already made a name for himself in classical scholarship by his masterly analysis of the technique of the formulaic epithets in the *Iliad* and the *Odyssey*.[3] This work had convinced him that the poems of Homer were traditional epics, and he soon came to realize that they must also be oral compositions.[4] He therefore set himself the task of proving, incontrovertibly if it were possible, the oral character of the poems, and to that end he turned to the study of the Yugoslav epics. In the autumn of 1935, he wrote: "the aim of the study was to fix with exactness the *form* of oral story poetry, to see wherein it differs from the *form* of written story poetry. Its method was to observe singers working in a thriving tradition of unlettered song and see how the form of their songs hangs upon their having to learn and practice their art without reading and writing. The principles of *oral form* thus gotten would be useful in two ways. They would be a starting point for a comparative study of oral poetry which sought to see how the way of life of a people gives rise to a poetry of a given kind and a given degree of excellence. Secondly, they would be useful in the study of the great poems which have come down to us as lonely relics of a dim past: we would know how to work backwards from their form so as to learn how they must have been made."[5]

In Part I of this book I shall attempt to fulfill Parry's purpose of setting forth with exactness the form of oral narrative poetry, drawing my illustrative material from this collection; in Part II I shall use the principles presented in Part I in studying the form of some of the great epic poems from the past. Because I intend to limit the scope of this book to a consideration of oral form and manner of composition, a discussion of a broader sort which would aim at seeing "how the way of life of a people gives rise to a poetry of a given kind and a given degree of excellence" will not be fully entered upon. Yet considerations of this kind will inevitably occupy us to some extent in this book. It is hoped that what is said here will be of use for future comparative study of oral poetry.

*　　*　　*

The burden of the first few chapters of Part I will be to work out in fullness of detail a definition of oral epic song. Stated briefly, oral epic song is narrative poetry composed in a manner evolved over many generations by singers of tales who did not know how to write; it consists of the building of metrical lines and half lines by means of formulas and formulaic expressions and of the building of songs by the use of themes. This is the technical sense in which I shall use the word "oral" and "oral epic" in this book. By formula I mean "a group of words which is regularly employed under the same metrical conditions to express a given essential idea." This definition is Parry's.[6] By formulaic expression I denote a line or half line constructed on the pattern of the formulas. By theme I refer to the repeated incidents and descriptive passages in the songs.

These definitions are but the bare bones of the living organism which is oral epic. We shall peer into the structural heart of the formulas to discern the various patterns which merge to give them form. We shall see that the formulas are not the ossified clichés which they have the reputation of being, but that they are capable of change and are indeed frequently highly productive of other and new formulas. We shall come to realize the way in which themes can be expanded and contracted, and the manner in which they are joined together to form the final product which is the song. We shall note the difference both in the internal structure and in the external connection of themes as they are used by different singers.

Finally we shall turn our attention to the song itself. We shall see that in a very real sense every performance is a separate song; for every performance is unique, and every performance bears the signature of its poet singer. He may have learned his song and the technique of its construction from others, but good or bad, the song produced in performance is his own. The audience knows it as his because he is before them. The singer of tales is at once the tradition and an individual creator.[7] His manner of composition differs from that used by a writer in that the oral poet makes no conscious effort to break the traditional phrases and incidents; he is forced by the rapidity of composition in performance to use these traditional elements.[8] To him they are not merely necessary, however; they are also right. He seeks no others, and yet he practices great freedom in his use of them because they are themselves flexible. His art consists not so much in learning through repetition the time-worn formulas as in the ability to compose and recompose the phrases for the idea of the moment on the pattern established by the basic formulas. He is not a conscious iconoclast, but a traditional creative artist. His traditional style also has individuality, and it is possible to distinguish the songs of one singer from those of another, even when we have only the bare text without music and vocal nuance.

* * *

The need for a clarification of the oral process of composition is reflected in the many terms which are used for oral narrative poetry. To no small degree difficulties have arisen because of the ambiguity of terminology and because each school has chosen a different facet of this poetry as distinctive. The term "oral" emphasizes, I believe, the basic distinction between oral narrative poetry and that which we term literary epic. But it too carries some ambiguity. Certain of the misunderstandings of Parry's oral theory arise from the failure to recognize his special use of the word "oral." For example, one often hears that oral poetry is poetry that was written to be recited. Oral, however, does not mean merely oral presentation. Oral epics are performed orally, it is true, but so can any other poem be performed orally. What is important is not the oral performance but rather the composition *during* oral performance.[9]

There may be ambiguity also when we say that the oral poet learns his songs *orally,* composes them *orally,* and transmits them *orally* to others. Like so many statements made in the debate on the oral theory, this one too is perfectly true if the word "oral" is understood in the technical sense in which it will be presented in this book. But if the reader interprets oral learning as listening to something repeated in exactly the same form many times, if he equates it with oral memorization by rote, then he will fail to grasp the peculiar process involved in learning oral epic. The same may be said for oral composition. If we equate it with improvisation in a broad sense, we are again in error. Improvisation is not a bad term for the process, but it too must be modified by the restrictions of the particular style. The exact way in which oral composition differs from free improvisation will, I hope, emerge from the following chapters. It is true also that oral epic is transmitted by word of mouth from one singer to another, but if we understand thereby the transmission of a fixed text or the kind of transmission involved when A tells B what happened and B tells C and so on with all natural errors of lapse of memory and exaggeration and distortion, then we do not fully comprehend what oral transmission of oral epic is. With oral poetry we are dealing with a particular and distinctive process in which oral learning, oral composition, and oral transmission almost merge; they seem to be different facets of the same process.

The word "epic," itself, indeed, has come in time to have many meanings. Epic sometimes is taken to mean simply a long poem in "high style." Yet a very great number of the poems which interest us in this book are comparatively short; length, in fact, is not a criterion of epic poetry. Other definitions of epic equate it with heroic poetry. Indeed the term "heroic poetry" is sometimes used (by Sir Cecil M. Bowra, for example) to avoid the very ambiguity in the word epic which troubles us. Yet purists might very well point out that many of the songs which we include in oral narrative poetry are romantic or historical and not heroic, no matter what definition of the hero one may choose. In oral narrative poetry, as a matter of fact, I wish to include all story poetry, the romantic or historical as well as the heroic; otherwise I would have to exclude a considerable body of medieval metrical narrative.

That whole body of verse that we have now agreed to designate as oral has been called by many names; the terminological battle is a serious one. Those who call it "folk epic" are carrying on a nineteenth-century concept of composition by the "folk" which has long since been proved invalid. At one time when "folk epic" referred to a theory of composition, it was a justifiable term. It pointed to a method of composition as the distinction between oral narrative poetry and "written" poetry. It was looking in the right direction. But when its theory of composition was invalidated, because no one could show how the people as a whole could compose a poem, then the technical meaning of the term was lost and it came to be equated in a derogatory sense with "peasant." The attention was then shifted from the way in which the poetry was made, first to the social status of those who practiced it, and then to the content and quality of the poetry itself. Although it may be true that this kind of poetry has survived longest among peasant populations, it has done so not because it is essentially "peasant" poetry, but rather because the peasant society has remained illiterate longer than urban society.[10] Indeed this poetry has more often been aristocratic and courtly than of the folk. It would seem even from its origins to have belonged to serious ceremonial occasions, to ritual, to celebration. The term "folk poetry" becomes more and more inadequate, more and more restricted in time and place. To apply the term to the medieval epics or to the Homeric poems is ever more inadmissible.

Another reason why this poetry should cease to be denominated as "folk epic" is that outside the circle of folklore enthusiasts the connotations of "folk" in many countries tend to be derogatory. One thinks of the simple peasant with his "quaint" ideas, his fairy stories, and children's tales. The use of folk stories as entertainment for young children has its ironic aspects; we are beginning to realize the serious symbolism and meaning of folk tales, which, if rightly understood, would be far from proper fare for children. Moreover, if we mean by "folk epic" to indicate that oral epic shares some of its subject matter with folk tale and all that is seriously implied in that term, we are ignoring or underestimating all the other subjects of oral epic, historical, legendary, and heroic: we have outgrown the appellation "folk epic." It is no longer exact, and in time it has come to misrepresent oral epic poetry rather than to describe it.

Similar objections can be brought against the term "popular," the Latin derivative equivalent to "folk." While this term avoids the "simple peasant" connotations of "folk," its literal meaning has been overlaid with another set of unfortunate implications from its use in English to denote "popular music" and "popular songs."

The fever of nationalism in the nineteenth century led to the use of oral epics for nationalist propaganda. The poems glorified the heroes of the nation's past; they depicted the struggles of the nation against outside foes. Hence the hero emerged as a "national" hero, and the poems themselves were labeled "national" epics. In some of the Slavic countries the word *narodni* has a useful ambiguity, since it means both "folk" and "national." As a term to designate oral epic "national" is woefully inadequate and an insidious imposter.

Some scholars have sought to avoid the pitfalls of the three terms already discussed, folk, popular, and national, by recourse to the word "primitive." It sounds somehow more "scientific" because it has been borrowed from the social science of anthropology. But here too the ambiguity is great and the connotations hardly less flattering than those of "folk" in some countries. If the idea behind the use of "primitive" for this poetry is that oral epic poetry precedes written poetry in time in the cultural growth of a society, then its use would be legitimate, because as a rule oral poetry does precede written poetry, but it would, like the other terms, still miss the fundamental difference in form between the two.

In summary, any term that is used to designate oral narrative poetry in an attempt to distinguish it from written narrative poetry must contain some indication of the difference in form. It is because the terms which we have discussed above failed to comprehend this distinction that they have proved themselves to be inadequate. Any terms, also, carrying implications derogatory to either oral narrative poetry or written poetry (as, for example, such terms as "authentic" and "artificial"; "primary" and "secondary") must be abandoned, for they represent an attitude that is neither scholarly nor critical. Both these forms are artistic expressions, each with its own legitimacy. We should not seek to judge but to understand.

If the need for a clarification of the process which produces oral narrative poetry is reflected in the confusion of terms which have been used to designate that poetry, this need is even more apparent, of course, in the variety of theories put forth in the last two centuries (and which still survive in one form or another today) to explain the peculiar phenomenon of oral epic. On the one hand there has been a solid block of loyalists to the literary tradition who have maintained through thick and thin that the

Homeric poems, as well as the great epics from medieval times, are written literary productions by a single author.

These loyalists have found themselves defending their position from attacks by those who from time to time raised annoying questions. One of the earliest questions posed was whether writing existed in the ninth century B.C., the traditional date of Homer. This was first raised by Josephus;[11] it came to the fore again in D'Aubignac[12] in the early eighteenth century and reached its classic expression in Friedrich August Wolf's famed *Prolegomena* (1795). A second problem was formulated during the seventeenth century and played a great role in the Querelle des Anciens et des Modernes; this was the problem of the "errors" or inconsistencies in the Homeric poems. D'Aubignac, Perrault, Giambattista Vico, Robert Wood, and others led once again to Wolf and the later Separatists. A third question concerned the unusual length of the Homeric poems. If there was no writing in Homer's time, how could such long poems be preserved until the time of writing? In fact, how could poems of such length come into being at all without the aid of writing? Clearly this was a corollary of the first question raised. Among the earlier scholars who attempted to answer this question the name of Robert Wood stands out. A fourth problem arose from the increased knowledge of and interest in medieval minstrelsy and contemporary oral poetry during the eighteenth century and later. Here again we may begin with D'Aubignac and continue with Thomas Blackwell, Percy, Macpherson, Herder, Goethe, and a host of others. There was, fifthly, also the problem, inherited from ancient times, of the meaning of the Peisistratean legend about the recension of the Homeric poems. And finally with the development of linguistic studies in the nineteenth century the question was raised about the possibility of one man using dialect forms from several regions and archaisms from different periods.

These were the chief questions that were current in Homeric scholarship and still are. In answering them some scholars have gone so far as to deny even the existence of Homer, but the usual answer has been some form of multiple authorship for the poems with Homer at one end or the other of a series of poets. Sometimes he was the originator whose poems were carried through oral tradition or whose works were modified by later poets; more often he was the last of the redactors or compilers or, in an attempt to bridge the gap between Unitarians and Separatists, he was the great poet who reworked oral tradition into a "literary" poem. The concept of multiple authorship led scholars naturally to the dissection of the Homeric poems in an attempt to see what parts were done by different authors. They were thus led also to seek the "original" or archetype of the poems.

The doubt as to the existence of writing in Homer's time has given Homerists three choices: to seek proof that the doubt was ill founded and that there was writing as early as the traditional date of Homer; to change Homer's date, bringing it down to a period when writing was possible; to leave Homer's date where it was and to cover the intervening years to the age of writing by oral transmission of Homer's poems.

The most significant step in proving that writing was possible and indeed existed not only in the ninth century but earlier has been made only recently in the discovery that Linear B is Greek. Although none of the texts yet deciphered is literary,[13] the old argument of Josephus and Wolf has had the ground cut from under it. Ironically enough, however, the proof has come at a time when many scholars realize that the existence of writing or even of a literary tradition does not necessarily mean that Homer's poems belong in the category of "written" literature; and many realize, and have realized for some time, that obviously our Homeric texts could not have been preserved had there not been writing in Homer's day. Valuable as the decipherment of Linear B is, it is no longer relevant to the Homeric problem.

Unless not only literary texts are discovered in Linear B but also some evidence can be unearthed to prove that epic poetry was being written down during the period of Linear B, its decipherment cannot help us much in determining Homer's date. Some Homeric names seem to have been deciphered, Hector and Achilles, for example, but this might indicate no more than that these were common names or that songs about these heroes existed; it tells us nothing about our poems. There is no evidence at all at this point that Homer was written down in Linear B and later copied in the Greek alphabet that we know. Were there such evidence, we would be justified in moving Homer's date back. So the problem of the date of Homer still remains with us.

Wolf and some of his predecessors turned to the Peisistratean legend to answer the question of date, as has Carpenter in our own century, although the latter's reasons are different from those of Wolf. Carpenter reflects our growing knowledge of oral literature and seeks a time when the writing down of the poems would make sense in the context of this knowledge. To him Peisistratus seems the most likely person to sponsor this. Certainly he is right that the Peisistratean legend is an invaluable clue, one that cannot be ignored but which demands explanation and interpretation. But Carpenter has been little heeded, and the date accepted now by most scholars is the second half of the eighth century.

Those scholars who made the third choice were moving in the right direction, namely towards oral tradition, but in putting the poet of our Homeric texts before the period of writing, they were unwittingly creating more problems than they were as yet equipped to handle. Their choice was a compromise. Oral tradition was a fickle mistress with whom to flirt. But scholars could call in to their help the "fantastic memories" so "well attested" of illiterate people. They felt that a text could remain from one generation to another unaltered, or altered only by inconsequential lapses of memory. This myth has remained strong even to the present day. The main points of confusion in the theory of those scholars who made the third choice arose from the belief that in oral tradition there is a fixed text which is transmitted unchanged from one generation to another.

The quarrel about the errors and inconsistencies in the Homeric poems, inherited from the seventeenth century, has continued steadily until our own times. In its narrower aspects the strife has resulted in a stalemate; the real inconsistencies still remain unexplained in spite of the ingenuity of the Unitarians, who have to their credit the checking of the excesses of the Separatists.[14] The picture of the great Homer nodding has looked more like an excuse than an explanation. Bowra's remark in *Tradition and Design in the Iliad* that the oral poet concentrates on one passage at a time is closer to the truth. We have been gaining much perspective on the inconsistencies, despite the hard core of apologist opinion. Of far greater importance than the labeling of the inconsistencies themselves has been the theory of multiple authorship which emerged when the quarrel over the "errors" began to find added fuel from the attention paid to still living bards and bardic traditions and to medieval minstrelsy. The many theories of multiple authorship of the Homeric poems have contributed more to Homeric scholarship than any other single concept. Not that they were right. But they led in productive directions. They were honest attempts to meet the challenge offered by the growing body of oral ballads and epics as well as of medieval epic.

The theories of multiple authorship can be divided into two general classes. The first, and the earliest, saw the Homeric poems as compilations of shorter songs, stitched together by their compiler. D'Aubignac presented this in his *Conjectures* in 1715, but it was Lachmann and his followers in the nineteenth century who made serious attempts to dissect the poems according to this *lieder theorie*. The attempts were unsuccessful and unconvincing; for the dissectors could not agree on where to use the scalpel. The theory was discredited.

A second general approach moved in vertical rather than horizontal lines. The scholars who used this approach abandoned the idea of a compilation, even of poems of different times and places, and conceived of an original kernel which was modified by a succession of later authors. Usually to them Homer was not a compiler but the last and greatest of the redactors. They too whisked out the scalpel and began to peel off the layers in the Homeric poems. Linguistic and dialect evidence came to their assistance. But they were equally unsuccessful and their theories too have been discarded, although with considerably less finality than those of the first group.

The work of the first group of dissectors led to several valuable compilations. Lönrot put together the Finnish *Kalevala,* the Estonians entered the competition with the *Kalevipoeg,* and the Serbs attempted a number of "national" epics on the Kosovo theme. But nothing comparable to the Homeric poems was produced. The problem of the way in which the

Homeric poems had attained their length, if they were not literary productions of a single author, remained unsolved.

So also did the problem of the variety of dialect and archaic forms in the poems. One of the attempts to solve this problem was the theory of a special poetic language, a kind of artificial dialect which was the property of epic poets. This of course did not solve anything. It merely put a label on the diction as found in the poems and pushed into the background the question of how such a diction could have been formed.

Hand in hand with the theory of multiple authorship went the emphasis on a search for the archetype. Leaf's work is typical of this trend. His five strata began with an original and then discerned expansions and interpolations of later periods. One still hears echoes of this kind of dissection, for example, in MacKay's *The Wrath of Homer*.

The work of all these theorists should not be dismissed as without avail, certainly not with the tired yet vituperative cynicism of Allen in his *Origins and Transmissions*. The service of these scholars has been in essence to point out the peculiarities of language and structure of the Homeric poems, peculiarities that we now recognize to be those of oral poetry. The inconsistencies, the mixture of dialects, the archaisms, the repetitions and epic "tags," and even the manner of composition by addition and expansion of themes have been noted and catalogued by these scholars. The questioned existence of writing led them to use the word "oral" and their experience of folk epic seemed further to justify this term. The elements that were needed to crystallize the answers to their questions were there. It is a strange phenomenon in intellectual history as well as in scholarship that the great minds herein represented, minds which could formulate the most ingenious speculation, failed to realize that there might be some other way of composing a poem than that known to their own experience. They knew and spoke often of folk ballad and epic, they were aware of variants in these genres, yet they could see only two ways in which those variants could come into being: by lapse of memory or by wilful change. This seemed so obvious, so much an unquestioned basic assumption, that they never thought to investigate exactly how a traditional poetry operated. They always thought in terms of a fixed text or a fixed group of texts to which a poet *did* something for a reason within his own artistic or intellectual self. They could not conceive of a poet composing a line in a certain way because of necessity or because of the demands of his traditional art.

I believe that the greatest moment in recent Homeric scholarship was expressed by Milman Parry when he wrote his field notes for his collection of South Slavic texts and spoke of his growing realization that what he had been calling traditional was in fact oral: "My first studies were on the style of the Homeric poems and led me to understand that so highly formulaic a style could be only traditional. I failed, however, at the time to understand as fully as I should have that a style such as that of Homer must not only be traditional but also must be oral. It was largely due to the remarks of my teacher M. Antoine Meillet that I came to see, dimly at first, that a true understanding of the Homeric poems could only come with a full understanding of the nature of oral poetry." [15]

The real impact of this revelation of Milman Parry has not yet been fully felt in Homeric scholarship, which has chosen to disdain oral epic and to move into the more abstruse kinds of literary criticism.[16] Although often referred to, the oral theory of Milman Parry is at best but vaguely understood. It is the purpose of this book to present that theory as fully and yet as simply as possible. Parry himself did not live long enough after making his monumental collection to think out his theory in detail, let alone to develop it and present it to the learned world in completeness. Working from the clues that he left, I have tried to build an edifice of which he might approve.

CHAPTER TWO

SINGERS: PERFORMANCE
AND TRAINING

Were we to seek to understand why a literary poet wrote what he did in a particular poem in a particular manner and form, we should not focus our attention on the moment when he or someone else read or recited his poem to a particular audience or even on any moment when we ourselves read the poem in quiet solitude. We should instead attempt to reconstruct that moment in time when the poet wrote the lines. Obviously, the moment of composition is the important one for such study. For the oral poet the moment of composition is the performance. In the case of a literary poem there is a gap in time between composition and reading or performance; in the case of the oral poem this gap does not exist, because composition and performance are two aspects of the same moment. Hence, the question "when *would* such and such an oral poem be performed?" has no meaning; the question should be "when *was* the oral poem performed?" An oral poem is not composed *for* but *in* performance. The implications of this statement are both broad and deep. For that reason we must turn first in our analysis of oral epic to the performance.

We must grasp fully who, or more correctly what, our performer is. We must eliminate from the word "performer" any notion that he is one who merely reproduces what someone else' or even he himself has composed. Our oral poet is composer. Our singer of tales is a composer of tales. Singer, performer, composer, and poet are one under different aspects *but at the same time*. Singing, performing, composing are facets of the same act.

It is sometimes difficult for us to realize that the man who is sitting before us singing an epic song is not a mere carrier of the tradition but a creative artist making the tradition. The reasons for this difficulty are various. They arise in part simply from the fact that we are not in the habit of thinking of a performer as a composer.[1] Even in the realm of oral literature most of us in the West, at least, are more accustomed to the ballad than to the epic; and our experience has been formed in large part by "folk" ballad singers who are mere performers. The present vogue of revival of folk singing on the concert stage and elsewhere has distorted our concept of the essence of oral composition. The majority of such "folk" singers are not oral poets. The collector even in a country such as Yugoslavia, where published collections have been given much attention for over a century, some of which have become almost sacrosanct, must be wary; for he will find singers who have memorized songs from these collections. In spite of authentic manner of presentation, in spite of the fact that the songs themselves are often oral poems, we cannot consider such singers as oral poets. They are *mere* performers. Such experiences have deceived us and have robbed the real oral poet of credit as a creative composer; indeed to some extent they have taken from epic performance an element of vital interest. Our task in this chapter is to restore to performance and performer their true significance.

When we realize that the performance is a moment of creation for the singer, we cannot but be amazed at the circumstances under which he creates. Since these circumstances influence oral form we must consider them. Epic poetry in Yugoslavia is sung on a variety of occasions. It forms, at the present time, or until very recently, the chief entertainment of the adult male population in the villages and small towns. In the country villages, where the houses are often widely separated, a gathering may be held at one of the houses during a period of leisure from the work in the fields. Men from all the families assemble and one of their number may sing epic songs. Because of the distances between the houses some of the guests arrive earlier than others, and of course this means that some leave earlier. Some very likely spend the whole night, as we learn from a conversation with Alija Fjuljanin (I, p. 291).* The singer has to contend with an audience that is coming and going, greeting newcomers, saying farewells to early leavers; a newcomer with special news or gossip may interrupt the singing for some time, perhaps even stopping it entirely.

What is true of the home gathering in the country village holds as well for the more compact villages and for towns, where the men gather in the coffee house (*kafana*) or in the tavern rather than in a private home. The taverns are entirely male establishments, whether the district is predominantly Moslem or not. Neither Moslem nor Christian women are ever allowed in these places. This is a man's world. Here the men gather at the end of the day. The farmers of the nearby villages may drop in for a short while to sit and talk, sip coffee or raki, and listen to songs. They come and go. The townspeople join them. There are shopkeepers and caravan drivers who

---

* In this book the texts of songs, conversations, and music in the Parry Collection as yet unpublished will be referred to by their number as catalogued in the Collection in Widener Library (for example, Parry 427). Those texts published in *Serbocroatian Heroic Songs*, Parry and Lord, Cambridge and Belgrade, 1954, will be referred to by volume number (I for the English translations and II for the Serbocroatian texts) and by their number within that volume (for example, II, No. 24). Conversations with singers, published in *Serbocroatian Heroic Songs*, will be referred to by volume and page number (for example, I, p. 63). Texts collected by Lord, beginning in 1950, will be referred to by their number as listed in the Collection in Widener Library (for example, Lord 102).

For information about the Parry Collection, see Chapter One, note 2.

have come in with merchandise from other districts or are stopping on their way through. Frequently the tavern is also an inn, a "han," and here the drivers will spend the night. Many of these men are also singers and the carriers of tradition from one district to another. They are a critical audience.

In market centers such as Bijelo Polje, Stolac, Novi Pazar, and Bihać, market day, the one day in the week when the town is crowded with people from the countryside who have come in to buy and sell, will be the busiest day in the han or in the kafana. Some of the business is done there during the day, and some of the money which has changed hands will be spent in the kafana at night before the men return to their own villages. They may even stay the night there and return the next morning, if they feel so inclined, or if the day has been particularly profitable. This is a good opportunity for the singer because, although his audience may not be stable, it does have money and is willing to reward him for his pains. He is not really a professional, but his audience does buy him drinks, and if he is good they will give him a little money for the entertainment he has given them.

When the singing takes place, as it occasionally does, at a wedding festival, the amount of confusion is increased by the singing of lyric songs and dancing carried on by the young people. The evenings offer the best opportunity for the singer of the old songs, when the older men are not watching the games or gossiping with their neighbors and are content to relax and sit back and listen to the bard.

Among the Moslems in Yugoslavia there is a special festival which has contributed to the fostering of songs of some length.[2] This is the festival of Ramazan, when for a month the men fast from sunrise to sunset and gather in coffee houses all night long to talk and listen to epic. Here is a perfect circumstance for the singing of one song during the entire night. Here also is an encouragement to the semiprofessional singer to attain a repertory of at least thirty songs. It was Parry's experience that such Moslem singers, when asked how many songs they knew, frequently replied that they knew thirty, one for every night of Ramazan. Most Moslem kafanas engage a singer several months in advance to entertain their guests, and if there is more than one such kafana in the town, there may be rivalry in obtaining the services of a well-known and popular singer who is likely to bring considerable business to the establishment.

In Novi Pazar Đemo Zogić kept a kafana, and Salih Ugljanin and Sulejman Makić had at one time or another been engaged in it as singers. Đemo paid the singer a hundred dinars in advance, or a hundred oka of grain for the singer to leave with his family for food, because the singer stayed in town and ate at Đemo's house. After the bard had sung a song in the kafana, Đemo circulated among the guests and took up a collection for him. According to Đemo some gave one dinar and some five, but Sulejman told us that they usually gave two dinars and that he made as much as sixty dinars a night (I, p. 238 and p. 265). Murat Žunić was much sought after in the district of Cazin and Bihać in the north, both places competing for his talent. He had sung in Banja Luka for six years during Ramazan (Parry 1915). Đemo Zogić was himself a singer and would sometimes sing for his own company, but he told us he was generally so busy serving coffee and greeting guests and talking that he had to hire someone to do the singing. Once when the singer had been indisposed during his engagement, Đemo had taken over, and the guests had given him great praise for his singing, so he tells us (I, p. 240).

In an account of the occasions for singing and of the audience which fosters it, mention at least should be made of the courtly entertainment of the earlier days in Yugoslavia. What we have been describing up to this point was in existence in Yugoslavia in the 1930's and to an extent still continues. In medieval times, before the Turkish conquests, the Christian courts had undoubtedly fostered the minstrel's art as had the courts of other countries in Europe at that time. When these courts re-emerged, however, after the expulsion of the Turks, they were no longer interested in the bards but sought their entertainment from abroad or from other sources. Hence in the Christian courts oral narrative poetry played no role for many generations. The local Moslem nobility on the other hand with its rich estates had fostered the art, and since this local nobility was still alive in some districts, such as Novi Pazar, Bijelo Polje, and Bihać in the 1930's, it was still possible to obtain firsthand information about the practice. It actually differed little from our account above except that everything was on a grander scale; the settings were more luxurious and the gifts to singers richer.

The records of the Parry Collection abound in stories, some fairly full, of how the Moslem bards used to sing at the "courts" of the Turkish nobility. Here the professional or semiprofessional singer was afforded the best opportunity for practicing his art. There seems to be little evidence, however, that the beys and aghas actually maintained a court minstrel. They not infrequently called in singers for special occasions when they entertained guests, but they did not keep a singer in their courts. In the old days the ruling class of Moslems celebrated the feast of Ramazan in its courts rather than in the kafana. When the Turkish rule was overthrown, the celebration took place more commonly in the kafana than in private Moslem homes.

Whether the performance takes place at home, in the coffee house, in the courtyard, or in the halls of a noble, the essential element of the occasion of singing that influences the form of the poetry is the variability and instability of the audience.

The instability of the audience requires a marked degree of concentration on the part of the singer in order that he may sing at all; it also tests to the utmost his dramatic ability and his narrative skill in keeping the audience as attentive as possible. But it is the length of a song which is most affected by the audience's restlessness. The singer begins to tell his tale. If he is fortunate, he may find it possible to sing until he is tired without interruption from the audience. After a rest he will continue, if his audience still wishes. This may last until he finishes the song, and if his listeners are propitious and his mood heightened by their interest, he may lengthen his tale, savoring each descriptive passage. It is more likely that, instead of having this ideal occasion the singer will realize shortly after beginning that his audience is not receptive, and hence he will shorten his song so that it may be finished within the limit of time for which he feels the audience may be counted on. Or, if he misjudges, he may simply never finish the song. Leaving out of consideration for the moment the question of the talent of the singer, one can say that the length of the song depends upon the audience. One of the reasons also why different singings of the same song by the same man vary most in their endings is that the end of a song is sung less often by the singer.

.*   *   *

If we are fully aware that the singer is composing as he sings, the most striking element in the performance itself is the speed with which he proceeds. It is not unusual for a Yugoslav bard to sing at the rate of from ten to twenty ten-syllable lines a minute. Since, as we shall see, he has not memorized his song, we must conclude either that he is a phenomenal virtuoso or that he has a special technique of composition outside our own field of experience.[3] We must rule out the first of these alternatives because there are too many singers; so many geniuses simply cannot appear in a single generation or continue to appear inexorably from one age to another. The answer of course lies in the second alternative, namely, a special technique of composition.

The major part of this book is concerned with the special technique of composition which makes rapid composing in performance possible. For an understanding of this technique it is necessary to introduce the Yugoslav singer and to examine the way in which he learns his art of singing. Let the singers speak for themselves from the phonograph records of the Parry Collection.

"My name is Sulejman Fortić, and I am Salih agha Forta's grandson. . . . Today I am a waiter in the coffee house" (I, p. 225).

"My name is Đemail Zogić. . . . I am thirty-eight years old. . . . I keep a coffee house" (I, p. 235).

"Nikola (the interrogator): What is your name? Sulejman (the singer): Sulejman Makić. . . . N: How old are you? S: Fifty years old. . . . N: What do you do at home? S: I plow and I reap. N: Do you have any sheep? S: I cut wood. No, by Allah, I have cattle" (I, p. 263).

"My name is Alija Fjuljanin. . . . I am a farmer. . . . I'm twenty-nine years old. . . . We occupy ourselves with stock and with the land" (I, p. 289).

"Nikola: What's your name, old man? Salih: Salih Ugljanin. N: How old are you? S: Eighty-five. . . . N: Tell me what your life has been like, Salih. S: My life has been good. I lived like a bey. I had cattle, and I traded. . . . I drove my cattle and sheep to Salonika, and up until the wars I had plenty. . . . Afterwards I came to Novi Pazar. . . . I kept a coffee house. . . . N: But how do you live now? S: We live well enough. God sends me my daily bread. Someone asks for me to help him with something, and he gives me something. Another calls me, and I help him, and he gives me something. N: How can you help anyone at your age? S: I help him with my brains . . . I fix up a deal for someone, which is to his advantage, and he sees. I buy oxen or sheep for him, if they're worth while. If anyone breaks his leg, I set it so you can't tell where it was broken. N: What, you're a doctor? S: Doctor, practitioner, whatever you like. . . . N: When you stopped trading, what did you do after that? S: For a while after that I worked the land, reaped and ploughed, and worked as a farmer. . . . I would sell the hay which I cut and take the money and buy cattle, and then buy grain, plough in a little, get some grain, feed my family, and all was well" (I, pp. 59, 62).

The example of Ahmet Musović in Bijelo Polje shows that even well-to-do Turkish beys used to sing. In 1934 he was sixty-four years old and until 1912 he had had his own land and tenant farmers and had been a merchant; he kept a store. He had two servants, one a Christian, the other a Moslem. Every Ramazan Ahmet and his family kept singers at their house. In fact, even a Christian tenant farmer used to come during Ramazan and sing both Christian and Moslem songs. These singers were paid, but when Ahmet himself used to sing it was not for pay. Only after the wars in 1912 when he lost everything had he himself gone from town to town and sung for pay (Parry 12390).

We can thus see that no particular occupation contributed more singers than any other, and professionalism was limited to beggars. There was a kind of semiprofessionalism among the Moslems during Ramazan, but only beggars lived completely by singing. In our field experience beggars, blind or otherwise, were not very good singers. In Yugoslavia in 1934–35 blind singers were not important carriers of the tradition. Our experience would not tend to verify the romantic picture of the blind bard. Nikola Janjušević in Gacko and Stjepan Majstorović in Bihać were both blind, but although they were picturesque characters, they were not skilled singers, either in respect to the outward aspects of their performance or in the fullness of development of their texts.

Majstorović's story is worth relating. He had been blind since he was a year and a half old (in 1935 he was fifty-five). He had had to care for his father and mother since the time he was fourteen. When he was twenty he had learned to sing to the *gusle* (the one-stringed bowed instrument used to accompany the singing) which he kept always with him in a bag, to prevent pranksters from putting soap on the string and thus spoiling it so that he would have to get a new string for it. He lived as a beggar and had not done badly for a number of years. When hard times came with the wars, the merchants in town had helped him and given him credit. In spite of his blindness he had married and had a married son. After the war his situation improved, and up to around 1928 or so all had gone well again, but for six or seven years prior to 1935 his luck had changed for the worse. He admitted that he could no longer sing very well because he was getting old and was not strong. He therefore liked short songs, because they did not tax his energies and he could sing them all the way through. Now, however, nobody listened to him, and in only one village (Bosanska Krupa) was he able to pick up any money. He sang his songs according to the company he was in, since he had to please his audience or else expect no reward. Thus when he was with Turks he sang Moslem songs, or his own songs in such a way that the Moslems won the battles. When he was with Serbs, whose company was more congenial to him, he sang their songs.[4] Although he had learned most of his songs from listening to singers, he told us that he had also learned at least three or four songs from the songbooks, strangely enough. A neighbor, or whomever he could find with some schooling, had read them to him. Occasionally some kind soul would tell him that a particular song would be pleasing to his audience, and though they had not been able to sing it for him, they had related it to him, I do not know whether in verse or prose, but I suspect the latter. He knew of some singers who had made up new songs, and he himself sang a new one about King Wilson. He told us that another singer had composed it, written it down, and had read it to him. When he was young, he had had to hear a song only once in order to pick it up, but now he found it hard to learn new songs (Parry 1912).

We do not mean to say, of course, that blind singers may not play an important role in the practice of their art in other cultures, or that they may not have done so in the past even in this one, but, for what it is worth, our experience in those years seemed to indicate that blind singers were not usually good singers. Against that evidence, however, one should place the information which we heard indirectly concerning the blind singer Ćor Huso, whose name has become closely associated with the Parry Collection in this country. He was blind in one eye (though some say blind in both, in spite of the fact the name Ćor means blind in one eye), and was a really professional singer according to the accounts which the collection contains. Huso was from Kolašin in Montenegro, and he wandered from place to place singing to the gusle. His fame spread abroad, and some of our best singers had learned songs from him. According to Salih Ugljanin's story, Huso had even gone to the court of Franz Josef and had been richly rewarded by him. He seems to have been a good showman. His dress and the trappings of his horse were distinctive, and he cut a romantic figure.

It is a great pity, of course, that someone did not collect songs from him a couple of generations ago, but he seems to have escaped the attention of collectors — just why would be interesting to know. Hörmann did not get so far west as Kolašin in gathering material for his most excellent volumes on the songs of the Moslems in Bosnia and Hercegovina, and Luka Marjanović was working in the north for the *Matica Hrvatska*. From later accounts of singers who learned from him, we can get some picture, however inaccurate, of the songs which he sang and of the influence which he had on the tradition. His example demonstrates the role which the prestige of a singer plays in the life of a song or of a theme; for the singer of fame will make a deeper impression on the tradition than will others of less repute.

What I believe is significant in this survey of the occupations which singers follow is that the singers do not seem to form a special class. They can belong to any group in society. The oral singer in Yugoslavia is not marked by a class distinction; he is not an oral poet because he is a farmer or a shopkeeper or a bey. He can belong to the "folk," the merchant class, or the aristocracy. His place in society tells us nothing about him as an oral poet. We must look elsewhere, then, for what distinguishes this man who sits before us and creates epic song from his fellow men and from those who write epics.

There seem to be two things that all our singers have in common: illiteracy and the desire to attain proficiency in singing epic poetry. If the second of these sets them apart from their fellows, it is the first, namely their illiteracy, which determines the particular form that their composition takes, and which thus distinguishes them from the literary poet. In societies where writing is unknown, or where it is limited to a professional scribe whose duty is that of writing letters and keeping accounts, or where it is the possession of a small minority, such as clerics or a wealthy ruling class (though often this latter group prefers to have its writing done by a servant), the art of narration flourishes, provided that the culture is in other respects of a sort to foster the singing of tales. If the way of life of a people furnishes subjects for story and affords occasion for the telling, this art will be fostered. On the other hand, when writing is introduced and begins to be used for the same purposes as the oral narrative song, when it is employed for telling stories and is widespread enough to find an audience capable of reading, this audience seeks its entertainment and instruction in books rather than in the living songs of men, and the older art gradually disappears. The songs have died out in the cities not because life in a large community is an unfitting environment for them but because schools were first founded there and writing has been firmly rooted in the way of life of the city dwellers.

In order best to appreciate and to understand the process of composition that we call oral, and thus to eliminate our prejudice against the "illiterate" singer, we must follow him during the years which he devotes to learning the art. If we take our future oral poet in his unlettered state at a tender age, let's say fourteen or fifteen, or even younger (singers tell us that this was the age at which they learned, although they usually mean by it only "when I was just a young boy"), and watch him learning the art, we can understand what this process is.

We can trace three distinct stages in his progress. During the first period he sits aside while others sing. He has decided that he wants to sing himself, or he may still be unaware of this decision and simply be very eager to hear the stories of his elders. Before he actually begins to sing, he is, consciously or unconsciously, laying the foundation. He is learning the stories and becoming acquainted with the heroes and their names, the faraway places and the habits of long ago. The themes of the poetry are becoming familiar to him, and his feeling for them is sharpened as he hears more and as he listens to the men discussing the songs among themselves. At the same time he is imbibing the rhythm of the singing and to an extent also the rhythm of the thoughts as they are expressed in song. Even at this early stage the oft-repeated phrases which we call formulas are being absorbed.

One of the best accounts of the learning process is to be found in Parry Text 12391 from Šećo Kolić. As a boy he used to tend sheep alone on the mountain. Here are his own words: "When I was a shepherd boy, they used to come for an evening to my house, or sometimes we would go to someone else's for the evening, somewhere in the village. Then a singer would pick up the gusle, and I would listen to the song. The next day when I was with the flock, I would put the song together, word for word, without the gusle, but I would sing it from memory, word for word, just as the singer had sung it. . . .[5] Then I learned gradually to finger the instrument, and to fit the fingering to the words, and my fingers obeyed better and better. . . . I didn't sing among the men until I had perfected the song, but only among the young fellows in my circle [družina] not in front of my elders and betters." Šećo here roughly distinguishes all three stages of learning; first, the period of listening and absorbing; then, the period of application; and finally, that of singing before a critical audience.

The second stage begins when the singer opens his mouth to sing, either with or without instrumental accompaniment. It begins with establishing the primary element of the form — the rhythm and melody, both of the song and of the gusle or the *tambura* (a two-stringed plucked instrument). This is to be the framework for the expression of his ideas. From then on what he does must be within the limits of the rhythmic pattern. In the Yugoslav tradition, this rhythmic pattern in its simplest statement is a line of ten syllables with a break after the fourth. The line is repeated over and over again, with some melodic variation, and some variation in the spacing and timing of the ten syllables. Here is a rhythmic fixity which the singer cannot avoid, and which gives him his first real difficulty when he sings. His problem is now one of fitting his thoughts and their expression into this fairly rigid form. The rigidity of form may vary from culture to culture, as we shall see later, but the problem remains essentially the same — that of fitting thought to rhythmic pattern.

It will be argued that this is what the literary poet does also. This may be true, but there are two factors in oral composition that are not present in a written tradition. We must remember that the oral poet has no idea of a fixed model text to serve as his guide. He has models enough, but they are not fixed and he has no idea of memorizing them in a fixed form. Every time he hears a song sung, it is different. Secondly, there is a factor of time. The literate poet has leisure to compose at any rate he pleases. The oral poet must keep singing. His composition, by its very nature, must be rapid. Individual singers may and do vary in their rate of composition, of course, but it has limits because there is an audience waiting to hear the story. Some singers, like Ćamil Kulenović in Bihać, begin very slowly with fairly long pauses between lines, working up gradually to very rapid rhythmic composition. Others insert many musical interludes of brief duration while they think of what is coming next. Still others have a formulaic phrase of general character addressed to the audience which they use to mark time, like Suljo Fortić with his *Sad da vidiš, moji sokolovi,* "Now you should have seen it, my falcons." But these devices have to be used sparingly, because the audience will not tolerate too many of them.

If the singer has no idea of the fixity of the form of a song, and yet has to pour his ideas into a more or less rigid rhythmic pattern in rapid composition, what does he do? To phrase the question a little differently, how does the oral poet meet the need of the requirements of rapid composition without the aid of writing and without memorizing a fixed form? His tradition comes to the rescue. Other singers have met the same need, and over many generations there have been developed many phrases which express in the several rhythmic patterns the ideas most common in the poetry. These are the formulas of which Parry wrote. In this second stage in his apprenticeship the young singer must learn enough of these formulas to sing a song. He learns them by repeated use of them in singing, by repeatedly facing the need to express the idea in song and by repeatedly satisfying that need, until the resulting formula which he has heard from others becomes a part of his poetic thought. He must have enough of these formulas to facilitate composition. He is like a child learning words, or anyone learning a language without a school method; except that the language here being learned is the special language of poetry. This is the period in which the teacher is most important.

In the first stage it generally happens that the neophyte has chosen one singer, perhaps his father, or a favorite uncle, or some well-known singer of his neighborhood, to listen to most closely, but he hears other singers, too. Sometimes, as we have seen in the case of Šećo Kolić, he has no single model, but picks up what he can from all whom he hears. Sulejman Makić, however, told us that he learned all his songs from a certain Arif Karalješak, who had stayed an entire year at Suljo's house when the boy was about fifteen years old. According to Suljo, he had brought this man to his house and kept him there to teach him to sing, but Arif also worked on the farm for them. Alija Fjuljanin said that his grandfather had given him a gusle when he was ten or twelve years old, and that he had learned most of his songs from three singers.

Sometimes there are published versions of songs in the background. Šaban Rahmanović in Bihać told us that he did not learn to sing until he was about twenty-eight (he was forty-five in 1935), and that he had learned his songs from the song books, the *Matica Hrvatska* collection in particular. Although he could not read, somebody had read them to him. But he had also heard the older singers in his district (Parry 1923). The entrance of these song books into the tradition is a very interesting phenomenon, and one that is open to gross misinterpretation. Yet as long as the singer himself remains unlettered and does not attempt to reproduce the songs word for word, these books have no other effect on him than that of hearing the song. In the case of Šaban it is very possible that he had heard many singers when he was young. He admits having heard his uncle sing, but says that he did not attempt to learn the art until later. Thus the first period in his learning was unusually long and casual, and the second period was taken up largely with having songs read to him from the song book.

More typical is the case of old Murat Žunić from the same district, a district which has been strongly influenced by the song books. Murat had learned his songs from singers, not from the song book versions being read to him, but he was aware of the song books, knew the names of the singers who had contributed songs to be published in them, and was conscious that some of those from whom he had learned had picked up their songs from the books. He had heard songs from Hercegovina read from books and was very critical of the singers of that province. He said that they made mistakes in geography because they didn't know where Kladuša, the home of the famous Hrnjići, was. His own songs he had learned chiefly from two members of his family (Parry 1915).

Franje Vuković knew only that he had first learned to sing from a cousin, Ivo Mekić Jerković, but he couldn't remember from whom he had learned each song which he knew. Like Šaban Rahmanović, he too had been a little late in learning. Until he was nineteen or twenty he had been too busy about the farm, but when he married, his wife took over the work, and he had leisure in which to listen to singers and to learn to sing himself. Strangely enough, Franje sang without any musical accompaniment. He told us that he had learned to sing to the gusle, but that when his house and mill had been burned to the ground he had lost his gusle, and since that time he had sung without it (Parry 1912).

Learning in this second stage is a process of imitation, both in regard to playing the instrument and to learning the formulas and themes of the tradition. It may truthfully be said that the singer imitates the techniques of composition of his master or masters rather than particular songs.[6] For that reason the singer is not very clear about the details of how he learned his art, and his explanations are frequently in very general terms. He will say that he was interested in the old songs, had a passion (*merak*) for them, listened to singers, and then, "work, work, work" (*goni, goni, goni*), and little by little he learned to sing. He had no definite program of study, of course, no sense of learning this or that formula or set of formulas. It is a process of imitation and of assimilation through listening and much practice on one's own. Makić was a bit more explicit than some. He said that his teacher would sing a song for him two or three times until he learned it (I, p. 264). Fjuljanin said that he sometimes asked a singer to sing a song for him (I, p. 292). Since the singer hears many songs, he uses the language and formulas that belong to them all; for the accomplished singer whom he has been imitating does not have one set of expressions for one song and another for another, except when there are themes in the one that are not in the other, and even in these cases the formulas and formulaic techniques are the same in all songs.

The second stage ends when the singer is competent to sing one song all the way through for a critical audience. There are probably other songs that he can sing partially, songs that are in process of being learned. He has arrived at a definite turning point when he can sit in front of an audience and finish a song to his own satisfaction and that of the audience. His job may or may not be a creditable one. He has very likely not learned much about "ornamenting" a song to make it full and broad in its narrative style. That will depend somewhat on his model. If the singer from whom he has learned is one who uses much "ornamentation," he has probably picked up a certain amount of that ornamentation too. Whether his first song is fully developed or not, it is complete in its story from beginning to end and will tend to follow the story as he heard it from his master. If, however, and this is important, he has not learned it from one singer in particular, and if the stories of that song differ in the various versions which he has heard, he may make a composite of them. He may, on the other hand, follow one of them for the most part, taking something from the others too. Either way is consistent with the traditional process. One can thus see that although this process should not be described as haphazard, which it is not, it does not fit our own conceptions of learning a fixed text of a fixed song. Already at this second stage, and to an extent also in the first, the singer has found, though the knowledge may not be conscious, that the tradition is fluid. His unlettered state saves him from becoming an automaton. Yet, in this period he is also closer to his originals in themes and possibly in language also than he will ever again be in his experience as a singer. Even the songs that he learns at this time will change as his repertory increases and his competence grows.

This increase in repertory and growth in competence take place in the third and last stage of the learning process. We can easily define its beginning as the point at which he sings his first song completely through for a critical audience, but it is much more difficult to set the other limit. That is a question of when a singer is an accomplished practitioner of the art, a matter to be considered shortly. Let us look more closely at what goes on in the third stage. First the singer learns to sing other songs all the way through. If he has already learned them in part, he finishes the process. But again this does not involve memorizing a text, but practicing until he can compose it, or recompose it, himself.

Our proper understanding of these procedures is hindered by our lack of a suitable vocabulary for defining the steps of the process.[7] The singers themselves cannot help us in this regard because they do not think in terms of form as we think of it; their descriptions are too vague, at least for academic preciseness. Man without writing thinks in terms of sound groups and not in words, and the two do not necessarily coincide. When asked what a word is, he will reply that he does not know, or he will give a sound group which may vary in length from what we call a word to an entire line of poetry, or even an entire song. The word for "word" means an "utterance." When the singer is pressed then to say what a line is, he, whose chief claim to fame is that he traffics in lines of poetry, will be entirely baffled by the question; or he will say that since he has been dictating and has seen his utterances being written down, he has discovered what a line is, although he did not know it as such before, because he had never gone to school.

While the singer is adding to his repertory of songs, he is also improving the singing of the ones he already knows, since he is now capable of facing an audience that will listen to him, although possibly with a certain amount of patronizing because of his youth. Generally speaking, he is expanding his songs in the way I have indicated, that is, by ornamenting them. This process will be treated in a later chapter, but it will suffice here to say that this is the period in which he learns the rudiments of ornamentation and expansion. The art of expanding the old songs and of learning new ones is carried to the point at which he can entertain his audience for a full evening; that is one of his goals.

Here, then, for the first time the audience begins to play a role in the poet's art. Up to this point the form of his song has depended on his illiteracy and on the need to compose rapidly in the traditional rhythmic pattern. The singers he has heard have given him the necessary traditional material to make it possible for him to sing, but the length of his songs and the degree to which he will ornament and expand them will depend on the demands of the audience. His audience is gradually changing from an attitude of condescension toward the youngster to one of accepting him as a singer.

It is into the world of kafana, informal gatherings, and festival that our young singer steps once he has mastered the singing of a song. Here he learns new songs. The form of his singing is being perfected, and its content is becoming richer and more varied. This audience and this social milieu have had an effect on the length of the songs of his predecessors, and they will have a similar effect on the length of his songs.

We might say that the final period of training comes to an end when the singer's repertory is large enough to furnish entertainment for several nights. Yet it is better to define the end of the period by the freedom with which he moves in his tradition, because that is the mark of the finished poet. When he has a sufficient command of the formula technique to sing any song that he hears, and enough thematic material at hand to lengthen or shorten a song according to his own desires and to create a new song if he sees fit, then he is an accomplished singer and worthy of his art. There are, to be sure, some singers, not few in number, who never go beyond the third stage in learning, who never reach the point of mastery of the tradition, and who are always struggling for competence. Their weakness is that they do not have enough proficiency in formula-making and thematic structure, nor enough talent, to put a song together artistically. Although such singers can show us much about the workings of the practice and of the tradition, it is the finest and longest songs and the most accomplished singers in whom we are interested for comparative purposes in the study of individual singers and individual songs.

The singer never stops in the process of accumulating, recombining, and remodeling formulas and themes, thus perfecting his singing and enriching his art. He proceeds in two directions: he moves toward refining what he already knows and toward learning new songs. The latter process has now become for him one of learning proper names and of knowing what themes make up the new song. The story is all that he needs; so in this stage he can hear a song once and repeat it immediately afterwards — not word for word, of course — but he can tell the same story again in his own words. Sometimes singers prefer to have a day or so to think the song over, to put it in order, and to practice it to themselves. Such singers are either less confident of their ability, or they may be greater perfectionists.

Sulejman Makić, for example, liked to have time to put his song in order. In Parry Text 681, Records 1322–23 (I, pp. 265–266) we can hear his own words: "Nikola: Could you still pick up a song today? Sulejman: I could. N: For example, if you heard me sing a song, let's say, could you pick it up right away? S: Yes, I could sing it for you right away the next day. N: If you were to hear it just once? S: Yes, by Allah, if I were to hear it only once to the gusle. N: Why not until the next day? . . . What do you think about in those two days? Isn't it better to sing it right away than later, when you might forget it after so long a time? S: It has to come to one. One has to think . . . how it goes, and then little by little it comes to him, so that he won't leave anything out. . . . One couldn't sing it like that all the way through right away. N: Why couldn't you, when it's possible the second or third day afterwards? S: Anybody who can't write can't do it. N: All right, but when you've learned my song, would . . . you sing it exactly as I do? S: I would. N: You wouldn't add anything . . . nor leave anything out? S: I wouldn't . . . by Allah I would sing it just as I heard it. . . . It isn't good to change or to add."

Đemo Zogić also gave us information on this point (I, pp. 240–241).

"N: We have heard — we've been in those places in our country where people sing — and some singers have told us that as soon as they hear a song from another singer, they can sing it immediately, even if they've heard it only once, . . . just as it was word for word. Is that possible, Đemail? Đ: It's possible. . . . I know from my own experience. When I was together with my brothers and had nothing to worry about, I would hear a singer sing a song to the gusle, and after an hour I would sing his whole song. I can't write. I would give every word and not make a mistake on a single one. . . .

"N: So then, last night you sang a song for us. How many times did you hear it before you were able to sing it all the way through exactly as you do now? Đ: Here's how many times I heard it. One Ramazan I engaged this Suljo Makić who sang for you here today those songs of the Border. I heard him one night in my coffee house. I wasn't busy. I had a waiter and he waited on my guests, and I sat down beside the singer and in one night I picked up that song. I went home, and the next night I sang it myself. . . . That singer was sick, and I took the gusle and sang the whole song myself, and all the people said: 'We would rather listen to you than to that singer whom you pay.' N: Was it the same song, word for word, and line for line? Đ: The same song, word for word, and line for line. I didn't add a single line, and I didn't make a single mistake. . . .

"N: Tell me this, if two good singers listen to a third singer who is even better, and they both boast that they can learn a song if they hear it only once, do you think that there would be any difference between the two versions? . . . Đ: There would. . . . It couldn't be otherwise. I told you before that two singers won't sing the same song alike. N: Then what are the differences? Đ: They add, or they make mistakes, and they forget. They don't sing every word, or they add other words. Two singers can't recite a song which they heard from a third singer and have the two songs exactly the same as the third.

"N: Does a singer sing a song which he knows well (not with rhymes, but one of these old Border songs), will he sing it twice the same and sing every line? Đ: That is possible. If I were to live for twenty years, I would sing the song which I sang for you here today just the same twenty years from now, word for word."

In these two conversations we have accomplished singers discussing under guidance the transmission, not of the art of singing, but of songs from one well-trained singer to another. They are also telling us what they do when they sing a song. Here the creative performer speaks. In the case of Đemo Zogić we can test his statements and thus we can learn how to interpret this information that singers can give us about their own art.

Note that both singers express some attitude toward writing. Makić gives the opinion that only a person who can write can reproduce a song immediately; whereas Zogić's boast is that although he can't write he can reproduce a song an hour after he has heard it. In other words, one says that the man with writing is superior; and the other, that he is as good as the man with writing. They reflect the unlettered man's admiration of the lettered, but their statements are inaccurate. Their admiration goes too far, for the man with writing cannot do what they believe he can and what they in actuality can do.

Both singers stress that they would sing the song exactly as they heard it, Zogić even boasting that he would sing the song in the same way twenty years later. Makić indicates that changing and adding are not good, implying that singers do change and add; and Zogić states plainly that two singers won't sing the same song alike. How do we disentangle these contradictions?

Zogić learned from Makić the song under discussion in his conversation, and both versions are published in Volume I of the Parry Collection (Nos. 24–25 and 29). Zogić did not learn it word for word and line for line, and yet the two songs are recognizable versions of the same story. They are not close enough, however, to be considered "exactly alike." Was Zogić lying to us? No, because he was singing the story as he conceived it as being "like" Makić's story, and to him "word for word and line for line" are simply an emphatic way of saying "like." As I have said, singers do not know what words and lines are. What is of importance here is not the fact of exactness or lack of exactness, but the constant emphasis by the singer on his role in the tradition. It is not the creative role that we have stressed for the purpose of clarifying a misunderstanding about oral style, but the role of conserver of the tradition, the role of the defender of the historic truth of what is being sung; for if the singer changes what he has heard in its essence, he falsifies truth. It is not the artist but the historian who speaks at this moment, although the singer's concept of the historian is that of a guardian of legend.

Although Makić's and Zogić's versions of the same song differ considerably, Zogić's version itself changes little in the course of years. It was my good fortune to record this song from him seventeen years later, and it is remarkably close to the earlier version, though hardly word for word. It even still contains a glaring inconsistency in the story which was not in Makić's version.

But when Zogić is not defending himself as a preserver of the tradition, when he is thus freed to speak of the art of singing as such, in other words when he can talk about someone else's practice, he can be more objective. Then he states that two singers won't sing the same song alike; then he can recognize changes, additions, and mistakes, and give us a clearer picture of what happens in transmission.

And the picture that emerges is not really one of conflict between preserver of tradition and creative artist; it is rather one of the preservation of tradition by the constant re-creation of it. The ideal is a true story well and truly retold.

CHAPTER THREE
THE FORMULA

There came a time in Homeric scholarship when it was not sufficient to speak of the "repetitions" in Homer, of the "stock epithets," of the "epic clichés" and "stereotyped phrases." Such terms were either too vague or too restricted. Precision was needed, and the work of Milman Parry was the culmination of that need. The result was a definition of the "formula" as "a group of words which is regularly employed under the same metrical conditions to express a given essential idea." [1] By this definition the ambiguity of "repetitions" was eliminated; we were henceforth to deal with repeated word groups, not with repeated scenes, although Bowra uses the term "formula" still to apply to both. [2] At the same time, Parry's definition broadens "formula" to include within its scope more than the repeated epithets. Furthermore, the opprobrium attached to "clichés" and "stereotyped" has been removed.

Students of epic have now willingly applied themselves to the study of the repeated phrases by textual analysis, by counting repetitions, classifying similar phrases and thus extracting the technique of composition by formula manipulation. Yet in following this method they tend to treat all texts alike, whether by the same singer or not, whether sung or dictated, whatever, indeed, the circumstances of their collection may have been. Much has been gained from this type of analysis, and from it surely much more remains to be learned concerning the details of the process in any given tradition. Yet it seems to me that in confining ourselves to this method we tend to obscure the dynamic life of the repeated phrases and to lose an awareness of how and why they came into being. Are we not conceiving of the formula as a tool rather than as a living phenomenon of metrical language? In this chapter we shall attempt to look at the formula not only from outside in terms of textual analysis, but also from within, that is, from the point of view of the singer of tales and of the tradition.

The stress in Parry's definition on the metrical conditions of the formula led to the realization that the repeated phrases were useful not, as some have supposed, [3] merely to the audience if at all, but also and even more to the singer in the rapid composition of his tale. And by this almost revolutionary idea the camera's eye was shifted to the singer as a composer and to his problems as such.

At all stages in our musings about oral epic we find it necessary to re-create in our imagination not a general but a specific moment of perform-ance. The singing bard must be our guide; and the singing bard is never a type but an individual. Whenever we say "the singer does this or that," we must make it clear that our statement is based on experience with a specific singer, or on the combined experience of various singers. Our method will be to follow the developing career of the young singer, beginning even from the time when he starts to absorb the tradition by much listening to the songs about him and continuing with each advance of his own flight of song.

It may seem strange that we have very few texts from singers in the earliest stage of apprenticeship, as it were, in their art. But collectors seek the best singers, and the best singers are usually the older men. Their reputa-tion is great; they are brought forward by those whom the collector ques-tions. On occasion a younger singer in his twenties or thirties may be suggested, often because he has a good voice or a fine manner of singing, more rarely because he is a narrator of quality. Yet it should surprise us that it has not occurred to anyone to make a special study of the youngest group. It is a commentary, indeed, on the force of the belief that the songs are set and that younger singers have not had time to memorize a song as well as an older man. Perhaps exposing this belief as false will encourage giving more attention to songs of the youngest singers, imperfect though they may be.

Surely the formula has not the same value to the mature singer that it has to the young apprentice; it also has different values to the highly skilled and to the unskilled, less imaginative bard. We may otherwise think of the formula as being ever the same no matter from whose lips it proceeds. Such uniformity is scarcely true of any element of language; for language always bears the stamp of its speaker. The landscape of formula is not a level steppe with a horizon which equalizes all things in view, but rather a panorama of high mountains and deep valleys and of rolling foothills; and we must seek the essence of formula at all points in the landscape. Moreover, with the penetrating eye of the mind we must look for this essence backward through the centuries which formed the mountains and the valleys. For the singing we hear today, like the everyday speech around us, goes back in a direct and long series of singings to a beginning which, no matter how difficult it may be to conceive, we must attempt to grasp, because otherwise we shall miss an integral part of the meaning of the traditional formula.

Or to use another figure, the formula is the offspring of the marriage of thought and sung verse. Whereas thought, in theory at least, may be free, sung verse imposes restrictions, varying in degree of rigidity from culture to culture, that shape the form of thought. Any study of formula must therefore properly begin with a consideration of metrics and music, particularly as confronted by the young singer first becoming aware of the demands of his art. Later we shall have to consider the question of why story becomes wedded to song and verse, to ask ourselves what kind of tale finds its expression in these very special methods of presentation. These are not problems that the contemporary singer of tales faces; for he has inherited the answers. The fact of narrative song is around him from birth; the technique of it is the possession of his elders, and he falls heir to it. Yet in a real sense he does recapitulate the experiences of the generations before him stretching back to the distant past. From meter and music he absorbs in his earliest years the rhythms of epic, even as he absorbs the rhythms of speech itself and in a larger sense of the life about him. He learns empirically the length of phrase, the partial cadences, the full stops.

If the singer is in the Yugoslav tradition, he obtains a sense of ten syllables followed by a syntactic pause, although he never counts out ten syllables, and if asked, might not be able to tell how many syllables there are between pauses. In the same way he absorbs into his own experience a feeling for the tendency toward the distribution of accented and unaccented syllables and their very subtle variations caused by the play of tonic accent, vowel length, and melodic line.[4] These "restrictive" elements he comes to know from much listening to the songs about him and from being engrossed in their imaginative world. He learns the meter ever in association with particular phrases, those expressing the most common and oft-repeated ideas of the traditional story. Even in pre-singing years rhythm and thought are one, and the singer's concept of the formula is shaped though not explicit. He is aware of the successive beats and the varying lengths of repeated thoughts, and these might be said to be his formulas. Basic patterns of meter, word boundary, melody have become his possession, and in him the tradition begins to reproduce itself.

In the months and years of boyhood, not very long indeed after he has learned to speak his own language, the future singer develops a realization that in sung stories the order of words is often not the same as in everyday speech. Verbs may be placed in unusual positions, auxiliaries may be omitted, cases may be used strangely. He is impressed by the special effect which results, and he associates these syntactic peculiarities with the singing of tales. Moreover, the linking of phrases by parallelism, balancing and opposition of word order become familiar to him; the verb, which occurs, for example, just before a syntactic pause, is repeated at the beginning of the next phrase or is balanced by a verb just before the following stop: (The verbs in the passage are italicized.)

Đe *sedimo*, da se *veselimo*,	Where we sit, let us make merry,
E da bi nas i Bog *veselio*,	And may God too make us merry,
Veselio, pa *razgovorio!*	Make us merry and give us entertainment!

In these pre-singing years, together with a sense of new arrangements of ideas and the words which express them, the boy's ear records the repetitions of the sounds of the words. His instinctive grasp of alliterations and as-sonances is sharpened. One word begins to suggest another by its very sound; one phrase suggests another not only by reason of idea or by a special ordering of ideas, but also by acoustic value.

Thus even before the boy begins to sing, a number of basic patterns have been assimilated in his experience. Their form may not be precise — the precision will come later — but it can be truly said that in this youth the idea of the formula is in process of becoming. What we shall soon designate as melodic, metric, syntactic, and acoustic patterns are forming in his mind.

The chief reason, of course, that the formula does not take precise shape at this stage, is that only the necessity of singing can produce a full-fledged formula. The phenomenon of which it is a manifestation arises from the exigencies of performance. Only in performance can the formula exist and have clear definition. Besides, not all the singers whom the boy hears in his family or community have the same formulas for a given idea or the same manner of treatment of formulas. There is no rigidity in what he hears.

What has been described so far has been an unconscious process of assimilation. Consciously the boy has been thinking of the stories them-selves which are related in this unusual way. But when he begins to sing, the manner of presentation comes for a long time to the fore. Then the formula is born for him and his formula habits are acquired.

One of the first problems for the young singer from the very beginning is to learn to play the instrument which accompanies the song. This is not a really difficult task, since most of the instruments which accompany chant are not intricate. In the Yugoslav case, the boy has to learn to bow a one-stringed instrument, the gusle, the range of which is open string plus four fingers, an ambitus of five notes. The rhythm is primary; the grace notes are ornamental. Some older singer may show him how to finger the in-strument, or the boy may simply imitate his elders by himself in private. He may make a small gusle for himself, because the grown-up size is too big for his hands, or his father or mentor may make one for him. He imitates the fingering, the melody, and the manner of his elder. Rade Danilović in Kolašin has told us how his father, Mirko, used to put the boy's hand on his own as he fingered the string (Parry 6783).

Thus begins the stage in which the rhythmic impressions of the earlier period of listening are fitted to the restrictions of the instrument and of a traditional melodic line. Usually the rhythms and melodies that the youth learns at this period of initial specific application will stay with him the rest of his life. He may acquire others from singers of great reputation or striking manner of performance, but they will be in addition to the earlier ones or, at most, they will only modify, not replace them.

At the same time, the boy is trying to sing words. He remembers the phrases he has heard, sometimes whole lines, sometimes only parts of lines.

From now on, for a considerable period of time, he will listen to his elders with more attention to the lines and phrases. He will pick them up from any singer whom he hears. As he practices singing by himself he realizes the need for them and he uses them, sometimes adjusting them more or less consciously to his own needs, sometimes unconsciously twisting them. They are not sacred, but they are useful. In this way he acquires the formulas of his elders and establishes his own formula habits. He is doing what all singers before him have done.

The most stable formulas will be those for the most common ideas of the poetry. They will express the names of the actors, the main actions, time, and place. Thus in the line, *Vino pije Kraljeviću Marko*, "Kraljević Marko is drinking wine," *Kraljeviću Marko* presents the hero in a complete second-half-line formula. Kraljević, properly a title, "king's son," or "prince," is treated as a patronymic. In another line, *Sultan Selim rata otvorio*, "Sultan Selim declared war," the title "Sultan" makes it possible to name Selim in a four-syllable initial formula. The young singer learns that patronymics, titles, and indications of city of origin, for example, *od Orašca Tale*, "Tale of Orašac," are of great use in naming his heroes. Epithets are not so frequent in this tradition because the shortness of the line does not present a need for them that cannot be fulfilled by title or patronymic. They come into usage either when there is no title or because the make-up of the line does not allow a long patronymic, or when the singer wishes to express the actor in a whole line, frequently a vocative, as in *Sultan Selim, od svijeta sunce*, "O Sultan Selim, light [sun] of the world."

The most frequent actions in the story, the verbs, are often complete formulas in themselves, filling either the first or the second half of the line, as in GOVORIO *Kraljeviću Marko*, "Kraljević Marko spoke." If the verb is a syllable short, a conjunction often completes the formula, as in PA ZASEDE *svojega dorata*, "Then he mounted his brown horse." The length of the action formula is naturally in part determined by whether the subject is expressed in the same line and by the length of the subject. The singer finds that he can say, "Marko said," in the first half of the line with subject expressed, *Marko kaže*, or in the second half line, *govorio Marko*, or in the whole line, *govorio Kraljeviću Marko*. Obviously here the length of the subject is influenced by the length of the verb. If the subject is not expressed, if the singer wants to say merely, "he said," *govorio* does very well for the first half of the line; the addition of a conjunction and the personal pronoun come to his aid in the second half line, *pa on govorio*, as does also very frequently a change of aspect of the verb, *pa odgovorio*, "then he replied." But in order to accomplish this in a whole line, the singer must repeat the idea in the second half of the line: *Govorio, riječ besedaše*, "He spoke, he uttered a word." This example illustrates that the object of a verb forms an integral part of the verb formula, and shows as well how and why pleonasm is so common in oral style. Many of the formulas for the second half of the line are made up of verb and object: *rata otvorio*, "opened war"; *knjigu napisao*, "wrote a letter." By a change of tense this last formula is often expressed in the first half of the line as *Knjigu piše*, "writes a letter." In both cases the other half of the line is left for the subject.

A third common set of formulas indicates time when the action occurs. A typical example, with Homeric overtones, is: *Kad je zora krila pomolila*, "When dawn put forth its wings," or *Kad je zora i bijela dana*, "When it was dawn and white day," or *Kad je sunce zemlju ogrijalo*, "When the sun had warmed the earth."

The singer must learn another category of common formulas indicating the place where an action occurs. "In Prilip," for instance, can be expressed in the first half of the line *U Prilipu*, in the second half of the line by *u Prilipu gradu*, and in the whole line by *U Prilipu gradu bijelome*, "In Prilip, that white city." Similarly, "in the tower" can be expressed in the first half of the line by *A na kuli*, with the conjunction *a* as a filler; in the second half line by *na bijeloj kuli*, "in the white tower," and in the whole line by *Na bijeloj od kamena kuli*, "In the white tower of stone."

The formulas represented by the preceding examples are the foundation stone of the oral style. We have seen them from the point of view of the young singer with an essential idea to express under different metrical conditions. Their usefulness can be illustrated by indicating the many words that can be substituted for the key word in such formulas. For example, in the Prilip formulas above, any name of a city with a dative of three syllables can be used instead of Prilip: *u Stambolu, u Travniku, u Kladuši*. Instead of *a u kuli*, "in the tower," one can say *a u dvoru*, "in the castle," or *a u kući*, "in the house." These formulas can be grouped together in what Parry, when studying the traditional epithets in Homer, termed "systems."[5] It is often helpful to write them as follows:

$$a\ u \begin{cases} \text{kuli} \\ \text{dvoru} \\ \text{kući} \end{cases}$$

Such a substitution system expresses graphically the usefulness and the relationship of a group of formulas.

A style thus systematized by scholars on the foundation of analysis of texts is bound to appear very mechanical. Again we may turn to language itself for a useful parallel. The classical grammar of a language, with its paradigms of tenses and declensions, might give us the idea that language is a mechanical process. The parallel, of course, goes even further. The method of language is like that of oral poetry, substitution in the framework of the grammar. Without the metrical restrictions of the verse, language substitutes one subject for another in the nominative case, keeping the same verb; or keeping the same noun, it substitutes one verb for another. In studying the patterns and systems of oral narrative verse we are in reality observing the "grammar" of the poetry, a grammar superimposed, as it were, on the grammar of the language concerned. Or, to alter the image, we find a special grammar within the grammar of the language, necessitated by the versification. The formulas are the phrases and clauses and sentences of this specialized poetic grammar. The speaker of this language, once he has mastered it, does not move any more mechanically within it than we do in ordinary speech.

When we speak a language, our native language, we do not repeat words and phrases that we have memorized consciously, but the words and sentences emerge from habitual usage. This is true of the singer of tales working in his specialized grammar. He does not "memorize" formulas, any more than we as children "memorize" language. He learns them by hearing them in other singers' songs, and by habitual usage they become part of his singing as well. Memorization is a conscious act of making one's own, and repeating, something that one regards as fixed and not one's own. The learning of an oral poetic language follows the same principles as the learning of language itself, not by the conscious schematization of elementary grammars but by the natural oral method.

Any thorough grammar of a language notes exceptions to "rules," dialectal differences, "irregular" nouns and verbs, idioms — in fact those divergences from the systematized rules that arise in usage and in the normal organic change constantly in operation in a living spoken language. If we analyze oral epic texts that are recorded from actual performance rather than texts taken from dictation and normalized to some extent, we can observe the oral poetic language in its pure state, with its irregularities and abnormalities arising from usage. Then it is clear that the style is not really so mechanical as its systematization seems to imply.

The value to us of drawing up a number of substitution systems is that we immediately begin to see that the singer has not had to learn a large number of separate formulas. The commonest ones which he first uses set a basic pattern, and once he has the basic pattern firmly in his grasp, he needs only to substitute another word for the key one. The actual basic formulas which any given singer may learn first would be practically impossible to determine; it would vary from singer to singer. Probably if the first song learned by the singer concerned Marko Kraljević, Marko's name and the varieties of it used in making lines would set the basic pattern for similar names, which would fall into a four-syllable plus two-syllable pattern. The fundamental element in constructing lines is the basic formula pattern. There is some justification for saying indeed that the particular formula itself is important to the singer only up to the time when it has planted in his mind its basic mold. When this point is reached, the singer depends less and less on learning formulas and more and more on the process of substituting other words in the formula patterns.

Although it may seem that the more important part of the singer's training is the learning of formulas from other singers, I believe that the really significant element in the process is rather the setting up of various patterns that make adjustment of phrase and creation of phrases by analogy possible. This will be the whole basis of his art. Were he *merely* to learn the phrases and lines from his predecessors, acquiring thus a stock of them, which he would then shuffle about and mechanically put together in juxtaposition as inviolable, fixed units, he would, I am convinced, never become a singer. He must make his feeling for the patterning of lines, which he has absorbed earlier, specific with actual phrases and lines, and by the necessity of performance learn to adjust what he hears and what he wants to say to these patterns. If he does not learn to do this, no matter how many phrases he may know from his elders, he cannot sing. He does this in performance, not before an audience at first, of course, but by himself. This style has been created and shaped in performance; it has been so with all singers since time immemorial, and it is so with him. The habit of adjustment, the creation of lines in performance, this is acquired from the moment the boy begins to try to sing.

What is meant by "adjustment" can best be comprehended in terms of the establishment of various kinds of patterns and rhythms of expression. These the boy has picked up in his pre-singing years and he now finds his own means of forming them naturally and readily. We may begin again with the melodies of the singing itself. The boy learns that there is a special pattern for the opening of a song, with its own beginning and cadence. There is at least one oft-repeated melodic pattern for sustained narrative. Sometimes in the course of his life the singer acquires from one to three variations of this most important pattern. It is quite possible that he has discovered that by changing the melody he rests his voice. On occasion, but by no means regularly, the melodic pattern shifts for dramatic emphasis. There is a modified version of the singer's main pattern for stopping before a rest and another somewhat modified version for reprise after a pause. The song also has its concluding cadence. An example of these patterns can be seen in the appendix to Volume I of *Serbocroatian Heroic Songs* in the musical transcriptions of the "Captivity of Đulić Ibrahim," sung by Salih Ugljanin in Novi Pazar with music notations from the records by Béla Bartók.

From these musical examples one can see also the rhythmic patterns, generally trochaic. Here the play or "adjustment" between melody and meter can be observed in operation. We note the inadequacy of our texts without music in presenting a picture of epic song. The line is syllabic, or better, syllabo-tonic, a trochaic pentameter with an invariable break after the fourth syllable. It is simple, yet subtlety has entered from the interplay between melody and text. There is a tension between the normal accent and the meter. The accent of the meter does not always fall on the normal prose accent,[6] nor are all five stresses of the same intensity. The ninth syllable is the most prominent, has the strongest beat, and is held longest; the seventh and eighth are the weakest. The tenth may be lost entirely, completely swallowed, or hopelessly deformed. It may be carried over to the beginning of the following line,[7] or it may be an ordinary short beat. The first and the fifth syllables tend to be of the same intensity because they are the initial beat in the line and the first after the break; but when a proclitic stands in these positions, as is very common at the beginning of the line and not unusual in the fifth syllable, the first and third feet are sometimes iambs rather than trochees, and the melody follows this rhythm. Occasionally the first foot, sometimes even the second or third foot, is a dactyl in the regular practice of some singers; and they have sets of formulas adjusted to this rhythm.[8] In these cases the extra syllable is often supplied by a word without meaning.

It is noteworthy also that Serbocroatian maintains a pitch accent, rising or falling, and pays much attention to long and short vowels. The subtlety of the rhythms is, of course, further complicated by these characteristics of the language. The metric differences here demonstrated required at an early stage an adjustment of formula by the singer, or perhaps were called into being because of an adjustment. Individual variations in melody and rhythm are greater than one might expect, and only when the actual melodies of recorded songs are published will this fact be properly realized.[9] Some idea of the range of variation can be obtained from sample lines from three singers (see pages 39–41).*

Under the pressure of rapid composition in performance, the singer of tales, it is to be expected, makes occasional errors in the construction of his lines. His text line may be a syllable too long or a syllable too short. This does not trouble him in performance, and his audience scarcely notices these lines, since they have an understanding of the singer's art and recognize these slight variations as perfectly normal aberrations. The singer himself adjusts his musical line to the text by making a dactyl out of a trochee or by holding one syllable for two rhythmical beats rather than for one.

An additional set of patterns, related to the rhythmic patterns, which the singer must learn to control in these first years, is that of word boundaries, or more properly, length of accentual groups (that is, a word plus proclitics and enclitics). This need is especially important to the singer because the feeling for the mid-line break is very real. An accentual group cannot, and in practice only very rarely does, bridge the fourth and fifth syllables, although neither the melodic nor rhythmic patterns show this. When listening to the song one hears no pause at the break. The end of the line is very clearly marked, and run-on lines are few. In the first half of the line the most common word-boundary patterns are 2-2, 1-3, and 4: *vino pije*, "he

---

* A. "The Captivity of Đulić Ibrahim," sung by Salih Ugljanin (1, pp. 437, 439)
  B. "Osman Delibegović and Pavičević Luka," sung by Avdo Međedović (Parry 12389)
  C. "Junaštvo Đerđelez Alije," sung by Avdo Međedović (Parry 12379)

INTRODUCTION

LINE 1

Ej!___ Đe se-dɪ - mo, aj! da se ve - se - ljim - [o]

Oj, Ri - hi- ječ pr - va Bo-že nɪ po-mo-zi

Oj, Ri - ječ pr - va Bo- že ni po- mo - zi

LINE 12

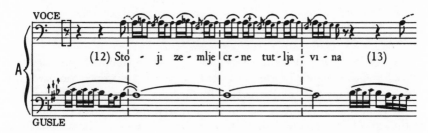

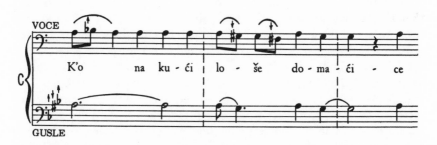

drinks wine"; *pa govori*, "then he says"; *Kraljeviću,* or *a vodi ga,* "and he leads him" (where *a* is proclitic and *ga* is enclitic). In the second half of the line the most common patterns are 2–4, 4–2, and 3–3: *juriš učinio,* "he made an attack"; *zametnuše kavgu,* "they started strife"; and *besedi serdaru,* "he says to the sirdar." Most of the formulas that the singer hears are in these patterns, and he will make new ones on the basis of them.

Closely allied to the word-boundary patterns, to no small extent helping to form them, are the syntactic patterns of the formulas. The order in which the parts of speech appear, hence the relation of ideas, is involved. In a style in which actions or things are added one to another in series, the conjunction plays a large role, and the most common patterns for the beginning of the line naturally begin with a conjunction. In fact conjunction-verb in the first half line is very frequent. For example:

A ćesar se na me naljutijo,	And the emperor was angered at me,
Pa na mene naljetljemu dao,	And he inflicted outlawry upon me,
Pa me danas surgun učinijo,[10]	And today he has exiled me,
A prati me k tebe u Bagdatu,	And sent me to you in Bagdad,
(II, No. 1:1194–1197)	

There are many initial formulas beginning with a conjunction, especially when an uncompounded form of the verb is used, for example, the narrative present, the imperfect, or the aorist. In the case of compound tenses, the auxiliary appears in the first half of the line and the participle or infinitive in the second. In the latter half of the line one finds most of the noun-epithet combinations: *knjigu šarovitu,* "well-writ letter"; *visoku planinu,* "high mountain"; *gradu bijelome,* "white city." [11]

A tasevi od srme bijele,	The cups were of white silver,
A sinđiri od žežena zlata.	And the chains were of 'fined gold.
Ej, Spanula bagdatska kraljica;	Ej, Then appeared the Queen of Bagdad.
(II, No. 1:1143–1145)	

Such are the syntactic patterns which the boy now begins to store in his experience and to use as a basis for new phrases.

The second half of the line is dependent not only syntactically on the first, but is also to some extent suggested by the sound patterns with which the line opens. There are a number of lines that have become set through the pattern of internal rhyme: "Kud god *skita,* za Aliju *pita,*" "Wherever he wanders, he asks for Alija"; *"Zveknu* halka, a *jeknu* kapija," "The knocker resounded, and the gate echoed." The importance of alliteration is apparent in such a line as "Kazaše ga u gradu Kajniđu," "They pointed him out in the city of Kajniđa," in which the k-g alliteration is arranged in chiastic order, k-g-g-k. Nothing would seem to have hindered the singer from using *u Kajniđu gradu* in the second half of the line, but he appears to have preferred the chiastic order, in part also perhaps under the influence of the a-u-a-u assonance in the middle of the line. The singers have a sensitivity to proportion and completeness of form even within the limits of a single line. Whatever feeling for such sound patterns the boy has absorbed in his pre-singing days is crystallized when he begins to perform.

This period in his training is pre-eminently one of learning to produce lines. Part of the process is accomplished by remembering and using phrases heard from other singers. This constitutes one element in the continuity of oral epic style. The phrases help to establish in the singer's experience a series of patterns, and these patterns are also an element in the continuity of the style. At the same time, by necessity, because he does not remember all the phrases which he needs, he is forced at the moment of his private performances to form phrases on the basis of the patterns. Since they follow the traditional patterns, they are indistinguishable from the other phrases that he has remembered, and may unconsciously be actually identical with them. To him the first matter of importance is certainly not the source of the phrase but the phrase itself at the critical time. For anyone, however, who is trying to understand how a particular style comes into being, it is necessary to note that there are two ways by which a phrase is produced; one is by remembering it, the other is through creating it by analogy with other phrases; and it may well be impossible to differentiate between the two. While both remembering and creating (in the sense of making, not necessarily "originating") play important roles, the latter, creating, is especially significant. The singer cannot, and does not, remember enough to sing a song; he must, and does, learn to create phrases. Hence the most important elements in the style are the basic patterns which we have illustrated, and which are established at this period.

In the course of time and of much practice, the need for a particular phrase arises over and over again. Whether it is one remembered from other singers or one created anew (and perhaps re-created several times as the need recurs), a phrase becomes set in the poet's mind, and he uses it regularly. Then, and only then, is the formula really born. The remembered phrase may have been a formula in the other singer's songs, but it is not a formula for our singer until its regular use in his songs is established. The remembered phrases from other singers are more numerous, of course, in the early years of training, and decrease gradually as the ability to make phrases is developed, although both processes continue during the singer's lifetime. The phrases for the ideas most commonly used become more securely fixed than those for less frequent ideas, with the result that a singer's formulas are not all of the same degree of fixity. Indeed, the creating of phrases continues always as well. I believe that we are justified in considering that the creating of phrases is the true art of the singer on the level of line formation, and it is this facility rather than his memory of relatively fixed formulas that marks him as a skillful singer in performance.

The very fact that the practice of oral narrative song has endured so long is proof enough that it can absorb new ideas and construct new formulas. But the process of building formulas is so quiet and unspectacular and so slow that it is almost imperceptible. Since the patterns of thought and the rhythm of presentation remain unchanged, the new words in the formulas are not noticed except when the ideas behind them are in striking contrast to the surroundings in which they occur. Thus proper names, recent foreign or international words, and the inventions of a mechanized age, when they find their way into the songs, as they do and must, provide us with the means of studying new formulas. It would be nonsense to suppose that the singer in whose songs these novelties are found is their originator. He may be, but the chances are against it.

New formulas are made by putting new words into the old patterns. If they do not fit they cannot be used, but the patterns are many and their complexity is great, so that there are few new words that cannot be poured into them. Salih Ugljanin's song of the Greek War (I, No. 10), a song which he claimed to have made up himself, contains some new ideas. He uses the word *Avropa* in the sense of "the rulers of Europe," *Avropa me odi zatvorila,* "Europe imprisoned me here," and *Avropa me* is only a variation of *Ibrahim me* or *Mustafa me.* The Queen of England, although a newcomer, is perfectly at home in the line *Misir daše ingliskoj kraljici,* "They gave Egypt to the Queen of England"; we are familiar with both the *moskovska kraljica,* "the Queen of Moscow," and the *bagdatska kraljica,* "the Queen of Bagdad." When, however, we come upon *Ti načini sitne teligrafe,* "Prepare short telegrams," the newness strikes us in the face. Salih is singing of a new age and he has simply substituted the new means of communication for the old type of official document, the *bujruntija. Ti načini sitne bujruntije* was his model. But when he tries to use the three-syllable nominative singular *teligraf* he runs into difficulty. The nominative singular *bujruntija* has four syllables, and the other most common missives, *knjiga* and *ferman,* have two. Formulas for communication have been built with either four- or two-syllable words in mind. He is thinking of *Od sultana brže knjiga dođe,* or *Od sultana brže ferman dođe,* "A ferman came swiftly from the sultan," when he sings *Od sultana brže teljigraf dođe.* In the last appearance of the word in his song he has solved the problem and found the right pattern: *Pa kad takav teljigraf dolazi,* "When such a telegram arrived."

Even in a song of olden times new words have crept in. Avdo Međedović uses terms that he must have picked up when he was in the army. In Parry Text 12389, the action of which, at least in Avdo's imagination, is placed in the days of Sulejman the Magnificent, we find *Moja braćo, moje dve* KOLEGE, "My brothers, my two colleagues" (line 415), *O* KOLEGA, *Fetibegoviću,* "O my colleague, Fetibegović" (line 2376), *Ja sam na to* RISKIRAO *glavu,* "It is for that that I risked my life" (line 1570), *A na njima careva* NIFORMA, "They were wearing imperial uniforms" (line 4085), and *Sve* SOLDATA, *sve pograničara,* "All soldiers, all men of the border" (line 6794). One can thus observe that the Yugoslav tradition was still very much alive in 1935 and still receptive to new ideas and new formulas.[12]

We have seen a bard's formulas coming into existence from the earliest period of his singing and we have noted the significant fact that they are not all alike either in their genesis or in their intensity of "formulicity." We have also suggested that the formulas themselves are perhaps less important in understanding this oral technique than the various underlying patterns of formulas and the ability to make phrases according to those patterns.

In order to avoid any misunderstanding, we must hasten to assert that in speaking of "creating" phrases in performance we do not intend to convey the idea that the singer *seeks originality* or fineness of expression. He seeks expression of the idea under stress of performance. Expression is his business, not originality, which, indeed, is a concept quite foreign to him and one that he would avoid, if he understood it. To say that the *opportunity* for originality and for finding the "poetically" fine phrase exists does *not* mean that the *desire* for originality also exists. There are periods and styles in which originality is *not* at a premium. If the singer knows a ready-made phrase and thinks of it, he uses it without hesitation, but he has, as we have seen, a method of making phrases when he either does not know one or cannot remember one. This is the situation more frequently than we tend to believe.

*   *   *

Thus far we have attempted to show the way in which the formulaic style enters into the consciousness of a young singer as he learns to use it for the telling of tales. Such a living art, so closely united to individual experience, cannot help but leave its peculiar stamp upon the songs and their texts. Because of this mark left upon them we can with a high degree of certainty determine whether any text that is before us was formed by a traditional bard in the crucible of oral composition.

Formula analysis, or even more generally textual analysis, must begin with a scrutiny of a sample passage in order to discover the phrases in it that are repeated elsewhere in as much of the work of an individual singer as there is available. In doing this we are following Parry's example. He took the first twenty-five lines of the *Iliad* and of the *Odyssey* and underlined those groups of words which he found repeated elsewhere in Homer. One needs only to glance at his charts[13] to see how many formulas there are in those samples. Chart I does the same for the Yugoslav material.

From Volume II of the Parry Collection we have chosen a passage of fifteen lines from the "Song of Bagdad," which was sung for phonograph recording by Salih Ugljanin in Novi Pazar in 1934 (II, No. 1). The singer was an old man at the time of recording and an accomplished performer with a large repertory, which he claimed included one hundred songs. His style, therefore, is not that of a beginner. The sample has been selected from the middle of the song rather than from the very beginning, because many of the Yugoslav songs open with an invocation which can be used for any song. Most Yugoslav epics are shorter than the Homeric poems, and we have had to use several of Salih's songs for corroborative purposes, rather than just two, in order to have sufficient material for analysis.

We have attempted, moreover, to choose a passage that did not contain one of the more frequently recurring themes such as those of letter-writing or of the arrival of an army on the field of assembly. In other words, the sample has been selected with an eye to making the experiment as valid as possible and to anticipating any objection which might be brought that the passage is of a sort that would be more formulaic by the very nature of its position or of its contents. For a similar reason, we have not admitted as supporting evidence for establishing a formula any repetition which occurs in the same passage in the two other versions of the same song by the same singer which are included in the material analyzed.

CHART I [14]

Jalah reče,/zasede đogata;	With "By Allah" she mounted her horse;
790 Đogatu se/konju zamoljila:	790 She implored the white horse:
"Davur, đogo,/krilo sokolovo!	"Hail, whitey, falcon's wing!
Četa ti je/o zanatu bila;	Raiding has been your work;
Vazda je Mujo/četom četovao.	Ever has Mujo raided.
Vodi mene/do grada Kajniđe!	Lead me to the city of Kajniđa!
795 Ne znam đadu/ka Kajniđi gradu."	795 I know not the road to the city of Kajniđa."
Hajvan beše,/zborit' ne mogaše,	It was a beast and could not talk,
Tek mu svašta/šturak umijaše.	But the steed knew many things.
Ode gljedat'/redom po planini.	He looked over the mountains
Uze đadu/ka Kajniđi gradu,	And took the road to the city of Kajniđa,
800 Pa sliježe/planinama redom,	800 And crossed one range after another,
Pa ga eto/strmom niz planinu,	Until lo he rushed down the mountain,
I kad polju/sliježe kajnićkome,	And when he descended to the plain of Kajniđa,
Kome stati/polje pogljedati,	Were anyone to look out over the plain,

In Chart I we have underlined the four-, six-, and ten-syllable phrases found more than once in the perusal of about 12,000 lines from the same singer. The chart is designed to show that in relation to 12,000 lines of diverse material from a given singer a certain number of phrases in a given passage are formulas. Twelve thousand lines is the approximate length of the longest of songs and will serve as a basis for comparison with the Homeric poems and others. These 12,000 lines constitute eleven different songs, three of which are recorded on the phonograph discs, four recited, but not sung, for the records, and four taken down from dictation. They give a good cross section of the more than 30,000 lines available from this singer.

From the chart we can see at a glance the number of repeated phrases that without any hesitation can be called "formulas." These phrases we know by demonstration that the singer has come in time to use regularly. Even within the limited number of lines used in the experiment, that is, 12,000, one quarter of the whole lines in the sample and one half of the half lines are formulas. It is most significant that there is no line or part of a line that did not fit into some formulaic pattern. In certain instances the pattern was a very common one and there was no difficulty in proving the formulaic character of the phrase. In a few instances the evidence was not so abundant, but it was still sufficient to make one feel certain that the phrase in question was formulaic. A number of the formulaic expressions could very easily have been classified as formulas, had we relaxed our established principles and standards. For example, *davur đogo* in line 791 misses being a formula because the evidence lists only *davur šturan* and *davur doro*. But *đogo, šturan,* and *doro* are all terms for horses. We could thus have easily increased the number of formulas.

Had we gone beyond 12,000 lines, the number of formulas would have continued to mount, and had we included material from other singers it would have increased still further, until it became clear that almost all, if not all, the lines in the sample passage were formulas and that they consisted of half lines which were also formulas. In other words, the manner of learning described earlier leads the singer to make and remake phrases, the same phrases, over and over again whenever he needs them. The formulas in oral narrative style are not limited to a comparatively few epic "tags," but are in reality all pervasive. There is nothing in the poem that is not formulaic.

Moreover, the lines and half lines that we call "formulaic" (because they follow the basic patterns of rhythm and syntax and have at least one word in the same position in the line in common with other lines or half lines) not only illustrate the patterns themselves but also show us examples of the systems of the poetry. Thus, although the beginning of line 790 was not found repeated exactly in the material analyzed, it belongs in a system of initial formulas made up of a three-syllable noun in the dative followed by the reflexive. Another example of the system is *junaku se.* The system would be written:

$$\left.\begin{array}{l} \text{đogatu} \\ \text{junaku} \end{array}\right\} \text{se}$$

Similarly, in line 791 *davur đogo* belongs in a system with

$$\text{davur} \left\{\begin{array}{l} \text{doro} \\ \text{šturan} \end{array}\right.$$

Any two-syllable word for a horse can fit into this system with *davur*. Finally, around the second half of the first line in the chart a lengthy system can be formed:

$$
\left.\begin{array}{l} \text{zasednu} \\ \text{zasedem} \\ \text{zasede} \\ \text{zasedi} \\ \text{zaseo} \end{array}\right\} \left\{\begin{array}{l} \text{đogata} \\ \text{kočiju} \\ \text{dorata} \\ \text{paripa} \\ \text{hajvana} \\ \text{maljina} \\ \text{binjeka} \\ \text{mrkova} \\ \text{vranina} \\ \text{menzila} \\ \text{šturika} \\ \text{zekana} \\ \text{eždralja} \end{array}\right.
$$

Since the singer learns his art from other singers and in his turn influences them, there are many formulas which are used by a large number of singers. For example, the following formula, line 789 from Chart I, is to be 'found in the songs of other singers from Novi Pazar:[15]

Jalah reče, zasede đogata.
"By Allah," she said, she mounted the white horse.

Sulejman Fortić

Jalah reče, posede đogina. (II, No. 22:433)	"By Allah," he said, he mounted the white horse.
Jalah reče, posede hajvana. (II, No. 23:308)	"By Allah," he said, he mounted the animal.

Đemail Zogić

Jalah reče, sede na dorina. (II, No. 24:746)	"By Allah," he said, he mounted the brown horse.
Jalah reče, posede hajvana. (II, No. 25:31)	"By Allah," he said, he mounted the animal.

Sulejman Makić

I to reče, posede dorata. (Parry 677:714)	And he said this, he mounted the brown horse.

Alija Fjuljanin

A to reče, zasede hajvana. (Parry 660:435)	And he said this, he mounted the animal.

One should not conclude, of course, that these singers learned these formulas from Salih or he from them. Salih learned them bit by bit from the singers whom he heard, and they from all whom they heard, and so forth back for generations. It would be impossible to determine who originated any of them. All that can be said is that they are common to the tradition; they belong to the "common stock" of formulas.

Although the formulas which any singer has in his repertory could be found in the repertories of other singers, it would be a mistake to conclude that all the formulas in the tradition are known to all the singers. There is no "check-list" or "handbook" of formulas that all singers follow. Formulas are, after all, the means of expressing the themes of the poetry, and, therefore, a singer's stock of formulas will be directly proportionate to the number of different themes which he knows. Obviously singers vary in the size of their repertory of thematic material; the younger singer knows fewer themes than the older; the less experienced and less skilled singer knows fewer than the more expert. Even if, individually, every formula that a singer uses can be found elsewhere in the tradition, no two singers would at any time have the same formulas in their repertories. In fact, any given singer's stock of formulas will not remain constant but will fluctuate with his repertory of thematic material. Were it possible to obtain at some moment of time a complete repertory of two singers, no matter how close their relationship, and from that repertory to make a list of the formulas which they know at that moment of time, there would not be complete identity in the two lists.

What is true for individuals is true also for districts. Differences of dialect and vocabulary, of linguistic, social, and political history will be reflected in thematic material and in formulas. The songs of Christian groups will have themes and formulas distinctive from those of Moslem groups, and *vice versa*. The formula stock of the Serbocroatian speaking district as a whole will be the sum total of the formulas known to its singers, but not all the singers will know all the formulas. One is ever being forced to return to the individual singer, to his repertory of formulas and themes, to the quality of his practice of the traditional art. One must always begin with the individual and work outwards from him to the group to which he belongs, namely to the singers who have influenced him, and then to the district, and in ever enlarging circles until the whole language area is included.

There would, however, be a large group of formulas known to all singers, just as in any speech community there are words and phrases in the language known to and used by all the speakers in that community. Even as these represent the most common and most useful ideas of the community, so too the stock of formulas known to all practitioners of the art of traditional narrative poetry represents the most common and most useful ideas in the poetry. Again they can be correlated with the thematic material. This common stock of formulas gives the traditional songs a homogeneity which strikes the listener or reader as soon as he has heard or read more than one song and creates the impression that all singers know all the same formulas.

The question whether any formula belongs to the common stock of formulas cannot be decided merely on the basis of its relative frequency in the songs of any given singer. In order to find the answer we must know its distribution among the singers of the tradition. For work of this sort a formula index is necessary, but this is a labor of many hands over many years. Only by compiling such an index could we determine with any degree of accuracy the frequency and distribution of formulas and the number of different formulas within a tradition. It would readily show us what formulas comprise the common stock of two or more individual singers, of a given district, or of a group of districts, and of the language tradition as a whole. This would do for formula study what the great motif indexes have done for thematic study.

Once a singer has solved a particular problem in verse-making, does he attempt to find any other solution for it? In other words, does he have two formulas, metrically equivalent, which express the same essential idea? Parry has shown how "thrifty" Homer was in this respect. Bowra has indicated that this thrift is not found in other oral poetry.[16] What facts can we deduce from our Yugoslav songs in the Parry Collection?

In order to test the possibilities, we have taken one of the formulas in Chart I and traced the instances in some nine thousand lines of Salih Ugljanin's songs of the essential idea of the formula. The purpose was to discover whether Salih had only one formula to express that idea under any one set of metrical conditions or whether he had several. This would show his "thrift," if any. The essential idea chosen was that of the second half line, "zasede đogata" (line 789), "he [or she] mounted his [or her] white [or black, or gray, etc.] horse." Horses play a very large part in Yugoslav traditional poetry, and the action of mounting them is frequently mentioned in Salih's songs.

In 3–3 rhythm in the last half line, with another clause ending at the break, and with a singular verb, Salih uses the following:

Jalah reče, zasede đogata. (II, No. 1:789; No. 2:912)	"By Allah," he said, he mounted his white horse.
Jalah rekni, zasedi đogata! (II, No. 1:1103)	Say "By Allah" and mount your white horse!

Under the same conditions but in 4–2 rhythm, he uses:

Jalah reče, zasednuo vranca. (II, No. 18:795)	"By Allah," he said, he mounted his black horse.

This change of rhythm was necessitated by the use of a two-syllable word for horse. In 2–4 rhythm, with a clause ending at the break, and with a plural verb, he uses:

Pa skočiše, konje zasedoše. (II, No. 17:323)	Then they leaped up, they mounted their horses.

Here the first question arises. Since *zasednuo vranca* and *konje zasedoše* both contain a four-syllable word and a two-syllable word, why is the rhythm of one 4–2 and of the other 2–4? There is a sound answer to this question. *Zasednuo vranca* is used in conjunction with *jalah reče* in the first half line, and the balanced chiastic pattern (object-verb, verb-object) of this common whole-line formula is in Salih's mind, so that *jalah reče, zasednuo vranca* follows along in the series with all the other instances of this full line. On the other hand, as we shall see shortly, when Salih uses *konje* he invariably puts it in this position in the line, and he is also following a different syntactic pattern. He has in mind such lines with *skočiše* as *Svi skočiše, seljam prifatiše,* "They all leaped up, they received the greeting" (II, No. 2:248), where another balance of verbs prevails, namely subject-verb, object-verb, as well as internal rhyme. When the subject of the verb "to mount" is expressed, it must be put in the first half line:

Svi konjici konje zasedoše.	All the horsemen mounted their horses.
(II, No. 1:880)	
A svatovi konje zasedoše.	And the wedding guests mounted their
(II, No. 4:1282)	horses.
Ta put hajduk šajku zasednuo.	Then the hajduk mounted his mare.
(II, No. 11:593)	
A Mujo svoga pojaše đogata.	And Mujo mounted his white horse.
(II, No. 11:694)	
Jalah Suka sede na menzila.	With a cry to Allah, Suka mounted his
(II, No. 2:99)	post horse.

The two instances of *konje zasedoše* here bear out what we said in the preceding paragraph. Salih always uses *konje* in this rhythmic pattern. But with *šajku zasednuo* we think back to *zasednuo vranca* and wonder why he did not say *zasednuo šajku,* following the same pattern in the second half of the line. First, however, we see that the syntactic pattern of the whole line is different from that of *jalah reče, zasednuo vranca,* the chiastic arrangement of which has already been indicated. Second, *šajku* usually occurs in this penultimate position in Salih's singing, especially in the common noun-epithet formula, *šajku bedeviju,* in the second half of the line. Added, then, to the pull of a whole-line syntactic pattern of subject, object, verb, is the influence of other formulas with *šajku.* In fact, such formulas begin in line 575, *I sa šnjime šajku bedeviju,* and continue with *Helj da ostane šajka u aharu* (576), *No najprijem šajku izvodićeš* (580), and *Pa odriješi šajku bedeviju* (584). In one of these cases the syntactic pattern of the second half line is the same as *šajku zasednuo;* namely, object, verb, *šajku izvodićeš* (580). Third, the two preceding lines end with the syntactic pattern, object, verb, and the rhythmic pattern, 2–4: *Jedno hebe zlata napunili* (591), and *Pro konja hebe proturiše* (592). Fourth, the vowel pattern discloses a chiastic order in the repetition of aj-u in the third to the sixth syllables, a-u-aj-u-aj-u-a-e-u-o. *Šajku* nicely repeats *hajduk* in the play of vowel sounds. *Zasednuo šajku* had no chance of breaking into such an aggregation of forces.

With *Mujo svoga pojaše đogata,* the principle of vowel alternation is again operative. Although *pojaše đogata* and *zasede đogata* mean essentially the same thing and the metrical conditions are identical, the back vowels of the first half of the line and the "o-a" pattern of *svoga,* repeated in *đogata* at the end of the line, call forth *pojaše* rather than *zasede.* We can see that the two formulas are not real equivalents in the phonological context. The next line, *Jalah Suka sede na menzila,* is a peculiar one. *Sede na menzila* and *zasede menzila* both have the same meaning, although they are not true alternates, because the rhythm is different; the former is 2–4 and the latter, 3–3. The second half of the previous line was *careva fermana,* "imperial firman"; the 3–3 might have called forth a 3–3 in the following line, but not necessarily. The intrusion of the subject *Suka* in the first half of the line has caused a change in the line. *Suka* has taken the place of *reče;* the singer has in his mind *jalah reče* and also *Suka reče* and *Suka sede.* The two-syllable *sede* plays not only its own role but also that of *reče,* with the same vowel arrangement. The line is an irregular and awkward one. In line 242 of the same song, *E! Jala, sede, krenu ka Budimu,* "With a cry to Allah, he mounted, and set out for Budim," one also finds the omission of the verb *reče,* and further adjustment in the line because of its absence. So far we have found no true alternates.

When a modifier is added to the idea "horse" or when an adverbial idea is to be added to the idea "mounted," the verb moves to the first half line. Or to state it in another way, if the verb is put in the first half line, some modifier must be added to the idea "horse" or an adverbial idea must be added to the idea "mounted." Thus we have:

Pa zasede krilata đogata.	Then he mounted his winged white horse.
(II, No. 1:1121)	
Pa posede šajku bedeviju.	Then he mounted his bedouin mare.
(II, No. 11:627)	
Eh, zasede njezina đogata.	Well, she mounted her white horse.
(II, No. 2:862)	
Zasedoše konje u avliju.	They mounted their horses in the court-
(II, No. 4:1538)	yard.
Pa zaseše konje na jaliju.	Then they mounted their horses on the
(II, No. 17:702)	bank.
Zasedoše dva konja menzila.	They mounted two post horses.
(II, No. 1:248)	

Here there is only one violation of the principle of thrift. *Posede* and *zasede* are interchangeable. There is so slight a difference in meaning between these two perfective aspects of the verb that they can be considered as identical. Very likely the alliteration of *posede* with *pa* and *bedeviju* has played a role in its choice. Thus far there has been variation, but no clear-cut departure from the principle of thrift.

There are three more instances of mounting in the material studied:

El Jala sede, krenu ka Budimu. (II, No. 2:242)	With a cry to Allah, he mounted and departed for Budim.
Đulić sede svojega dorata. (II, No. 4:1541)	Đulić mounted his brown horse.
A gotove konje zasednuše. (II, No. 13:112)	They mounted their ready horses.

In the first line *Jalah reče zasede đogata* has been telescoped into the first half of the line by omitting the verb "said" and the idea "horse," and by using the uncompounded verb *sede*, "he sat." Strictly speaking, the "essential idea" is not the same as the one that we are investigating, because the idea "horse" is omitted, but even if it had been expressed, as in the line which follows it above, it would not break the principle of thrift, because the uncompounded verb is forced on the singer by the preceding two-syllable word. The following line bears this out. Nor does *konje zasednuše* affect our thesis. It is the same as *konje zasedoše* except that it uses the momentary aorist instead of the simple aorist. The singer undoubtedly had in his mind the verb *krenuše*, "they departed," in the third and fourth syllables of the following line, so that the last two syllables of one line rhyme with the third and fourth of the following line.

When our judgment concerning thrift takes into consideration the acoustical context, there are few if any instances where substitution of one word for another even if they have the same essential meaning and metrical value is justified.

There has been a tendency to come to conclusions from an examination of all the songs in a collection regardless of whether they are from the same singer or even from the same district. Under such circumstances one would scarcely expect to find thrift. A *singer's* thriftiness is significant; that of a district or tradition less so (if it exists) for our purposes.

Indeed, it seems to me that the thriftiness which we find in individual singers and not in districts or traditions is an important argument for the unity of the Homeric poems. Homer's thriftiness finds its parallel in the individual Yugoslav singer, but not in the collected songs of a number of different singers.

Our brief excursion into the principle of thrift in actual oral composition among Yugoslav singers has served to emphasize the context of the moment when a given line is made. In order to understand why one phrase was used and not another, we have had to note not only its meaning, length, and rhythmic content, but also its sounds, and the sound patterns formed by what precedes and follows it. We have had to examine also the habits of the singer in other lines, so that we may enter into his mind at the critical creative moment. We have found him doing more than merely juggling set phrases. Indeed, it is easy to see that he employs a set phrase because it is useful and answers his need, but it is not sacrosanct. What stability it has comes from its utility, not from a feeling on the part of the singer that it cannot or must not be changed. It, too, is capable of adjustment. In making his lines the singer is not bound by the formula. The formulaic technique was developed to serve him as a craftsman, not to enslave him.

In the foregoing, for the sake of clarity, we have spoken only of single lines and their parts. In actuality, lines cannot be isolated from what precedes them. The singer's problem is to construct one line after another very rapidly. The need for the "next" line is upon him even before he utters the final syllable of a line. There is urgency. To meet it the singer builds patterns of sequences of lines, which we know of as the "parallelisms" of oral style. As we have said, some sense of these is gained in the pre-singing period, but when the singer begins to practice and to train himself the patterns here too must become specific. Moving from one line to another is not merely, perhaps not even correctly, the adding of one ready-made phrase, or group of ready-made phrases, to another. Oddly enough, because of the variety of patterns for sequences of lines there is greater flexibility possible and greater skill is needed than in pure juxtaposition of formulas. The complexity and artistry of the result are often surprising to anyone who feels that illiterate singers can produce only simple structures. The passages below, chosen almost at random, will serve to illustrate the potentialities of the style.

In South Slavic song, the end of a line is marked by a pause for breath, by a distortion of the final syllable or syllables, frequently by an ornamental turn in the musical accompaniment. Since it is the close of a unit of composition, it is clearly emphasized. Very rarely indeed does a thought hang in the air incomplete at the end of the line; usually we could place a period after each verse. Of 2400 lines of Yugoslav epic analyzed, 44.5 per cent showed no enjambement, 40.6 per cent showed unperiodic enjambement (that is, the sense was complete at the end of the line, but the sentence continued) and only 14.9 per cent involved necessary enjambement. The greatest number of exceptions in Yugoslav epic involve a preceding subordinate clause, or a line consisting of a noun in the vocative case plus modifiers,[17] and even in these cases a thought, even if it is not the main thought of the sentence, has been presented whole by the end of the line. This absence of necessary enjambement is a characteristic of oral composition and is one of the easiest touchstones to apply in testing the orality of a poem. Milman Parry has called it an "adding style"; the term is apt.

In rapid, almost staccato, style the singer may add together a series of actions, moving the story quickly forward: (I have italicized the verbs.)

Kud god *skita* za Aliju *pita*.	Wherever he went, he asked for Alija.
Kazaše ga u gradu Kajniđu.	They said he was in the city of Kajnida.
Kad tatarin pod Kajniđu *dođe,*	When the messenger came to Kajniđa,
Pa eto ga uz čaršiju *prođe,*	He passed along the main street,
Pa *prilazi* novom bazdrđanu,	Then he approached the new shopkeeper,
Te *upita* za Alino dvore.	And he asked for Alija's court.

Bazdrđan mu dvore *ukazao*. — The shopkeeper pointed out the court to him.

Kad tatarin na kapiju *dođe*, — When the messenger came to the gate,
Pa *zadrma* halkom na vratima. — He beat with the knocker on the door.
Zveknu halka a *jeknu* kapija. — The knocker rang and the gate resounded.
(II, No. 3:108–117)

Or he may break in on a series of actions with description, providing at one and the same time a more leisurely tempo and a richness of detail. The following passage has an almost Homeric touch:

Tevabije *brže* u podrume; — The retainers went quickly to the stable;
Iznijeśe takum na đogata, — They brought forth the trappings on the white horse,

Vas u srmi i u čisto zlato, — All in silver and in pure gold.
Pa konjičko *preturu* oruže, — Then they placed on the weapons for fighting from horseback,

S obe strane dvije puške male — On each side two small pistols
Sa dva grla a zrna četiri. — With two barrels which take four bullets.
Preložu hi surom međedinom, — Over them they placed a brown bearskin,
Da mu rosa ne kvari oruže. — That the dew might not rust the arms.
Pa *preložu* pulu abrahiju; — Then they placed on a blanket with sequins;

Zlatna pera biju niz đogata. — Its golden tassels beat against the white horse's flank.

Vezlje su je četiri robinje — Four slave girls had woven it
U Dubrovnik za četir' godine. — In Dubrovnik for four years.
Pa *udriše* đema nemačkoga. — Then they put a German bit into the horse's mouth.

Ej! Stasa đoga, žešće bit' ne more! — The white horse stood there, he could not
(II, 1:737–750) — have been prouder or fiercer!

This last line, beginning with a shout and sung in a different and cadential rhythm, marks the close of the passage. We have italicized the series of verbs which carry along the actions of caparisoning the horse, and also the lines which break this forward movement by providing ornamental, descriptive details that add color and poetry to the actions themselves. The vivid adornments may be added one to another: to the idea of the sequined blanket is added that of the golden tassels striking against the horse; then the blanket is made more glorious by the story of its creation by four slave girls; and finally, this detail is heightened by the fact that they were in the famed city of Dubrovnik and that they worked on this blanket for four years! When we reach the last line of the passage, we cannot but admit that the white horse "could not have been prouder and fiercer!" The method of addition seems simple; yet in the hands of a skillful singer it has a cumulative effect that is telling.

The total impact, however, is due to more than the adding style. The connections between the parts of lines and between lines and between groups of lines is far more intricate and subtle than that. The singer has a strong sense of balance which is shown by the patterns of alliteration and assonance and by the parallelisms.[18] Take the first passage, for example. Note the positions of the italicized verbs. There is internal end rhyme in *skita* and *pita* in the first line; and an internal initial rhyme in *zveknu* and *jeknu* of the last line. The play of "k" alliteration, caused, no doubt, by the proper name *Kajnida* is clear in the first three lines, which have two "k's" in each line. This same "k" alliteration recurs at the end of the passage, namely in the last three lines, where the key word is *kapija*, "the gate"; line 115 has two, line 116, one, and line 117, four "k's." The central part of the passage, lines four to seven, is dominated by "p," "b," and "z" alliteration around the dominant word *bazdrdan*. In lines three and four the verb comes at the end of the line; in lines five and six the verb is in second position after the conjunction; in lines seven and eight the verb is again at the end of the line; and in lines nine and ten, as in lines one and two, the verb is in the first half line. Moreover, in lines three and four, *dode* and *prode* rhyme, and the second half of line four is syntactically parallel to that of line three: *Pod Kajnidu dode* and *uz čaršiju prode*. Both have the pattern: preposition, noun, verb. This pattern is repeated in line eight, *na kapiju dode*. Indeed, line eight is the same as line three in the first half of the line as well.

The singer in this passage is guided for his acoustic patterns not only by the alliteration but by assonance also. The vowel patterns are set by *Aliju, Kajnidu,* and *kapiju*. "A-i" and its opposite "i-a" predominate: but "a-u" plays a role also, influenced by the key words as well as by *gradu* and *bazdrdanu*. Its opposite, "u-a," is found, but is not so important. *Dode, prode,* and *dvore* establish an "o-e" pattern, which modulates via "u-o-e" and "o-o-e" to an opposite, "e-u" in the last line. But this pattern is subsidiary to the "a" and "a-i" patterns. The following table, columns one and two, will make the chief alliterations and assonances apparent at a glance.

K-D, G-Ð, sK-T-, Z-, -l--, P-T-	u-o-I-A-a-A-I-ju-I-A	2-2, 4-2
K-Z-š-, G-, -, Gr-D-, K-n-Ð-	a-a-e-a-u-a-u-AJ-I-u	4, 3-3
K-D, T-T-r-n, P-D, K-n-Ð-, D-Ð-	a-a-A-I-o-AJ-I-U-O-E	1-3, 4-2
P-, -T-, G-, -Z, č-rš-, PR-Ð-	a-e-o-a-u-A-I-JU-O-E	1-3, 4-2
P-, PR-l-Z-, n-v-m, B-ZD-Ð-n-	A-I-A-I-o-o-A-R-A-U	1-3, 2-4
T-, -P-T-, Z-, -l-n-, Dv-r-	e-u-I-A-A-A-I-O-O-e	1-3, 4-2
B-ZD-Ð-n, m-, Dv-r-, K-Z--	A-R-A-U-o-e-u-a-a-o	4, 2-4
K-D, T-T-r-n, n-, K-P--, D-Ð-	a-a-A-I-A-A-I-JU-O-E	1-3, 4-2
P-, Z-D-m-, h-lK-m, n-, Vr-T-m-	a-a-r-a-a-o-a-A-I-A	1-3, 2-4
Zv-Kn-, h-lK-, -, -Kn-, K-P--	e-u-a-a-a-je-u-A-I-JA	2-2, 3-3

The singer is also influenced by the rhythmic and word-boundary patterns as he moves from line to line. The analysis of this passage continues, in the third column, with a list of rhythmic sequences.

The alternation of the patterns of the second half of the lines is worthy of particular notice. After the parallelism of 1–3, 4–2 in lines three and four of the passage, there follows a series of 2–4 alternating with 4–2, which is not broken until the 3–3 of the last line. The pattern is too persistent and regular to be accidental. Moreover, it forms a nice counterpoint to the syntactic parallelisms; there is, indeed, a kind of syncopation between the syntactic parallelisms and the word-boundary patterns. Lines three and four are parallel both in respect to word-boundary patterns and syntactic patterns, but whereas the first half of five and six are both syntactically and rhythmically parallel, the second halves are 2–4 and 4–2 respectively, following an alternation beginning in line four with a 4–2 pattern. One has, therefore:

.......dođe	4–2
.......prođe	4–2
.prilazi......	2–4
.upita......	4–2
......ukazao	2–4
.......dođe	4–2
.zadrma......	2–4

The syntactic and rhythmic parallelism of lines three and four modulates into a pattern of syntactic and rhythmic opposition in lines four and five, six and seven, eight and nine, at the same time that syntactic parallelism is kept between five and six, seven and eight. Had Ugljanin been a literate poet who sat down with pen in hand to devise these lines with their inner balances and syncopations, he could not have done better. One can even fancy the overliterate "interpreter of literature," innocent of Salih's ignorance of such matters, extolling the syncopation as the artful intent of the poet to indicate the zigzag search of the messenger for Alija!

A perfectly natural consequence of building passages by syntactic parallelisms and acoustic patterns is that passages so built tend to have a comparative stability, or better, a continuity in time both in the habit of the single singer and, to a lesser degree, in the current of a tradition. Just as formulaic lines with internal rhyme or with a striking chiastic arrangement have a long life, so couplets with clearly marked patterns persist with little if any change. For example:

Bez eđelja nema umiranja,
Od eđelja nema zaviranja.
  (II, No. 24:631–632)

Without the fated hour there is no dying,
From the fated hour there is no escape.

or:

A zečki je polje pregazio,
A vučki se maši planinama.
  (II, No. 24:41–42)

Like a rabbit he crossed the plain,
Like a wolf he ranged along the mountains.

It seems preferable to keep such couplets in a class by themselves and not to call them formulas, reserving that term for the components of a single verse. Some singers, however, have a tendency to sing in couplets, and in their songs the cadence really comes at the end of the second line; with them it would be perfectly defensible to extend the formula to the couplet.

There are, in addition, larger groups of lines which the singer is accustomed to use often, and through habit they are always found together. The repetition of these groups is sometimes word-for-word exact, sometimes not. Often enough the order of the lines is different. But these clusters of formulas or of lines, which are frequently associated together and are recurrent, also mark one of the characteristic signs of oral style.[19] They are useful to the singer; for they emerge like trained reflexes. The example (in Chart II) from Zogić's favorite song about the rescue of the children of the bey by Bojičić Alija will illustrate. The first passage is from a version sung and recorded in 1934, and the second is the parallel passage in the dictated version of the same year.

CHART II

Pa proklinje careva fermana:	I proklinje careve fermane:
"Bor ubijo careva fermana!	
Ferman care od Stambola sprema,	"Ferman care od Stambola sprema,
Oprema ga Alibegu mome,	
Pa mi bega traži u Stambolu.	Pa mi bega traži u Stambolu.
Hasi mu se narod učinio,	Hasi mu se narod učinijo;
Nit' mu porez ni vergiju daje,	Nit' mu porez daje ni vergiju,
Nit' mu asker ni mazapa daje,	Nit' mu asker daje ni mazapa,
Da bi l' malo narod umirijo.	Da bi l' kako narod umirijo.
Od fermana nema varakanja.	Od fermana nema varakanja.
Pa kad begu ferman degdisao,	Kad mu begu ferman degdisao,
Beg se spremi na bijelu kulu,	Beg se spremi na bijelu kulu,
	A pripasa silah i oružje,
	I opremi široka dorata.
Na njegova široka dorina,	Navali mu pusat i saltanet,
	Jalah reče, posede hajvana,
Isprati' ga do dimir kapije.	Pa ga nagna preko polja ravna.
Ode beže preko polja ravna,	
A zečki je polje pregazio,	Oh zečki je polje pregazijo,
A vučki se maši planinama,	A vučki se maši planinama,
Dok preskoči dvije tri planine,"	Preturijo dvije tri planine,"
(II, No. 24: 26–43)	(II, No. 25: 18–35)

CHART II, TRANSLATION

Then she cursed the imperial firman:	And she cursed the imperial firmans:
"God destroy the imperial firman!	
The sultan sent the firman from Stambol,	"The sultan sent the firman from Stambol,
He sent it to my Alibey,	
And he sought my bey in Stambol.	And he sought my bey in Stambol.
The people were in revolt against him;	The people were in revolt against him;
Neither tax nor tribute do they give him,	Neither tax do they give him nor tribute,
Neither soldier nor sailor do they give him,	Neither soldier do they give him nor sailor,
That he might quiet the people a little.	That he might somehow quiet the people.
There is no avoiding a firman.	There is no avoiding a firman.
And when the firman reached the bey,	When the firman reached the bey,
The bey prepared himself in his white tower;	The bey prepared himself in his white tower,
	And girded on his belt and arms,
And mounted his broad-backed chestnut horse,	And prepared his broad-backed chestnut stallion.
	He put on him his arms and trappings,
	With a cry to Allah he mounted his beast,
I accompanied him to the iron gate.	
The bey departed across the level plain.	And he drove him across the level plain.
Like a rabbit he crossed the plain,	Like a rabbit he crossed the plain,
Like a wolf he ranged along the mountains,	Like a wolf he ranged along the mountains,
Until he had leaped over two or three mountains."	He passed over two or three mountains."

How persistent such a "run" may be can be seen from the same passage sung for the records in 1951, seventeen years after the two excerpts in Chart II.

Pa proklinje careva fermana:	Then she cursed the imperial firman:
"Bog ubijo careva fermana,	"God destroy the imperial firman,
Što ni care ferman opremijo!"	Which the sultan sent to us!"
Pa mi traži Alibega mlada.	He sought my young Alibey.
Traži bega care u Stambolu.	The sultan in Stambol sought the bey.

From *Hasi mu se* through the line *Na njegova široka dorina* in Chart II the 1951 text is word-for-word the same as the 1934 sung text in the first column above. Then it continues:

Krenu beže preko polja ravna.	The bey set out across the level plain.

The next two lines are the same in all three texts. And the last line in 1951 is:

Dok preturi dvije tri planine.	Until he passed over two or three mountains.
(Lord 200:21–37)	

Another excellent example of a cluster of formulas, or a "run," is afforded by the following six lines from Ugljanin's colorful description of the hero Tale and his horse:

Na kulaša sedla ni samara,	On the mouse-gray horse was neither saddle nor pack-carrier,
Sem na kula drvenica gola.	But only a bare wooden frame on the mouse-gray.
S jedne strane topuz od čeljika;	From one side (hung) a steel mace;
On ga tiče, on mu se spotiče.	It struck the horse and caused him to stumble.
A na Tala od jarca ćakšire,	Tale was wearing goatskin trousers,
Dlake spolja; sva koljena gola.	The hairy side out; his whole knee was
(II, No. 1:627–632)	bare.

This description is word-for-word the same in the song, "Ženidba Ćejvanović Meha" (II, No. 12:485–490).

If one takes two texts of the same song, as we have above, and underlines the verses that are common to both, one discovers a characteristic picture. There will be a series of lines unmarked followed by a series of underlined verses with occasional small breaks perhaps, followed in turn by another "clear" spot. If a singer sings a song many times the underlinings, as in Zogić's case, will be many, but this will not be the case with a song infrequently sung. One obtains thus a photograph of the individual singer's reliance on habitual association of lines and of the degree to which habit has tended to stabilize, without fixing or petrifying, passages of varying length. One might well contrast, for example, the comparative stability of Zogić's passage from his favorite song with the fluctuation and sparseness of underlining in the following passage (Chart III) from Halil Bajgorić's song of Alijaga Stočević, sung for the records in 1935 and again for the records in 1950 at Stolac, Hercegovina.

CHART III

1935	1950
Razbolje se Stočević Alija	Razbole se Stočević Alija
——————————	——————————
Usred Stoca grada kamenoga.	Usred Stoca grada bijeloga.
—————— – – – – – – –	—————— – – – – –
Pa boluje za punu godinu.	
Vazda misle age Stolačani,	
5 Da j' Alija svijet mijenijo.	
Pa boluje za dvije godine,	Te boluje za dvij' godine dana.
– – – – – – – – – – – – – –	– – – – – – – – – – – – – –
Pa boluje i treću godinu.	
Vazda misle age Stočevljani,	
Da j'Alija i umiro davno.	

1935

1950

Bože mili, na svemu ti fala!
No Alija nikoga ne ima,
Samo imade sestru svoju Fatu.
Niko ne zna u bijelu gradu,
Da li Alija boluje al' ne boluje.
Neko misli da ga tuka nema,
10 Da je Alija izgubijo glavu.
To se čudo na daleko čulo.
Za to začu crni Arapine

10 Za to začu sivi Arapine
───── ─ ─ ─ ─ ─ ─

Preko sinja mora debeloga,   Preko mora sinja debeloga,
─ ─ ─ ─ ─ ─ ─ ─ ─ ─   ─ ─ ─ ─ ─ ─ ─ ─ ─ ─ ─
Pa on jaše svoju bedeviju,
A crna je kako gavran crni,

Da je umro Stočević Alija,
15 I zakuči sebe i kobilu,
I ovako junak progovara:
"Hajte, sić' ću Stocu kamenome,
Tome Stocu na Hercegovinu.
Ima tamo ljepih devojaka,
20 Kako čujem u bijelu Stocu,
A danas nema nikakova junaka,
Da će meni stanut' na mejdanu.
Ja ću sići u polje Vidovo.
U njemu ću čador razapeti,
25 I nametnut' namet na vilajet,
Svaku nojcu po jalovu ovcu,
I po kab'o preljetne rakije,
Sedam oka crvenoga vina,
Rujna vina od sedam godina,
30 I ljubiću svaku nojcu po jednu
đevojku.
Kad se svane i ograne sunce,
Ja je ocu i materi spremam,
Ali drugu do večera tražim."
Što govori Arapine crni,
35 On je tako isto učinijo,
Te zapuči sebe i kobilu,
I on vodi četiri sejiza,
Što mu nose skute i rukave.
Silan Arap pa se posilijo.
40 'Oće Arap da mejdana traži,
'Oće Arap da đevojke ljubi,
'Oće Arap pa da vina pije,
'Oće Arap i rakiju da pije,
'Oće Arap da je junak na mejdanu.
45 Eto ga kamenome Stocu.
─── ─ ─ ─ ─ ─ ─ ─

Pa eto ga Stocu kamenome.
─ ─ ───── ─ ─ ─ ─ ─
15 Dođe Arap u Vidovo polje.   (Lord 83: 1–45)
(Parry 6697: 1–15)

CHART III, TRANSLATION

Stočević Alija fell ill
Midst Stolac, stony city.
He was ill for a full year.
Ever the aghas of Stolac think
5   That Alija has changed worlds.
He was ill for two years,
And he was ill also a third year.
Ever the aghas of Stolac think
That Alija has long since died.

10   A dark Arab heard of this
Across the dark blue sea, the deep,
And he mounted his bedouin mare,
Black as a black raven she was.

Stočević Alija fell ill
Midst Stolac, white city.

And he was ill for two years of days.

Dear God, thanks to Thee for all
     things!
5   But Alija has no one,
Except his sister Fata.
No one knows in the white city,
Whether Alija is ill or not.
Some think that he is not there,
10   That he has lost his life.
That marvel was heard afar.
A black Arab heard of this
Across the sea, dark blue, deep,

That Stočević Alija had died,
15   And he secured himself and his mare,
And thus the hero spoke:
"Come, I shall go to stony Stolac,
To that Stolac in Hercegovina.
There are beautiful maidens there,
20   As I hear in white Stolac,
And today there is no hero,
To meet me in single combat.
I shall go to Vidovo plain.
On it I shall pitch my tent,
25   And impose tribute on the province,
Every night a gelding sheep,
And a bucket of fine brandy,
Seven pounds of ruddy wine,
Red wine seven years old,
30   And every night I shall love a maid.
When it dawns and the sun rises,
I shall send her to her father and
     mother,
But I shall seek another by evening."
What the black Arab said,
35   The same he did,
And he secured himself and his mare,
And he took with him four squires,
Who carried his sleeves and train.
The mighty Arab strengthened his
     might.

40 The Arab will seek single combat,
    The Arab will seek to love maidens,
    The Arab will seek to drink wine,
    The Arab will seek to drink brandy
    too,
    The Arab will seek to be a hero in
    combat.

    And lo, here he is in stony Stolac. 45 Lo, here he is in stony Stolac.
15 The Arab came to Vidovo plain.

It is clear that Bajgorić is actually re-creating the song with little reliance on habitually and frequently sung passages. The importance of these observations for the comparatist lies in their possible application to divergent manuscripts of the same song which we may be fortunate enough to have from medieval or ancient times. The answer to the question of how the divergences arose may possibly be found in some cases in the fact that one is dealing with two oral texts rather than with a text modified by a scribe or by a second poet working from an already written text.

All singers use traditional material in a traditional way, but no two singers use exactly the same material in exactly the same way. The tradition is not all of one mold. We can differentiate individual styles in the epic technique of oral verse-making. The significance of this for the Homeric songs is clear. It should be apparent that if we make proper use of our knowledge gained from testing the Yugoslav sample, we should be able at some time to answer with some degree of certainty the question of whether the *Iliad* and *Odyssey* are by the same singer.

We have three texts from Zogić (all of the same song), two from 1934 and one from 1951, totalling 3495 lines, and from Makić four texts (all of different songs) from 1934, totalling 2873 lines. One could be sure that these two groups are by different singers, in spite of many similarities, by noting that the formula series consisting of conjunction, plus *evo* or *eto,* plus a personal pronoun in the genitive, for example, *pa eto ga,* is used only twice by Zogić but twenty-two times by Makić.

Zogić	Makić
Kad eto je hanka na kapiju (II, No. 24:370)	Kad eto ga jedna sirotinja (II, No. 26:585)
Pa eto je kafezli odaje (Lord 200:157)	Pa eve ga šarena kafaza (26:31)
closely related:	Pa eve ga na odaju dođe (26:36)
Eto ti je kafezlji odaji (II, No. 24:649)	Pa eve ga na planinu dođe (26:582)
Eto ti ga kafezlji odaje (Lord 200:734)	A eve ga muhur sahibija (26:8)
	E eve ga đadi dolazijo (26:584)

Ej eve ga do Bagdata priđe
(26:597)
Pa eve ga na kapiju siđe
(27:39)
Eh, eve ga kod vezira dođe
(27:429)
Helj eve ga kralje Rakocija
(27:144)
Pa eve je kod devljeta stigla
(27:268)
Pa evo ga među đamovi[ma]
(27:17)
Pa eve ga boja najgornjega
(28:772, 29:325)
I eve je na noge skočila
(28:14)
Pa eve je u avliju siđe
(29:94, 128)
Pa eve ga do kapije dođe
(29:361)
Pa eve ga kod kočije dođe
(29:548)
I eve ga pijanoj mehani
(29:508)
I eto ga poljem zelenijem
(29:545)
I eto je na kapiju prođe
(29:129)

closely related:
On, eve ga pod ravnu Semen[tu]
(27:336)

The use of this formula in the material from the two singers is a clear and statistically measurable mark of a difference between the two men.

Another distinguishing mark between the same two singers is the form of the couplet expressing the idea "he who was nearby looked at the ground; he who was farther off pretended not to hear." Zogić says:

Ko je bliže, ka zemlji gledaše,
Ko je dalje, čini se ne čuje.
 (II, No. 24:463–464, 588–589; 25:297–299; Lord 200:440–441)

He who was nearby looked at the ground,
He who was farther off pretended not to hear.

In No. 25 he inserts the line *Kako raste trava na zavojke,* "To see how the grass was growing in spirals" between the two lines of the couplet. Makić's form of the couplet is:

Ko bi dalje, čini se ne čuje,

Ko bi bliže, zemlji pogleduje.
 (II, No. 29:260–261)

He who was farther off pretended not to hear,
He who was nearer looked at the ground.

The two lines are reversed, the aorist is used instead of the present, *ka* is omitted in the second line, and an aspect of the verb *gledati* is used which allows rhyme between *pogleduje* and *čuje*. Although we have only one instance of this couplet from Makić, it is of the kind that becomes fixed in a singer's usage, and one can be certain that he would not change it. These are but samples to illustrate one kind of distinguishing characteristic in individual formula styles.

*   *   *

The poetic grammar of oral epic is and must be based on the formula. It is a grammar of parataxis and of frequently used and useful phrases. Usefulness in composition carries no implication of opprobrium. Quite the contrary. Without this usefulness the style, and, more important, the whole practice would collapse or would never have been born. The singer's mode of composition is dictated by the demands of performance at high speed, and he depends upon inculcated habit and association of sounds, words, phrases, and lines. He does not shrink from the habitual; nor does he either require the fixed for memorization or seek the unusual for its own sake. His oft-used phrases and lines lose something in sharpness, yet many of them must resound with overtones from the dim past whence they came. Were we to train our ears to catch these echoes, we might cease to apply the clichés of another criticism to oral poetry, and thereby become aware of its own riches.

For while I have stressed usefulness and necessity in composition as essential considerations in studying formulas and the whole formulaic style, it may well be that these characteristics belong to the preservation and development of that style and of the formula rather than to their origins. It is certainly possible that a formula that entered the poetry because its acoustic patterns emphasized by repetition a potent word or idea was kept after the peculiar potency which it symbolized and which one might say it even was intended to make effective was lost — kept because the fragrance of its past importance still clung vaguely to it and kept also because it was now useful in composition. It is *then* that the repeated phrases, hitherto a driving force in the direction of accomplishment of those blessings to be conferred by the story in song, began to lose their precision through frequent use. Meaning in them became vestigial, connotative rather than denotative. From the point of view of usefulness in composition, the formula means its essential idea; that is to say, a noun-epithet formula has the essential idea of its noun. The "drunken tavern" means "tavern." But this is only from the point of view of the singer composing, of the craftsman in lines.

And I am sure that the essential idea of the formula is what is in the mind of the singer, almost as a reflex action in rapid composition, as he makes his song. Hence it could, I believe, be truly stated that the formula not only is stripped to its essential idea in the mind of the composing singer, but also is denied some of the possibilities of aesthetic reference in context. I am thinking especially of what might be called the artistically weighted epithet: what later literary critics find "ironic" or "pathetic." Indeed one might even term this kind of criticism "the pathetic fallacy" in that it attributes to an innocent epithet a pathos felt only by the critic, but not acknowledged or perhaps even dreamed of by either the poet or his audience. Being part of the tradition, they understand its characteristics and necessities. Nevertheless, the tradition, what we might term the intuitions of singers as a group and as individuals who are preserving the inherited stories from the past — the tradition cannot be said to ignore the epithet, to consider it as mere decoration or even to consider it as mere metrical convenience. The tradition feels a sense of meaning in the epithet, and thus a special meaning is imparted to the noun and to the formula. Of course every adjective and epithet can be said to do this, but I am not thinking in this case about the surface denotative meaning of the adjective, but rather of the traditional meaning, and I would even prefer to call it the traditionally intuitive meaning. For it is certain that the singer means on the surface "drunken tavern" to mean a tavern in which men drink and become drunk, but it could well be argued that the epithet is preserved in the tradition because it was used in stories where the tavern was the symbol for an entrance into the other world and the drinking involved is the drinking of the cup of forgetfulness, of the waters of Lethe, and that the drunkenness involved is not that of the ordinary carousel, but is itself a symbol for consciousness in another world, perhaps even death. This meaning comes to it from the special, peculiar purpose of oral epic song at its origin, which was magical and ritual before it became heroic.

This sense of "drunken" becomes clear when one follows the various stories of Marko Kraljević and his brother Andrija, for example, in which Andrija is lured by a tavern maid into her tavern, where he is made drunk by a band of Turks and then killed. Some of the variants have him asking for water rather than wine because he has been contending with his brother to determine which could stand thirst the longer; and Andrija breaks a taboo imposed by his brother in that he dismounts from his horse although instructed not to do so, and enters the tavern. Other variants have Marko reporting his brother's death to their mother according to the elaborate instructions given by the dying Andrija, and saying that Andrija has fallen in love with a girl in a far-off country who has given him of the waters of forgetfulness so he will not return. This last is from our earliest version in the sixteenth century; other examples can be found in the songs in Volume I of the Parry Collection.[20]

Webster may well be correct in regard to his tracing of the meaning of formulas, such as "ox-eyed Hera" and "bright-eyed Athene" to cult songs,[21] although it is not entirely clear what he means by them. These epithets do seem to refer to the epiphanies of the goddesses and thus to strengthen the power of the invocation of the goddess by the repetition of the goddess in several different ways, that is to say, not only by invoking her by her name but also by her epiphany. I think we are safe in assuming that the repetition was there in two forms originally, not for the sake of meter, nor for the sake of convenience in building a line, but rather for the sake of redoubled prayer in its hope of surer fulfillment. The metrical convenience, or even better, the metrical necessity, is probably a late phenomenon, indispensable for the growth of epic from what must have been comparatively simple narrative incantations to more complex tales intended more and more for entertainment. This was a change concomitant with the gradual shift toward the heroic and eventually the historic. It is quite likely that the later stages could not have developed until the formula became a compositional device; yet because of its past it never could become merely a compositional device. Its symbols, its sounds, its patterns were born for magic productivity, not for aesthetic satisfaction. If later they provided such satisfaction, it was only to generations which had forgotten their real meaning. The poet was sorcerer and seer before he became "artist." His structures were not abstract art, or art for its own sake. The roots of oral traditional narrative are not artistic but religious in the broadest sense.

CHAPTER FOUR
THE THEME

Formulas and groups of formulas, both large and small, serve only one purpose. They provide a means for telling a story in song and verse. The tale's the thing.

Anyone who reads through a collection of oral epic from any country is soon aware that the same basic incidents and descriptions are met with time and again. This is true in spite of the fact that editors seek diversity of story and actually avoid variants of any one story, relegating them at best to the notes, in spite of the fact also that collections usually contain songs from many singers from many parts of a country. The reader's impression of repetitions would be closer to the experience of the singer himself and to that of the singer's audience were he to read first the songs in the repertory of a single singer and then those from singers in the same small district. The arrangement of the texts in the published volumes of the Parry Collection is intended to afford just such an experience.

Following Parry, I have called the groups of ideas regularly used in telling a tale in the formulaic style of traditional song the "themes" of the poetry.[1] The first major theme in the "Song of Bagdad" (I, No. 1) is a council, one of the most common and most useful themes in all epic poetry. This one is surprisingly like the opening theme of the *Chanson de Roland*. The sultan has received a letter from his field commanders who have been besieging Bagdad for twenty years without avail. He summons his councilors together, asks them what to do, receives evil advice from one of them and good advice from another, and the theme is concluded with the writing of an imperial letter to Bosnia and dispatch of the messenger.

Incidents of this sort occur in song after song, and from much hearing the pattern of the theme becomes familiar to the youthful bard even before he begins to sing. He listens countless times to the gathering of an army or of a large number of wedding guests (the two are often synonymous). He hears how the chieftain writes letters to other chiefs; he comes to know the names of these leaders of the past and of the places where they dwelt; he knows what preparations are made to receive the assembling host, and how each contingent arrives, what its heroes are wearing and what horses they are riding and in what order they appear. All this and much more is impressed upon him as he sits and is enthralled by his elders' singing of tales. He absorbs a sense of the structure of these themes from his earliest days, just as he absorbs the rhythms and patterns of the formulas, since the two go hand in hand. And we can to some extent reproduce this process of absorption by reading (or even by listening to) as many songs as possible from a given district or group of singers.

There is nothing in the poet's experience (or in ours if we listen to the same song from several singers and to the same singer telling the same song several times) to give him any idea that a theme can be expressed in only one set of words. Those singers whom he has heard have never reproduced a theme in exactly the same words, and he has no feeling that to do so is necessary or even normal practice.[2] The theme, even though it be verbal, is not any fixed set of words, but a grouping of ideas. Some singers, of course, do not change their wording much from one singing to another, especially if the song is one that they sing often. The beginning of Zogić's much loved song of the rescue of Alibey's children (I, No. 24) is comparatively stable, and remained so over a period of seventeen years (Chart IV).

CHART IV

Bojičić Alija Rescues the Children of Alibey, sung by Đemail Zogić

A (1934) sung	B (1934) dictated	C (1951) sung[3]
Hej! Ej! Vikni, druže, haj, pomogni, Bože!	Vikni, druže, a pomozi, Bože!	Hej! Prva riječ, Bože ni pomože!
Amin Bože hoće, ako Bog da,	Sad velimo da malo pevamo,	Evo druga, hoće ako Bog da!
Pomognuti pa razgovoriti,	Što je nekad u zemanu bilo,	A za ime Boga milosnoga,
Od svake ne muke zakloniti,	Šta su naši stari rabotali.	A u zdravlje
5 Od zle muke i dušmanske ruke.		5 Od kada je svijet postanuo,
Sad veljimo pjesmu da pjevamo.		Nije bolji cvijet
Jedno jutro kad je zora bila,	5 Jedno jutro tek je osamnulo,	
Studena je rosa udarila,	Studena je rosa osamnula,	Studena je rosa udarila,
Zeljena je bašča beherala,	Zeljena je bašča beherala,	Zelena je bašča beherala,
10 Ljeskovina mlada preljistala,	Leskovina mlada prelistala,	Ljeskovina mlada prelistala,
E svakoja pilad prepevala.	A svakoja pilad zapevala.	10 O svakoja pilad prepevaše.
Sve pevahu, jedan zakukaše.	10 Sve pevahu a jedna kukaše.	Sve pevahu, jedna zakukaše.
To ne beše tica lastavica,	To ne beše tica lastavica,	To ne beše tica lastavica,

A (1934) sung

No to beše sinja
　kukavica,
15 Kukavica, Alibegov-
　ica.
Kroz kukanju vako
　govoraše:
"Hala njojzi do Bora
　jednoga,

B (1934) dictated

No to beše sinja kuka-
　vica,
Kukavica, Alibegov-
　ica.
Kroz kukanje Bosnu
　proklinjaše:
15 "Ravna Bosna kugom
　pomorena,

C (1951) sung[3]

No to beše sinja kuka-
　vica,
Kukavica, Alibego-
　vica.
15 Kroz kukanju vako
　govoraše,
Sve proklinje Bosnu
　cip cijelu:

CHART IV, TRANSLATION

Shout, comrade, and
　help us, God!
So it shall be, if God
　grants,

To help and enter-
　tain,
To protect us from
　all torment,
5 From evil torment
　and enemy hand.
Now we say that we
　sing a song.
One morning when it
　was dawn,
The chilly dew fell,

The green garden
　blossomed,
10 The young hazel-
　wood leaved in
　abundance,
And all the little
　birds began to sing.
They all sang, one
　lamented.
It was not a swallow,
But it was a gray
　cuckoo-bird,
15 A cuckoo-bird, the
　wife of Alibey.
In her lamenting she
　spoke thus:
"Woe to her by the
　one God,

Shout, comrade, and
　help us, God!
Now we say that we
　sing a little,

What was once in
　time,
What our elders ac-
　complished.

5 One morning when
　it had just dawned,
The chilly dew
　dawned,
The green garden
　blossomed,
The young hazel-
　wood leaved in
　abundance,
And all the little
　birds began to sing.
10 They all sang, but
　one lamented.
It was not a swallow,
But it was a gray
　cuckoo-bird,
A cuckoo-bird, the
　wife of Alibey.
In her lamenting she
　cursed Bosnia:
15 "Level Bosnia, may
　you be devastated
　by plague,

The first word, God
　help us![3]
Here is the second, it
　shall be, if God
　grants!
In the name of God
　the merciful,
And the health

5 Since the world be-
　gan
No better flower has

The chilly dew fell,

The green garden
　blossomed,
The young hazel-
　wood leaved in
　abundance,
10 And all the little birds
　began to sing.
They all sang, one
　lamented.
It was not a swallow,
But it was a gray
　cuckoo-bird,
A cuckoo-bird, the
　wife of Alibey.
15 In her lamenting she
　spoke thus,
Ever she cursed en-
　tire Bosnia:

We can see the other extreme most graphically if we look at the beginning of a song as it was sung or dictated by a singer on six different occasions. One of the best known songs of the Marko Kraljević cycle, one that has been published many times and exists even in an eighteenth-century version,[4] is "Marko and Nina of Kostur." The Parry Collection has four full versions of it from Petar Vidić of Stolac in Hercegovina. One was written down by Dr. Kutuzov from dictation in August, 1933 (Parry 6); another text was written by Nikola Vujnović from dictation on December 7, 1934 (Parry 805); a third was recorded on the phonograph records on the same date (Parry 804); and a fourth was recorded on December 9, 1934 (Parry 846). In addition, the first twenty or so lines of the song were recorded twice (Parry 803a and b) as a trial run for the dubbing of Parry Text 804. The four versions vary in length: No. 6 has 154 lines; No. 804, 279 lines; No. 805, 234 lines; and No. 846, 344 lines. Chart V (pages 72–73) shows the variations in wording in the six versions of the beginning of the song (cf. Appendix II).

One can see a similar variety in the passages from the "Song of Bagdad" shown in Chart VI (page 76) from singings of it by Salih Ugljanin and by Suljo Fortić, the texts of which are published in Volume II.

Such examples are typical of what the young singer hears. The degree of "improvisation" varies from singer to singer and depends as well on the song itself.

The beginner works out laboriously the themes of his first song. I know, because I have tried the experiment myself. Even as one is learning to build lines, one thinks through the story scene by scene, or theme by theme. Let us say that the young man has decided to learn the "Song of Bagdad" first and that Salih Ugljanin is his main teacher. We can follow the apprentice for a while and see what he learns and how.

Above we have given a bare statement of the council theme with which the song opens. The theme ends with the suggestion by the wise councilor that the sultan send to Bosnia for Đerđelez Alija and the Bosnian armies, a suggestion which is accepted, and a messenger is sent with a letter to the hero. This is the framework on which the singer will build. Although he thinks of the theme as a unit, it can be broken down into smaller parts: the receipt of the letter, the summoning of the council, and so forth. Yet these are subsidiary to the larger theme. They will be useful perhaps in other contexts later on, but the singer learns them first for use in the specific council of the specific song, with the appropriate names of people and places and their characteristics. The names are attached in minor themes of calling the council, introducing speeches, in question and answer. All this the learner thinks through before he can be satisfied with his singing and before he can move on to the next larger theme.

CHART V

No. 6	No. 803a*	No. 803b
Pije vino Kraljeviću Marko	A urani Kraljeviću Marko	O urani Kraljeviću Marko
A sa svojom ostar-jelom majkom,	Na bijeloj načinjenoj kuli	Na bijeloj načinjenoj kuli
I sa svojom vjereni-com ljubom,	U Prilipu gradu bije-lome,	Prije zore i bijela dana,
I sa svojom jedinicom sejom.	Podranijo, kahvu po-trošijo,	Ah do njega ostarjela majka,
5 Kad se Marko nakitio vina,	5 A nastavi žeženu ra-kiju,	5 Ah do majke ljuba vjerenica,
Tada Marko čašu uto-čio,	A kod njega ostarjela majka,	A do ljube kitna An-đelija,
Pak nazdravlja osta-rjeloj majci,	Ostarjela majka bijaše mu,	To je njemu vjerenica seka.
I ljubovci i jedinoj seji.	A do majke ljuba Kraljevića,	A kad viknu Kra-ljeviću Marko:
"Nadajte se suncu i mjesecu,	A do ljube kitna An-đelija,	"Čuješ li me, ostarjela majko!
10 Meni Marku nemojte nikada!"	10 To je njemu vjerenica seka.	10 Evo jesam rakiju po-troši'.
A pita ga ostarjela majka:	Onda Marko rakiju popijo,	Čuješ li me šta ću besjediti!
"De ćeš, Marko, moj jedini sinko?"	Pa zapjeva tanko gla-sovito:	A tako mi svašta do svijeta,
Progovara Kraljeviću Marko:	"Moja majko, mooj roditelju!	Dosta ti sam jada učinijo,
"Odoh, majko, caru u vojništvo	Evo tebi sina Kra-ljevića.	I junaštva na crnoj zemljici.
15 Za zemana devet godin' dana."	15 Dosta ti je. . . .	15 A čuješ li, ostarjela majko!
Kad je Marko došo u vojništvo,		Juče mi je sitna knjiga stigla
Tri se puta preklonijo Marko,	* This is the only one of these texts begin-	Od našega sultan cara moga,
Dok je caru ruci pri-stupio;	ning with a "pripjev." It covers six lines, and	Cara moga, sunce iza gore,
Pa je caru ruku po-ljubio.	has been omitted here since it has no bear-	I ovako knjiga naki-čena,
20 Car mu odmah sablju oduzeo,	ing on the comparison of the texts.	20 U knjigi, majko, za-pisano,
Oduzeo sablju i Ša-rina,		Pa me care u voj-ništvo zove
Da ga služi devet godin' dana,		Za zemana devet godin' dana,
Kad izsluži devet godin' dana,		A i moga Šarca od mejdana,
Da mu dade sablju i Šarina.		I u njojzi sablju po-sjeklicu.

CONTINUATION OF CHART V

No. 804

A urani Kraljeviću
Marko
Na bijeloj od kamena
kuli,
Uranijo, rakiju na-
stavi,
A rakiju Marko po-
trošijo,
5 Ah do njega ostarjela
majka,
A do majke ljuba
vjerenica,
A do ljube kitna An-
đelija.
A kad Marko lakrdiju
viknu:
"Moja majko, đutu-
rume stari!
10 Dosta ti sam jada
učinijo,
A junaštva na zemlji
uč'nijo.
Čuješ li me, milosnice
majko!
Došla mi je sitna
knjiga juče,
A u knigi meni za-
pisano.
15 Zove mene care u
vojništvo,
Sultan care, iza gore
sunce:
'Da si došo k na
Bjelicu, Marko,
I dovedi plemića Ša-
rina,
I donesi posjeklicu
krivu,
20 Od godine do petnejes
dana.'
A što ću tu, đutu-
rume, kazat'?"
"Da li ću ti čekat'
petnes dana?"
"Moja majko, mili
roditelju!
Ako Nina na Koštunu
čuje,

No. 805

Uranijo Kraljeviću
Marko
U Prilipu na bijeloj
kuli,
I do njega ostarjela
majka,
I do majke ljuba vje-
renica,
5 I do ljube sestra An-
đelija.
Nazdravi im bistri-
com rakijom:
"Juče mi je sitna
knjiga stigla
Od sultana cara česti-
toga.
Zove care mene u
vojništvo,
10 Da ga služim devet
godin' dana."
To se čudo na daleko
čulo,
I začuo Nina od
Koštuna.
Reče Marko ostarjeloj
majci:
"Da će Nina do Pri-
lipa doći,
15 I porobit' u Prilipu
kulu,
I odvesti Kraljevića
ljubu,
I uz ljubu Kraljevića
Anđu,
A majku mi nogam'
pogaziti,
Kad ti dođe Nina od
Koštuna,
20 Piši meni knjigu šaro-
vitu,
Pa je meni po sokolu
spremi,
Soko će mi knjigu
donijeti."
Kad evo ti Nine od
Koštuna,
Su njegova brata sva
tri pusta,

No. 846

Aj urani Kraljeviću
Marko
Na bijeloj od kamena
kuli,
A do njega ostarjela
majka,
A do majke ljuba vje-
renica,
5 A do ljube vijernica
mlada.
Što ću vami dugo
besjediti?
Kad se njimam dade
poslušati,
Kad evo ti knjigonoše
mlade.
Ona nosi knjigu šaro-
vitu
10 Gospodaru Kraljeviću
Marku.
Bože mijo, od kog' li
je grada?
Niko neće ni riječi
tuka.
Kad je Marko knjigu
prifatijo,
A na knjizi pečat pre-
lomijo,
15 I vidijo što mu sitno
piše,
Marko štije, ne be-
sjedi ništa.
Zavika mu ostarjela
majka:
"O moj sine, Kralje-
viću Marko!
I prije su knjige sala-
zile,
20 Ama nisu tako žalo-
vite.
Kaži meni od kog' ti
je grada."
"Ovo mi je knjiga
šarovita
Od našega čestitoga
cara,
Sultan cara iza gore
sunca,

No. 6	No. 803a	No. 803b
Marko Kraljević is drinking wine	Marko Kraljević arose early	Marko Kraljević arose early
With his old mother,	In his white well-built tower	In his white well-built tower,
And with his true love,	In Prilip the white city.	Before dawn and white day.
And with his only sister.	He arose and drained his coffee,	Next to him his old mother,
5 When Marko had drunk his wine,	5 And began refined brandy;	5 Next to his mother his true love,
Then Marko brimmed the glass	With him was his old mother,	And next his love, the well-adorned Anđelija.
To the health of his old mother,	His old mother it was,	This was his true sister.
And his love and his only sister.	And next the mother Kraljević's wife,	And when Kraljević Marko shouted:
"Expect the sun and the moon,	And next his wife the well-adorned Anđelija,	"Listen to me, aged mother!
10 But me Marko never!"	10 This was his true sister.	10 Lo I have drained my brandy.
And his old mother asked him:	Then Marko drank the brandy,	Listen to what I shall say!
"Whither are you going, Marko, my only son?"	And began to sing, shrill and loud:	In the name of everything on earth,
Marko Kraljević spoke:	"My mother, you who bore me!	I have caused enough sorrow,
"I am going, mother, to the sultan's army	Here is your son Kraljević.	And I have performed enough heroic deeds on the black earth.
15 For a period of nine years."	15 Enough. . . .	15 But listen, aged mother!
When Marko arrived at the army,		Yesterday a brief letter arrived
Marko bowed thrice,		From our sultan, my czar,
Before he approached the sultan's hand;		My czar, sun from above the mountains,
Then he kissed the sultan's hand.		And thus was the letter embellished,
20 The sultan immediately took away his sword,		20 In the letter, mother, was written,
He took away his sword and horse Šarac,		And the sultan calls me to the army
That he serve him for nine years,		For a period of nine years,
When he had served nine years,		And also my battlewise Šarac,
That he return to him the sword and Šarac.		My saber and blade.

No. 804

Marko Kraljević arose
early
In his white tower of
stone.
He arose, began his
brandy,
And Marko drained
the brandy.
5   Next to him his old
mother,
Next his mother his
true love,
And next his love, the
well-adorned Anđe-
lija.
And when Marko
shouted something:
"My mother, old
shrew!
10 I have caused enough
sorrow,
And I have per-
formed enough he-
roic deeds on this
earth.
Listen to me, merciful
mother!
A brief letter arrived
yesterday,
And in the letter
there was written:
15 The sultan summons
me to the army,
Sultan, czar, sun from
above the moun-
tains:
'Come to Bjelica,
Marko,
Bring the noble Šarac,
And bring your
curved blade,
20 For the space of fif-
teen days.'
What, shrew, shall I
say to that?"
"Shall I wait for you
for fifteen days?"
"My mother, dear one
who bore me!
If Nina in Koštun
hears,

No. 805

Kraljević Marko arose
early
In Prilip in his white
tower,
And next him his old
mother,
And next the mother
his true love,
5   And next his love his
sister Anđelija.
He toasted them in
clear brandy:
"Yesterday a brief
letter arrived
From the sultan, il-
lustrious czar.
The sultan summons
me to the army,
10 To serve him for nine
years."
This marvel was
heard afar,
And Nina of Koštun
heard of it.
Marko said to his old
mother:
"If Nina comes to
Prilip,
15 And captures the
tower in Prilip,
And carries off Kra-
ljević's love,
And with her Kra-
ljević's Anđa,
And treads on my
mother with his
feet,
When Nina of Koš-
tun comes,
20 Write me a well-writ
letter,
And send it to me by
falcon.
The falcon will bring
me the letter."
Then lo there came
Nina of Koštun,
With all three of his
cursed brothers,

No. 846

Kraljević Marko arose
early
In his white tower of
stone,
And next him his old
mother,
And next his mother
his true love,
5   And next his love his
true young wife.*
Why should I
lengthen my tale?
Then they listened,
And lo a young letter-
bearer.
He was carrying a
well-writ letter
10 For the master, Kral-
jević Marko.
Dear God, from what
city is it?
None will speak a
word.
When Marko had
taken the letter,
He broke the seal on
the letter,
15 And he saw what the
brief letter said.
Marko read and said
nothing.
His old mother cried
out to him:
"O my son, Kraljević
Marko!
Letters have come be-
fore,
20 But they were not so
sad.
Tell me from what
city it is."
"This is a well-writ
letter
From our illustrious
sultan,
Sultan, czar, sun from
above the moun-
tains,

* A mistake for sister.

CHART VI

Excerpts from "The Song of Bagdad"

Ugljanin (II, No. 1: 96–110) (Sung, Nov. 22, 1934, Novi Pazar)	Ugljanin (II, No. 2: 79–96) (Sung, July 24, 1934, Novi Pazar)	Fortić (II, No. 22: 61–76) (Sung, Nov. 24, 1934, Novi Pazar)
Pa sad viknu Suku čohadara,	Suka* zovnu Suku čohadara;	Pa saziva Ibra surudžiju:
Čohadara, carskog tatarina:	Zovnu sultan svoga tatarina:	"O moj sine, Đulić Ibrahime!
"Đe si, Suka, carev tatarine?	"Siđi, Suka, u tavlu sultansku!	Nosi ferman u Kajnidžu ravnu,
Ti siljezi u tavlu carevu!	Bira' ate, a bira' paripe!	Pravo kuli Đerđelez Alije!"
5 Bira', Suka, ate i paripe,	5 Hoćeš, sine, Bosni silaziti!"	5 Sad da vidiš Đulić Ibrahima!
Koji će te Bosni prenositi!	Kad tatarin sabra lakrdiju,	Teke side u tople podrume,
Da prifatiš careva fermana,	Pa silježe u tavlu sultansku,	Na dorina timar udarijo,
Da ga Bosni nosiš halovitoj,	Pa izbira konje menzetile,	Na dorina ćebe privalijo,
Na gaziju Đerđelez Aliju!"	Izvede hi pred gradsku kapiju.	Na dorina sedlo udarijo.
10 Ej! Kad Suka sabra lakrdiju,	10 U sultana stasaše fermana.	10 Priteže mu četiri kolana,
Pa u carsku tavlu dolazijo.	Sam je sultan muhur udarijo,	A on uze pletenu kandžiju,
Bira ate, a bira paripe,	Na gaziju Đerđelez Aliju;	Pa on sade caru na divanu,
Pa menzilske konje izvodijo	Gradi njega komendar Alijom.	Pa mu care ferman opružijo.
Pod takumom i pod saltanetom.	Traži š njime sto hiljada vojske,	Sad je Ibro ferman prifatijo,
15 Pa sniješe careva fermana.	15 Da mu s vojskom pođe u Bagdatu,	15 Pa poljubi turalji fermana,
	Da prifati bijela Bagdata.	Dva za cara, treći za fermana.
	Pa sniješe careva fermana,	
	Tesljimiše carskom tatarinu.	

* A slip of the tongue for *sultan*.

CHART VI, TRANSLATION

Excerpts from "The Song of Bagdad"

Ugljanin (II, No. 1: 96–110) (Sung, Nov. 22, 1934, Novi Pazar)	Ugljanin (II, No. 2: 79–96) (Sung, July 24, 1934, Novi Pazar)	Fortić (II, No. 22: 61–76) (Sung, Nov. 24, 1934, Novi Pazar)
And now he summoned Suka the chamberlain, The chamberlain, the imperial messenger: "Where are you, Suka, imperial messenger? Go to the imperial stable! 5 Choose stallions, Suka, and steeds, Which will carry you to Bosnia! Take the imperial firman, And carry it to enchanted Bosnia, To the hero Đerđelez Alija!" 10 When Suka understood these words, Then he went to the imperial stable. He chose stallions and he chose steeds, And led forth the post horses Caparisoned and panoplied. 15 Then they brought forth the imperial firman.	Suka* summoned Suka the chamberlain, The sultan summoned his messenger: "Descend, Suka, to the imperial stable! Choose stallions and choose steeds! 5 You will, son, go to Bosnia!" When the messenger understood these words, He descended to the imperial stable, And chose post horses. He led them before the castle gate. 10 The firman was with the sultan. The sultan himself put his seal on it, For the hero Đerđelez Alija; He made him commander Alija. He sought with him an army of a hundred thousand men, 15 To go with the army to Bagdad, To capture white Bagdad. Then they brought forth the imperial firman, They delivered it to the imperial messenger.	Then he summoned Ibro the messenger: "My son, Đulić Ibrahim! Carry the firman to level Kajnidža, Straight to the tower of Đerđelez Alija!" 5 Now see Đulić Ibrahim! When he descended to the warm cellars, The chestnut he rubbed down, On the chestnut he placed a blanket, On the chestnut he put the saddle. 10 He tightened the four girths And took the braided whip, Then he went to the sultan's council, And the sultan handed him the firman. Now Ibro took the firman, 15 And kissed the firman with the imperial seal, Twice for the sultan, a third time for the firman.

* A slip of the tongue for *sultan.*

The building of a theme in a singer's repertory of themes begins already at this period to consist of a core greatly influenced by the single singer, perhaps his father, who is his prime teacher. To this core are added elements first from other singers' performances of the theme in the same song and then from other singers' performances of the theme in other songs, and finally, as time goes on, elements that he may add himself, usually unconsciously or under the inspiration of the moment, although, again it should be stressed that there is no compulsion upon him from outside to do so. Thus a theme grows and reaches a normal development in the practice of a singer. Much of the growth probably occurs after the singer's repertory includes more than one song, when songs within his own repertory begin to influence one another. But the foundation is laid early, and growth starts before the first song is well learned. At the beginning it will be much like that of his prime mentor, but it may change in time. It is not surprising, therefore, that themes of the pupil may not eventually be at all close to those of the teacher. Transmission at this early stage must be differentiated from transmission of a song at a later period in the singer's development.

With years of experience the singer becomes an active listener to the songs of others. The really talented oral poet combines listening and learning in one process. The listening is then dynamic and can be said to constitute in itself the first rehearsal of the new song. Singers who can do this are, however, rare. Many may boast, but their boast is a heroic one and belongs to the hyperboles of epic poetry. That it is possible I am sure; for I have seen and heard this marvel accomplished.

When Parry was working with the most talented Yugoslav singer in our experience, Avdo Međedović in Bijelo Polje, he tried the following experiment. Avdo had been singing and dictating for several weeks; he had shown his worth and was aware that we valued him highly. Another singer came to us, Mumin Vlahovljak from Plevlje. He seemed to be a good singer, and he had in his repertory a song that Parry discovered was not known to Avdo; Avdo said he had never heard it before. Without telling Avdo that he would be asked to sing the song himself when Mumin had finished it, Parry set Mumin to singing, but he made sure that Avdo was in the room and listening. When the song came to an end, Avdo was asked his opinion of it and whether he could now sing it himself. He replied that it was a good song and that Mumin had sung it well, but that he thought that he might sing it better. The song was a long one of several thousand lines. Avdo began and as he sang, the song lengthened, the ornamentation and richness accumulated, and the human touches of character, touches that distinguished Avdo from other singers, imparted a depth of feeling that had been missing in Mumin's version.

The analysis of the first major theme in Mumin's and in Avdo's text (see Appendix I) illustrates how well Avdo followed his original and yet how superbly he was able to expand it and make it his own.[5]

morning coffee, and his proceeding with his servant to the ramparts of Osek
to sit and smoke and look out over the plain. This peaceful scene of everyday life is interrupted. Osman sees a cloud on the horizon and from it
emerges a rider; Osman wonders who it may be. The rider is described as
he approaches the wall. He hails Osman and from the conversation one
learns that the new arrival is Osman's nephew. Osman goes down to greet
him, he is brought into the court, and then Osman assembles the nobles of
Osek to celebrate the arrival of the youth. There follows an assembly theme,
which differs from those we have already seen because there is no one unhappy in the group. Osman asks them all to spend the night and on the
following day they continue their festivities. At this point the assembly is
interrupted. Osman looks out over the plain and sees the usual cloud, from
which emerges a rider. This rider turns out to be a messenger. The news
that he brings initiates the action of the song, action in which the nephew
who has been introduced to the listener plays a leading role. This assembly
breaks up with the decision to gather an army, and the assembly theme gives
way immediately to the theme of the summoning of a host.

It is to be noted that Avdo differed from Mumin in the description of the
arrival of the messenger in the assembly. Mumin simply said that the door
creaked and a messenger entered. Avdo described how Mustajbey looked
out the window and saw a cloud of dust from which emerged a rider
bearing a message on a branch. From a consideration of the arrival scenes
in the tale of Osman, one can see that Avdo has used his own firmly en-
trenched method of describing arrivals.

The poor and despised hero at the foot of the assembly is no stranger
to Avdo, as we have seen from the song of Vlahinjić Alija. There is a
difference between Alija and Bećiragić Meho, however. Alija is dressed in
glorious armor and decorations for bravery in single combat, whereas Meho
was in the simplest of clothes, except for his two pistols. It is even possible
that Avdo had Alija in mind when he began his description of Meho; for
he started with the lines: "The youth was not wearing breastplate or arms,
but only cotton trousers and a shirt." Both these heroes are mocked by one
of the members of the assembly. Yet the mocking is different in each case
since the persons uttering the reproaches are themselves distinctive.

One could multiply examples of assembly themes from other songs of
Avdo, but it is now abundantly clear that in the retelling of the "new"
song of Bećiragić Meho, Avdo had other models in addition to Mumin's
song. He was not re-creating out of whole cloth. His many years of experience in building themes, a technique inherited from the generations of
singers before him, made possible what seemed on the surface to be an
incredible feat.

A major theme, then, can take several possible forms in a singer's repertory.
When he hears such a theme in a new song, he tends to reproduce it ac-

cording to the material already in his possession. Minor themes also have a number of forms suitable to several different situations. Such a minor theme, indispensable to narrative, is that of writing a letter.

Within the limits of the 578 lines of his short version of "The Battle at Temišvar" (II, No. 27) Sulejman Makić makes frequent use of the theme of writing a letter or a decree. As the story runs, the populace complain to Avdi and Seidi Pasha about the damage that King Rákóczy has been inflicting in his raids across the border into Turkish land. The pashas promise to send an ultimatum to the king. Seidi Pasha, who is the elder, tells Avdi to write the letter:

"Malji sine, Avdi paša mladi!	"My little son, young Avdi Pasha!
Deder knjigu šarovitu piši!	Hasten and write a well-writ letter!
Kaži svinji kralji Rakociji:	Say to that swine, King Rákóczy:
'Digni ruke s moje sirotinje, . . .' "	'Keep your hands from my poor peo-
(lines 67–70)	ple, . . .' "

Then he dictates the contents of the letter (lines 70–75), and the singer continues:

Kade začu Avdi paša mladi,	When young Avdi Pasha heard,
Avdi paša do hastala priđe,	Avdi Pasha went to the table,
Eh ufati murećepa crna.	And he took black ink.
Knigu šara, kralja razgovara:	He penned a letter and said to the king:
"O ti svinjo, kralje Rakocijo!	"You swine, King Rákóczy!
Miči ruke s moje sirotinje, . . ."	Take your hands from my poor peo-
(lines 76–81)	ple, . . ."

The letter ends in line 87 and a new theme begins, namely the dispatching of the letter. The letter as written by Avdi Pasha is not exactly the same as it was dictated by Seidi Pasha, but it is close:

"Digni ruke s moje sirotinje,	"Keep your hands from my poor people,
Helj, tako mi hljeba carevoga,	For, by my imperial bread *sic,*
Katal ću te," kaže, "učiniti.	I shall destroy you," he said.
Pokupiću moju carevinu,	"I shall gather my empire,
Rakoću ću tebe prevrnuti,	I shall raze your Rakoća,
A za tebe dobro biti neće!"	And it will not be well for you!"
(lines 70–75)	

"O ti svinjo, kralje Rakocijo!	"You swine, King Rákóczy!
Miči ruke s moje sirotinje,	Take your hands from my poor people,
Helj, tako mi hljeba bijeloga,	For, by my white bread,
Za nekoga dobro biti neće!	It will not be well for someone!
Pokupiću moju carevinu,	I shall gather my empire,
A ću sići do tvoje stoljice.	And I shall attack your throne.
Ja ću tvoju prevrnut' stoljicu,	I shall overturn your throne,
Al ću moju izgubiti glavu!"	Or I shall lose my own head!"
(lines 80–87)	

For this theme the letter is first dictated in full and then written in full. Over a hundred lines later the answer to the ultimatum is received.

Rákóczy has appealed to the emperor in Vienna, an army has been gathered, and it is now before the walls of Temišvar. The emperor writes to the pashas, and the singer says:

Eve ćesar knjigu opremijo: Lo, the emperor sent a letter:
(line 214)

The letter itself, demanding surrender, follows in lines 215–220. The singer here says nothing about the process of writing the letter; it is not dictated to anyone, and hence its contents are not repeated. This is a simple form of the theme.

Following the demand for surrender further exchange of correspondence takes place. Avdi Pasha's wife advises him as to what reply he should make to the emperor. "Send another letter and ask the old emperor for a truce of three months in which you may evacuate Temišvar" (lines 227–230).

I Avdija knjigu našarao,   And Avdi penned a letter,
I ćesara starog zamoljijo: And implored the old emperor:
(lines 231–232)

The letter itself covers lines 233–239. In this instance of the theme the letter is given in indirect form first, and when it is written, it is presented in full.

The answer to this letter comes immediately and it is in a simple form:

O natrag mu knjigu povratio: He sent back a letter in reply:
(line 242)

The letter, granting a truce of half a year, is given in lines 243–245.

After the truce has been declared, Avdi's wife tells him to write a letter to the sultan asking for help. Again she gives the contents of the letter in indirect form. The letter itself is introduced by:

Pa kad začu Avdi paša mladi,   Then when young Avdi Pasha heard,
Načineo turalji fermana: He prepared a firman with his seal:
(lines 258–259)

and it is given in full in lines 260–265.

This letter to the sultan has the desired effect, and Ćuprilić the Vizier arrives at Temišvar with troops. He asks the pashas if they have informed Rustembey in Sarajevo of what is happening, and when they reply in the negative another letter is written, the last in the song, this time to Rustembey imploring him to send troops. Its form is the simple one we have already seen.

I on piše knjigu šarovitu,   And he wrote a well-writ letter,
I spremi je šehru Sarajevu: And sent it to the city of Sarajevo:
(lines 310–311)

The letter itself covers lines 312–322.

In the compass of 322 lines of a short version of a single song six letters have been written.[10] Each letter has been given in full; in one case it was dictated and then written; in two instances the general contents of the letters were given in indirect form and then the letter was written; in three cases the singer merely states that someone wrote a letter, and he gives the letter in full.

In Makić's song of the taking of Bagdad by Sultan Ibrahim (I, No. 26) the first writing in the song occurs in the story-within-a-story. On his death-bed Sultan Sulejman tells his son Ibrahim of his vain attempts to take Bagdad. "My son, I declared war and I prepared a firman with my seal and summoned my empire. I sent a firman to Medina, to the Shah of the Kaaba, and I sent a firman to Abdullah, the Shah of Egypt," and so Sulejman continues for two more firmans (lines 82–97). The letters, or firmans, are not quoted in full as in previous cases. Their contents are left to be inferred from the situation.

This same theme occurs later in the song, not in the direct discourse of the story-within-a-story but as part of the singer's narrative. Sulejman dies and Ibrahim succeeds him. After liquidating his father's enemies, Ibrahim seeks out the elder Ćuprilić and they prepare once again to attack Bagdad. Ćuprilić summons the imperial Sheh Islam to write several letters. "He prepared a firman with his seal and sent it to the Shah of the Kaaba, and the *imam* penned the firman and sent it; and then they prepared another and sent it to Abdullah, the Shah of Egypt," and so forth (lines 340–351).

In none of the above examples has Makić employed the full form of the writing of a series of letters summoning an army or inviting guests to a wedding. He has done it briefly and indirectly in his song of Bagdad, but without disclosing the contents of the letters themselves. Makić is not much given to expansion and elaboration. His narrative is generally simple, and his songs are correspondingly short. We can illustrate the longer versions of this letter-writing theme from two other singers, one from the same district as Makić, that is, Novi Pazar, and the other from Gacko in Hercegovina.

In Salih Ugljanin's song of the wedding of Bey Ljubović, the theme of summoning wedding guests by letter is more extended than in Makić's songs.

Beg sad priđe đamu do penđera,	Now the bey went to the window,
Pa dofati knjige i hartije,	And he took letter paper,
Kaljem drvo što se knjiga gradi,	A quill with which letters are made,
A mastila što se knjiga piše,	And ink with which letters are written,
Pa načinje knjigu šarovitu,	And he prepared a well-writ letter,
Sprema knjigu ljićkom Mustajbegu: itd.	He directed the letter to Mustajbey of the
(Parry 651, lines 744–749)	Lika: etc.

The invitation is quoted in full in lines 750–762; then the singer continues:

Pa sad drugu knjigu načinijo.	And now he prepared another letter.
Opremi je Šali sa Mostara.	He sent it to Šala of Mostar.
Sudi Šala s trides i dva grada.	Šala governed thirty and two cities.

Te sad Šalu u svatove zove: itd. (lines 766–769)	And now he invited Šala to join the wedding guests: etc.

The invitation is given again in full in lines 770–777. The process is repeated five more times, and each time the letter of invitation is given in full, but with variation. Here are the other introductory lines:

Pa sad drugu knjigu naredijo. On je gradi kladuškome Muju: (lines 780–781)	Now he set in order another letter. He prepared it for Mujo of Kladuša:
Pa je opet drugu načinijo. Opremi je Bojković Aljiji: (lines 789–790)	Then again he prepared another. He directed it to Bojković Alija:
Sad je drugu knjigu načinijo. Opremi je kovaćkome Ramu: (lines 796–797)	Now he prepared another letter. He directed it to Ramo of Kovač:
Pa je drugu knjigu načinijo. Opremi je Tanković Osmanu: (lines 801–802)	Then he prepared another letter. He directed it to Tanković Osman:
Opet drugu knjigu načinijo. Opremi je Talu Ljićaninu: (lines 806–807)	Again he prepared another letter. He directed it to Tale of the Lika:

The length of each of the letters is different; in order they are 13, 8, 5, 3, 2, 2, and 8 lines long. It can be seen that the length diminishes as the writing continues and as the singer wishes to avoid monotonous repetition. The increase in the number of lines in the last letter is explained by the fact that Tale of the Lika, to whom it is addressed, is a special person who "rates" a longer letter. Generally speaking, the first letter in such a series is fairly long, since it explains the situation to the addressee for the first time, and the last letter is longer than the others because it is usually to some outstanding individual.

We can detect the germ of even further expansion of this letter-writing theme contained in the second letter of the series just given, that addressed to Šala of Mostar. The singer stops for a line to comment that Šala governed thirty and two cities. By the addition of more information about the people invited or about the people to whom the letters are addressed, the number of men they have at their command, and details of this sort, this theme can be elaborated even further.

For a final example of the letter-writing theme with its series of letters we turn to the song of the wedding of Smailagić Meho in the version dictated by Hajdar Habul of Gacko in Hercegovina (Parry 905). Meho's father, Smailagha, sits down to write invitations. It is expected that the wedding will involve a bloody battle and it is necessary to gather an army. The process of preparation for the writing is fuller than we have seen before.

Pa na mlađe viku učinijo:	Then he summoned the youths:
"Dones'te mi divit i hartiju!	"Bring me writing table and paper!
Valja sade knjige rasturiti,	I must now send out letters,
Pokupiti kićene svatove."	To gather the well-dight wedding guests."
Od kako je svijet postanuo,	Ever since the world began,
Vazdi mlađi sluša starijega.	Youth has ever obeyed its elder.
Donesoše divit i hartiju.	They brought writing table and paper.
Vid' staroga! Poče knjige pisat'.	See the old man! He began to write letters.
Prvu šalje begu Mustajbegu	He sent the first to Mustajbey
Na široku Liku i Ribnika,	To the broad Lika and Ribnik,
I ovako begu besjedaše:	And thus he spoke to the bey:
(lines 933–943)	

The letter follows in the next seventeen lines, and the singer continues:

Pa je drugu odma prifatijo,	Then immediately he took another,
Pa je piše Hasan paši Tiru:	And wrote it to Hasan Pasha Tiro:
(lines 962–963)	

After eleven lines of letter, the singer moves on to the next:

Tu puštijo, drugu prifatijo,	He left that one, and took up another,
Pa je šalje Kuni Hasanagi:	And sent it to Kuna Hasanagha:
(lines 975–976)	

This letter has only two lines. The old man writes six more letters, bringing the total to nine. He introduces these last six with the same brief form used in the last two examples, but again the letters vary in length. In order they are 17, 11, 2, 7, 6, 7, 7, 7, and 25 lines long. The last letter is to the famous Mujo of Kladuša who is to be the leader of the wedding guests and commander in chief of the army.

Usually the singer invites the same heroes in each song in which this theme is used. He does not learn a special set of names for each song. When he finds it necessary to gather an army or wedding guests, he has the theme ready in his mind. For example, we have seen that Ljubović in Ugljanin's version of the song of his wedding invited the following in order: Mustajbey of the Lika, Šala of Mostar, Mujo of Kladuša, Bojković Alija, Ramo of Kovač, Tanković Osman, and Tale of the Lika. In his version of the taking of Bagdad the same singer has Đerđelez Alija summon the following in the order given: Šala of Mostar, Mustajbey of the Lika, Mujo of Kladuša, Bojković Alija, Tanković Osman, Tale of the Lika, and Ramo of Kovač. The order is different, but the personnel is the same. The theme is always at hand when the singer needs it; it relieves his mind of much remembering, and leaves him free to think of the plan of the song itself or of the moment of the song in which he is involved.

The quality of an oral epic tradition depends in no small measure on the singer's skill in fashioning descriptions of heroes, horses, arms, and castles. In them the forward march of the story is halted while the listener sits and marvels at the scenes presented. Yet they are as recurrent as any other theme in the tradition. Compare the two following descriptions of the arming of the hero before he sets forth to do mighty deeds. The first is from Salih Ugljanin's song of the rescue of Mustajbey by Hasan of Ribnik (I, No. 18, p. 180); the hero being prepared is Osek Osmanbey, who is about to set out on his first raid. He is donning a disguise.

Now the old woman went to the chest and took from it a bundle of clothing. First there were linen breeches and a shirt — not made on a loom, nor spun, but woven of gold from Stambol. Then she gave him a breastplate and vest. The breastplate was made throughout of golden chain mail. On his shoulders she placed two golden caftans and on them two gray falcons. All this billowed on the young man's shoulders. Then she gave him a cloak, with twelve buttons, each one containing a liter of gold. And she gave him breeches of fine cloth, even of green Venetian velvet. They were of Bulgarian make. All the seams were covered with gold braid. Along the calves of his legs were concealed fasteners, and on them were woven serpents, their heads embroidered on the knees. At every step he took the snakes yawned, and they might well have frightened a hero! Then she gave him his belt and weapons, in the belt two mother-of-pearl pistols, neither forged nor hammered, but cast in Venice. The butts were decorated with golden ducats, and their barrels were of deadly steel. The sights were of precious stones. Two small pistols they were, which shoot well. Then he girded on golden powder boxes, and above them a curved saber. The whole hilt was of yellow ducats, and the scabbard of deadly steel. On the hilt was a precious stone. He put on his head a four-cornered hat with twelve crosses. On one of them was the name of Niko the standard-bearer, from Ćpanur hard by the Turkish border. Then he drew on his boots and leggings and took the saddlebags of Moroccan leather.

The second passage is from the "Song of Smailagić Meho" by Avdo Međedović (Parry 6840). Meho himself is being prepared for the journey to Buda.

From the basket she [Meho's mother] took a bundle of silk embroidered with gold. It was not tied with knots but had been pierced by golden pins. She untied the golden bundle, and garments of gold poured forth. May God be praised! — It was as if the sun were shining! First of all his mother put upon him linen of finest cloth. Every third thread in it was of gold. Then she gave to him a silken vest, all embroidered with pure gold. Down the front of the vest were buttons fashioned of gold pieces, which reached to his silk belt. There were twelve of them, and each contained half a liter of gold. As for the button at his throat, it shone even as the moon, and in it was a full liter of gold. The vest had a gold-embroidered collar whose two wings were fastened by the button. At the right side of the collar, above the button, was the likeness of Sulejman the Magnificent and on the other side, that of the imperial pontiff of Islam. Then she gave him his cylindrical breastplate. It was not of silver but of pure gold and weighed full four stone. On his back she fastened it with a buckle. Then she put upon him his silken breeches, of Damascus make, all embroidered with gold, with serpents depicted upon his thighs, their golden heads meeting beneath his belt and beneath the thong by which his sword was hung. Then she girded on him two Tripolitan sashes and a braided belt of arms, which was not like other belts of arms, but braided of golden threads and embroidered with white pearls. Therein were his two small Venetian pistols, forged of pure gold; the sights were diamonds and the ornaments were of pearl. They shone even as the moon. Both pistols fire without flint and take a full liter of powder, breaking fierce armor and burning the hearts of heroes. Between them was a scimitar, an angry blade which severs heroes' hearts. Its whole scabbard was decorated with pearls, and its hilt was forged of gold. Upon his shoulders was a silken cloak, its corners heavy with gold. Gilded branches were embroidered round about and upon his shoulders were snakes whose heads met beneath his throat. Down the front hung four cords, braided of 'fined gold, all four reaching to his belt of arms and mingling with his sword-thong, which held his fierce Persian blade.

Then his mother took an ivory comb and combed his sheaf-like queue and bound it with pearl. She put on his fur cap with its twelve plumes, which none could wear, neither vizier nor imperial field marshal, nor minister, nor any other pasha except the alajbey under the sultan's firman. She put upon him his boots and leggings. On his head waved the plumes, and the golden feathers fell over his forehead. The imperial plumes were made after two fashions; half of them were stationary and half mobile. Whenever he rode or marched, the stationary plumes twanged, even as an angry serpent, and the moving plumes revolved. The hero needed no watch; for the plumes revolved thrice or four times an hour.

Although singers speak of such passages as "ornaments" and, indeed, boast of their ability to "ornament" a hero or a horse, or even a song, there is a strongly ritualistic flavor to these descriptions. They do not seem to be used indiscriminately. The poet has a choice of using a short form of these themes (or of omitting them entirely) or of elaborating them. The arming of a hero may be accomplished in a single line: "Then Osman prepared himself within his chamber" (Međedović, "Smailagić Meho," line 1859). On the other hand, it may be ornamented as we have just seen in the arming of Meho above from the same song.

The longer version seems to be reserved for the main protagonist when he is preparing himself to go forth on a special mission, in this case to receive his credentials as alajbey, succeeding his father and uncle in that office, and also, incidentally, to woo a maiden. It may well be that the presence of the elaboration at this point and in connection with this particular hero is a survival from rites of initiation or dedication.

The singer almost pointedly omits the detailed description of the arming of the companion and squire, Osman. Were he decorating the song merely for decoration's sake or merely to lengthen it, he would surely have included Osman's arming as well. Later in the song, when the wedding guests have assembled and are ready to leave on their journey to fetch the maiden, Međedović says only: "Lord Mehmed prepared himself in the very gold array in which he had assumed the commission of alajbey and in which he had wooed Fatima" (lines 9339ff.). The investiture belongs to Meho. But Osman is an important character in the song, and the description of his accoutrements is not neglected. We see him, however, already dressed and armed. Just as Meho was told by his elders what clothes and arms he was to don, so Osman is instructed by Meho's father, Smail: "Array yourself in those garments that you wear only twice in the year, on both Bajrams, even the Day of Pilgrims and the Bajram of Ramazan, and that you wore when we went before the sultan" (lines 1811ff.). And later some fifty lines are devoted to a description of Osman, which begins: (lines 2050ff.)

Then they quieted the horse, and from the house, from the coffee room came Osman, the standard-bearer, dressed in silk and gold. On his head was a golden cap with seven plumes, three steadfast and four mobile. The steadfast plumes hissed like angry snakes, while the mobile ones turned on their pivot four times an hour. When the hero was journeying afar or fighting in the wars, he needed no timepiece; for the plumes turned and told him what hour it was of day or night. The golden feathers fell over his forehead and some backwards over his neck. They trailed over the young man's shoulders like a dragon's scales. Osman's cloak was woven and had upon it bands of gold. Golden branches were embroidered on all sides, and serpents were woven on his shoulders, their heads meeting beneath his throat. Had you not seen them before, you would have sworn the snakes were living. The breastplate upon young Osman's chest was gilded. His breeches were of scarlet Venetian cloth, with golden stripes upon his thighs and golden branches embroidered between the stripes. The embroidery was of gold and the fabric of scarlet; the two colors met and mingled. . . .

This is not an investiture; for Osman has already been "invested." He is Meho's standard-bearer, squire, and protector. In ritual terms he is the sponsor of the neophyte, and his regalia are worthy of attention. But the theme of donning them does not belong to him. The theme of description is shorter than that given to Meho himself and thus indicates the degree of importance of each person in the story. The length, or even the presence, of "ornamental" themes cannot be said, therefore, to depend solely on the whim of the singer. In some cases, at least, there seems to be a deeper significance, perhaps deriving from ritual.

A parallel to the dressing and arming of Meho can be found in the medieval Greek epic of *Digenis Akritas*. The young Basil has proved his strength and bravery by killing wild beasts. His father and uncle then take him to a spring to wash:

> And afterwards the boy changed his clothing;
> Thin singlets he put on to cool himself,
> The upper one was red with golden hems,
> And all the hems of it were fused with pearls,
> The neck was filled with southernwood and musk,
> And distinct pearls it had instead of buttons,
> The buttonholes were twisted with pure gold;
> He wore fine leggings with griffins embellished,
> His spurs were plaited round with precious stones,
> And on the gold work there were carbuncles.[11]

In the Russian prose version of *Digenis* this scene of investiture comes before the fight with the serpent that emerges from the spring in which Digenis has bathed, and there are overtones of ritual dedication.

The more obvious parallels in the *Iliad* are the arming first of Patroclus and then of Achilles himself. These scenes should not be taken by themselves, but should be compared with other arming scenes in the *Iliad*. The first example is in Book III, lines 330–338, describing the arming of Alexandros for single combat:[12]

> First he placed along his legs the fair greaves linked with
> silver fastenings to hold the greaves at the ankles.
> Afterwards he girt on about his chest the corselet
> of Lykaon his brother since this fitted him also.
> 5 Across his shoulders he slung the sword with the nails of silver,
> a bronze sword, and above it the great shield, huge and heavy.
> Over his powerful head he set the well-fashioned helmet
> with the horse-hair crest, and the plumes nodded terribly above it.
> He took up a strong-shafted spear that fitted his hand's grip.

The short form of the arming theme follows in the very next line:

> In the same way warlike Menelaos put on his armour.

The arming of Alexandros, proceeding as the challenger, seemed worthy of lengthier treatment to Homer, whatever the reason may be, than that of Menelaos. The arming of Patroclus in XVI, 131–144, follows that of Alexandros word for word for the first eight lines, except that the line "starry and elaborate of swift-footed Aiakides" takes the place of line 4 above. To this core of eight lines is added:

> He took up two powerful spears that fitted his hand's grip [a
> variant of line 9 above]
> only he did not take the spear of blameless Aiakides,
> huge, heavy, thick, which no one else of all the Achaians
> could handle, but Achilleus alone knew how to wield it;
> the Pelian ash spear which Cheiron had brought to his father
> from high on Pelion to be death for fighters . . .

Patroclus' arming seems by this much to be more important than that of Alexandros, and chiefly for what he did not take, the distinctive mark of Achilles himself, the ashen spear.

The arming of Achilles (XIX, 369–391) begins with the very same lines as that of Alexandros and Patroclus through line 6 above, but eliminating the line (4) about the borrowed corselet; and it ends with the last four lines, which we have quoted from Patroclus' arming, about the ashen spear. Between these two and beginning with the reference to the great shield, which has previously been described, come these lines that mark the arming of Achilles as of vaster significance than that of Patroclus:

> . . . and from it [the shield] the light glimmered far, as from the moon.
> And as when from across water a light shines to mariners
> from a blazing fire, when the fire is burning high in the mountains
> in a desolate steading, as the mariners are carried unwilling
> by storm winds over the fish-swarming sea, far away from their loved ones;
> so the light from the fair elaborate shield of Achilleus
> shot into the high air. And lifting the helm he set it
> massive upon his head, and the helmet crested with horse-hair

shone like a star, the golden fringes were shaken about it
which Hephaistos had driven close along the horn of the helmet.
And brilliant Achilleus tried himself in his armour, to see
if it fitted close, and how his glorious limbs ran within it,
and the armour became as wings and upheld the shepherd of the people.
Next he pulled out from its standing place the spear of his father, . . .

Impressive as this scene of arming surely is, it is still not the most ornate as such in the *Iliad*. That distinction belongs, curiously enough, to the passage describing the arming of Agamemnon in Book XI (lines 17–44). It begins with the same three lines that are used in all the other passages, but with the mention of the corselet it diverges:

[the corselet] that Kinyras had given him once, to be a guest present.
For the great fame and rumour of war had carried to Kypros
how the Achaians were to sail against Troy in their vessels.
Therefore he gave the king as a gift of grace this corselet.
Now there were ten circles of deep cobalt upon it,
and twelve of gold and twenty of tin. And toward the opening
at the throat there were rearing up three serpents of cobalt
on either side, like rainbows, which the son of Kronos
has marked upon the clouds, to be a portent to mortals.
Across his shoulders he slung the sword, and the nails upon it
were golden and glittered, and closing about it the scabbard
was silver, and gold was upon the swordstraps that held it.
And he took up the man-enclosing elaborate stark shield,
a thing of splendour. There were ten circles of bronze upon it,
and set about it were twenty knobs of tin, pale-shining,
and in the very centre another knob of dark cobalt.
And circled in the midst of all was the blank-eyed face of the Gorgon
with her stare of horror, and Fear was inscribed upon it, and Terror.
The strap of the shield had silver upon it, and there also on it
was coiled a cobalt snake, and there were three heads upon him
twisted to look backward and grown from a single neck, all three.
Upon his head he set the helmet, two-horned, four-sheeted,
with the horse-hair crest, and the plumes nodded terribly above it.
Then he caught up two strong spears edged with sharp bronze
and the brazen heads flashed far from him deep into heaven.
And Hera and Athene caused a crash of thunder about him,
doing honour to the lord of deep-golden Mykenai.

The varying degrees of elaboration of the theme of arming used by Homer are similar to those of the Yugoslav singers, extending from the single line to longer passages. As with the South Slavic poets, the very presence of the theme has a meaning beyond that of description for description's own sake. If the ritual in the Yugoslav poems and in the *Digenis Akritas* seems to be one of initiation, that in the *Iliad* is probably one of dedication to the task of saving the hero's people, even of sacrifice. Each of these men is about to set out upon a mission of deep significance, and the "ornamental" theme is a signal and mark, both "ritualistic" and artistic, of the role of the hero.

In building a large theme the poet has a plan of it in his mind beyond the bare necessities of narrative. There are elements of order and balance within themes. The description of an assembly, for example, follows a pattern proceeding from the head of the assembly and his immediate retinue through a descending hierarchy of nobles to the cupbearer, who is the youngest in the assembly and hence waits upon his elders, but ending with the main hero of the story. This progression aids the singer by giving him a definite method of presentation. A similar plan can be seen in the gathering of an army. Here the order is often an ascending one. And almost invariably the last hero to be invited and the last to arrive is Tale of Orašac, a man of great individuality. Sometimes the singer merely adds one name after another as they occur to him until he has exhausted his store and then he caps the list with Tale.

The living eye of the singer's imagination moves in the theme of dressing a hero or in that of caparisoning a horse in the natural order of the action being described. In the first case he begins with shirt and trousers and ends with headdress and weapons, the latter being described also in the order in which they are put on. In the case of the horse, the singer begins with the blanket under the saddle and ends with the bit in the horse's mouth. He is ready to be led forth. The descriptions are vivid because they follow the action.

In all these instances one sees also that the singer always has the end of the theme in his mind. He knows where he is going. As in the adding of one line to another, so in the adding of one element in a theme to another, the singer can stop and fondly dwell upon any single item without losing a sense of the whole. The style allows comfortably for digression or for enrichment. Once embarked upon a theme, the singer can proceed at his own pace. Wherever possible he moves in balances: from boots to cap, from a sword on the left side to powder box on the right. Moreover, he usually signals the end of a theme by a significant or culminating point. The description of an assembly moves inexorably to focus on the chief hero of the song; the description of a journey moves toward its destination; headdress and armor are the most glorious accoutrements of a warrior; the larger assembly theme proceeds onward to the decision which will itself lead to further action. The singer's mind is orderly.

This orderliness can be further illustrated in the question and answer technique so commonly used either in an assembly or when two heroes meet after many years. In "Smailagić Meho," Meho is asked by his uncle a series of questions to which the answers are all negative. Meho replies with a series of negative answers and finally states the real reason why he is sad. In Ugljanin's song of Đulić Ibrahim, Đulić questions the newly-arrived prisoner concerning affairs back home, beginning with general questions about the Border, proceeding to questions about his own house and household, and ending with the inquiry about his wife. The answers of the prisoner follow the same pattern. Here again the end of the theme is clear and the structure within is balanced.

It might be expected, since the singer works out both in performance and in his solitary practice his own form of a theme, that the themes of one singer could be distinguished from the themes of another. The flexibility of formula structure allows us to determine individuality of style on that level. We can, I believe, do the same on the level of the theme. In spite of the variety that we have seen in Avdo's different handlings of the assembly, one could make no mistake about his individual style in them.

It is not merely the fullness of treatment of the assembly theme that distinguishes Avdo's version from Šemić's. This is an important difference, of course. Avdo elaborates more than Šemić does. But Avdo can sing the same theme with less elaboration, just as all singers can, although it is Avdo's habit to be fuller. In the telling of the writing of the petition, indeed, Šemić is not sparing of details. If we compare these two versions of this subsidiary theme, we note that Šemić has Hasanagha leave the assembly and go to the market place for a *hodža,* who then writes the petition at the dictation of Hasanagha. In Avdo's song, four scribes are already present, who fashion the petition themselves. Moreover, Šemić uses a different method of having the signing done. The petition is handed from one member of the assembly to another. Each reads it and each puts his seal upon it. This text was read to Avdo, yet he made no attempt to imitate it. The theme of signing regularly used by Avdo, a form that does not tell of handing the petition from one hero to another or of the heroes' reading it, came to the fore and took the place of the one that the singer from whom he learned the song had employed. A singer ordinarily has one basic form for such a minor theme; it is flexible and within limits adaptable to special circumstances. But when such circumstances are absent, the singer makes no attempt to alter its general pattern.

In the two versions of the assembly in Vlahovljak's and Avdo's songs of Bećiragić Meho we can also note a difference in technique between the two, especially as regards the arrival of the messenger. Vlahovljak tells how the door creaked and a messenger entered. Avdo, on the other hand, it will be remembered, described how the heroes looked out the window, saw a cloud of dust in the distance, from which emerged a rider. Standard-bearers were sent to meet the messenger, who was brought in by them to the assembly. This is Avdo's normal way of describing the arrival of messengers. He uses it, for example, in his song of Osmanbey Delibegović and Pavičević Luka (Parry 12389 and 12441).

Differences in working out the same subsidiary theme mark compositions as belonging to different singers just as surely as the more spectacular qualitative distinctions of length and fullness.[13] This method is obviously of importance to the Homerist, plagued as he is with the question as to whether the *Iliad* and *Odyssey* are by the same author.

One might legitimately ask whether the differences noted could possibly appear in the work of a single singer over a period of years. Would he change his technique as he grew older and more experienced? There is always a possibility that he might do this, of course. We shall see an example in the next chapter of the change in a song in the hands of a single singer over a period of some years,[14] but it is noteworthy that this was between the ages of twenty-nine and forty-six, when the singer was still growing in his art. From the time that maturity is reached and the singer has established the general outlines of a theme, evidence seems to indicate that he changes it little if at all. (One might add that young singers do not produce *Iliads* and *Odysseys!*) Avdo's version of the assembly theme in the song of Bećiragić Meho, which he recited for the records in 1951, sixteen years after he first sang it (and he swears that he had not sung it at all in the interval), still contains the distinctive feature that I have already marked; namely, the arrival of the messenger is narrated in the same way as in 1935.

*　　*　　*

Although the themes lead naturally from one to another to form a song which exists as a whole in the singer's mind with Aristotelian beginning, middle, and end, the units within this whole, the themes, have a semi-independent life of their own. The theme in oral poetry exists at one and the same time in and for itself and for the whole song. This can be said both for the theme in general and also for any individual singer's forms of it. His task is to adapt and adjust it to the particular song that he is re-creating. It does not have a single "pure" form either for the individual singer or for the tradition as a whole. Its form is ever changing in the singer's mind, because the theme is in reality protean; in the singer's mind it has many shapes, all the forms in which he has ever sung it, although his latest rendering of it will naturally be freshest in his mind. It is not a static entity, but a living, changing, adaptable artistic creation.[15] Yet it exists for the sake of the song. And the shapes that it has taken in the past have been suitable for the song of the moment. In a traditional poem, therefore, there is a pull in two directions: one is toward the song being sung and the other is toward the previous uses of the same theme. The result is that characteristic of oral poetry which literary scholars have found hardest to understand and to accept, namely, an occasional inconsistency, the famous nod of a Homer.[16]

One of the most glaring inconsistencies of this sort within my experience of Yugoslav oral song occurs in Ðemail Zogić's song of the rescue of Alibey's children by Bojičić Alija (I, No. 24). The young hero has neither a horse nor armor with which to undertake his mission, and his mother borrows them from his uncle, Rustembey. Later in the poem there is a recognition scene in which Alija is recognized because he is wearing the armor of Mandušić Vuk, whom he overcame in single combat. Zogić has not made the necessary adjustment in the theme of recognition so that it would agree with the theme of the poor hero who borrows his armor. This theme of recognition we know was not in the version which Zogić learned from Makić. Zogić has used another form of the theme of recognition, and it was not right for the particular song. Yet seventeen years later when Zogić sang the same song it contained the same inconsistency. We know the cause of it. It is more difficult to understand its persistence.

It would be a mistake for us to attempt to palliate the continuance of this inconsistency. We must score this against Zogić as a singer of tales. The best of singers would not have allowed such an inconsistency ever to come into being, let alone become fixed over many years. Yet the case is instructive. It shows us that the ordinary singer is not always critical, is not looking for that consistency which has become almost a fetish with literary scholars. Bowra, in his book *Tradition and Design in the Iliad*,[17] has attributed some of the narrative inconsistencies to the fact that the poet was concentrating on one episode at a time. This is close to the truth but does not give the whole picture. It is not merely that the singer is concentrating on each episode as he sings it. Each episode has rather its own consistency.

I believe that it is accurate to say that the poet thinks of his song in terms of its broader themes. This is what Makić means by saying that the singer must "think how it goes, and then little by little it comes to him." He has to set in his mind what the basic themes of a song are and the order in which they occur. But that is not all. If it were, the process of making his song would be fairly mechanical. He would say to himself, "I begin with a 'council,' then go on with a 'journey,' another 'council,' the 'writing and sending of letters,' and so forth." In his bag of tricks would be a "council," a "journey," and other themes with suitable labels; he would pick out the appropriate one, change the names in it, and fit it into place. This is as false a concept as the notion that the singer has a common stock or index of formulas from which he draws. There is a common stock of formulas, as we saw, and there is a common stock of themes which we can conveniently label. But our neatly categorizing minds work differently from the singer's. To him the formulas and themes are always used in association one with another; they are always part of a song. To the singer, moreover, the song has a specific though flexible content.

Usually the singer is carried from one major theme to another by the demands for further action that are brought out in the developing of a theme. Thus the decision of the assembly in "Smailagić Meho" to send Meho to Budapest to obtain his credentials from the vizier leads inevitably to the theme of the journey, which in itself contains preparation and travel. This particular journey theme is distinctive in that Meho meets and rescues a maiden and discovers the treachery of the vizier. The action in this theme leads naturally to the next large theme of betrothal to the maiden and the return home to gather wedding guests. And so the poet moves forward. We might divide the "Song of Smailagić Meho" into five major themes: one, the assembly; two, the journey to Budapest and return; three, the gathering of an army; four, journey, battle, and return; five, the wedding.

In the "Song of Bagdad" there is no difficulty in proceeding from the council to the second theme, that of sending, carrying, delivering, and receiving a letter. The logic of the narrative draws the singer forward. The first two themes form a group: arrival of a letter, council; sending of a letter, arrival of a letter. This general pattern is repeated in the third and fourth themes of the song. The arrival of the sultan's message leads to the conversation between Alija and his mother in which the hero asks for advice. From this emerges the fourth theme of Alija's letter to Fatima, his betrothed. This is written and delivered, and her answer is written and returned to Alija, after which Alija returns his answer to the sultan. At this point a main section of the song is completed. The structure could be schematized as follows: a (council), b^1 (letter), c (conversation), d^1 (letter), d^2 (answer), b^2 (answer). Theme b is interrupted by themes c and d, which are counterparts of a and b. By the time the singer has learned this part of the song he has laid the groundwork for future themes of council and conversation, which are not unrelated, and for communication by letter writing or imperial decree.

The next larger complex of themes in the song that the singer must learn to express extends from the writing of letters summoning the chieftains to the arrival of the Bosnian army before Stambol. He begins with an expanded letter-writing theme, which is actually a catalogue. He has already used the simpler forms of letter writing several times and has a foundation for the more elaborate one, which is formed by repetition. This is followed by the sending of messengers for provisions of various kinds; then the arrival of the provisions and completion of preparations for receiving the host are related. The arrival of the contingents is another catalogue, richly adorned with description. The order of arrival is the same as that of invitation. The structure of the group of themes is a^1 (invitation catalogue), b^1 (ordering provisions), b^2 (arrival of provisions), a^2 (arrival catalogue). Such a catalogue, or series of catalogues, can and will be used by our singer, once he has formed it, in many songs.

The second half of the larger complex contains the theme of the arming and preparations of the main hero, the departure of the army, and its arrival. The departure is told in terms of order of march, and hence constitutes one more brief catalogue of forces. The arrival is told in terms of messengers bringing news to the sultan and of the rewards given them as bearers of good tidings. In the arrival catalogue the singer learns to describe horses and heroes as they are seen emerging onto a plain. He also learns to caparison a horse and to dress a hero.

These complexes are held together internally both by the logic of the narrative and by the consequent force of habitual association. Logic and habit are strong forces, particularly when fortified by a balancing of elements in recognizable patterns such as those which we have just outlined. Habitual association of themes, however, need not be merely linear, that is to say, theme b always follows theme a, and theme c always follows theme b. Sometimes the presence of theme a in a song calls forth the presence of theme b somewhere in the song, but not necessarily in an a-b relationship, not necessarily following one another immediately. Where the association is linear, it is close to the logic of the narrative, and the themes are generally of a kind that are included in a larger complex. I hesitate to call them "minor" or "nonessential" or "subsidiary," because sometimes essential ideas may be expressed in them. Where the association is not linear, it seems to me that we are dealing with a force or "tension" that might be termed "submerged." The habit is hidden, but felt. It arises from the depths of the tradition through the workings of the traditional processes to inevitable expression. And to be numb to an awareness of this kind of association is to miss the meaning not only of the oral method of composition and transmission, but even of epic itself. Without such an awareness the overtones from the past, which give tradition the richness of diapason of full organ, cannot be sensed by the reader of oral epic. The singer's natural audience appreciates it because they are as much part of the tradition as the singer himself.

What I mean may be illustrated by considering any single member of the complex of themes associated with, let us say, the return of the hero from captivity in enemy country, although the song itself may not necessarily be one of captivity and return. It is a curious fact in the Yugoslav tradition, that when a hero has been absent for a long period, or even when a long war is an element in the story, whether the hero has been in that war or not, a deceptive story, or its vestige, and a recognition, or its vestige are almost invariably to be found in the same song. Some force keeps these elements together. I call it a "tension of essences."

The Odyssean story of return after long absence entails disguise, deceptive story, and recognition. The Yugoslav return songs have the same grouping of elements. This grouping is, of course, to be expected because it is the basic narrative of the tale. There are, however, songs that are not fundamentally return songs but that contain some if not all of these elements. Thus, the "Song of Bagdad" by Ugljanin (I, No. 1) begins with the theme of a long and unsuccessful war. One of its chief characters, the hero's betrothed, Fatima, disguises herself as a standard-bearer and joins the hero's army. She tells him a false tale as to who she really is, namely, the outlaw Budimlija Mujo; and at the end of the song there is a scene of recognition in the marriage chamber. This group of themes (long war, disguise, deceptive story, recognition) tends to maintain an identity of its own even when it is not ostensibly the main theme of the story, which in this case is the capture of Bagdad by Đerđelez Alija.

Zogić's favorite song of the rescue of Alibey's children (I, No. 24) who have been long in captivity also has the theme of long absence. The hero disguises himself, and is recognized by a tavern maid in the enemy city. The second version of the Bagdad song (I, No. 26), the central episode of which is a single combat, also contains disguise, deceptive story, and recognition. The song of Mitrović Stojan (Parry 6796, 6777) tells how the hero has been many years with a band of raiders in the mountains, has a longing to see his wife, disguises himself in order not to be captured by the Turks, tells a deceptive story, but eventually is recognized and captured.

In our investigation of composition by theme this hidden tension of essences must be taken into consideration. We are apparently dealing here with a strong force that keeps certain themes together. It is deeply imbedded in the tradition; the singer probably imbibes it intuitively at a very early stage in his career. It pervades his material and the tradition. He avoids violating the group of themes by omitting any of its members. In the following chapter we shall see that he will even go so far as to substitute something similar if he finds that for one reason or another he cannot use one of the elements in its usual form.

CHAPTER FIVE
SONGS AND THE SONG

As long as one thought of the oral poet as a singer who carried in his head a song in more or less the exact form in which he had learned it from another singer, as long as one used for investigation ballads and comparatively short epics, the question of what an oral song is could not arise. It was, we assumed, essentially like any other poem; its text was more or less fixed. But when we look more closely at the process of oral composition and come to appreciate more fully the creative role of the individual singer in carrying forward the tradition, we must begin to query our concept of a song.

When the singer of tales, equipped with a store of formulas and themes and a technique of composition, takes his place before an audience and tells his story, he follows the plan which he has learned along with the other elements of his profession.[1] Whereas the singer thinks of his song in terms of a flexible plan of themes, some of which are essential and some of which are not, we think of it as a given text which undergoes change from one singing to another. We are more aware of change than the singer is, because we have a concept of the fixity of a performance or of its recording on wire or tape or plastic or in writing. We think of change in content and in wording; for, to us, at some moment both wording and content have been established. To the singer the song, which cannot be changed (since to change it would, in his mind, be to tell an untrue story or to falsify history), is the essence of the story itself. His idea of stability, to which he is deeply devoted, does not include the wording, which to him has never been fixed, nor the unessential parts of the story. He builds his performance, or song in our sense, on the stable skeleton of narrative, which is the song in his sense.

When one asks a singer what songs he knows, he will begin by saying that he knows the song, for example, about Marko Kraljević when he fought with Musa, or he will identify it by its first lines.[2] In other words, the song is the story of what someone did or what happened to some hero, but it is also the song itself expressed in verse. It is not just a story; it is not merely a tale divorced from its telling. Sulejman Makić said that he could repeat a song that he had heard only once, *provided that he heard it to the gusle* (I, p. 266). This is a most significant clue. The story in the poet-singer's mind is a story in song. Were it not for remarks like that of Makić, we might be led to think that the singer needs only "a story," which he then retells in the language of verse. But now we know that the story itself must have the particular form which it has only when it is told in verse.

Any particular song is different in the mouth of each of its singers. If we consider it in the thought of a single singer during the years in which he sings it, we find that it is different at different stages in his career. Its clearness of outline will depend upon how many times he sings it; whether it is an established part of his repertory or merely a song which he sings occasionally. The length of the song is also important, because a short song will naturally tend to become more stable the more it is sung.

In some respects the larger themes and the song are alike. Their outward form and their specific content are ever changing. Yet there is a basic idea or combination of ideas that is fairly stable. We can say, then, that a song is the story about a given hero, but its expressed forms are multiple, and each of these expressed forms or tellings of the story is itself a separate song, in its own right, authentic and valid as a song unto itself. We must distinguish then two concepts of song in oral poetry. One is the general idea of the story, which we use when we speak in larger terms, for example, of the song of the wedding of Smailagić Meho, which actually includes all singings of it. The other concept of song is that of a particular performance or text, such as Avdo Međedović's song, "The Wedding of Smailagić Meho," dictated during the month of July, 1935.

Our real difficulty arises from the fact that, unlike the oral poet, we are not accustomed to thinking in terms of fluidity. We find it difficult to grasp something that is multiform. It seems to us necessary to construct an ideal text or to seek an original, and we remain dissatisfied with an ever-changing phenomenon. I believe that once we know the facts of oral composition we must cease trying to find an original of any traditional song. From one point of view each performance is an original. From another point of view it is impossible to retrace the work of generations of singers to that moment when some singer first sang a particular song.

We are occasionally fortunate enough to be present at a first singing, and we are then disappointed, because the singer has not perfected the song with much practice and by the test of repeated performance.[3] Even after he has — and it may change much as he works it over — it must be accepted and sung by other singers in order to become a part of the tradition, and in their hands it will go through other changes, and so the process continues from generation to generation. We cannot retrace these steps in any particular song. There was an original, of course, but we must be content with the texts that we have and not endeavor to "correct" or "perfect" them in accordance with a purely arbitrary guess at what the original might have been.

Indeed, we should be fully aware that even had we this "original," let us say, of the wedding of Smailagić Meho, we would not have the original of the basic story, that is, the song of the young man who goes forth into the world to win his spurs. We would have only the application of this story to the hero Meho. Each performance is the specific song, and at the same time it is the generic song. The song we are listening to is "the song"; for each performance is more than a performance; it is a re-creation. Following this line of thinking, we might term a singer's first singing of a song as a creation of the song in his experience. Both synchronically and historically there would be numerous creations and re-creations of the song. This concept of the relationship between "songs" (performances of the same specific or generic song) is closer to the truth than the concept of an "original" and "variants." In a sense each performance is "an" original, if not "the" original.

The truth of the matter is that our concept of "the original," of "the song," simply makes no sense in oral tradition. To us it seems so basic, so logical, since we are brought up in a society in which writing has fixed the norm of a stable first creation in art, that we feel there must be an "original" for everything. The first singing in oral tradition does not coincide with this concept of the "original." We might as well be prepared to face the fact that we are in a different world of thought, the patterns of which do not always fit our cherished terms. In oral tradition the idea of an original is illogical.

It follows, then, that we cannot correctly speak of a "variant," since there is no "original" to be varied! Yet songs are related to one another in varying degrees; not, however, in the relationship of variant to original, in spite of the recourse so often made to an erroneous concept of "oral transmission"; for "oral transmission," "oral composition," "oral creation," and "oral performance" are all one and the same thing. Our greatest error is to attempt to make "scientifically" rigid a phenomenon that is fluid.

But if we are pursuing a will-o'-the-wisp when we seek an original, we are deluded by a mirage when we try to construct an ideal form of any given song. If we take all the extant texts of the song of Smailagić Meho and from them extract all the common elements, we have constructed something that never existed in reality or even in the mind of any of the singers of that song. We have simply then the common elements in this restricted number of texts, nothing more, nothing less.

It seems to me highly significant that the words "author" and "original" have either no meaning at all in oral tradition or a meaning quite different from the one usually assigned to them. The anonymity of folk epic is a fiction, because the singer has a name. We have created for ourselves in regard to both these terms problems that are not of any major importance.

It should be clear from the foregoing that the author of an oral epic, that is, the text of a performance, is the performer, the singer before us. Given normal eyesight on the part of the spectator, he is not multiple, but single. The author of any of our texts, unless an editor has tampered with it, is the man who dictated, sang, chanted, or otherwise gave expression to it. A performance is unique; it is a creation, not a reproduction, and it can therefore have only one author.

Actually, only the man with writing seems to worry about this, just as only he looks for the nonexistent, illogical, and irrelevant "original." Singers deny that they are the creators of the song. They learned it from other singers. We know now that *both* are right, each according to his meaning of "song." To attempt to find the first singer of a song is as futile as to try to discover the first singing. And yet, just as the first singing could not be called the "original," so the first man to sing a song cannot be considered its "author," because of the peculiar relationship, already discussed, between his singing and all subsequent singings. From that point of view a song has no "author" but a multiplicity of authors, each singing being a creation, each singing having its own single "author." This is, however, a very different concept of multiple authorship from that, or more properly those, in general use among Homerists.

Change and stability — these are the two elements of the traditional process that we must seek to comprehend. What is it that changes and why and how? What remains stable and why? In order to answer these questions, we should consider three groups of thematic analyses of songs, reports, as it were, on three groups of experiments. The first contains experiments on transmission of a song from one singer to another, the second illustrates the differences in a single singer's performances of a given song at brief intervals of time, and the third shows what happens to a song in a singer's repertory over a longer period, namely sixteen or seventeen years.

The cases of direct transmission without any intervening period of time (Salih Ugljanin from Nikola Vujnović, Avdo Međedović from Mumin Vlahovljak) demonstrate that the learner follows the text that he hears fairly closely in terms of basic story. The first of this pair of experiments ("The Wedding of Relja of Pazar," Parry 656) shows Salih Ugljanin omitting a number of details, but expanding two speeches and the marriage theme at the end.[4] Expansion is what one would normally expect from an old singer repeating the song of one much younger; in fact it is surprising that Ugljanin did not expand more. The omissions are interesting because the majority of them are concerned with the mountain spirits (*vile*). It would seem that these creatures of the imagination do not live in groups with a leader in Ugljanin's world. In his songs they appear alone and hence without a leader. His own picture of these spirits has, therefore, prevailed over that of Vujnović except for the necessary action of one of them attacking Relja and marrying him. The changes of detail, however, do not change the essence of the story. They follow the principle we have seen at work in the previous chapter; namely, that in learning a song the singer depends for details on his already habitual presentation of themes.

These changes in detail in Ugljanin's singing of the wedding of Relja of Pazar are minor, and perhaps of no great significance; but the changes that Međedović made in Vlahovljak's song of Bećiragić Meho attract our attention (Parry 12471, 12468; thematic analysis in Appendix I). The most striking difference between the two is, of course, the degree and quality of expansion in Avdo's performance, from 2294 lines to 6313 lines, nearly three times the length of Mumin's song. Naturally such expansion involves the addition of many details, and we have already seen in the previous chapter the kind of changes that are normal in transmission on the level of the individual theme. The learner usually employs his own form of any given theme rather than the form that he has heard from the other singer. Sometimes the singer who is learning has to restrain himself from doing this, that is, from following his own theme rather than another's. If he did not take care, he would fall into self-contradiction later. Avdo is trapped in this way briefly, and not very significantly, at the beginning of theme 5 (see Appendix I). According to his habit, when a letter is delivered, the recipient opens it and reads it and the head of the assembly asks about the letter. This Avdo causes to happen in our story, forgetting that the messenger is waiting for a reward; momentarily Avdo is carried on by habit and for a few lines neglects the theme of paying the messenger, a really important theme in this song, a distinctive part of it. Later Avdo has to repeat the theme of reading the letter, thus causing a minor inconsistency.

There was something also in the story of Meho's capture of Nikola Vodogazović (theme 7) that surprised Avdo. He *tells* us that he was surprised; that is to say, he underlines the fact that Meho went to Janok, not in disguise, but in the clothes of a Turkish border warrior. Avdo emphasizes this at the time of telling, and even makes it the lever for introducing the repetition of this part of the tale-within-a-tale when Meho stands before the vizier in Budim. Avdo underlines this lack of disguise, because expeditions to Janok are generally for rescue, not for capture, and they are accomplished in disguise. The tavern maid usually recognizes the hero as a blood brother by tokens of some kind, and aids in the rescue. Everything in Avdo's experience of the tradition at this point indicates that the hero should be in disguise, and Avdo must restrain himself from disguising him. He indicates his problem and his feeling about it; yet he follows his model.

Indeed, after the story-within-a-story, Avdo is still worried about the question of disguise; he still feels that he must "correct" Mumin's telling. When assistance is offered to Meho from others in the assembly (theme 8), Mumin is content with Meho's wearing the clothes and riding the horse of his uncle, or of Halil, or of Bećir; when one wears another's clothes, one is that man for the moment and is thus disguised. Avdo did not accept this method, and on Meho's second journey to Janok, Avdo is determined that he will be in disguise. The disguise is proper now, anyway, because he is going on a rescue mission, not one of capture. Therefore, in Avdo's singing, when Meho's uncle offers help to the youth, he states specifically that Meho must this time disguise himself and his horse. In the case of Halil's offer, Halil says merely that his sister will dress Meho as she does him when he goes on such raids. Later the dress is specified as that of a Viennese standard-bearer (theme 9).

Disguise must eventually involve recognition. The sense of "disguise" which must at one time have belonged to the borrowed horse and armor as we find it in Mumin's song has disappeared; so that when Meho in Halil's clothes and riding Halil's famous strawberry roan goes to Jela's tavern in Janok, she immediately recognizes him. There is no need for a recognition scene. In fact, all feel that Meho is not in disguise. But Avdo has restored to the theme a consciousness of disguise by adding a second disguising, the clothing and armor of the enemy country, in addition to borrowed horse and armor. The consequent recognition by Jela, the tavern maid, is not by elaborate signs; Meho simply tells her who he is. Yet one of the elements of recognition, one of those artifacts that constitute stage properties for such scenes, the musical instrument, together with a song, is present in Avdo's tale. Oddly enough the instrument is in the hands of the maid, not of the hero; the significant fact is that both it and the song are present at this moment in the tale. They were not in Avdo's model but have been added by him to the song as he heard it.

Another kind of change illustrated in this same experiment with Mumin and Avdo is concerned with a shift in the order of events. We have seen that Mumin listed three offers of assistance from members of the assembly; one from each of the following: uncle Ahmet, Halil, and Bećir, son of Mustajbey. Avdo lists only the first two. What is involved here is the boundary between themes. In Mumin's story the theme of assembly can be said to end at line 1320, when Meho departed for Kladuša. The scene in Kladuša follows, after which the story shifts back again to Udbina, Bećir, and Mustajbey; the shift is skillfully accomplished by having Meho pass through Udbina as he leaves for Janok, and by describing the aghas as watching him depart. The theme of assembly could also be said not to end until after the conversation between Bećir and his father; it might be thought of rather as being interrupted by the scene in Kladuša. Such a framing is one of the common methods of indicating concurrent actions. Avdo's technique is somewhat different at this point. With him the assembly theme does not end when Meho departs for Kladuša but continues through the conversation between Bećir and Mustajbey and the summoning of the Border. Then the scene is transferred to Kladuša, whence the hero departs directly for Janok without going by way of Udbina, or at least without any mention of that town.

A similar change is found toward the end of the song (theme 13). In this case, however, it is Avdo who interrupts the final scene before the great battle (the scene in which Meho leaves Jela and goes to join Anđelica at the crossroads) by returning to Udbina and to the Turks preparing to go to the assistance of Meho. Mumin had included the raising of the border army at the end of the conversation of Bećir with his father, Mustajbey (theme 10), but its scope was not so great as that of Avdo.

We have seen in this song changes stemming from addition of details and description, expansion by ornamentation, changes in action (such as those concerned with the disguise) that seem to stem from the tension of essentials preserving certain conglomerates or configurations of themes, changes in the order of appearance of the *dramatis personae,* shifting of themes from one place to another, forming new balances and patterns. Yet the story has remained essentially the same; the changes have not been of the kind that distort the tale. If anything, they have enhanced it.

In the two experiments so far discussed the "pupil" sang immediately after hearing the song from the "teacher." We have the exact text of both performances. In other instances in the Parry material, the "pupil's" text was taken down or recorded some period, usually many years, after the learning, and in only one case do we have, by chance, the exact text from which the learning was done. This is the case of Avdo Međedović and the twelve thousand-line dictated text of "The Wedding of Smailagić Meho" (Parry 6840). This remarkable song merits special comment. Expansion by ornamentation is obvious in this case throughout the song; the first theme, of which we have written in the previous chapter, illustrates this ornamentation extremely well. We have already observed that the description of the hero is not purely decoration, but is rather especially meaningful. Here Meho is the hero born of old age, the darling of family and empire, owner of special gifts, horse, sword, armor, and clothing. Avdo has emphasized, indeed brought into significant prominence, these characteristics of Meho by his expansion of this part of the theme.

There is one change that may have been brought about simply by Avdo's own personal sensitivity to human relations in a heroic society. In the song book the question as to why Meho is sad was posed by the uncle without any prompting by the head of the assembly. Avdo represents the leader as calling the uncle and suggesting that he interrogate the youth, with the caution that it not be done immediately but only after a short period, lest the boy be embarrassed.

As in "Bećiragić Meho," so in "Smailagić Meho," there are several cases of a change in the order of events. Thus, in the song book Meho talks first with the maiden in the coach at the Glina, hears her story, and then he and Osman fight with the guards. In Avdo's telling, Meho and Osman first fight with the guards and then Meho talks with Fata and hears her story. Moreover, Avdo has Fata ask for Meho's identity, and then has Meho ask Fata for her hand in marriage. She replies that her mother has told her she was destined for him anyway. There is none of this in the song book version, not at this point in the tale at any rate. In the song book, Meho asks Fata's mother for her daughter's hand when he first meets her in Budim bewailing the fate of her husband and child. He offers to give her good news of Fata, if she will give her to him. Avdo's version of the meeting between Meho and Fata's mother is somewhat more dramatic — even melodramatic! The mother is about to leap from the window to her death in the courtyard when Meho shouts to her that her daughter has returned with him.

Avdo has also added a detail that is worth noting, because he makes use of it again later in the story, namely the letter that Osman found on the body of the captain of the guard who was taking Fata by coach to General Petar. A letter or some sign proving betrayal is a not uncommon theme (cf. the cross falling from the turban of the pontiff in the story of the capture of Bagdad, I, p. 85). In this case the letter is used later when Meho and Osman are back with Smail in Kanidža to prove that they are not lying about the vizier's treachery.

Surely one of Avdo's most attractive qualities as a singer of tales — and he has many — is his sense of heroic ethic. In his elaboration of the theme of Meho's departure from Budim, he shows Meho presented by Fata's mother with two proposals, each of which has something to recommend it. First, Fata's mother suggests that he take Fata back with him immediately lest the vizier capture her during his absence. This is sensible, but he refuses on grounds that he does not wish the vizier to think him afraid. The second suggestion is that he stay with Fata a month to enjoy her love lest he be killed in the battle that is sure to come. This suggestion was taken from the song book, which merely stated, however, that Meho refused to stay overnight. This too Meho refuses as dishonorable.

Less attractive to us as expansion, but typical of epic, especially of dictated oral epic, is the extended catalogue. Avdo pulls out all the stops! Those who have maintained that the catalogue of ships in the *Iliad* must be a historical document of considerable accuracy and antiquity should pay close attention, I believe, to the "accuracy" with which Avdo has reproduced the song book! Had his sense of historicity been at all strong, he would 'at least have tried to follow the book with care. The book and his friend who could read were available, and he most certainly could have had this part memorized "cold." Obviously this did not concern him. His catalogue here is essentially the same catalogue as in his other songs! Note that the list of chieftains who arrive in response to the invitations contains names of some individuals who were not mentioned in the invitations themselves.

Avdo has felt it necessary to relate the final battle, or battles, at considerable length, giving special care to the attack on Budim. It is noteworthy that he has rejected the facts even of the song book story here. Avdo rejects Mustajbey as the captor of the vizier and as the new pasha. Moreover, after the battle has been described, Avdo has chosen to draw together with completeness many of the threads of the story otherwise left hanging. The sultan is informed of what has happened, new administrators and rulers are appointed, Fata's father and others are brought back from exile, and the wedding is finally held. The song book version left it to be taken for granted that all these details would have been worked out; Avdo has simply told in full what the other left to the imagination.

Making the imagination articulate is one of Homer's secrets also, and the following passage from Avdo's song, presented here as further illustration of his technique of expansion and elaboration, is reminiscent of Telemachus' journey in the *Odyssey* and not unhomeric in quality. On the second night of their journey to Budim, Meho and Osman stop at Knez Vujadin's house.

The corresponding section in the song book, *Smailagić Meho,* Mostar, 1925, tells of the stop at the house of Toroman Vuk and covers eleven lines (194–204):

They drove on their battle steeds and travelled that second day. They made their lodging far off in the small village of Veselica with the Vlah, Toroman Vuk. There they will spend the second night, and they will be lodged graciously, and graciously received, and graciously served. Then in the morning they will arise early. They pressed forward through the border country.

Here is Avdo's account:

They flew over the green plain even as a star in summer across the sky. They passed villages and crossed mountains. They travelled a whole day until nightfall, and they covered as much of Bosnia as they had planned to that day. They had come to the dwelling of Knez Vujadin. The Knez was at home with his wife and his two sons. They were looking from the window when the two imperial dragons came in sight, all glittering with gold and glorious in their plumes. The horses beneath them were in full panoply. Both heroes were like unto imperial pashas, and much better riders were they. Their array was much better than a pasha's or even a vizier's, or even, indeed, a great imperial general's. The Knez's two sons flew to the window and pressed their foreheads against it. When they saw, they wondered, and they cried out to their father: "O father, here is a wonderful sight that we have never seen before! Here are two heroes on two golden horses! They must be either pashas or viziers."

When the Knez looked and saw the son of Smail the Pilgrim with his plumed cap and the feather of an alajbey on it, and beneath him his winged horse, and when he saw the standard-bearer, that mighty hero, on his fine steed, then did Vujadin feel distressed, for here was the son of the Pilgrim in person. He recognized him because of Osman and his white horse, for all the Border knew Osman, and all the Kingdoms too. Then said Vujadin to his sons: "Run quickly to open the courtyard gate; open both portals wide before the two imperial dragons! Give them greeting and stand at attention, as if they were pashas or viziers, for to you they are indeed pashas and viziers. Tonight you shall neither sleep nor sit in their presence, but you must cross your arms upon your breast and speak no word, but serve these heroes in silence. Show that you honor them highly, both for my sake and for the prestige of your house, that in the years when I am no more you may bring it good repute!"

The Knez's two sons watched, and then they ran even as two mountain wolves and opened the courtyard gate. The two heroes drove in their horses. They said: "Good evening!" and the youths in the courtyard replied, and bowed low before them. Then they embraced the youths. Old Vujadin came flying from the house to the bottom of the stairs. He shouted greeting to the heroes and took them by their lordly hands. His two sons seized the horses by the bridle and walked them up and down. Then Lady Vujadin took the two spears from the saddlehorn and carried them to the upper chamber of the house to the master's room, where but few guests are admitted. That room was kept for such heroes as these. It was strewn with Venetian cloth, and round about were silk couches and fine pillows covered with white silk and embroidered in the center with gold. They parted the curtained doorway of the room and entered. Then came his two dear daughters-in-law, like unto two white mountain spirits. They took the men's boots and socks and the swords from their waists. When the two youths were seated, they gazed at the ornaments in the room, at the cushions on the couch, all silk and embroidered with gold. In the middle of the room was a table spread with Venetian cloth and on it a metal platter heaped with all sorts of food; and on the table were coffee-urns with golden handles, and cups of crystal. Next to this was a mother-of-pearl table with a six-winged cask holding forty stone, two pitchers adorned with mother-of-pearl, and four three-liter glasses covered with a silk napkin. Around the table were four chairs. . . .

[Glasses are filled, and talk begins. Vujadin says to Meho:]

"What is happening on the Austrian border? How are the lords of the Border? Do you still lead raiding bands over the hills, raiding bands and larger armies? Do you reach even as far as the Austrian Empire, broadening the borders of Sulejman's kingdom? Have the young men become better than their elders? What think you, Mehmed; are the old men better than the young?" And Mehmed answered: "Thoughts differ, but mine shall ever be that the old men are the better." . . . .

In the meantime the boys had brought back the tired horses from their walk, had taken off the golden saddles and the girths and all the trappings. They sponged the horses and dried their manes with a cloth. Then they covered them with blankets, gave them barley, and waited for the beasts to eat it. They put hay in the mangers, closed the door of the stable, and went into the house to continue to do service. Their hats they left on the pegs, and they stood bareheaded before Mehmed and his standard-bearer Osman. . . .

Finally the couches were spread for sleep, and the youths settled comfortably. All night the boys watched over their lords, lest, tired from drink, they should be disturbed and seek either wine or water.

When dawn broke, Osman called to Mehmed: "O Mehmed, we have slept too long." Vujadin and his sons tried as best they could to persuade their guests to stay longer, but it was of no avail. The Knez's sons prepared the horses. Meantime the youths were ready and descended to the courtyard. The maidens brought their spears, the boys led out their horses, and the youths mounted. The night had passed and now the day-star shone and dawn unfolded its wings.

Mehmed put his hand into his pocket and gave each of the maidens five gold pieces. But the Knez's children would not accept them: "No, Mehmed, you shall not pay for your lodgings. This is not an inn or a tavern, but a dwelling for men of breeding." But Mehmed would not listen: "This is not pay, my children, but a gift of love. Let the girls buy combs and powder!"

Then he rode to the courtyard gate, and behind him Osman on his white stallion, even as a star across a clear sky. Dawn spread its wings and soon the two youths were riding by the cool Klim near Budim, four hours away.

Avdo has gone to great lengths to elaborate this theme and the theme of the other overnight stop on Meho's journey. There is some evidence to indicate that singers do not ornament unimportant points in their stories.

Halting places on journeys, scenes of hospitality, both here and in Homer, may deserve the emphasis given them neither because they are realistic pictures of heroic life nor because they are artistically useful in showing passage of time, but because the archetypal journey in epic was of a ceremonial nature and its stages were marked by significant events and meaningful encounters. Perhaps in such changes Avdo is following a tribal and traditional sense of what is important, although he himself would merely claim that he knew how to "ornament" a song.

Certainly not all singers would make the changes that Avdo has. In the Parry Collection there are songs from singers who learned them from printed texts. Their songs, however, are very close to the printed versions, and one realizes that the singer was attempting consciously to memorize or at least to follow closely what was printed. Singers like Avdo, in whom the feeling of the traditional is still strong, make no attempt to memorize, as we know, even when a song is read to them, but singers imbued with the idea that the written text is the proper one strive to keep to it even verbally if possible. With them the tradition is dead or dying. It could be truly said, I believe, that the only way in which they can compensate for their lack of awareness of the tradition, that awareness that we are beginning to see as deeply conservative, religiously maintaining the meaning of a song, is to memorize or attempt to memorize. The true representative of the tradition has other methods of learning, unfamiliar to the nontraditional.

One might expect that when a son learns from his father, whom he hears at an early age and frequently during the most formative years, the song will not vary much if at all in the process of transmission. Although we do not have any texts from direct experiment of son and father at the period of learning, we do have texts at a later period, when the son is grown up and has become a singer in his own right. A study of these texts seems to indicate that the changes in transmission that we found characteristic of the experiments with Ugljanin and Međedović, both mature singers learning from mature singers, are present here as well. Two examples from Kolašin in Montenegro will illustrate these changes.

We have the song of "Čevljanin Rade and the Captain of Spuž" from Antonije Ćetković (Parry 6718), the seventy-year-old father, and also from Milan Ćetković (Parry 6714), the son, aged twenty-two. Both were literate. The year of recording was 1935. The son's song is shorter than the father's, 249 lines as compared to 445 lines. The father ornaments more than the son does. We note this from the very beginning as we read the two songs parallel to one another.

Antonije	Milan
Čevljanin Rade is drinking wine	Čevljanin Rade is drinking wine
In the midst of Čevo in the white tower.	In broad Čevo on the border.
An adorned mountain woman is serving the wine,	An adorned mountain woman is serving the wine,

Antonije	Milan
In her right hand a beaker and a golden cup.	
When Rade had his fill of wine,	When they had their fill of wine,
He began to talk of many things,	
How many Turks he had cut down	
Around Spuž the bloody town;	
And the adorned mountain woman listened to him,	
Listened and then said to him:	The adorned mountain woman asked him:
"My lord, Čevljanin Rade,	"My lord, Čevljanin Rade,
I know well that you are a good hero.	
So, my dear lord,	So, by the true God,
Are you afraid of any hero?	Are you afraid of any hero?
If he call you tomorrow to combat,	If he call you tomorrow to combat,"
Would you dare to go out to fight?"	

He answers that he is afraid only of the Captain of Spuž. At this moment a letter arrives from the Captain of Spuž. In the manner of its arrival we note the difference between the two singers; this is another case of the same theme being told in two different ways. Antonije, the father, simply tells of the letter arriving at the place where they were sitting and falling into Rade's lap; Rade takes it, breaks the seal, and reads it. Milan, the son, at this point expands the telling; Rade hears the knocker and asks the woman to go to see who it is; for it might be a letter-carrier. The woman obeys and goes down stairs to the courtyard, lets in the letter-carrier, who goes up to Rade's room, puts the letter on Rade's lap, and stands back to serve him. Rade reads the letter and is troubled. The woman asks him the reason, and he tells her the contents of the letter. At this point the son's song is slightly longer than the father's, 52 lines as compared with 34 lines.

Since the letter is important in starting the action of the song, Milan has paid closer attention to it, and the verbal resemblances between his text and that of his father are great, especially in the beginning. The captain says that he has heard of the worth of Rade's wife; he too has a worthy wife. He challenges Rade to single combat at Spuž in the presence of both their wives. The way in which the prize is stated differs noticeably in the two songs. The son says simply: "Let the winner take both women!" (line 71). The father elaborates: "If you cut off my head, take my white-throated lady to Čevo on the border, and love her whenever you awake. If I cut off your head, I shall take your adorned mountain woman to Spuž on the border, and love her whenever I awake" (lines 49–56). Here the father is distinguished by the *kind* of ornamentation which he favors. One might say that the moral qualities of the singers are herein reflected.

The next section of the song tells of the preparation of Rade and his wife to go to Spuž and of their journey there. Milan, the son, is not so skilled in description as his father, Antonije. Rade arrives at Spuž in line 94 in Milan's song, and at line 124 in Antonije's. The father relates how the captain is there already drinking wine, and how Rade too sits down to drink as his wife waits upon him. But Milan says nothing of Rade's drinking and omits the striking picture of the captain's horse as it stands impatiently waiting for its master: "Before the tent he had tied his bedouin mare; and what a horse she was — may the wolves devour her! She struck with her hoofs and scraped with her ears, and with her teeth she bit the black earth. She was awaiting her master. The mare was thirsting for blood, eager to drink the blood of heroes" (lines 129–135). Milan missed this magnificent and frightening creature.

Now the two opponents send their wives to the enemy to discover whether either man is wearing steel breastplate under his shirt. Rade's wife finds that the captain has on a breastplate, but the captain tells her that if she informs Rade, the captain will be killed and his wife will go to Rade, and Rade's wife will become her slave. Rade's wife, therefore, reports to him that the captain is not wearing steel. The captain's wife then makes trial of Rade and discovers that he has no breastplate and reports this truly to the captain. The two singers' versions of this theme are very close, although the father uses more ornamentation than the son (the theme ends at line 254 in the former and at line 154 in the latter). Antonije presents a conversation between Rade and the captain's wife in which Rade asks her why she seems sad when she discovers he has no breastplate. "Is the captain wearing one?" asks Rade. She tells him to ask his own wife; for she herself cannot be untrue to the captain. In Antonije's song this conversation balances that between Rade's wife and the captain; the balance is lacking in Milan's song.

The combat itself is not only much shorter in Milan's version (lines 155–213) than in his father's (lines 255–385) but it is also rather different. Antonije tells how they first fire their pistols and miss; then they fight with swords and Rade's sword strikes fire from the captain's breastplate, whereas the captain draws blood from Rade. Rade breaks the captain's sword, and they begin to wrestle. The foam from Rade's lips is bloody; he sees he will perish and he calls his wife to aid him (line 321). In Milan's song the two first fight with swords until Rade's foam is bloody and the swords are broken. Then they wrestle and Rade throws the captain and is about to cut off his head, when the captain shouts to Rade's wife to help him, saying that if she does not, Rade will win the captain's wife and she will become that woman's slave (line 181). The breastplate, about which there was so much time spent earlier in the song, is not even mentioned again by Milan.

In Antonije's tale Rade's wife takes a sword from the ground and wounds him, whereupon he asks the captain's wife for aid. She comes and kills the mountain woman and then helps Rade against the captain. Finally she cuts his belt and his trousers fall about his legs and trip him. Rade falls upon him, the captain's wife brings Rade a sword, and he kills the captain. He takes horse and wife home. Milan tells how Rade's wife comes to the aid of the captain and attacks Rade, who then appeals to the captain's wife, on the grounds that if he perishes the captain will make her a slave of the new wife. The captain's wife kills the woman with her teeth and gives a sword to Rade, who cuts off the captain's head. Milan avoids the rather cheap trick with the trousers.[5]

It would seem that the differences between the same song performed by a father and also by a son who learned it from him are the same in kind and even in number as in transmission between other individuals. This may be surprising at first blush. We should remember, however, that the social groups involved are small, and it often happens that the boy will hear other singers as frequently as he hears his father. Moreover — and this is the real point — the differences are inherent in the very process of transmission and composition.

At the end of the previous chapter we saw that some themes have a tendency to cling together, held by a kind of tension, and to form recurrent patterns of groups of themes. They adhere to one another so tenaciously that their use transcends the boundaries of any one song or of any group of songs. They are found in return songs, weddings, rescues, captures, and taking of cities. If, for one reason or another one of these themes is omitted or expressed only by implication or inadequately in the singing of one man, it will reappear in full bloom in the singing of another who has learned the song from him, but is already aware from other songs of the tensions binding the themes.

We can illustrate this phenomenon from the Novi Pazar material in Volume I. In Makić's song of the rescue of the Alibey's children (No. 24) he has omitted the theme of the disguise, possibly taking it for granted that the disguise is to be understood. The other elements of the thematic complex, long captivity, recognition, rescue, are present. In Zogić's version, the theme of disguise is made explicit and elaborated. Makić, of course, may have made this element more explicit in other singings than the single one which we have from him, but in a real sense Zogić's addition or elaboration here has not been a radical change in the story as he heard it, whether the disguise was expressed or implicit in Makić's performance. The point is that the disguise is there. Zogić has also used a different means of recognition, namely by the breastplate, than that employed by Makić, who simply has the hero declare his identity. These are two of the multiforms of this theme. The change is not basic.

While the foregoing example explains why a theme was added or elaborated, that is, in order to fill a gap which could not be left, it does not explain the particular form of the new material. Zogić could very well have had Alija go home, put on a disguise, and depart for enemy country. This form of the disguise theme is common and even usual in the group of themes in question. There is, however, another group of themes in which an orphan hero goes forth on adventure with borrowed armor and weapons, and the adventure involved is seeking to rescue someone (often a father) or to win a bride. This group is closely akin to the return group. Its hero is generally Sirotan (Orphan) Alija, and he and Bojičić Alija are frequently and understandably confused. Zogić has modulated, as it were, into the orphan group, whence he obtains the material for this theme. By doing so, however, he makes his narrative come into conflict with the form of the recognition theme that he has chosen. Alija is recognized by the breastplate which he always wears and which he won in single combat! Yet earlier he had no weapons or armor and had to borrow them from his uncle. The two themes do not go together because they belong in two different, though related, groups of themes. The strength of the association of Alija with the orphan group has brought into the return group a theme inconsistent with one of the multiforms of the recognition theme belonging in the return group.

The examples of transmission that have been given leave no doubt that it would be a fruitless task to attempt to reconstruct the text of a song purporting to be the model for any other given text. When we turn to the study of different performances of a song by a given singer, we usually find here also no small divergences in text, yet a conservativeness in regard to story. Several examples are to be found in the published volumes of the Parry Collection,[6] but I include here an example from the Christian tradition of Marko Kraljević songs in central Hercegovina in the district of Stolac.

Petar Vidić is no more than an average singer, and for that reason a comparison of his texts is not without significance. He is the type of singer who must carry the brunt of the transmission of the art. From the thematic analysis of his four versions of the song of Marko and Nina (Appendix II) we can see the changes in the content of a song that take place between performances. There are more Petar Vidić's in any tradition than there are Homers!

Petar's version of this song seems to have changed in the year intervening between Parry 6 (1933) and Parry 804 (1934). He did not know the song very well in 1933, but the encounter with the American collector had revived interest in it, and when Parry returned the next year Petar was prepared. He now sings a song of 279 lines rather than 154. Actually the expansion that has brought this length about occurs in the first part of the story, up to the entrance of Marko into Nina's tower. The expressed fear of Marko that Nina will attack his home while he is in the army and the instructions to his mother are additions, as are also the account of the harrowing of Marko's castle, the actual capture of his wife and sister, and the sending of the falcon with the letter to Marko. These elements are additions, but there is nothing especially new in them. Expanded also is the scene in Stambol of Marko's obtaining permission from the sultan and men to accompany him.

Petar had handled the disguising of Marko and his men in monks' clothing in a very summary manner in No. 6, but he made up for this the next year in No. 804. In so doing, however, he omitted the important scene of Marko's meeting at the spring Zloglav with his wife, who does not recognize him, although she does recognize his horse. In No. 804, instead of encountering her at the spring, Marko is questioned by her from a window when he arrives in the courtyard of Nina's castle. Marko's deceptive tale is given at the spring in No. 6 and in the courtyard in No. 804. Not that the spring is missing in the later text. It is there, but introduces not the scene with the wife but the scene at the nearby church where the monks' clothing is captured, the theme to which Petar had given short shrift the preceding year. In concentrating on this, he has forgotten about the women at Zloglav until it is too late. It is important, however, for Marko to tell his deceptive story to his wife, and Petar substitutes her for Nina in the courtyard scene.

Such are the main differences in the first part of these two texts from Petar Vidić. In 1933 his knowledge of the song was imperfect, and he was having great difficulty in dictating. In 1934 he was more at home singing No. 804 and seems possibly to have brushed up on the song in the meantime. But the expansion led him to forget an important scene; it may also be that the recording apparatus, which he saw for the first time in 1934, had excited him.

Parry 805 was dictated immediately after No. 804. Its comparative brevity stems undoubtedly from Petar's inability to dictate and the great feeling of discomposure that arose therefrom. He nevertheless straightened out the difficulty of the relationship between the scene of the church and the disguise, the deceptive story told to the wife, and the story told to Nina. When Petar sang the song again two days later (Parry 846), the early part of the story, the arrival of the letter from the sultan, Marko's experiences in Stambol, and the activity of Nina, are elaborated at greater length than in any of the other texts. And he has preserved the same order of disguise and deceptive stories as in No. 805.

There is a certain amount of confusion in the endings of all Petar's versions: the name of Marko's chief companion is different in each text; he and the other companions are killed in No. 6 but not in No. 804. Because the story of Marko and Nina is a form of the tale of the return of the hero to find his wife about to remarry, believing that he is dead, the question of whether the chief companion (and other companions) are killed is not without significance to the comparative study of this story. Odysseus' crew perishes, but his son and friends in Ithaca, who aid him in slaying the suitors, are untouched.

Petar's texts do not answer the question as to whether Marko's companions are to be equated with Odysseus' crew or with his friends, but they indicate that the question is a real one; for sometimes the companions are crew and sometimes friends. They are killed in No. 6 (crew), survive in No. 804 (friends), and in Nos. 805 and 846 they all survive except for the chief companion, who is missing (a compromise). From this score we can see that it is a point on which Petar was not very clear, but which he felt to be significant enough to be kept, even when he had forgotten it in one performance (a performance in which he also forgot about the scene at the spring with Marko's wife and the other women). It is possible that Petar's compromise was necessary. Return tales seem to involve the death of someone close to the returning hero; in Yugoslav tradition this person is generally the hero's mother. I believe that it is highly likely that the death of the chief companion here is a substitute for the death of the mother.

The experiment with Petar Vidić and his song of Marko and Nina is very helpful, because it illustrates the way in which a singer, even when faced with unfamiliar circumstances of performance such as dictating and singing for a microphone, struggles with the phenomena of stability and change. It also demonstrates the value of having not merely two, but even three or more texts of the same song from the same singer. Numbers 805 and 846, in spite of differences in amount of elaboration and hence in length, differences resulting from the dictating technique, show stability from performance to performance, not of text, but of thematic structure. On the other hand, at first glance, Numbers 6 and 804 seem to indicate change. It is to be noted, however, that the differences between them are of the same order as the differences discussed in the section on transmission; namely, elaboration or lack of it, shifts in sequence, substitution. Actually the singer is attempting to regain a lost stability of story. He regains it in No. 805. Once a singer learns a song it attains a kind of thematic stability as long as he keeps singing it; but when he sings it infrequently, it begins to suffer from reduced ornamentation, and lapses of memory of the story. We have seen that it can be restored to active duty from the moth-ball fleet.

Not all parts of the song appear to be equally shadowy when a song is inactive. It may well be that the elements that remain, no matter how lacking in elaboration, are the most significant in the story. Nothing vital to the tale is missing from Vidić's No. 6 in 1933. The essentials are all there.

We have observed the thematic changes that take place between versions of the same song sung by a single singer over varying intervals of time. The longest interval, however, was only a year. From the material that I collected in 1950 and 1951 we can examine the differences found in versions of the same song by the same singer separated by a period of fifteen or sixteen years. The translation below presents thematic analysis in parallel columns of such an experiment. The song analyzed is the same song of Marko and Nina analyzed above in Vidić's versions and thus incidentally offers opportunity to observe the thematic content of versions of the same song by different singers. The singer of the versions below is a Moslem, Halil Bajgorić, from Dabrica near Stolac. He is, in fact, a close neighbor of Vidić. In Dabrica are the ruins of a fortress called Koštun, and the inhabitants of this valley associate the song of Marko and Nina with the fortress which is ever in their sight. Parry 6695 was sung for the records in the spring of 1935; it contains 464 lines. Lord 84 was sung for the wire recorder June 7, 1950 and contains only 209 lines. The singer was in a hurry to finish and depart, since he had been called by the authorities from his work in the fields. The song must be considered as incomplete; otherwise the ending is unsatisfactory.

Parry 6695 (1935)	Lord 84 (1950)
Twelve days after his wedding, Marko receives a letter from the sultan telling him that the Arabs have attacked and asking Marko to come to his assistance. Marko prepares his horse and himself, tells his mother that he is going, says farewell to her and to his wife, and sets out for Stambol.	Marko goes to fight the Arabs for the sultan.
In Stambol the sultan greets Marko, explains the situation to him, and then Marko goes to Arabia where he fights with and overcomes the Arabs.	
The sultan recalls Marko to Stambol and gives him gifts. Again the sultan sends him out to fight with the Arabs.	
During the battle Marko receives a letter from his mother telling him that Nina has captured his tower, stolen his wife, and trodden upon his mother. She asks him to come to their help.	While Marko is away Nina captures his tower, steals his wife, and treads upon his old mother. His mother writes a letter to Marko telling him what has happened.
Marko goes to Stambol, tells the sultan about Nina, and asks for help.	Same
The sultan tells Marko that it is useless and that he will not give him help, but Marko asks only for Alilagha and 30 heroes. This the sultan grants.	Same
Marko disguises himself and his men as monks and they proceed to Dabrica.	Same, except that they go first to Prilip where Marko talks with his mother. Then they all go on to Dabrica.
At the spring of Zloglav they find 30 women washing clothes, among them Marko's wife. When she sees Marko's horse, she asks the monk where he got the horse. He explains that Marko has died in a fight with the Turks (!) and that Marko gave him his horse in return for burying him. Marko's wife weeps.	Same, except that there are 100 women instead of 30.

Parry 6695 (1935)	Lord 84 (1950)
They proceed to Koštun. Marko tells the guards that he is a monk who has come to marry Nina, and that he has 30 companions who will prune the vines. He is welcomed by Nina, who asks him if he has ever been in the Turkish army. Marko says that he has.	Arrived at Koštun, Marko leaves his companions at the gate while he goes to talk with Nina. He tells Nina that Marko is dead. Nina asks him if he will marry him to Marko's wife. Marko agrees.
Nina asks Marko if he will sing and dance. Marko dances and the tower trembles. Nina says that the monk must have learned to dance from Marko. As a gift he gives him Marko's sword, which nobody has been able to draw from its scabbard.	At the wedding feast Marko asks Nina for permission to dance a little. He dances and the tower trembles. Nina says that the monk must have learned to dance from Marko.
Marko reveals himself, draws the sword and cuts off Nina's head. A fight ensues. Marko sends Alilagha to the gate to prevent any of the enemy from escaping.	Marko reveals himself, draws the sword, and cuts off Nina's head. Marko drives his enemies to the gate where they are met by his companions.
Nina's three brothers escape and Marko pursues them. He kills Vidoje at Vidovo Polje; Stephen at Stephen's Cross; and Jasen at Jasena.	
Marko gives Koštun to Alilagha and makes him a bey. Then Marko returns with his wife to his mother in Prilip.	

As we might, indeed, have expected, the story has remained essentially the same in both versions. The main difference between the two is to be found at the beginning and at the end. In the earlier version the beginning was greatly elaborated and the end was given full treatment. The second version has reduced the beginning of the song to a minimum and the end has been clipped. It is very likely that the clipped ending is caused not by the period of time between the two versions but simply by the singer's eagerness to depart. Certainly the discrepancies between the two versions are not necessarily greater than the discrepancies possible between two singings under different circumstances. There is no evidence that time has much changed Bajgorić's version of this song. But we can observe the opposite of what we saw with the first two texts of Vidić's performances of the same song; namely the regression from an elaborated text to a reduced text. One could infer, I believe correctly, that Bajgorić had not sung this song for a considerable period of time, and the circumstances of performance were not ideal.

It will be useful to see the results of a similar experiment with another singer and another song. The singer is Sulejman Fortić of Novi Pazar, and the song is the taking of Bagdad. Parry 676 (II, No. 22) was sung for the phonograph records November 24, 1934, and Lord 10 (II, No. 23) was sung for the wires May 17, 1950. The former has 875 lines and the latter 812. The difference in length is negligible when compared with the difference in our first example.

With Fortić, also, the story is essentially the same in both the earlier and the later versions. It is instructive to note that sometimes the later version is fuller than the earlier and sometimes the opposite is true. One must bear in mind that the performer in this case was only twenty-nine years old at the time of the first version and that he was not yet a fully trained singer. Fifteen years later he was a more accomplished singer, although he is by no means a very good one even at his best. There are, however, two major differences between the two versions that cannot be explained as elaboration, or lack of it, but illustrate the substitution of one incident for another. In 1934 Fortić told how the messenger from the sultan went to Kajnidža, did not find Alija at home, and was directed by his mother to the mosque garden where Alija was assembled with the other men. In this he follows his master's, Ugljanin's, singing of the story faithfully. In 1951, possibly because he felt that as president of the National Front in Novi Pazar the mention of religious institutions such as mosques was not wise or fitting, he has omitted this incident, thus avoiding forbidden gatherings of Moslems at their churches. However, the feeling that Alija could be reached only through an intermediary was also very strong, and Fortić substituted another incident for the one with the mosque. The messenger must go first to Mujo and Halil in Kladuša and they will take him to Alija. Again the change is only apparently basic. The significant idea has been kept, and only the form of it has changed. The idea itself was felt to be so important that the simple solution of having the messenger proceed directly to Alija was avoided.

The second major difference between the two versions is in the ending. The way in which the earlier version ends is unorthodox. None of the other versions of this song has an unhappy and unsatisfactory ending. This ending may have been something that Fortić had himself improvised earlier at a time when he had not heard the song many times all the way through or when he had forgotten it. In other words, this unhappy ending may itself have been a change introduced into the song by Fortić himself. The later version of Fortić with its happy ending would seem to indicate that the singer had heard the more orthodox versions of the song since the earlier singing and had brought his own version more into conformity with them. The later version would then be an example of the corrective influence of the tradition. When a singer deviates too greatly from the traditional version of a song in regard to an essential theme, he is brought back into line, not by the audience but by the songs and singers of the tradition itself.[7]

For confirmation of the changes that take place over a period of time in oral narrative song, from another though closely related language district, I am deeply indebted to Professor and Mrs. St. Stojkov of Sofia, Bulgaria. In July 1958 the Bulgarian Committee for Friendship and Cultural Relations with Foreign Countries arranged for the Stojkovs to take me to two of the villages near Sofia to listen to and record epic singing. We went to hear singers whom the Bulgarians had recorded on tape seven years earlier and whose songs, transcribed from these tapes, I had read in the Ethnographic Museum in Sofia. Mrs. Stojkov brought carefully typed copies of these texts into the field, and we asked the singers to sing these songs while she and I followed the texts. She was surprised to find that the singers changed the texts even very considerably. In one case the changes were so great that it was impossible to follow the written text. There was no doubt that in the person of the aged Vasilenka a pure oral tradition was still alive and operative.[8]

If we cease to expect verbal identity between different performances of the same song, whether they be by different singers or by the same one, whether they be over a shorter or a longer period of time, we are bound to notice that there are a few simple types of differences between them: (1) elaboration or simplification; the same thing told with more or less detail; (2) different order in a series; usually the reverse order, but sometimes merely a different order. In respect to the first of these types, the elaboration is usually significant, whereas the simplification indicates either a limited scope on the part of the singer, a restriction of time, or lack of practice in the song. In any case, the elaboration, in spite of what the singer himself may think or say about it, is not "pure" ornamentation; it has meaning in terms of the tradition from which it stems. In regard to the second type, one might conjecture as to why the change of order is often to the reverse. It would seem to be a sort of "chiasmus." Singers often use a series of questions followed by the answers in reverse order. Such a shift of order is regular practice. We should not be too surprised, therefore, to find it in transmission from one singer to another, since it is common in the singing of a given individual. Neither of these two types is a change in the "essence" of a song. If the tradition moved from singing to singing, from singer to singer, only in these two ways, one would not arrive at the diversity of "versions" and "variants" of a single song which is so characteristic of oral traditional material. They account for some of the differences but not for all of them, and certainly not for the most radical.

But there are other types of change. The substitution of one multiform of a theme for another, one kind of recognition scene for another kind, for example, one kind of disguise for another, is not uncommon, we have seen, as songs pass from one singer to another. The endings of songs are less stable, more open to variation, than their beginnings. Here the tension between themes that arises from habitual association comes into operation. It may help to provide an ending when either there was none in the singer's experience of a given song or what there was seemed vague and hazy in his mind. The process may involve more than a mere ending to a song and actually lead the singer to mix songs, passing from one song pattern to another at a point at which the two patterns coincide. Singers recognize the fact that this kind of thing happens, because they criticize other singers for "mixing" songs. It is well for us to understand how this comes about. It is not haphazard, but the result of perfectly understandable and knowable forces. To the superficial observer, changes in oral tradition may seem chaotic and arbitrary. In reality this is not so. It cannot be said that "anything goes." Nor are these changes due in the ordinary sense to failure of memory of a fixed text, first, of course, because there is no fixed text, second, because there is no concept among singers of memorization as we know it, and third, because at a number of points in any song there are forces leading in several directions, any one of which the singer may take. If his experience of the particular song is weak, either as a whole or at any part, the force in a direction divergent from the one he has heard may be the strongest.

It is worth pointing out again that the changes of which we have been speaking have been brought about, not by forces seeking change for its own sake, nor by pure chance, but by an insistent, conservative urge for preservation of an essential idea as expressed either in a single theme or in a group of themes. Multiformity is essentially conservative in traditional lore, all outward appearances to the contrary.

The result of this multitudinous pattern of stresses and strains for the maintenance of stability is the typical multiformity of songs in oral tradition. The only way to make this multiformity graphic is to compare a number of texts of return songs from the Parry Collection. (See Appendices III and IV.)

The fact that the same song occurs attached to different heroes would seem to indicate that the story is more important than the historical hero to which it is attached. There is a close relationship between hero and tale, but with some tales at least the *type* of hero is more significant than the *specific* hero. It is convenient to group songs according to their story content, or thematic configurations, because songs seem to continue in spite of the particular historical hero; they are not connected irrevocably to any single hero.

If we classify the songs by their content we find a number of well-defined categories: weddings, rescues, returns, and captures of cities. They are well defined, and yet they overlap. We can illustrate this by isolating some of these groups and studying their basic patterns.

Parry was especially interested in the particular groups I have just mentioned and his collection is filled with examples of them. The reason for his concern for these groups lies in their obvious similarity to the Homeric poems and also, insofar as we have information about them, to the epics of the ancient Greeks called "cyclic." Because of the parallel with the *Odyssey*, let us begin with the return songs in Yugoslav tradition.

The focal point of the return song is the return itself, and this is always surrounded by (a) disguise, (b) deceptive story, and (c) recognition. Almost invariably in this group the return is preceded by (a) shouting of the hero in prison after a long period of years, and (b) release with stipulation of return to prison. The section of the story that precedes the return home usually contains within it, by flashback, or else it is introduced by, the tale of how the hero was summoned from home on his wedding night to go to war, and of how he was captured. On the other hand, almost invariably the return home is followed by (a) the return of the hero to the enemy prison, and (b) the rescue of someone else from that prison. These four essential elements, (1) tale of capture, (2) shouting and release, (3) return home, and (4) sequel, are roughly parallel to the story of Odysseus.

It is, I believe, very significant that, whereas the songs that contain the return home are preceded by a tale of capture, shouting, and release and are followed by a sequel in the form of a rescue, there is a group of songs beginning with a tale of capture and shouting that does *not* lead to release and return, but to *refusal of release* and to rescue of the hero by someone else. In other words, songs beginning with the first two elements can lead in two directions, either to release or to rescue. And we cannot help but be struck by the similarity here with the twofold plan of Athena at the beginning of the *Odyssey*, (a) to send Telemachus to seek news of his father, who is weeping on the shores of Ogygia, and (b) to send Hermes to release Odysseus.

We can see that the return songs proper are in reality part of a larger group that entails captivity, shouting, and rescue, for even the return group contains a sequel to the return home that relates a rescue. Those containing the return theme end with the rescue (a) of the other prisoners who had been with the hero, or (b) of the hero's son who had been captured during his absence, or (c) of the hero himself. In the first two instances the hero does the rescuing; in the last case he is himself rescued by his wife's suitor, by his friend, or by his son. Although the rescue is accomplished in several ways, the commonest is by capturing the enemy's son and negotiating an exchange of prisoners. In the subgroup which tells of refusal of release followed by rescue, the rescue of the hero is done by his wife or by the Turks of the Border in battle!

There is a group of rescue songs that begins with the arrival of a message from a prisoner or prisoners who have been in captivity for a long period of time, often announcing that they are soon to be executed and asking for help. This opening thematic group coincides with the situation of the return group in which the release is refused; only the shouting scene is missing. In the rescue group a hero undertakes the task of rescuing the long lost hero.

He first disguises himself and when he arrives, after a journey, in the enemy country, there is a recognition scene with someone who is friendly, usually a woman; there are games or tests of some kind, and then flight. Very often not only rescue but also a wedding is involved.

Although it would seem that we have changed heroes in midstream, from the imprisoned to the rescuer, the pattern of disguise, journey, deceptive story, recognition, games, is like that of the return songs proper. In this case the disguise, journey, recognition complex is associated with the trip *to* the enemy country, and in the return songs it is connected with the trip *from* that country. There is a change in personnel and in geographical direction but not in basic thematic material. One might say that this group of rescue songs is a group of return songs in reverse.

There is also a group of wedding songs which follow the same pattern as the group of rescue songs. Bride stealing, especially when the bride is willing, as she is in these cases, but hindered by the enemy, is basically the same as rescue. We have seen, moreover, that even the rescue songs in this category (and they seem to include all those in which the imprisoned has been absent for a long time) also involve a wedding.

We find this same complex (disguise, journey, deceptive story, recognition, games or tests, wedding) in one other group of songs, namely, in that concerned with capture of cities. This is particularly clear in the version of the "Song of Bagdad" (Parry 20, Lord 79, by Osman Mekić of Stolac) in which Dadić Omer, who has accepted the challenge of Kajtaz to meet him in single combat in place of the sultan, is accosted by some magic birds on his way to Bagdad. They advise him to change clothes with a beggar whom he will meet. In this disguise he meets the queen of Bagdad in the castle garden, there is a recognition scene, and this is followed by the combat, and finally by the abduction of the queen and the capture of the city. Characteristic of the group of songs concerned with the capture of a city is the fact that the siege has been going on unsuccessfully for a long period of time.

It would seem, then, that all these groups, return, rescue, wedding, capture of city, are the same song in respect to the pattern of captivity and freedom (release or rescue) that we have been studying, in many disguises! This is, moreover, not a subsidiary pattern, not a minor part of the story, but actually the central action.

It is clear now, therefore, that the songs of this whole group are basically one song, at any rate from the disguise and departure to the final rescue. But how about the beginnings of the songs in this category? The beginnings are centered in the captivity itself. It is a long period of captivity, usually in a far distant enemy country. And in one way or another the story of the capture, of how the hero happened to find himself in this predicament, is related. Sometimes this is told in direct narrative, but more often, especially in the return tales proper, it is in a flashback, that is to say, the hero tells a newly-arrived prisoner the story of his capture. In the other groups, especially the rescue group proper, the tale of capture is related in the message received from the prisoner, or sometimes the person who has received the message relates it to the group or individual who will undertake the rescue. In the case of wedding songs, the hero often gives an account of how he happened to meet or to know of the girl in the far country to whom he is now betrothed and whom he now wishes, venturing forth, to win back.

Any single performance that we may choose of a song in this group of interrelated families must be understood in terms of its brothers and sisters, and even its cousins of several removes. While recognizing the fact that the singer knows the whole song before he starts to sing (not textually, of course, but thematically), nevertheless, at some time when he reaches key points in the performance of the song he finds that he is drawn in one direction or another by the similarities with related groups at those points. The intensity of that pull may differ from performance to performance, but it is always there and the singer always relives that tense moment. Even though the pattern of the song he intends to sing is set early in the performance, forces moving in other directions will still be felt at critical junctures, simply because the theme involved can lead in more than one path.

When we look back over these examples of transmission, we are, I believe, struck by the conservativeness of the tradition. The basic story is carefully preserved. Moreover, the changes fall into certain clear categories, of which the following emerge: (1) saying the same thing in fewer or more lines, because of singers' methods of line composition and of linking lines together, (2) expansion of ornamentation, adding of details of description (that may not be without significance), (3) changes of order in a sequence (this may arise from a different sense of balance on the part of the learner, or even from what might be called a chiastic arrangement where one singer reverses the order given by the other), (4) addition of material not in a given text of the teacher, but found in texts of other singers in the district, (5) omission of material, and (6) substitution of one theme for another, in a story configuration held together by inner tensions.

In a variety of ways a song in tradition is separate, yet inseparable from other songs.

CHAPTER SIX
WRITING AND ORAL TRADITION

The art of narrative song was perfected, and I use the word advisedly, long before the advent of writing. It had no need of stylus or brush to become a complete artistic and literary medium. Even its geniuses were not straining their bonds, longing to be freed from its captivity, eager for the liberation by writing. When writing was introduced, epic singers, again even the most brilliant among them, did not realize its "possibilities" and did not rush to avail themselves of it. Perhaps they were wiser than we, because one cannot write song. One cannot lead Proteus captive; to bind him is to destroy him.

But writing, with all its mystery, came to the singers' people, and eventually someone approached the singer and asked him to tell the song so that he could write down the words. In a way this was just one more performance for the singer, one more in a long series. Yet it was the strangest performance he had ever given. There was no music and no song, nothing to keep him to the regular beat except the echo of previous singings and the habit they had formed in his mind. Without these accompaniments it was not easy to put the words together as he usually did. The tempo of composing the song was different, too. Ordinarily the singer could move forward rapidly from idea to idea, from theme to theme. But now he had to stop very often for the scribe to write down what he was saying, after every line or even after part of a line. This was difficult, because his mind was far ahead. But he accustomed himself to this new process at last, and finally the song was finished.

A written text was thus made of the words of song. It was a record of a special performance, a command performance under unusual circumstances. Such has been the experience of many singers in many lands, from the first recorded text, I believe, to present times. And what has been said of other performances can be said of it; for though it is written, it is oral. The singer who dictated it was its "author," and it reflected a single moment in the tradition. It was unique.

Yet, unwittingly perhaps, a fixed text was established. Proteus was photographed, and no matter under what other forms he might appear in the future, this would become the shape that was changed; this would be the "original." Of course, the singer was not affected at all. He continued, as did his confrères, to compose and sing as he always had and as they always had. The tradition went on. Nor was his audience affected. They thought in his terms, in the terms of multiformity. But there was another world, of those who could read and write, of those who came to think of the written text not as the recording of a moment of the tradition but as *the* song. This was to become the difference between the oral way of thought and the written way.

Before the advent of electrical recording machines, written texts of actual performance — not from dictation — were possible only in a very limited number of cases. Wherever the singing was done by two people and the second man repeated exactly what the first man sang there was time for someone writing rapidly to set down the line during the repetition, especially if the tempo of singing was slow and the verse not over long. This is the manner of singing in parts of northern Albania and Yugoslav Macedonia. Because of the slow tempo, such a manner is not conducive of long epic songs — it is too leisurely to sustain narrative interest. I have heard such singing in Albania (in 1937) and Macedonia (in 1950 and 1951), and have seen this method of writing down a text applied successfully in eastern Macedonia by Professor Rusić of Skoplje. Sometimes one singer repeats the line exactly and no assistant in the singing is called in, but this is merely a variation of a manner of singing that originally depended on two men. If the line is very long or the singing very rapid, it is difficult, if not impossible, to write down a song by this method. Wherever the assistant does not repeat the line exactly but repeats the idea in different words or adds another idea, as is the case in Finland,[1] this method is obviously impossible. It is restricted to very few special cases.

If the singer of oral epic always sang a song in exactly the same words, it would be possible, of course, to ask him to repeat the performance a number of times and thus to fill in on the second or third singing what was lost in notating the first singing. But bards never repeat a song exactly, as we have seen. This method, although it has been used often, never results in a text that truly represents any real performance. It produces a composite text even when a singer's song is fairly stable, as we know it may be with shorter epics. In a truly oral tradition of song there is no guarantee that even the apparently most stable "runs" will always be word-for-word the same in performance.

There are two methods of writing down a text from actual performance which I have not heard of being used, but which might be employed with some degree of success. One of these is to use shorthand. The resulting text might not have the exact niceties of odd forms or phonetic peculiarities that a more accurate method would provide, but a word-for-word text could be gotten in this way. Another method would be to have a battery of two or more scribes taking down alternate lines or every third line, depending on the number of scribes employed. There is no evidence to my knowledge that this means has been used at any time in the past. The idea of obtaining an accurate text of a given performance is comparatively recent, because heretofore the concept of a fixed text somewhere in the background tended to minimize the importance of any single given performance. Actually there is very little chance, if any, for the reasons given above, that our written texts at any time were taken down during performance. It is normal to expect that, on the other hand, the singer was asked to dictate his song without singing, pausing after each verse to give the scribe time to write. Since this is the case, we should do well to consider how this special type of performance by dictation affects the text.

From the recited texts from Novi Pazar published in Parry and Lord, II,[2] we can obtain some idea of the singer's difficulties in making normal verses when he is deprived of singing. These texts were recorded on phonograph discs but the singer was unable to sing to instrumental accompaniment because of the ban on singing during the period of mourning following the assassination of King Alexander I in Marseilles in early October of 1934. Parry was allowed to collect only by recitation without song. A mixture of prose and verse, parts of verses interspersed with parts of prose sentences and *vice versa,* are the result. This is true especially at the beginning of the song, but even when the singer has accustomed himself to reciting, the number of lines that are irregular or poorly formed rhythmically and formulaically still remains high.

A nemade majka da rodi junaka, (12 syllables)	No mother has borne a hero,
Niko da se nafati knjige. (9 syllables)	None to accept the letter.
Ta put Meho reče: (6 syllables)	Then Meho said:
"Ču lji me, begov kahveđija! (9 syllables)	"Hearken to me, coffee-maker of the bey!
Aj, suoči u Kajniđu gradu, (10 syllables)	Go to the city of Kajniđa,
Traži kulu Ajanević Meha! (10 syllables)	Seek the tower of Ajanević Meho!
Ćejvan deda kulu traži, Ćejvanage deda, (14 syllables)	Seek the tower of Ćejvan the elder, of Ćejvanagha the elder,
Pa otidi k dedu u odaji! (10 syllables)	And then go to the elder in his room!
Ako ti se on knjige nafati, (10 syllables)	If he accepts the letter from you,
I dobro i jes; ako ti se nafati dedo knjige, dobro će ti biti, a ne šćene se nafatit', ne znam ništa!" [prose] (II, No. 12:77–87)	Then it is well; if the elder accepts the letter from you, it will be well for you, but if he is not willing to accept it, then I know nothing!"

It is not to be wondered at that when the singer is asked to dictate, stopping at the end of each verse, he is uncertain at first where to stop, and hesitates also as to the number of syllables in a line. Frequently he will give a whole sentence in prose. He is, after all, telling a story. As regards the forming of verses, songs recited for the records and songs dictated but taken down by a scribe who does not seek to obtain good rhythmic lines are about the same. They look very much like the text of the Old Spanish *Cid* [3] or that of the Escorialensis manuscript of the medieval Greek *Digenis Akritas* [4] with their "irregularities" of meter.

One collector in the second half of the last century wrote of his difficulties in taking down songs from dictation: "Many cannot dictate songs without the gusle, even as Todor Vlatković from Visoko, who without the gusle cannot speak two lines; he gets lost without it." That there are singers to whom it does not matter, however, he also bears witness: "To Ilija (Divljanović) it did not matter whether he sang to the gusle or dictated without it, except that in the case of dictation one had to give him a little wine or brandy to fire his imagination; then the song would be clearer and more adorned." [5]

A well-trained and intelligent scribe, like Nikola Vujnović, Parry's assistant, seeks normal verses, trying at the same time not to suggest them to the singer. He simply indicates that what has been said is not right, sometimes goes back several lines and reads them to the singer to give him the continued rhythm, or even puts the musical instrument in his hands and asks him to sing the verses. By this laborious and patience-trying process regular lines can be obtained from even the most confused of singers. For the most part these lines are just as they would be sung. But careful analysis reveals some differences between sung and dictated lines within the limits of a single singer's works. The singer when dictating occasionally builds his lines somewhat differently from the way he would if he were singing. For example, in Parry and Lord, Volume II, Salih Ugljanin sings the line *Sultan Selim rata otvorijo* ("Sultan Selim declared war") in No. 1, line 12, but dictates it *Sultan Selim otvorijo rata* in No. 3, line 2. The rhythms are different.

Such cases are instructive because they indicate that a dictated text, even when done under the best of circumstances and by the best of scribes, is never entirely, from the point of view of the line structure, the same as a sung text. One should emphasize, however, that these changes or differences are not caused by the singer's conscious or deliberate choice of an order of words or of words themselves for any other reason than the influence of the surrounding rhythmic structure. This structure is broken by the dictating and such breaks may be indicated by differences in the line. The singer is struggling with the traditional patterns under unusual circumstances. He is not seeking *le mot juste* for any other purpose than that of the traditional line; he is, indeed, striving to maintain, not to depart from, the tradition.

It is vastly important that we do not make the unthinking mistake of believing that the process of dictation frees the singer to manipulate words in accordance with an entirely new system of poetics. Clearly he has time to plan his line in advance, but this is more of a hindrance than a help to a singer who is accustomed to rapid-fire association and composition. Opportunity does not make the singer into an e.e.cummings! not even if he is already a Homer! There is even the possibility that Homer would not feel complimented! It would, moreover, be easy to exaggerate the amount of *avant garde* musing which a scribe engaged in writing down a long epic would be willing to accept even were the singer capable of it. Nor is there any case on record — and I venture to submit there is none off the record either — of an oral singer going back in his song after it has been written down and changing words and lines. Opportunity there is, of course. But when an oral singer is through with a song, it is finished. His whole habit of thinking is forward, never back and then forth! It takes a vast cultural change to develop a new kind of poetic. The opportunity offered in dictating is not sufficient.

From the point of view of verse-making, dictation carries no great advantage to the singer, but from that of song-making it may be instrumental in producing the finest and longest of songs. For it extends almost indefinitely the time limit of performance. And with a little urging, under the stimulus of great accomplishment for a worthy audience, the singer of talent will apply every resource of his craft to adorn and enrich his song. The important element is that of time; there is nothing in the dictating process itself that brings this richness to bear. The collector who tells a singer that he can sing his song from day to day taking as many days, as much time, as he wants, can elicit the same results in sung performance, as we saw in the case of Avdo Međedović's songs in the last chapter. It should be stressed also that the additional time is of use only to the exceptional singer of great talent in a tradition rich in traditional themes and songs. The "ordinary" singer in a mediocre tradition will not have enough material at his command nor the imagination to avail himself of it. The extraordinary singer will enjoy the opportunity to the full.[6]

The use of writing in setting down oral texts does not *per se* have any effect on oral tradition. It is a means of recording. The texts thus obtained are in a sense special; they are not those of normal performance, yet they are purely oral, and at their best they are finer than those of normal performance. They are *not* "transitional," but are in a class by themselves.

It is necessary for us to face squarely the problem of "transitional" texts. Is there in reality such a phenomenon as a text which is transitional between oral and written literary tradition? This has become a vastly important question. Diplomatic Homerists[7] would like to find refuge in a transitional poet who is both an oral poet — they cannot disprove the evidence of his style — and a written poet — they cannot, on the other hand, tolerate the unwashed illiterate. Recent research in Anglo-Saxon and Middle English [8] indicates a strong desire on the part of medievalists also to seek a solution to the problems raised by the discovery of oral characteristics in some of the poems in their fields by recourse to the term "transitional." Even if one may have reservations about the ultimate results of the compromise, one is enormously encouraged by a development in the medieval sector that is a guarantee that the traditional association of Homeric and medieval scholarship is as alive and strong today as it was in the days of Lachmann.

It is worthy of emphasis that the question we have asked ourselves is whether there can be such a thing as a transitional *text;* not a *period* of transition between oral and written style, or between illiteracy and literacy, but a *text,* product of the creative brain of a single individual. When this emphasis is clear, it becomes possible to turn the question into whether there can be a single individual who in composing an epic would think now in one way and now in another, or, perhaps, in a manner that is a combination of two techniques. I believe that the answer must be in the negative, because the two techniques are, I submit, contradictory and mutually exclusive.[9] Once the oral technique is lost, it is never regained. The written technique, on the other hand, is not compatible with the oral technique, and the two could not possibly combine, to form another, a third, a "transitional" technique. It is conceivable that a man might be an oral poet in his younger years and a written poet later in life, but it is not possible that he be *both* an oral and a written poet at any given time in his career. The two by their very nature are mutually exclusive. We may in actuality discover what might be called special categories of texts, but it is more than doubtful that they should be labelled "transitional," that is, part way between oral and written techniques.

We might ask whether those oral poets who write their own texts (for there are such) [10] can under any circumstances produce an oral poem. The answer is affirmative. Yet an oral singer who has learned just enough writing to put down laboriously a song that he would ordinarily sing would do this only at the request of a collector. Such a text might be called "autograph oral," because the singer would follow his usual oral style, having great difficulty, however, in doing so in a new medium and under strange circumstances. For the collector this means merely a very poor method of obtaining an inferior text which does not do justice to either the song or the singer.

Such a singer will probably learn some songs from the book, but he will still retain a residue of songs that he learned from oral transmission, and hence his repertory will be mixed in origin. When he thinks of the written songs as fixed and tries to learn them word for word, the power of the fixed text and of the technique of memorizing will stunt his ability to compose orally. But this process is not a transition from an oral to a literary technique of composition. It is a transition from oral composition to simple performance of a fixed text, from composition to reproduction. This is one of the most common ways in which an oral tradition may die; not when writing is introduced, but when published song texts are spread among singers. But our singer does not necessarily blossom forth as a literary poet. He usually becomes . . . nothing at all.

When and how, then, does the "literary" technique start? The poet of whom we have been speaking can read and write, but he is still an oral poet. To become a "literary" poet he has to leave the oral tradition and learn a technique of composition that is impossible without writing, or that is developed because of writing. If I am not mistaken, the process can already be observed in the dictated and autograph texts; it is a process, or better the acceleration or aggravation or extension of a process that continually goes on in oral composition. It is a process of formula change and of change in thematic structure. Making new metrical expressions patterned on the old, is, as we have seen, a part of the oral technique. It is necessary for the introduction of new ideas into the tradition. If a man continues to use these expressions, they become formulas, and if they are taken up by another, they then enter the tradition and become traditional formulas. All this is within the realm of oral composition on the formula level. This is the way of oral poetry. The oral singer thinks in terms of these formulas and formula patterns. He *must* do so in order to compose. But when writing enters, the "must" is eliminated. The formulas and formula patterns can be broken, and a metrical line constructed that is regular and yet free of the old patterns. This breaking of the pattern occurs in rapid composition, but is always felt as wrong or awkward, or as a "mistake." When the point is reached that the break of the pattern is made consciously and is desired and felt to be "right," then we are in a "literary" technique.

Formula analysis, providing, of course, that one has sufficient material for significant results,[11] is, therefore, able to indicate whether any given text is oral or "literary." An *oral* text will yield a predominance of clearly demonstrable formulas, with the bulk of the remainder "formulaic," and a small number of nonformulaic expressions. A *literary* text will show a predominance of nonformulaic expressions, with some formulaic expressions, and very few clear formulas. The fact that nonformulaic expressions will be found in an oral text proves that the seeds of the "literary" style are already present in oral style; and likewise the presence of "formulas" in "literary" style indicates its origin in oral style. These "formulas" are vestigial. This is not surprising. We are working in a continuum of man's artistic expression in words. We are attempting to measure with some degree of accuracy the strength and mixture of traditional patterns of expression.

We should not be surprised to find a fair number of nonformulaic ex-pressions in such a talented oral singer as Avdo Međedović. It would be fantastic to expect that a gifted poet who has thought in poetic form all his life should not have sufficient mastery of that form to be able not only to fit his thought into it but also to break it at will. No more should we be surprised to find formulas in Chaucer or William Morris, or to learn that at some periods there are more "formulas" in the "literary" style than at others. Some ages think less about breaking tradition than others; some ages prefer a traditional flavor, others seek a "new" pattern of expression. And yet the two methods are clearly distinguishable, I believe, in the analysis.

The formula level is not the only one to be considered. Analyses of different kinds of enjambement in different styles are likewise helpful. We have seen that nonperiodic enjambement, the "adding" style, is character-istic of oral composition; whereas periodic enjambement is characteristic of "literary" style.[12] Obviously, then, the oral text will yield a predominance of nonperiodic enjambement, and a "literary" text a predominance of periodic. But enjambement cannot be used as the sole test in determining oral or "literary" style; it alone is not a reliable guide. This is because writing actually tends to emphasize composition by line equally as much as the music or the instrumental accompaniment does for the purely oral performance. Nonperiodic enjambement persists longer in an otherwise "literary" style than formula patterns, because the cause of it in oral style is replaced by an equally strong, but different, cause in "literary" style.

While these elements of formula pattern and enjambement are vastly important for stylistic analysis in determining whether any text is oral or "literary," of greater significance for an understanding of the development of literary epic is the change that takes place in the ideas, in the themes presented in epic by a literate oral poet. The oral epic poet needs well-established themes for rapid composition. But when he is of the caliber of Avdo Međedović, he is not bound by these themes, except as he wishes, and he usually so wishes, because he feels them to be right — they are the proper subject of epic poetry. Eventually, however, writing will free him from the need of the themes for purposes of composition. This will mean not only a freer opportunity for new themes, but also greater freedom in consciously combining and recombining themes.

Writing as a new medium will mean that the former singer will have a different audience, one that can read. Psychologically, he may at first be addressing himself still for some time to the audience of listeners to whom he has always been accustomed. But the new reading public, though it will be small at first, will undoubtedly have different tastes developing from those of the traditional nonliterate audience. They will demand new themes, or new twists to old themes.

The singer will no longer be bound by the tyrannous time limit of a performance, or by the fickleness of an immediate audience in a coffee house. This circumstance leads, as we have seen in the case of dictated oral songs, to longer songs than before. Coupled with greater thematic freedom, the freedom from the singer's audience produces long poems with greater variety of theme, tending frequently to episodic structure. It seems highly probable that the romance finds its origin in the oral dictated texts of epic at a stage when its solemn religious magic was less felt but when at least some of its practitioners were not wholly satisfied with "true history" and sought a degree of the marvelous and fantastic.

As I review the texts that over the years have given me pause as to whether they might be termed transitional, I find that in every case the answer is negative. They are either one or the other; they are either oral or written. Those poems that are written "in the style of" the oral epic, such as those in Kačić's *Razgovor*,[13] or of Njegoš in his *Ogledalo Srpsko*,[14] strikingly close though they may sometimes be to the folk epic, are nevertheless definitely written texts. I strongly suspect that in the very process of writing these songs both authors were psychologically out of the oral tradition of composition. In both cases, of course, they had heard oral epic from their earliest years. Yet they were after all educated men, learned in books. They could not compose an oral epic.

The songs of Kačić and of later writers in the style of the oral epic can be distinguished from truly oral epic, provided that one knows the oral tradition well. Sometimes the distinguishing marks are obvious. A few of Kačić's songs, for example, are written throughout in rhymed couplets.

Vesele se svita banov*ine,*	The countries of the world rejoiced,
I po svitu visoke plan*ine,*	And in the world the lofty mountains,
Sve pustinje i gore zel*ene,*	All the desert places and green forests,
Svako cviće, ružice rum*ene.*	Every flower, the ruddy roses.
Rodiše se četiri jedn*aka*	Four men alike were born
U istoku sveta imanj*aka,*	In the east, all with the same holy name.
Koji sjaju lipše neg Da*nica,*	They shine more brightly than the Day Star,
Žarko sunce oli prihod*nica.*[15]	The burning sun or its forerunner.

Moreover, this song, like the others in rhymed couplets, is written in four-line stanzas, with a full stop at the end of each stanza. This is not the way of the oral tradition of the region, which is purely stichic.

Among the songs written in the nineteenth century those which begin with the date are invariably from the hand of a writer and not from the lips of a singer. For example:

Na tisuću i sedme stotine	In the year one thousand and seven hundred
Devedeset i šeste godine	Ninety and six
Mahmut vezir sovjet učinio	Mahmut Vizier held an assembly
U bijelu Skadru na Bojanu.[16]	In white Scutari on the Bojana river.

This is perhaps the first instance of such dating, but it became a frequent mark thereafter.

Na hiljadu i osme stotine	In the year one thousand and eight hundred
Sedamdeset i pete godine	Seventy and five
Zbor zborilo dvanajest knezova	Twelve chieftains held council
Na šljemenu zemlje Hercegove,	On the heights of Hercegovina,
U širokom polju Nevesinju.[17]	On the broad plain of Nevesinje.

And also:

Braćo moja i družino draga,	My brothers and dear company,
Da vam pričam pjesmu od istine,	Let me sing you a true song
Za gospode i dobre družine.	For our lords and good comrades.
Od hiljade devete stotine	In the year one thousand nine hundred
Četrnaeste u ljetu godine,	And fourteen in the summer,
U junome, kada cvati trava,	In June when the grass blooms,
Sastala se dva silna vladara	There met together two mighty rulers
Habsburškoga roda i plemena.[18]	Of Hapsburg birth and family.

There seem always to be signs in the songs themselves that point to the fact that they are written and not oral. In a fully developed written tradition of literature the formulas are no longer present. They are not needed. There may be repeated phrases, but the proportion of them to the whole is small. Words are chosen for nontraditional effects and placed in patterns which are not those of the tradition. Thus the basic patterns behind the formulas are changed. Lines are unique, and are intended as such. The meter is strictly regular. If there are "runs" (which ordinarily do not occur) they are used by the author for a special effect and do not arise simply from the habitual association in composition. This is again impossible because of the uniqueness of each line. This kind of uniqueness can be balanced against the multiformity of the oral literary tradition on the level of the theme and the song. The uniqueness of a single performance in oral tradition is an element in the multiformity; for the single performance is a multiform. But the uniqueness of written literary tradition is stark. Virgil's *Aeneid* is unique; Ugljanin's *Captivity of Đulić Ibrahim* is unique and at the same time it is but one multiform of a large complex.

In most countries of Western Europe where there are traces of a change from an oral to a literary tradition having at least started, the development seems to have come about through the intermediary of those trained to some degree in a literary tradition that has itself entered from foreign sources. In other words the stimulus has come from an already existent, originally nonnative, literary tradition. Some member or members of that group applied the ideas of written literature to the native oral literature. Such are the cases of Kačić, Njegoš, Mažuranić, Karadžić, and Sima Milutinović.[19] In the Yugoslavia of the eighteenth and nineteenth centuries there were men of education who wrote epic poetry in the native ten-syllable

line. Njegoš and Mažuranić used it for what is clearly written literary purposes in *Gorski Vijenac* and *Smrt Smailage Čengića,* for example.[20] In the
works under consideration these authors are not *imitating* oral epic, not
writing "in its style." They have developed a native literary tradition of
epic.

Thus, Njegoš in Vladika Danilo's soliloquy with which the work opens:

Moje pleme snom mrtvijem spava,	My people sleep a sleep of death,
suza moja nema roditelja,	My tear has no parent,
nada mnom je nebo zatvoreno,	Above me the sky is barred,
ne prima mi plača ni molitve;	It does not accept my weeping or my prayer;
u ad mi se svijet pretvorio,	My world has been transformed into hell,
a svi ljudi pakleni duhovi! [21]	And all its men are demons of Hades!

Or, from a famous part of Mažuranić's *Smrt Smailage Čengića:*[22]

Kad al' eto inoga past'jera	When lo another kind of shepherd
gdjeno krotak k svome stadu grede.	Meekly approached his flock.
Ne resi ga ni srebro ni zlato,	He was not bedecked with silver or gold,
nego krepost i mantija crna.	But with strength and a black cassock.
Ne prate ga sjajni pratioci	A brilliant train did not accompany him
uz fenjere i dupl'jere sjajne,	With lanterns and shining crucifixes
ni ponosn'jeh zvona sa zvonika:	Or with proud bells from the towers:
već ga prati sa zapada sunce	But the sun from the west accompanied him
i zvon smjeran ovna iz planine.	And the measured bell of the ram from the mountains.
Crkva mu je divno podnebesje,	His church is the wondrous sky,
oltar časni brdo i dolina,	His holy altar the mountain and the valley,
tamjan miris što se k nebu diže	The fragrance of incense is that which rises to heaven
iz cvijeta i iz b'jela sv'jeta	From the flowers and from the bright world
i iz krvi za krst prolivene.	And from the blood shed for the Cross.

One of the difficulties in comprehending the change from oral to written
style lies in the fact that we think of the written always in terms of quality,
and that of the highest. We assume without thinking that written style
is always superior to oral style, *even from the very beginning*. Actually
this is an error in simple observation of experience, perpetrated alas by
scholars who have shunned experience for the theoretical. A superior written
style is the development of generations. When a tradition or an individual
goes from oral to written, he, or it, goes from an adult, mature style of
one kind to a faltering and embryonic style of another sort. The Homeric
poems could not possibly belong to a "transitional" or early period of written
style. Bowra's phrase that the richness of these poems "suggests reliance on
writing" [23] is ambiguous.

While the presence of writing in a society *can* have an effect on oral tradition, it does not *necessarily* have an effect at all. The fact of writing does not inevitably involve a tradition of written literature; even if it did, a tradition of written literature does not inevitably influence an oral tradition. The Southern Slavs had a tradition of written literature since the end of the ninth century; indeed they invented the alphabets used by the Slavs. Yet this written tradition had no influence on the form of the oral tradition until the nineteenth and twentieth centuries. The two existed side by side, not, of course, within the same group, but certainly within the same district. In medieval times, writing and written literature, first on foreign models but soon developing along its own lines, were cultivated in the monasteries, as in the rest of Europe. The carriers of oral tradition were the unlettered people outside the monasteries. Beginning in the fifteenth century on the Adriatic coast and on some of the islands, particularly in the cities of Split, Zadar, and Dubrovnik, again under foreign influence and with foreign models at first, a rich literary tradition arose not only among the clergy, but more especially among the wealthy merchant aristocracy. In the villages surrounding these cities and among the other classes of the population in the cities, that is, among those who were not of patrician families and not educated in the schools abroad, or later at home, oral tradition continued to flourish among the unlettered. In both these instances the literary tradition was not a development from the oral tradition. It was stimulated from outside, from Byzantium or from Italy.

In the medieval literature influenced by Byzantium there is a conspicuous lack of verse except for hymns or liturgical and didactic poetry.[24] On the coastland verse was cultivated in Latin and in Croatian, both in medieval and renaissance times, but the verse used for the Croatian poems was not the native meter but an Italian one. Some poets, indeed, showed a knowledge of the native oral literature (which can be seen from the epithets used), yet their works were of a purely literary rather than oral character; and there was a handful of Croatian poems (in part attributed to Šiško Menčetić and Džore Držić of the fifteenth century, and in part to others) which were close to oral lyric and possibly were such. They were not published until later in the nineteenth century.[25] A few narrative ballads from oral tradition appear inserted in literary works beginning in the sixteenth century.[26] The first oral epic texts are found in manuscript collections dating from the first decades of the eighteenth century, discovered and published during the nineteenth and twentieth centuries.[27] These private collections had no influence on oral tradition itself. Before the eighteenth century we meet with either collected songs or purely literary works springing from nonnative forms.

In the eighteenth century we find the first epic works that are in the style of the oral songs, yet were never sung but were written. The most significant and influential of these is the *Razgovor ugodni naroda slovinskoga* by Andrija Kačić-Miošić, of which we have already spoken.[28] Kačić (1704–

1760) was a Franciscan monk, and his *Razgovor* is a chronicle of the South Slavs from the beginning to his own day, partly in prose and partly in verse. The verse part consists of epic songs almost entirely in the ten-syllable line of oral tradition. Kačić knew the oral epic very well and he wrote his songs in its style. His sources were in part oral epics that he had heard, but even more the available chronicles and histories, documents, accounts of eye witnesses. He aimed at historical truth as he saw it. He has set out to praise the heroes who have not been praised in the tradition, or not sufficiently.

It is worth noting that the Abbé Fortis, collector of the famed *Hasana-ginica,* accepted Kačić's book as a collection of oral epics and through his translation of three of Kačić's songs into Italian they entered into Herder's *Stimmen der Völker in Liedern* (1778–79). In his *Saggio d'Osservazioni sopra l'Isola di Cherso ed Osero* (1771), Fortis compared Kačić's songs with the "translations" of Macpherson which had·begun to appear in 1760.

The *Razgovor* became an extremely popular book and some of its songs entered into the oral tradition whence they had not come. They could still be collected from singers in the 1930's and probably even today. Kačić was not primarily a collector, but the days of great collecting activity were not far off. Vuk Stefanović Karadžić's first book appeared in 1814, and he was followed by many other collectors down to the present day. The material in all these collections is somewhat uneven, but for the most part the songs were really noted down from singers and, in spite of editing, give a fair picture of the tradition. They are oral dictated texts. Songs have entered these collections that were written, as Kačić's poems were written, and like his they are not really oral traditional poems. Still other songs were made up for the first time by the singers at the moment of dictation probably at the urging of the collector, as was the case of the new songs by the famous singer Filip Višnjić.[29] We must probably consider these as oral epics. The collecting seems to have stimulated the creation of new songs. Nationalism was rife and the chauvinism of the day, a chauvinism not in-herent in the tradition itself but fostered by nationalistic and political forces outside the tradition, was unfortunately mirrored in the songs.

What has been the effect of the collections on the tradition itself? The larger, more expensive editions did not reach the communities in which the singing was cultivated, nor did they have any effect in places where there was no person who could read. But during the nineteenth century schools began to spread slowly, and after World War I schools were to be found in most communities. Since the establishment of the Communist regime a concentrated battle against illiteracy has been going on, and now in Yugoslavia only a comparatively small number of the older people are still unable to read and write. Common fare in all school books have been the songs from Vuk's collection or, to a lesser extent, from Njegoš's work. School teachers played a large role in collecting and they and the younger generation have been the chief purveyors of the songs in their printed forms. But inexpensive paper reprints of individual songs have also been circulated down to the present day.[30] They are still appearing. These contain texts again largely from Vuk. They were also the means for spreading the new songs — largely written and not taken from oral tradition — of the various uprisings against the Turks, the Balkan Wars, World War I, and the recent wars and revolutions. Between the two world wars the Serbs and the Montenegrins were especially active in this field. Printing establishments in Belgrade and Cetinje produced many small paper pamphlets with songs. In Sarajevo, too, the Moslems were busy reproducing songs from the Matica Hrvatska collection and from Hörmann.[31] Most of this activity has taken place since the turn of the century, particularly since 1918.

The effect on the younger generation which could read was that the young people began to memorize songs from the books. They still learned the art from their elders and could sing songs picked up from oral tradition, but they were moving away from that tradition by memorizing some of their repertory from the song books. The memorization from a fixed text influenced their other songs as well, because they now felt they should memorize even the oral versions. The set, "correct" text had arrived, and the death knell of the oral process had been sounded. There are very few younger singers, particularly among the Christian population, who have not been infected by this disease. This is somewhat less true among the Moslems, because none of their collections has been given the almost sacred authority of Vuk's or Njegoš's.

The song books have, of course, spread songs from one district to another, but this effect of the collections has been similar to what would happen, and has often happened, when a singer from one district migrates to another, or when songs are carried by caravan drivers along the routes of trade. So far as oral technique of composition is concerned this distribution of songs by the song books has not been in any way abnormal.

Actually older unlettered singers, even when they are exposed to the reading of song books to them, are not greatly influenced.[32] The learning of the song in this way is like the learning of it from a sung performance. Their habit of oral composition is too well inculcated to be changed.

Those singers who accept the idea of a fixed text are lost to oral traditional processes. This means death to oral tradition and the rise of a generation of "singers" who are reproducers rather than re-creators. Such are the men who appear in costume at folk festivals and sing the songs they have memorized from Vuk's collection. You or I could do the same with a certain amount of training and with a costume. These "singers" are really counterfeits masquerading as epic bards! They borrow the songs of real singers complete from first word to last; one can follow the text in the book. They are a menace to the collector. The idea of the fixed text has been established in them, but they are not by this token literary poets, even though they are now members of the community of those with written "mentality," in spite of the fact that some of them are still unlettered.

The change has been from stability of essential story, which is the goal of oral tradition, to stability of text, of the exact words of the story. The spread of the concept of fixity among the carriers of oral traditional epic is only one aspect of the transition from an oral society to a written society. Ironically enough, it was the collector and even more those who used his collection for educational, nationalistic, political, or religious propaganda who presented the oral society with a fixed form of its own material. This aspect of the transition can be dated, therefore, from the period of collecting or more exactly from the spread of the collected songs among the oral singers in one form or another as outlined above. Today in Yugoslavia the transition under this aspect is nearly complete. The oral process is now nearly dead.

But this is only one aspect of the transition and it is the easiest one to treat. The written epic traditions of renaissance times in Yugoslavia were not developments from oral tradition. They were extensions of Italian literary traditions and were not autochthonous. This does not mean that a real Yugoslav literary tradition did not arise from them. They did, of course, produce a real Yugoslav literature, just as real and as distinctive as those of other peoples. But they did not come in a straight line from the oral tradition of the Yugoslavs even when they borrowed the subject matter, as they did more and more as time went on. The existence of such literary traditions adjacent to oral traditions may or may not be necessary for the transition from an oral literature to a written literature, but these borrowed forms are in no way themselves transitional.

There is nothing peculiarly Yugoslav in this picture except that among the Yugoslavs oral tradition has lasted until the present time and was flourishing only yesterday. Beginning with the Romans, the peoples of Europe have borrowed a literary tradition and made it their own. It supplanted their native oral traditions; it did not develop out of them. There is no direct line of literary development from the *chansons de geste* to the *Henriade,* or from *Beowulf* to *Paradise Lost.*[33] Our Western literary tradition of epic stems from Homer through Apollonius and Virgil. Virgil did not write in Saturnians, nor in any direct descendant of them; nor did Milton write in alliterative Germanic verse, nor in any direct descendant of it, because there were no real direct descendants of these native oral traditional meters. Oral tradition did not become transferred or transmuted into a literary tradition of epic, but was only moved further and further into the background, literally into the back country, until it disappeared.

PART II. THE APPLICATION

CHAPTER SEVEN

HOMER

The practice of oral narrative poetry makes a certain form necessary; the way in which oral epic songs are composed and transmitted leaves its unmistakable mark on the songs. That mark is apparent in the formulas and in the themes. It is visible in the structure of the songs themselves. In the living laboratory of Yugoslav epic the elements have emerged and they have been segregated. We have watched singers in the process of learning songs, we have seen them change songs, and we have seen them build long songs from short ones. A panorama of individual singers, some of them true artists, has passed before us, and the details of their art no longer mystify us. With this new understanding, which further research will eventually deepen, we must turn again to the songs that we have inherited from the past in precious manuscripts. Do they also show the marks of oral composition as we have come to know them? To investigate this question is the problem of the succeeding chapters of this book.

At last we find ourselves in a position to answer the question as to whether the author of the Homeric poems was an "oral poet," and whether the poems themselves are "oral poems." We now know exactly what is meant by these terms, at least insofar as manner of composition is concerned. We have cleared away and discarded some false notions of "oral tradition," "oral composition," and "oral transmission," and installed in their stead knowledge gained from observation and analysis of oral tradition in action.

We realize that what is called oral tradition is as intricate and meaningful an art form as its derivative "literary tradition." In the extended sense of the word, oral tradition is as "literary" as literary tradition. It is not simply a less polished, more haphazard, or cruder second cousin twice removed, to literature. By the time the written techniques come onto the stage, the art forms have been long set and are already highly developed and ancient.

There is now no doubt that the composer of the Homeric poems was an oral poet. The proof is to be found in the poems themselves; and it is proper, logical, and necessary that this should be so. The necessity of oral form and style has been discussed; their characteristic marks have been noted. What marks of formulaic technique and of thematic structure does examination of the Homeric poems reveal?

Parry's analyses have, I believe, answered the first part of this question.[1] His discovery of the intricate schematization of formulas in the Homeric poems has never been challenged; though there have been critics who have not been willing to accept his interpretation of the meaning and implication of the phenomenon of formula structure. It is highly important to emphasize the fact that the formulas are not limited to the familiar epithets and oft-repeated lines, but that the formulas are all pervasive. In Chart VII it will be noted that about 90 per cent of the 15 lines analyzed are formulas or formulaic. Considering the limited amount of material available for analysis — only two poems, approximately 27,000 lines — the percentage of demonstrably formulaic lines or part lines is truly amazing. It is even more to be wondered at because of the subtlety and intricacy of the Greek hexameter. The task before the ancient Greek bards was not easy, and one should have the most profound respect for their accomplishment in creating a formulaic technique so perfect and rich in expressive possibilities. It is a complex and delicately balanced artistic instrument.

The Greek hexameter is probably the best known meter in all literature, and for this study of formulas it needs no further elucidation than has already been given it. But something must be said about formula length so that the divisions in Chart VII may be understood. In the Yugoslav poems there are formulas of four, six, and ten syllables in length. The structure of the Yugoslav line, with its strict break after the fourth syllable, is comparatively simple. The Greek hexameter allows for greater variety, because the line may be broken at more than one place by a caesura. It is probably correct to say that this flexibility is closely allied to the musical pattern in which the poetry was sung or chanted, but since we know nothing of this music, any such statement is speculative. The caesura can occur in any one of the following points in the line: (a) after the first syllable of the third foot, (b) after the second syllable of the third foot if it is a dactyl, and (c) after the first syllable of the fourth foot. To these should be added (d) the bucolic diaeresis (after the fourth foot) and (e) the pause after a run-over word at the beginning of the line, which occurs most frequently after the first syllable of the second foot. One can, therefore, expect to find formulas of one foot and a half, two feet and a half, two feet and three quarters, three feet and a half, four feet, and six feet in length measured from the beginning of the line, and complementary lengths measured from the pause to the end of the line.

The only satisfactory way to analyze formulaic structure is the one which Parry used and which has been employed in Chapter Three of this book: to select a number of lines (in our case fifteen), and to analyze each of them for its formulaic content. I shall use the first fifteen lines of the *Iliad* for Chart VII, and since my divisions differ slightly from Parry's, I invite

CHART VII²

ΙΛΙΑΔΟΣ Α

Μῆνιν ἄειδε, θεά, Πηληϊάδεω Ἀχιλῆος

— — — — — — — — — — — — — — — —¹

— — — — — — — ?————————————³

οὐλομένην, ἣ μυρί' Ἀχαιοῖς ἄλγε' ἔθηκε,

— — — — — — — — — — — — — — — —⁴

————⁵ — — — — — — — ————————⁶

πολλὰς δ' ἰφθίμους ψυχὰς Ἄϊδι προΐαψεν

— — — — — — — — — — — — — — — —⁷

— — — — — — — — ————⁸————————⁹

ἡρώων, αὐτοὺς δὲ ἑλώρια τεῦχε κύνεσσιν¹⁰

———— — — —¹¹   12

5 οἰωνοῖσί τε πᾶσι, Διὸς δ'ἐτελείετο βουλή,¹³

— — — — — —¹⁴ ————————————¹⁵

ἐξ οὗ δὴ τὰ πρῶτα διαστήτην ἐρίσαντε

— — — — — — — — — — — — —¹⁶

———————— ————————¹⁷ — — — — — — —¹⁸

Ἀτρεΐδης τε ἄναξ ἀνδρῶν καὶ δῖος Ἀχιλλεύς.

— — — — — — — — — — — — — — — —¹⁹

————————²⁰ ————————²¹ ————————²²

Τίς τ'ἄρ σφωε θεῶν ἔριδι ξυνέηκε μάχεσθαι;

— — — — — — — —²³ — ————————————²⁴

————————²⁵

Λητοῦς καὶ Διὸς υἱός· ὁ γὰρ βασιλῆϊ χολωθεὶς

— — — ————————²⁶ — — — — — — — — —²⁷

10 νοῦσον ἀνὰ στρατὸν ὦρσε κακήν, ὀλέκοντο δὲ λαοί,

— — — — — — — — —²⁸ — — — — ————————·⁹

οὕνεκα τὸν Χρύσην ἠτίμασεν ἀρητῆρα

— — — — — — — — — — — — — — —³⁰

———————— — — — — —³¹   32

Ἀτρεΐδης· ὁ γὰρ ἦλθε θοὰς ἐπὶ νῆας Ἀχαιῶν

————————³³ — — ————————————————³⁴

λυσόμενός τε θύγατρα φέρων τ' ἀπερείσι' ἄποινα,

————————————————————³⁵

———————— — — — — —³⁶ ————————————³⁷

στέμματ' ἔχων ἐν χερσὶν ἑκηβόλου Ἀπόλλωνος³⁸

— — — — ————————³⁹ ————————————⁴⁰

15 χρυσέῳ ἀνὰ σκήπτρῳ, καὶ λίσσετο πάντας Ἀχαιούς,

————————————————————⁴¹

— — — — — — — — —⁴² — — — — — ————————⁴³

comparison with his table. As in the analysis of the Yugoslav poetry, an unbroken line indicates a formula, and a broken line a formulaic expression. A list of the supporting passages from the Homeric corpus is given in the notes to the chart.[2]

The divisions of the lines do not always agree with those of Parry, and it is very likely that someone else would divide them in still another way. Without dwelling on these details, but considering the chart as a whole, we notice that well over 90 per cent of the sample is covered by either an unbroken line or a broken one. In the case of the two half lines which are labelled as nonformulaic, I believe that I have erred on the side of being overcautious, and this is probably true for the six whole lines which are put in the same category. The concordances do not furnish any examples of the patterns under the key words of these passages. But it is almost certain that a line-by-line search of the two poems would reveal other instances of these rhythmic and syntactic patterns. It is not necessary to do this, however, because the formula structure is clear enough from what has been underlined.

The formula technique in the Homeric poems is, indeed, so perfect, the system of formulas, as Parry showed, is so "thrifty," so lacking in identical alternative expressions, that one marvels that this perfection could be reached without the aid of writing.[3] We have already shown that the thrift of the Yugoslav poetry is greater than was previously believed. To determine the thrift of a poetry, one should confine oneself to the work of a single singer, as we have done in the foregoing chapters, and one should take into consideration all the poetic elements in a formula, including its acoustic pattern. The misunderstanding of Yugoslav thrift has come about by reading hastily through collections from many different singers from different regions and from different times. This method is not precise enough to yield reliable results. Moreover, even were one to limit oneself to a single singer and make use of only sung texts, one would still not arrive at a just picture of the situation for comparison with the Homeric poems. One must always make allowances and adjustments for sung texts and their deviations which arise from the pressure of rapid composition. Dictated texts of a carefully controlled type must be used for the comparison. When this was done, we saw that we had statistics comparable to those for the Homeric poems, which must of necessity be dictated and not sung texts. By making one's methods more exact, by considering the nature of the texts chosen in the Yugoslav experiment, and by understanding the type of text represented in the Homeric poems, one sees that the discrepancies between the statistics for the two traditions disappear.

The formulaic techniques, therefore, in the Greek and South Slavic poetries are generically identical and operate on the same principles. This is the surest proof now known of oral composition, and on the basis of it alone we should be justified in the conclusion that the Homeric poems are oral compositions. But there are other characteristics which can corroborate this conclusion.

In his study of enjambement in the Homeric poems Parry indicated that necessary enjambement is much less common in the epics of Homer than in Virgil or Apollonius.[4] The line is a metrical unit in itself. In Yugoslav song necessary enjambement is practically nonexistent. The length of the hexameter is one of the important causes of the discrepancy between the two poetries. It is long enough to allow for the expression of a complete idea within its limits, and on occasion it is too long. Then a new idea is started before the end of the line. But since there is not enough space before the end to complete the idea it must be continued in the next line. This accounts for systems of formulas that have been evolved to fill the space from the bucolic diaeresis to the end of the line, with complementary systems to take care of the run-over words in the following line.

Parry pointed out the situation in the Homeric poems, and I have already compared this with statistics from the Yugoslav poetry in a separate article.[5] Here, too, it was necessary, as always, to be aware of the differences of language, length of line, and possible influence of a different type of musical accompaniment in order to understand the discrepancy between the Greek and Yugoslav poetries in the higher instance of end-stop lines in the latter than in the former. Again, by paying particular attention to matters of method, one was able to arrive at an understanding of this basic stylistic feature. The test of enjambement analysis is, as a matter of fact, an easily applied rule of thumb that can be used on first approaching a new text to determine the possibility of oral composition. It should be done, however, with a knowledge of the musical background, if such information is available, and with an awareness of differences that may be brought about by length of line and peculiarities of the languages involved.

Another corroborating test for oral composition is less easily applied — though just as decisive — because it requires a greater amount of material for analysis than is usually available from the poetries of the past. This is the investigation of thematic structure.[6]

The Homeric poems have probably been analyzed more often and more variously than any other poems in world literature. It would be a brave man who would undertake another analysis of them, unless he were convinced that there are really new and significant grounds for so doing, and that the analysis would bring decisive results.

The first step in thematic analysis must be to prove the existence of themes in the poem under consideration. In other words we must find, either in the poem under scrutiny or in other poems by the same singer or otherwise belonging to the same tradition, the same situations repeated at least once. The method is the same used for formula analysis; but the units are larger and exact word-for-word correspondence is not necessary. In fact, exact word-for-word correspondence, as we have seen, is not to be expected.

One of the more readily isolated themes in the Homeric poems, indeed in all epic literature, is that of the assembly. It is easily isolated because it has an obvious beginning and an obvious end. Let us observe this theme in Books I and II of the *Iliad*. The first assembly in the *Iliad* is an informal and unofficial one, and it is brief. Chryses comes to the Achaean fleet, and makes his petition to the people in general and to the Atridae in particular. The people applaud, but Agamemnon sends the priest away with harsh words. This form of the theme of the assembly is a hybrid. It is halfway between the general theme of interchange of words between two characters and the general theme of the formal assembly, because it takes place in the presence of the people, yet it lacks the calling and dismissing of an assembly.

The next assembly in the poem is a full-dress affair, called by Achilles at the instigation of Hera, complete with the risings and sittings of the speakers and with the dismissal of the assembly. This assembly can serve as a model for the full use of the theme.

The third assembly in Book I, and the final scene in the book, is that of the gods, where Hera and Zeus bandy words and Hephaestus takes his mother's part. Here again is a special form of the general theme, because this group of gods is usually always together except for individuals away on a mission. It needs to be called into formal council only when there is special and important business. It is like a family scene, or like the aghas of the Border in the Yugoslav Moslem songs, who are always gathered together in the green bower in Udbina. There is no need usually to call an assembly, hence no need to dismiss one. It is not unlike the first assembly described above, except that in that case the conversation was started by a newly arrived stranger, and in this instance it is confined to the family group.

The relationship between these three examples of the assembly theme in Book I could be expressed as A (the assembly called by Achilles), B_1 (the assembly of the gods), and B_2 (the quarrel between Chryses and Agamemnon).

Book II furnishes a number of instructive cases of this theme. First comes the council of elders called by Agamemnon as a result of the deceptive dream. It is a formal affair and belongs in the A category. If we designate the full assembly of the people as A_1, we may call the council of elders A_2, although structurally there is no difference between them. In the example under consideration in Book II, however, the council of elders is introduced within the framework of the full assembly. Heralds are sent out to summon an assembly of the people, and while the men are gathering together a council of elders is held. A_2 is here included in A_1. This popular assembly is not formally dismissed for some time; it is broken up by the men themselves, who have to be brought back by the efforts of Odysseus. We might term this interrupted and reconvened assembly of the people A_{1a}.

There are two more examples of our theme in Book II. The first may be considered as a special variety of A₂, the council of elders. Agamemnon calls together the elders and chief men; there is a sacrifice and dinner (both of which are themselves themes, of course), followed by a brief speech of instruction and command by Nestor. We might call this A₂ₐ. Although I am including this theme with the assembly themes, it might perhaps more properly belong with feasting and sacrifice themes. This ambiguity emphasizes the overlapping of themes, or, more precisely, the way in which minor themes are useful in more than one major theme. The summoning of the elders is a minor theme in point, as is also the speech of Nestor. This can be seen again in the lines that immediately follow the speech and tell of the sounding of the call to battle and the assembling of the army. The lesser theme of summoning is itself useful in numerous situations: in this case in the larger theme of summoning an army, which is the prelude to the theme of the catalogue. The architectonics of thematic structure are wondrous to observe.

The final assembly in Book II is one already in progress on the Trojan side. It is a popular assembly, and hence a form of A₁. It has been addressed by Iris and will be dismissed by Hector. We see only the end of the assembly.

Thus, in the first two books of the *Iliad* we find some seven examples of the theme of the assembly. The second example in Book I provides a good model. The rest seem to be variations in different tonalities on this theme. We have already become aware in this analysis of the interweaving and overlapping of major themes; we have begun to glimpse the complexity of thematic structure in the *Iliad*.

We have now applied the three sets of tests that we recognize as valid in determining whether any given poem is oral or not. The Homeric poems have met each of these tests. We now realize fully that Homer is an oral poet. Some of the implications of that fact have already been apparent from our thematic analysis. But we cannot leave it at that.

First, this knowledge places Homer inside an oral tradition of epic song. He is not an outsider approaching the tradition with only a superficial grasp of it, using a bit here and a bit there, or trying to present a "flavor" of the traditional, yet ever thinking in terms essentially different from it. He is not a split personality with half of his understanding and technique in the tradition and the other half in a parnassus of literate methods. No, he is not even "immersed" in the tradition. He *is* the tradition; he is one of the integral parts of that complex; for us, as undoubtedly for his own audiences, he is the most gifted and fascinating part of that tradition. His vividness and immediacy arise from the fact that he is a practicing oral poet. Those who would make of Homer a "literary" poet, do not understand his "literariness"; he has none of the artificiality of those who use traditional themes or traditional devices for nontraditional purposes. From ancient times until the present we have been misled about the true nature of

Homer's art and greatness. And the reason has been that we have tried to read him in our own terms, which we have labelled "universal terms of art."

We have exercised our imaginations and ingenuity in finding a kind of unity, individuality, and originality in the Homeric poems that are irrelevant. Had Homer been interested in Aristotelian ideas of unity, he would not have been Homer, nor would he have composed the *Iliad* or *Odyssey*. An oral poet spins out a tale; he likes to ornament, if he has the ability to do so, as Homer, of course, did. It is on the story itself, and even more on the grand scale of ornamentation, that we must concentrate, not on any alien concept of close-knit unity. The story is there and Homer tells it to the end. He tells it fully and with a leisurely tempo, ever willing to linger and to tell another story that comes to his mind. And if the stories are apt, it is not because of a preconceived idea of structural unity which the singer is self-consciously and laboriously working out, but because at the moment when they occur to the poet in the telling of his tale he is so filled with his subject that the natural processes of association have brought to his mind a relevant tale. If the incidental tale or ornament be, by any chance, irrelevant to the main story or to the poem as a whole, this is no great matter; for the ornament has a value of its own, and this value is understood and appreciated by the poet's audience.

Each theme, small or large — one might even say, each formula — has around it an aura of meaning which has been put there by all the contexts in which it has occurred in the past. It is the meaning that has been given it by the tradition in its creativeness. To any given poet at any given time, this meaning involves all the occasions on which he has used the theme, especially those contexts in which he uses it most frequently; it involves also all the occasions on which he has heard it used by others, particularly by those singers whom he first heard in his youth, or by great singers later by whom he was impressed. To the audience the meaning of the theme involves its own experience of it as well. The communication of this supra-meaning is possible because of the community of experience of poet and audience. At our distance of time and space we can approach an understanding of the supra-meaning only by steeping ourselves in as much material in traditional poetry or in a given tradition as is available.

But we are getting ahead of our story. Having determined that the method of composition of the Homeric poems is that of oral poetry, we must next decide what degree of oral composition they represent. What degrees can we distinguish? First, there is the *actual performance*.

Let us make one thing clear at this point. An interested audience, with time and desire to listen for a long period and from one day to another, coupled with a singer of talent in a rich tradition might produce songs as long as the Homeric poems. But our texts as we have shown in a previous chapter could not have been written down during performance. Actual performance is too rapid for a scribe. One might possibly suggest that the scribe might write as much as he could at one performance, correct it at the next, and so on until he had taken down the text of the whole from several singings. I mention this because Parry had an assistant in the field at the beginning who thought that he could do this, but the variations from one singing to another were so great that he very soon gave up trying to note them down. It should be clear by now that such a suggestion makes sense only when there is a fixed text being repeated. In oral epic performance this is not the case. Without recording apparatus, it is impossible to obtain an exact text of actual performance, and hence we cannot say that our texts of the Homeric songs represent oral poetry in the first degree.

The second degree is close to the first in matter of composition. This degree is the dictated text. This is the nearest one can get to an actual performance without the use of a recording machine, but there are important differences. In the hands of a good singer and competent scribe this method produces a longer and technically better text than actual performance, for reasons that we have already analyzed. It seems to me that this is where we should most logically place the Homeric poems. They are *oral dictated texts*. Within this class of texts, we can differentiate between those skillfully and those ineptly done. The first will have regular lines and fullness of telling. The second will have many irregularities in lines and the general structure will be apocopated. Even allowing for later editing, we must see in the Homeric texts models of the dictating and scribal technique.

The third degree of oral composition is when the oral poet is literate and himself writes down a poem. At best the result may be the same as in the second degree described above, except that the pen is in the hand of the singer, and there is no scribe involved. This may be attractive to those who must have a literate Homer writing. Theoretically, it makes little difference, if any, in the results at this stage. Yet it is not a normal situation, and the experience which we have of such cases would indicate that texts thus produced (which we have termed *oral autograph texts*) are inferior in all respects to oral dictated texts. There seems to be little sense in grasping at this solution for purely sentimental reasons. In putting a pen into Homer's hand, one runs the danger of making a bad poet of him. The singer not only has a perfectly satisfactory method of composition already in the highly developed oral technique of composition, but is actually hampered and restricted by writing. The method he knows came into being for the very purpose of rapid composition before a live audience, as we have said. Writing is a slow process even at best, and the oral poet would find it annoying, indeed, not worth the bother.[7] I cannot accept Homer as semi-literate, whatever that may mean. His skill demands that he be either the best of oral poets or the best of literary poets, not a nondescript hybrid. Anyone actually acquainted with "semiliterate" texts would, I believe, strongly resist any pressure to place Homer in such a category.

Those who wish may seek to find comfort and corroboration in the discovery of pre-Homeric literacy as shown by Linear B. They will be prone to "discount" and ignore the wise caution of Professor Sterling Dow,[8] who has pointed out the limited use of Linear B and the disappearance of the script on the mainland perhaps around 1200 B. C. He writes (p. 128):

> Four or five hundred years the Greeks had lived in Greece before they learned to write. In other skills and arts, including those of power, they had advanced tremendously. In literacy — the very nerve of Classical civilization — the Mykenaian Greeks, after they once got it, made no advance at all. . . . Literacy arrived tightly associated with practical day-by-day bread and butter purposes. Created for these purposes, it was all too adequate for them. . . . The origin was in government and commerce, not in *belles lettres*. When, with the coming of the Dorians and the Dark Ages, the purposes which writing served — commerce and elaborate government — were choked off, writing ended; whereas literature — oral, that is — went on. . . .
>
> Europe's first taste of literacy was comparatively brief, meager, and unpromising. However severe the cataclysm that caused it, the loss of that literacy was not itself an unqualified disaster. The oral tradition which gave us the Homeric poems may well have been saved at an early stage (i.e. before the twelfth century) by the restricted nature of Mainland literacy, which doubtless excluded it from the field of heroic poetry; and heroic poetry remained oral, i.e. unthreatened, during its great period of growth, because in that period literacy, instead of expanding, perished.

And in the same article (p. 108) Professor Dow has indicated our tendency to naïveté concerning literacy:

> Literacy is usually spoken of, for instance, as a simple indivisible essence (so that we say "the Mykenaians were literate"), whereas in reality literacy is a complex skill applicable to a wide variety of purposes, in fact, to practically all the purposes of human communication. It would obviously be hazardous to assume that as soon as a person — child, barbarian, or Minoan — learns to write, he will use writing for the full range of purposes familiar to us.

But even were we to assume that writing flourished in the service of literature in Homer's day, it does not follow that we must also assume that Homer wrote. We have already seen that oral literature can and does exist side by side with written literature. The discovery of an entire literature, including written epics, in Linear B would not in any way alter the fact that the Homeric poems are oral.

* * *

And so we see Homer as the men of his own time saw him, a poet singer among poet singers. That there was a Greek tradition of oral epic we have abundant reason to believe. The *Odyssey* gives us a picture of the practice, and what we know of the Cyclic epics gives us some idea of what kind of stories were told in this tradition. Homer was one of many singers in his own day; he was preceded by generations of singers like him; and certainly, scanty though our evidence may be here, the tradition of oral epic in Greece scarcely stopped with Homer. It would be the height of naïveté to conceive of Homer as the inventor of epic poetry in Greece or in our Western culture. The tradition in which he belonged was a rich one. He heard many good singers, and he himself had great talent, so that he was well known wherever songs were sung.

The singer who performed the *Iliad* and the *Odyssey* was obviously no novice in the art. Both poems are too well done, show too great a mastery of technique (and by this I mean oral technique) to be by a young man in the stages of learning. To attain such mastery, Homer must have been a singer with a large repertory of songs. He must also have performed his songs, and especially the tale of Achilles and that of Odysseus, many times. He was not a two-song man; nor was he one who sang but once a year at a festival. He sang these two songs often. It is normal to assume that he learned them from other singers. The songs were current in the tradition; Homer did not make them up. We do not have to depend on the analogy with Yugoslav epic or with any single Yugoslav singer to come to this conclusion. The songs themselves betray the fact that they have been long in the tradition. If Separatist scholarship has taught us nothing more, if it has not proved the kind of multiple authorship which it had ever in its mind, it has brought to our attention the mingling of themes, which is an indication of a long period of existence in the traditional repertory. It should be understood, however, that we are speaking about the songs, the tales of Achilles and of Odysseus, and not about the *Iliad* and the *Odyssey,* which are fixed texts (at a given period) by a given singer whom we call Homer. We shall consider that moment and those texts shortly, but it is necessary first to see what can be said about the two songs before they became the *Iliad* and the *Odyssey.*

We shall never be able to determine who first sang these songs, nor when they were first sung, nor where, nor what form they had. We can only be sure that it was a long time before Homer's day; for, as I have said, the songs themselves show that they have had a long history. We can with some certainty assume that their original form, their first singing, was crude as compared with our texts and only in basic story similar.[9] And it is only fair to recognize that the generic tales and many of the themes were already formed and in Greek tradition long before they were applied to Achilles and to Odysseus. Our *Iliad* and *Odyssey* were many centuries in the making.

The poet who first sang these songs changed them in the second singing in the manner which we have already demonstrated in the Yugoslav tradition, and this change continued in each successive singing. He never thought of his song as being at any time fixed either as to content or as to wording. He was the author of each singing. And those singers who learned from him the song of Achilles or that of Odysseus continued the changes of oral tradition in their performances; and each of them was author of each of his own singings. The songs were ever in flux and were crystallized by each singer only when he sat before an audience and told them the tale. It was an old tale that he had heard from others but that telling was his own. He did not claim it, yet all could see that it was his; for he was there before them.

This is the way of oral tradition. To call it multiple authorship is to belittle the role not only of Homer but of all the singers in an oral tradition. It is based upon a false premise, namely, that at one time someone created a fixed original for each song in the tradition and that thereafter whatever happened to the tales was a change of something that had been formed from a marble monolith. As long as scholars felt that they were dealing with firm entities, they could speak of multiple authorship and of interpolation. A part of one monolith could be chiseled away and set upon another. But it should be clear from our investigation of oral tradition in the field in Yugoslavia that one is not dealing with monoliths but with a pliable protean substance. When the same or similar ideas are properly useful in many tales, they belong to none, or perhaps even better, they belong to all of them. Interpolation implies, I believe, that an element belonging to only one song is moved consciously into another. In the flux of oral tradition where a theme is fitting in many tales, the term interpolation is misapplied. And the same may be said for multiple authorship. Once Homer's texts of a particular performance of our two songs were set in the *Iliad* and in the *Odyssey*, interpolations were possible; for here for the first time probably in Greek epic tradition were two definite monoliths. But that belongs to the story of what happened to the manuscripts of the Homeric poems after Homer had sired them.

He must have sung them many times before and many times after those momentous occasions that gave us the *Iliad* and the *Odyssey*. And then came one of the greatest events in the cultural history of the West, the writing down of the *Iliad* and the *Odyssey* of Homer. We know the results of that moment of history, but other than the poems themselves we know nothing about the actual moment. We are in the dark about why the poems were written down. We may be fairly certain, however, that it was not Homer's idea. He would have no need for a written text; he would not know what to do with it. Surely, as master of the oral technique, he needed no mnemonic device. That he might wish to see his songs preserved may seem a valid reason for us, but no oral poet thinks even for a moment that the songs he sings and which others have learned from him will be lost. Nor has he a concept of a single version which is so good that it must be written down to be kept. In suggesting such reasons we are putting into the mind of an oral poet something logical for us but foreign to him. I feel sure that the impetus to write down the *Iliad* and the *Odyssey* did not come from Homer himself but from some outside source.

One reads such statements as "Homer composed the *Iliad* and the *Odyssey* for performance at a festival." [10] Homer did not need a written text. He indeed may have and probably did sing the tales of Achilles and of

Odysseus at festivals. At a much later period, once the poems were written down, there were singers who memorized the written text and performed them at festivals. But these were not oral poets. A festival might give an oral poet an opportunity to sing a song over several days and thus to sing a long song. Homer might have sung these songs long at such a festival. But I am afraid that even here we are straining to explain the length of the *Iliad* and the *Odyssey*. In some ways it seems to me that a festival would be the least likely circumstance to afford opportunity for a long song. There is too much going on at a festival. The audience is constantly distracted and is constantly moving about. A long song seriously delivered to an appreciative audience can be produced only in peace and quiet.

Our texts of Homer can have come only from an ideal condition of dictating, inasmuch as there were no recording apparatuses in ancient Greece! Since there is only one way in which the *Iliad* and the *Odyssey* could have been taken down from our oral epic singer, Homer, the problem of the festival lasting several days to allow time for Homer to sing his songs becomes irrelevant. I have already suggested that such festivals or circumstances which would allow for the singing of moderately long songs are important only for the development of a rich tradition; hence they would have only an indirect influence on the actual texts of the poems we have. It is more likely that epics were sung in brief or in moderately long versions on such occasions. What we can be sure of is that in the course of Greek oral tradition there must have been opportunity for the singing of epics of several thousand lines. A tradition does not become as rich in ornamental themes as the ancient Greek tradition if singers have opportunity to perform songs of only a few hundred lines. Yet the length of the *Iliad* and of the *Odyssey* must have been exceptional.

The length of the songs in the Epic Cycle may provide a rough measurement of the length of the ordinary songs in the tradition in ancient Greece. They seem to belong to a collection that someone made from various singers, or possibly from a compilation of several manuscript collections of various dates.[11] We are told that the *Oidipodeia* had 6,600 verses, the *Thebaid* (ascribed to Homer), 7,000 verses, and the *Epigonoi* (also ascribed to him), 7,000 verses. Other indications of length are in terms of books. If we compare them with the Homeric poems, then the *Cypria*, with its eleven books, was a little less than half the length of those poems; and so proportionately with the five books of the *Aithiopis* and the *Nostoi*, the four books of the *Ilias Mikra*, and the two books of the *Sack of Ilium* and of the *Telegonia*. In other words the longest of the poems in the Epic Cycle were not more than half as long as the *Iliad* and *Odyssey*. To Homer belongs the distinction of having composed the longest and best of all oral narrative songs. Their unusual length predicates exceptional circumstances of performance. If I be not mistaken, dictation to a scribe provides this opportunity. Would not the fact that Homer was the man who dictated the "long songs" account for the reputation which both he and the songs came to enjoy? Would not the city-states have vied with one another for the credit of having nurtured this unusual man?

Yet we still have no answer to the question of why someone chose to ask Homer to dictate 27,000 Greek hexameters to him. The most recent conjecture is found in Cedric Whitman's *Homer and the Heroic Tradition.*[12] After recognizing the fact that "Homer's mode of composition seems to be, from beginning to end, strictly that of the oral poet" (p. 79), Whitman continues by excluding the possibility that Homer himself wrote down his songs. Whitman then points to an example noted by J. Notopoulos[13] previously, of a Greek revolutionary who from being an oral singer became a writer of his own memoirs, as an indication of "a dissatisfaction with the improvised accounts in verse which he had formerly sung to his companions. In an age when the art of writing has gone far toward thrusting back the boundaries of illiteracy, it can hardly fail to strike a creative artist sooner or later that the medium of pen and paper has something new to offer. One might even say that, with writing, a new idea of permanence is born; oral communication is shown for what it is — inaccurate and shifting. Writing has a godlike stability, and to anyone with an eye for the future, its significance is scarcely to be mistaken. . . . If one seeks the motivation for the transference of oral verse to written form it must lie in the disseminated knowledge of writing itself, in its disintegration of the belief that unwritten songs never change, and in the promise of real fixity. One ought, therefore, to associate the great epic, in contrast to the short epic song, not only with festal audiences, but also with writing, not because writing is necessary for its creation, but because the monumental purpose of the large epic is profoundly served by anything which bestows fixity of form. In the century which saw the rise of the city-state, the festivals, and the first flowering of the great colonial movement, the Greek mind cannot have failed to recognize that written characters have a peculiar permanence, whatever had been commonly believed about the immutability of oral tradition" (pp. 80–81). I have quoted Whitman at some length for convenience in analyzing his thinking on this subject.

First, the example of the Greek revolutionary is not really apt for Homer, unless we assume much more writing in Greece in Homer's time, and that of a literary sort, than there is evidence of, at the moment at least. Revolutionary Greece had a rich tradition of written literature, and Makriyannis' progress from illiteracy to literacy was a progress from a more backward, peasant social group to a more advanced, and more privileged social stratum. It is to be doubted that his dissatisfaction with the older oral songs (which was probably very real) sprang at all from any recognition of the possibilities of a fixed text as against the lack of them in an oral text. It is far more likely that he was dissatisfied with them because they belonged to the peasant society and he had now graduated into the company of the elite. Are we to assume that there was such a literate and elite group of littérateurs in Homer's day? If so, where is the evidence for it? Makriyannis moved into a milieu with a long-established tradition not only of writing (we might even say from Homer's day), but of fine writing in the form of literature. "The boundaries of illiteracy" were of a different kind in modern Greece from what they were in ancient, more specifically, late eighth century B.C. Greece, and the gulf between the oral singer and "the creative artist" was both broad and deep in Makriyannis' time. In Homer's day, on the contrary, the oral singer was a creative artist; in fact there was no distinction — I believe that the idea of the "creative artist," the "inspired poet," and so forth, is derived from the mantic and sacred function of the singer. In assessing the situation in Homer's day in Greece, we must reckon with the fact that we have no other literary texts from that time, no written literary tradition. Yet suddenly 27,000 Greek hexameters appear! Are we supposed to believe that Homer, or someone else, saw the lists of chattels and, realizing what this meant for epic, sat down to record the *Iliad* and *Odyssey*? Makriyannis had much more than jar labels to read when he learned his ABC's. A slow progress with small written beginnings in the field of literature, recording short pieces, over a long period of time is believable, and Whitman allows for some possibility of this later when he says, "For all we know, some of his [Homer's] predecessors may have committed their work to paper somehow." Without interference from outside of Greece, this is the only way one could have arrived at the point of writing down so many lines of verse.

The trouble with Whitman's "creative artist" is that, in spite of the fact that he is said to compose entirely as an oral poet, he is not in the tradition; he is not an oral *traditional* poet. *And oral poets who are not traditional do not exist.* With this in mind, if one should substitute "the best oral traditional singer" for "creative artist" in Whitman's statement, it would read, "it can hardly fail to strike the best oral traditional singer sooner or later that the medium of pen and paper has something new to offer." I cannot help, when the statement reads this way, but ask *why* the idea of "something new" is so inevitable for the oral poet, even the greatest and best of them. Why should permanence and fixity be so attractive to an oral poet? And how does he come to recognize and to distrust oral communication as "inaccurate and shifting?" Remember that the man with whom we are dealing is an oral poet in a society with writing, but no extensive writing in literature, if any at all. Whitman has tacitly and naturally assumed that the oral poet has the same sense of propriety for the "form" of his song, even for "his song" that the written poet has. He hears the "creative artist" saying, "This is *my* song, *my* masterpiece, every word of it"; but the oral poet does not say this because he is in the tradition. What he says is, "I learned this song from someone else, and I sing it as he sang it." Does this man with his sense of the tradition see permanency so readily, if at all, for the tradition's song? It is not in the psychology of the oral poet to concern himself with stability of form, since stability of meaning and story already exist for him. Oral communication is not "inaccurate and shifting" until you have the idea that a given *form, one* given performance, is worth fixing. And this idea may come readily to the "creative artist" who is self-consciously creating something which he is accustomed to think of as his very own, but it is a large order for the oral poet who is intent upon preserving a meaningful traditional song. We must not suddenly endow the oral poet with the mentality of the developed literary artist in a written tradition, with his sense of ownership.

Perhaps we shall never have a certain solution to the riddle of the writing down of the Homeric poems, but we can hypothesize on what is most likely. We have already seen that the idea would not have come from Homer, and it is logical that the group to which he belonged and which regularly listened to him would not have had any reason (other than what we might project backward from our own thinking) for wanting these two songs, or any songs, written down. We should do well, therefore, to look about in the world of ancient Greece, before, let us say, 700 B.C., if perchance we might discover people who were recording or had already recorded in writing their literature, people with whom the Greeks may well have come into contact.

In the ninth century in Palestine the oldest of the documents of the Old Testament seems to have been written, namely, the J Document, and in the following century the E Document came into being.[14] These writings or records told of the creation of the world and of the history of the founders of the Jewish people or of man in general. They contained the epics and myths of these people. In the eighth century Sargon II (722–705) established the library at Nineveh and under him the Assyrian Empire was at its greatest extent. His library contained tablets inscribed with epic, mythic, magic, and historical material in several languages, including Sumerian, and dating from as early as 2000 B.C. Here were to be found the Epic of Creation and the Epic of Gilgamesh, among other texts.[15] Two bodies of recorded lore, one already ancient in ancient times, the other new and exciting in its serious intensity, were thus available to any Greeks who might turn in their direction. And it seems that it would be normal for them to look to the East during these centuries; for it was in the East that the cultural center was then located.

Hence, I should like to suggest that the idea of recording the Homeric poems, and the Cyclic epics, and the works of Hesiod, came from observation of or from hearing about similar activity going on further to the East. The list of works on Sumerian tablets given by Kramer in his *Sumerian Mythology*[16] reminds one of the kind of literature recorded at the earliest period in both Palestine and Greece: "epics and myths, hymns and lamentations, proverbs and 'wisdom' compositions." And the wisdom compositions consist of "a large number of brief, pithy, and pointed proverbs and aphorisms; of various fables, such as 'The Bird and the Fish,' 'The Tree and the Reed,' 'The Pickax and the Plow,' 'Silver and Bronze'; and finally of a group of didactic compositions, long and short, several of which are devoted to a description of the process of learning the scribal art and of the advantages which flow from it." The Greeks and the Hebrews were reliving in their own terms the cultural experiences of older civilizations. The scribe who wrote down the Homeric poems was doing for the Greeks what the scribes of Sumer had done for their people many centuries before.

CHAPTER EIGHT

THE ODYSSEY

In reading the *Odyssey* or the *Iliad* we are at a distinct disadvantage because we are reading isolated texts in a tradition. The comparison with
other traditions shows us very clearly that songs are not isolated entities, but
that they must be understood in terms of other songs that are current. Had
we an adequate collection of ancient Greek epic songs, we could view the
Homeric poems from a truer perspective. Much of the difficulty in interpretation in the past has arisen from this lack. Yet the situation would be even
worse had only one song survived, and that a short one; at least there are
two poems adding up to some 27,000 lines, and the two poems are on
different subjects. Hesiod and especially the Cyclic fragments may be of
some help in supplying a hint of other thematic material current in Homer's
day.[1] And the poems themselves may point to still more such themes. We
can even, with some caution, appeal to the Greek dramatists for versions
of epic stories. Dares and Dictys[2] should not be completely ignored. Our
task is not then entirely hopeless. Other traditions can assist us particularly
in indicating what we should look for.

Of great interest and value for Homeric study are the texts on clay
tablets that have been unearthed in Mesopotamia and the nearer Near
East.[3] Their deciphering and interpretation are marvels of scholarship,
imaginative scholarship at its best. Homer is no longer the earliest epic
singer whose songs we know. Rather he stands perhaps a little before the
midpoint, chronologically, of our knowledge. For we now have epic tales
going back to the third millennium B. c. from peoples and cultures contiguous
to Greek and with which the Greeks had contact. In other words, we have
access to thematic material of Homer's neighbors before his day; we know
the story climate of the Near East which taught Greece so much. If we find
parallel tales and themes among these peoples they may be of service in
interpreting Homer; they may verify or even help us to discover story
patterns in the Homeric songs.

We should be daring enough, as well, to make use of later epic stories
which follow the same or similar patterns, provided that they are traditional
and oral.[4] Medieval and modern songs, if our theory of composition and
transmission is correct, are extremely conservative in regard to essential
story pattern, as we have seen in the case of the Yugoslav songs from the

Parry Collection. Our best material will be in the Homeric songs themselves and in what we know of Greek Cyclic poets and Greek drama. Next in importance is the Near Eastern corpus. And last, but by no means least, the medieval and modern parallels can be useful. For it is the essential pattern and the significant detail that concern us, not the accidental and incidental.

The *Odyssey* was one of many return songs told in the time of Homer. Some of them were surely in Homer's own repertory. It is clear that he had the tale of the return of Agamemnon in his mind while composing the *Odyssey,* and also the return of Menelaus. A son played no vital role in this story,[5] but it contained wanderings and strange adventures, shipwreck and storm, and a visit to the "other" world in the many shapes of Proteus. The romance of the journey of the Argonauts was known to Homer.[6] These songs were all, and many more, in the repertory of epic singers in his day. They surround the *Odyssey*. Together with it they make up a body of related thematic material.

Yet the *Odyssey* does not draw from the tradition; it is a part of it. I do not wish to imply that Homer used these other songs as sources, borrowing here and there, modeling this or that incident on one in another song. We should not forget the lesson from the Yugoslav tradition that songs are fluid in content. The question as to whether an incident "belongs" in a song, the question of proprietary rights, as it were, is relative in oral tradition. It is vastly important for us to understand the place of the *Odyssey* in the repertory of Homer and in the repertory of other singers. It is the place of one song among many others with related themes in an oral epic tradition.

*   *   *

After an invocation which stresses the wanderings of Odysseus and the loss of his men (but has no mention of Telemachus), the *Odyssey* opens with a council of the gods in which we find Zeus meditating on the story of the return of Agamemnon. Such a reference to another tale is highly sophisticated and unusual for oral epic. In the Yugoslav tradition stories are kept separate and, to the best of my knowledge, singers never refer in one song to the events of another.

Such a device of reference is, of course, far from inconsistent with the analogical thinking or associative thinking of oral poets everywhere. But I do not believe that this explains the presence of these references in the *Odyssey*. They make sense, however, if they are taken as part of a song telling the story of the return of the heroes of Troy, a song, in other words, that would include both the events of the Cyclic epic, the *Nostoi,* and the *Odyssey,* and possibly also the *Telegony.* They are not an anomaly in such a setting. Indeed, they presuppose it. This larger song with which we are dealing is the song of the returns of the Greek heroes from the Trojan War, including Agamemnon, Menelaus, Nestor, Odysseus, and, to a lesser extent, others. Perhaps the returns of the Atridae and the return of Odysseus were sometimes sung as a single song, and without the extensive ornamentation of Homer this would not have to be an inordinately long song. We know that Odysseus, Telemachus, and Telegonus all appeared in the Greek return stories in some way. We can therefore postulate that we could have (a) a song including all the heroes, not emphasizing one above another, (b) a song including all, but emphasizing the return of the Atridae, and (c) a song including all, but emphasizing Odysseus. This is thoroughly consistent with oral technique. Homer probably sang the return of the Atridae as a separate song as well as the *Odyssey,* and it is very likely that he may sometimes have sung them together. The opening of the *Odyssey,* I believe, indicates just that.

The allusion to the return of Agamemnon points, then, to the scope of tales in the tradition of ancient Greece. It also provides later generations of readers, who are no longer listeners to the old songs, with an indication of another pattern of return story from that of the tale of Odysseus. Moreover, we know not only of the existence of this different pattern, but also that Homer started his *Odyssey* with an awareness of that pattern. The divergences in the two stories are clear: Agamemnon returns home openly and is murdered by his wife's lover, whereas Odysseus returns in disguise and murders his wife's suitors; Clytemnestra is unfaithful to her husband, but Penelope is a model of fidelity. Later in the *Odyssey* Homer emphasizes these *differences* between the two stories. But in the opening of the song Homer is thinking of the parallels, of Aegisthus and Orestes, of the violator and the avenger, of suitor and son. And as soon as the plan is laid for the release of Odysseus from Ogygia, the singer turns to the suitors of Odysseus' wife and to the actions of Odysseus' son. The pattern of release and return is scarcely begun before Homer has shifted emphasis to enclose within that pattern a multiform of the related suitor and son theme.

In the South Slavic tradition the role of the son is highly variable. Most frequently he is not present at all in the story. Of the twelve return songs in Appendix III, the son plays a part in only three.[7] Two of those three (Parry 1920 and 6229) are unusual in that the wife is not about to marry again. The son in these two provides a marriage, a theme basic to the story; the returning father finds his son about to marry. In them the son can be said, therefore, to be taking the place of the wife. He is not playing the part of an Orestes aiming to avenge his father's death or of a Telemachus who is seeking news of his father. In these two songs, at any rate, the son *qua* son, is not important; the son is used, by substitution, as the wife in the basic tale, to bring in the element of marriage. In fact these songs themselves are mavericks, because they contain no remarrying wife. In the second of these (Parry 6229) the son plays another role in addition to providing the marriage theme. He is the ransom stipulated by his father's captor, and after his marriage the son returns with his father to the enemy, his father is released, and the son escapes by his own efforts. This song is more interesting in that it shows the son as an aid in the final freeing of the father, but it is the sort of role that in some other songs is given to the wife's suitor (see, for example, Parry and Lord, I, No. 4, in which suitor Halil helps Đulić Ibrahim in returning to Zadar). In the last analysis the son in this song is playing someone else's part as ransom; all sentiment aside he performs the same function as the head of the dead suitor, which is the promised price of freedom in some songs. He is not an avenging Orestes nor even a father-seeking Telemachus.

Only in Avdo Međedović's song (Parry 12465), which belongs in the category of the faithless wife, does the son's role approach that of Greek tradition. The significant element for the present analysis is that the son years later rescues the father from prison, a prison to which the father had returned in fulfillment of his oaths. Like Orestes, he avenges wrongs done to his father; only this time not by his mother but by the enemy. Like Orestes, the son in this story is neglected by a mother who is intent on marrying again.

In this Yugoslav song one sees the son as rescuer rather than avenger, a role interestingly enough often played in the return-rescue songs by the hero's wife' (see Appendix IV, Parry 1921 (1940), 923 (sister), and 275A). Once again the son's role seems ultimately to be a substitution for the wife's role. In other words, an analysis of the Yugoslav songs seems to indicate that the son is not a basic, essential person in the drama of the Return. Only in the Agamemnon type is the son a necessary element. The evidence of traditional patterns, therefore, points in the direction of a story of the return of Odysseus in which Telemachus played no vital role as son, even though he might be present.

It may be that Telemachus enters the *Odyssey* because of the parallel between the story of Agamemnon and the story of Odysseus, the two return stories par excellence involving return to wife and family. The plan of Athena to send Telemachus away from Ithaca so that he will not be present when Odysseus lands on the island has a certain parallel in the exiling of Orestes, which results in his absence at the time of Agamemnon's return and murder. It is noteworthy too that when Telemachus returns, like Orestes, he brings a friend. Theoclymenus has been thought of as being a vestige of many people,[8] but I am not sure that anyone has suggested him as a Pylades. Theoclymenus thus considered is an extension of Peisistratus, son of Nestor, who makes a better Pylades to Telemachus' Orestes. Moreover, the attitude of the suitors to Telemachus as they plot to kill him is like that of Aegisthus. Since Homer opens his song with reference to the Agamemnon pattern we may not be far wrong in suggesting that this pattern was at some time influential in introducing Telemachus as the son plotted against and absented first by the suitors and then, in a later interpretation, sent by Athena to seek news of his father.

Yet as soon as Telemachus becomes an "exile," he also falls into the pattern of the young hero who sets forth to win his own spurs in the world with borrowed equipment. Like Beowulf, Telemachus is thought a weakling, and like the Sirotan Alija of Yugoslav Moslem tradition[9] he must borrow the means of his transportation. The word *sirotan* in Serbian means "orphan" and is connected also with the word meaning "poor." Invariably the young man who sets out on adventures is fatherless and aided by mother, uncle, or friend. The usual pattern is that the equipment and the assistance are denied by one group and granted, often through intervention, by another group.

Telemachus is scorned in the assembly of the lords of Ithaca even as Bećiragić Meho is scorned by Mustajbey; both young men are refused assistance by the mighty of the realm. Telemachus in his frustration may be compared also to the boyish hero, Smailagić Meho, who, about to set forth on his first exploit, complains of his sheltered youth:

Just listen, Cifrić Hasanagha, to the boasts of the Turks in the tavern. One says that he has raised a band, another that he has joined one. One boasts that he has raised an army, another that he has enlisted. One says that he has broadened the border, or won in combat, or taken captives. But, O uncle, Cifrić Hasanagha, by the health of my father, Smailagha, and of my uncle, Cifrić Hasanagha, I have known nothing of raiding and campaigning, not to mention single combat. The broadening of borders is unknown to me. I do not even know where the border is, nor where our ancient battle grounds are. How then could I have crossed the border to raid and take captives, and so marry off a friend? Although I am a man, there has been nothing heroic in my life. No one will say that I am a man. I have nothing more to boast about than that I can take off these men's clothes and put on those of our girls — since I have neither beard nor mustache, and my pigtail is like a maiden's tresses — and embroider and spin. Let them all say that I am a woman (Parry 6480:429–457).

Athena has said that she will go to Ithaca in order to arouse Telemachus to more vigorous action and that she will send him on his journey "to win a good report among mankind." She has thus emphasized the journey as a maturing — should we say initiatory — adventure for the young man. The pattern of the tale of the youthful hero setting out on his first adventure sometimes contains the rescue of someone from the hands of an enemy,[10] often by killing the enemy, who is possibly a supernatural monster. Sometimes the journey takes the hero into the other world, and as such entails experience with the guardians, entrances, and exits of that world. Sometimes, too, the purpose of the journey is to obtain power-bestowing knowledge or information,[11] to be used on the return by the hero, or perhaps, if not used in a specific situation, to make a powerful magician or simply "a man" of the hero. This last is actually Athena's avowed purpose in sending Telemachus to the mainland:

Near him came Athene, likened to Mentor in her form and voice, and speaking in winged words she said:

"Telemachus, henceforth you shall not be a base man nor a foolish, if in you stirs the brave soul of your father, and you like him can give effect to deed and word. Then shall this voyage not be vain and ineffective. But if you are no son of him and of Penelope, then am I hopeless of your gaining what you seek. Few sons are like their fathers; most are worse, few better than the father. Yet because you henceforth will not be base nor foolish, nor has the wisdom of Odysseus wholly failed you, therefore there is a hope you will one day accomplish all. . . ." [12] (2.267–280).

It makes extraordinarily good sense that the son of Odysseus of many wiles should seek knowledge in his first journey from home. His visit to Nestor and to Menelaus is, therefore, not a vain one in the deeper meanings of such journeys.

On the most obvious level Telemachus discovers from Menelaus where his father is, namely, on an island with Calypso. This was the information he was seeking; he knows now that his father is not dead. From Nestor and Menelaus Telemachus has also heard the full story of the return of the other Greeks and especially of Agamemnon. The parallel between Telemachus and Orestes has been almost painfully pointed out to Telemachus; likewise emphasized is the correspondence between affairs in Ithaca and affairs in Argos before Agamemnon's return. Orestes has proved his worth, and Homer's audience can be optimistic about Telemachus' future once Nestor's doubts of Telemachus' promise are cleared away with the knowledge that Athena is at the boy's side.

It is at Book 4, line 624, in the *Odyssey* that we are faced, I believe, for the first time, with a really serious problem. As long as we were following the Telemachus portion of Athena's plan, we were forgetful not of Odysseus, who is actually always in our minds, but of Athena's intention of releasing him from Calypso's island and of bringing him home. Even though it was never promised that Telemachus would find Odysseus and return with him — in fact we knew very well that this would not be so and we had been told that Telemachus' journey even overtly was merely for news — the realization that we were in a tale of the young man's first adventure, the exploit that would make a man of him, led us subconsciously to expect a rescue. There were, it would seem, versions in which Telemachus did meet his father and return to Ithaca with him. In the tale of Dictys the Cretan, Telemachus hears of his father's presence as a guest of Antenor and goes to meet Odysseus there.[13] In this tale Telemachus is married to Nausicaa, daughter of Antenor, after he and Odysseus have slain the suitors. With Telemachus feasting in Sparta and ready to return home we are now prepared for the release of Odysseus, which might well be followed eventually by the meeting of father and son. In reality this is what happens, but so much intervenes that we tend to lose sight of the fact that Telemachus' meeting with Odysseus at Eumaeus' hut (Book 16) is in essence a meeting of the two before either of them returns to the palace of Odysseus in Ithaca. Meeting there is, but postponed almost to the last moment. Yet the traditional bard has too deep a feeling for the meanings and forces in the story patterns to allow himself to violate them altogether.

When we analyze the recognitions later in this chapter we shall note Homer postponing actions because other material, chiefly that related to Telemachus, interrupts. In the second half of Book 4 there is such an interruption, which postpones briefly the expected release of Odysseus from Ogygia. The scene shifts from Sparta back to Ithaca and to the discovery by the suitors and by Penelope of Telemachus' absence. Antinous now lays the plot to ambush Telemachus on his return voyage from Pylos, and Penelope's fears are allayed by a dream in which her sister assures her that the gods will protect her son. The plot against Telemachus comes, I believe, from the Agamemnon-Orestes story pattern, which is ever on Homer's mind in these early books, and it is that pattern which interrupts the action at this point.

And here a question comes to mind, consideration of which may add further depth to our understanding of the first four books of the *Odyssey*. Telemachus is a parallel to Orestes, but he is also in part a parallel to his own father Odysseus, especially insofar as the Odysseus pattern coincides with the Agamemnon pattern. It is not mere chance that in Greek tragedy Orestes returns to Argos in disguise and tells a deceptive tale about his identity.[14] Here Orestes and Odysseus both share the same thematic complex, that is, that of return of the hero in disguise. It is a thematic complex fraught with latent mythic meanings, the disguise being the weeds of the other world which still cling to the hero; this complex is not merely narrative framework. Orestes' return is like Odysseus' return. There is trouble awaiting both. Telemachus as he returns circumspectly to Ithaca shares with Orestes and his father Odysseus the dangers of encounter with the forces of evil at home. At the other end of Telemachus' journey he has been given instructions in regard to Penelope, and he himself repeats them, instructions that mimic the counsel given by a departing husband on his way to war. "If I do not return, then go back to your father or marry again." On the journey Telemachus is honored as his father, and first Nestor, then Helen, and then Menelaus point out how strikingly like his father he is. The patterns of Odysseus, Telemachus, Agamemnon, and Orestes merge and separate and then merge again.

Homer begins the *Odyssey* again in Book 5. He has let Telemachus and Orestes get a little out of hand; he has enjoyed the story and the weaving of its telling. But he is aware that it has gone a little far. Facetiously we might say that he tricked himself by that initial speech of Zeus with its introduction of the Agamemnon parallel. So Homer takes up the story of the release of Odysseus by a return to the gods in council with Athena starting off as if she had never mentioned Odysseus to Zeus before. Zeus' reply is Homer chiding Homer:

"My child," replied the Gatherer of the Clouds, "I never thought to hear such words from you. Did you not plan the whole affair yourself? Was it not your idea that Odysseus should return and settle accounts with these men? As for Telemachus, you are well able to look after him: use your own skill to bring him back to Ithaca safe and sound, and let the Suitors sail home again in their ship with nothing accomplished" [15] (5.21–27).

At any rate we leave Agamemnon, Orestes, and Telemachus until Book 11, where Odysseus meets Agamemnon in the lower world, and inquires from his mother Anticlea about his son.

If the return of Agamemnon has been a potent influence in shaping the part of the *Odyssey* that concerns Telemachus, the return of Menelaus, narrated in *Nostoi*[16] and also in Book 4 of the *Odyssey,* has been effective in fashioning the Circe and Underworld episodes. Menelaus, it will be recalled, was detained on an island off the coast of Egypt waiting for favorable winds. He meets the daughter of Proteus, Eidothea, who advises him to question her father as to why he is kept from proceeding further with his ships. She tells him how to capture the old man of the sea. Proteus, when finally subdued, first answers Menelaus' questions as to who of the gods is keeping him in Egypt and what his homeward way is. After this Menelaus asks Proteus about the returns of the other heroes from Troy, and Proteus prophesies Menelaus' own future.

The points of coincidence of pattern with the story of Odysseus are clear: (1) Menelaus and Odysseus are both being detained on an island; (2) they are both advised by a supernatural female to seek information from an aged second-sighter; (3) there is a certain ritual to be gone through in order to get the seer to talk; (4) the seer tells them both why they are having difficulty with the immortals, how they can overcome these difficulties, and he prophesies the nature of the death of each.

Menelaus first asks Eidothea: "Rather tell me — for gods know all — which of the immortals chains me here and bars my progress; and tell me of my homeward way, how I may pass along the swarming sea" (4.379–381). In her advice about her father she says: "He would tell you of your course, the stages of your journey, and of your homeward way, how you may pass along the swarming sea. And he would tell you, heaven-descended man, if you desire, all that has happened at your home, of good or ill, while you have wandered on your long and toilsome way" (4.389–393). This last has more relevance to Odysseus, it will be noted, than it does to Menelaus. At the close of her instructions to Menelaus as to how to capture Proteus, Eidothea tells him: "Then, hero, cease from violence and set the old man free, but ask what god afflicts you, and ask about your homeward way, how you may pass along the swarming sea" (4.422–424). Menelaus' actual question to the captive Proteus is word-for-word the same as his original question to Eidothea, given above.

Odysseus on his part in Book 10 is told by Circe, when he asks her permission to return home, that he "must first perform a different journey, and go to the halls of Hades and of dread Persephone, there to consult the spirit of Teiresias of Thebes, the prophet blind, whose mind is steadfast still" (10.490–493). Odysseus objects and asks who will pilot them, and Circe gives full instructions which end: "Thither the seer will quickly come, O chief of men, and he will tell your course, the stages of your journey, and of your homeward way, how you may pass along the swarming sea" (10.538–540). Odysseus then tells his men that they are to leave, saying: "For potent Circe has at last made known to me the way" (10.549) — and later when they were mustered: "But Circe has marked out for us a different journey, even to the halls of Hades and of dread Persephone, there to consult the spirit of Teiresias of Thebes" (10.563–565). In the land of the dead, after the ritual, after talking with Elpenor, Teiresias comes up and speaks to Odysseus, without the latter asking him any questions (11.99).

It will be noted that the reason for the journey to the lower world to consult Teiresias is given only once, at the end of Circe's instructions about the ritual to be performed. Odysseus himself, incidentally, does not ask why he must go. The journey is imposed by Circe, not suggested as the consultation with Proteus is suggested by Eidothea. Hence one has the impression of a labor, like that of Heracles. In the case of Menelaus there is a plethora of questions and reasons for the journey. The closest version in the Menelaus passage (Book 4) to the words of Circe in Book 10 about inquiring concerning the journey home occurs at the close of Eidothea's first advice (not the ritual instructions) to Menelaus, in which she uses exactly the same words: "He would tell you of your course, the stages of your journey, and of your homeward way, how you may pass along the swarming sea" (4.389–390). And it is here that she adds . . . "and he would tell you, heaven-descended man, if you desire, all that has happened at your home, of good or ill, while you have wandered on your long and toilsome way" (4.391–393). This would have made sense in reference to Odysseus. Of the three questions which Odysseus might have been sent to ask, the three, indeed, that the seer answers without being asked, namely, (1) who of the gods is angry, (2) how can I get home, and (3) what is going on at home, only one is made explicit in the instructions. We know the others partly from the answers given by Teiresias and partly from the parallel with another multiform of the theme, the questioning of Proteus by Menelaus. Actually it would have been better on the part of the bard to let us infer from the answers what the questions to be asked were. The first question would not make much sense under the circumstances, because the only immortal holding Odysseus and his men back at this point seems to be Circe herself, and she will release them (if they go to Hades?). The second question would make sense if Teiresias really answered it, but he doesn't, and Odysseus gets the answer when he returns from Circe herself. In other words, the question which is really listed is not answered. And even if the third question had been asked, no one could have been less interested than Odysseus in the answer, to judge from his reaction to what Teiresias tells him of affairs at home. Odysseus says: "Teiresias, these are the threads of destiny the gods themselves have spun (referring to the prophecy of his own death). Nevertheless, declare me this, and plainly tell: I see the spirit of my dead mother here . . . (11.139–141). He completely ignores the information given him. This is in contrast to the weeping of Menelaus in the earlier passage.

From the parallel of the Menelaus-Proteus passage we understand why Teiresias gives the "replies" he does — to questions that are not asked. But we are still left with several difficult questions ourselves: (1) Why did Circe send him to consult Teiresias, if not to find out how to get home? (2) What is the role of Elpenor? (3) Why does Odysseus ignore the information about affairs at home? and (4) Why does his mother's account of things at home differ from that of Teiresias?

The parallel with Menelaus-Proteus may suggest an answer to the question of why Odysseus ignores Teiresias' information about things at home. The earlier passage has influenced the inclusion of this account in the speech of the seer, but it does not belong as things stand because it duplicates the questions and answers of Odysseus and his mother. (It contradicts them, too, of course.) In regard to this question and answer, in other words, Teiresias is a duplication of Odysseus' mother (or *vice versa?*). And note, please, that the account of affairs at Ithaca in that it describes an evil situation at home parallels the Agamemnon tale. Once again the Agamemnon pattern, with its Telemachus-Orestes correspondence, interrupts the story of Odysseus. Now, from the account of Ithacan affairs given by Anticleia, one would judge that Odysseus was not supposed to learn about the suitors from anyone in Hades. This part of the scene indicates either that there was no trouble at home, or else that Odysseus was to find out about it elsewhere. In the Dictys version, it is worth mentioning, he finds out about it from Telemachus, who meets him at Antenor's home! [17] We have several patterns conflicting at this point, each one contributing something to the story. Just as there were forms of the story in which Odysseus did not find out about the suitors from anyone in Hades, so there may well have been versions of the Return in which all was well at home and the wife was not besieged by suitors, as Anticleia's tale would seem to indicate. We are reminded that such versions are to be found in the Yugoslav tradition (see Appendix III, Parry 1920 and 6229).

The story of Menelaus may help us in other parts of our puzzle also. Elpenor has at least a partial counterpart in Nestor's tale of Menelaus' journey as related to Telemachus in Book 3. Thus: "Now as we came from Troy, the son of Atreus and myself set sail together full of loving thoughts; but when we were approaching sacred Sunion, a cape of Athens, Phoebus Apollo smote the helmsman of Menelaus and slew him with his gentle arrows while he held the rudder of the running ship within his hands. Phrontis it was, Onetor's son, one who surpassed all humankind in piloting a ship when winds were wild. So Menelaus tarried, though eager for his journey, to bury his companion and to pay the funeral rites" (3.276–285). This incident is like the death of another helmsman, even Tiphys in the Argonauts;[18] and all together are the ancestors of Palinurus in the *Aeneid* and a host of others. True, Elpenor is not a helmsman, and he is not buried until later. But the loss of a man who must be given burial rites, occurring in a story in which there are other more striking parallels, tends to confirm what we have said about the force of thematic correspondences.

Corroborative also is another detail from Menelaus' journeyings, this time as told by the hero himself in Book 4. After the prophecy of Proteus: "So back again to Egypt's waters, to its heaven-descended stream, I brought my ships and made the offerings due. And after appeasing the anger of the gods that live forever, I raised a mound to Agamemnon, that his fame might never die" (4.581–584). Thus also Odysseus and his men returned to Circe's island and there buried Elpenor with due ceremony and piled a mound for him, topped by the oar he pulled when alive.

Professor Whitman's analysis of Odysseus' *Adventures*[19] exhibits the kind of geometric scheme that he has found elsewhere in Homer, particularly in the *Iliad*. In it Elpenor frames the all-important central episode of the Journey to the Dead. The picture that emerges is neat, but a question arises when we consider the *connections* between the several parts. The implication of Whitman's scheme is that Homer had the pattern, CIRCE, Elpenor, NEKYIA, Elpenor, CIRCE in his mind and was fitting the events to this configuration. Are we to infer that Elpenor remains unburied so that Homer can fulfill his program of returning to Aeaea, to the Elpenor theme, and hence to Circe, purely for the aesthetic effect of geometric regularity? It does not seem likely that the force of the artistic pattern, *qua* artistic pattern, in a traditional oral song would be great enough in itself to cause either the placing or displacing of incidents. I doubt if the artistic pattern is dynamic to this degree and in this way. This is not to deny that such balances of pattern are felt by the singers — we have seen them operative on the level of interlinear connections, where they play a part in determining the position of words in a line and perhaps even thereby the choice of words. But to suppose that such patterns would be the cause of changes of essential idea and meaning may be carrying their influence too far.

There is real difficulty, I think, with understanding the role of Elpenor, unless we try to analyze his part in the story on the basis of the dynamic mythic patterns involved. Only these have the power needed. The difficulty begins when Elpenor is left unburied. The Menelaus pattern to which we referred above supplies room for the loss of a companion, but time is taken for burial. It may well be that the death of a companion in this configuration is sacrificial and a necessary element for the successful journey to the land of the dead. I think that in a sacrificial death, due burial would be expected, and thus it happens in the Menelaus pattern.

The Menelaus pattern, however, does not provide for the return of the hero to the woman who sends him into the other world to consult with a seer. We are left with one question for which no answer has been suggested: why did Circe send Odysseus to the Underworld? There are two parts to that question: why Circe? and why the Underworld?

The parallel with the Menelaus episode suggests that the excursion to the world of mystery belongs to the story pattern wherein the journey is planned or ordered by the daughter of a sage or sorcerer, herself a sorceress. Any hero who has been away a long period from home and returns is fit subject for the lower world journey, because he has already followed the pattern of the myth by reason of a long absence in the other world and a return to this. The journey to the Underworld is but a microcosm of the macrocosm. *Nostoi*,[20] we are told, also contained a visit to Hades — we do not know just where in *Nostoi* — a Hades that probably included Tantalus, hence of the old-fashioned kind similar to the end of the Underworld narrative in the *Odyssey*. Odysseus visited there a seer, one, indeed, whose death and burial are narrated in *Nostoi*.[21] There is no journey to the Underworld in Dictys, but it is related that Odysseus went to an island on which was a certain oracle and that the oracle answered his questions about everything except what happens to the souls of men in the hereafter. It is not recorded what the questions and answers were, nor where the oracle was. But the event occurred after his visit to Circe and Calypso, sisters who lived in Aulis, whose realms he visited in the order given, Circe's and then Calypso's. It is not said that Calypso sent him to the oracle; it is said rather "and then I came to an island. . . ."[22]

In these two sections we have seen how a knowledge of other traditional multiforms in the charged atmosphere of oral literature helps to explain the structure and even the "inconsistencies" of any given multiform. Just as any single return tale elaborated in Appendix III must be understood in terms of the others which surround it, and, in a real sense, are contained in it themselves, so the *Odyssey* must be read with an awareness of the multiforms operative in its own structure.

*   *   *

From the time that Odysseus leaves the farm with Eumaeus for his own house until the recognition of the wanderer by his wife, the singer of the *Odyssey* is elaborating the central and most vital portion of the return story. We shall shortly be concerned with the recognitions before the hero enters the town of Ithaca and after he has left it for his father's farm. Now let us examine the central core, which is to say, the recognition of Odysseus by his wife. At his home Odysseus is recognized by or revealed to a dog, a nurse, two farm hands, and his wife, in addition, of course, to the suitors. The dog recognizes him instinctively; the nurse knows him by the scar; the suitors find out about his identity by the trial of the bow; he tells the farm hands who he is. His wife recognizes him by three different methods: (a) by the trial of the bow, (b) by the bath,[23] and (c) by the token of the bed. Any one of these means would have been sufficient, but Homer, or the tradition before him, has woven them all together, making only the last final. The singer renders many lines of story before he finally reaches this recognition. Odysseus departs from the swineherd's hut and arrives at his own palace in the middle of Book 17, but recognition is consummated near the close of Book 23. It is, I believe, legitimate to ask why the narration takes so long, why the recognition is postponed several times, including a last minute delay while Odysseus bathes and his wife waits.

It should first be noted that there are two returns to the palace recorded here: that of Telemachus and that of Odysseus. The two returns are kept separate. That of Telemachus deserves special scrutiny. The opening scene of Book 17 (Telemachus asks Eumaeus to take the stranger, Odysseus, to the city to beg his living, while he, Telemachus goes ahead to tell his mother of his return) parallels in part the scene in Book 15 when Telemachus arrives on the shores of Ithaca and sends Peiraeus with Theoclymenus on to the city while he goes to Eumaeus' hut. In both passages Telemachus is sending to the city someone whom he has met before his own return to Ithaca, and this stranger is accompanied by a friend. These two scenes look like multiforms of the same theme, and it is not surprising that scholars[24] have sometimes thought that Theoclymenus is a duplication of Odysseus. The impression that this is so is strengthened when we see that Telemachus goes home and awaits the coming first of Theoclymenus and then of Odysseus. In fact, Book 17 begins with a twofold plan, the first part of which is concerned with Telemachus and the second with Odysseus. As at the beginning of the *Odyssey,* the first plan is followed, Telemachus goes home and the narrative continues with his return with Theoclymenus, and then the second plan, the return from the farm of Odysseus and Eumaeus, is fulfilled.

The parallel between these two plans in Book 17 and those set forth in Book 1 is made even more compelling by the similarity in the technique of moving from plan one to plan two in both parts of the song. In Book 4 Menelaus has concluded his account of his meeting with Proteus and has invited Telemachus to stay for a while with him, then he will send him forth with goodly gifts. Telemachus has requested him to let him go, and asks for some small gift rather than horses and chariot, and Menelaus has said he will give him a bowl of silver with a rim of gold. At this moment the singer says: "So they conversed together. But banqueters were coming to the palace of the noble king. Men drove up sheep, and brought the cheering wine, and their veiled wives sent bread. Thus they were busied with their dinner in the hall. Meanwhile before the palace of Odysseus the suitors were making merry, throwing the discus and the hunting spear upon the level pavement, holding riot as of old" (4.620–627).

Compare with this passage that in Book 17 which is the transition from Telemachus at home with Penelope and Theoclymenus to the suitors. Telemachus has reported to Penelope (and Theoclymenus) his conversation with Menelaus in Sparta; Theoclymenus has prophesied that Odysseus is already in Ithaca, when Penelope says with a sigh that she wishes this were so; if it were she would give him, Theoclymenus, many a gift. "So they conversed together. Meanwhile before the palace of Odysseus the suitors were making merry, throwing the discus and the hunting spear upon the level pavement, holding riot as of old" (17.166–169).[25]

The two passages given above are like watersheds between the plot of Telemachus' journey to the mainland and the suitors at home. On the other hand the subsequent passages about the suitors lead to, or are at the least themselves followed by, the narrative which directly concerns Odysseus. It is true that there is great difference in length between the passage about the suitors in Book 4 and that in Book 17; the former is over two hundred lines long and the latter less than twenty. Nevertheless, they have the same plot material before them, and the same after them.

The scene in Book 17 ending with the passage given above begins with the arrival of Telemachus at the palace of his father. Because this entire theme has affinities with the final recognition theme between Odysseus and Penelope in Book 23, we may learn something of importance by analyzing the theme in Book 17 and its earlier relatives. Let us first, however, note the points of similarity between the scene in Book 17 and that in Book 23, the goal of our present investigation. Telemachus returns to the palace and is greeted first by Eurycleia, then by the other maids, and after this his mother enters, greets him, and asks what he saw on his journey. At the end of Book 22, after the slaughter of the suitors, Odysseus talks with Eurycleia, has a fire lighted and the house fumigated, and next is greeted by the faithful maids; then Eurycleia, at the beginning of Book 23, goes and finally brings Penelope to meet Odysseus. Although the conversation between Eurycleia and Penelope is of some length and, therefore, has no parallel itself in the earlier passage, nevertheless, there is a similarity of pattern in the order of persons greeted. Father and son follow the same pattern, in the beginning of the two scenes.

In both these passages something strange happens after the entrance of Penelope. In Book 17 she asks, as we have seen, for a report from Telemachus. Instead of giving her a report, he tells her to take a bath, change, and pray to Zeus while her son goes to the market place to pick up a stranger to bring home for supper! Penelope does as he orders, he fetches Theoclymenus, they bathe and eat with Penelope nearby spinning. Finally she says that she is going to bed and she asks him for the report, stating that he had not dared to give it before because of the suitors — yet the suitors were not present at the time of his return. At any rate, now at last Telemachus tells his mother what he learned from Nestor and Menelaus.

So much at the moment for Book 17. In Book 23 at this point Penelope and Odysseus sit staring at one another until Telemachus upbraids his mother for not speaking to his father after so many years. Penelope says that she and Odysseus have ways of knowing one another; then he suggests that he and Telemachus carry out a ruse to protect them against the suitors' relatives. He takes a bath and then comes back to where Penelope is sitting patiently. There is clearly hugger-mugger of some sort at both these points! Penelope is kept waiting first for the report of her husband from her son and then for a report from her husband. In both passages the report is delayed by one or more baths, by the departure and return of the person who is to give the report.

Conversations between Telemachus and his mother (and it is a conversation of mother and son that is the focal point of the difficulty in both these passages) have had special significance since the very beginning of the song. It could also be said that the arrival of a stranger at the palace of Odysseus, or elsewhere, for that matter, has also been of significance from the opening of the *Odyssey*. Moreover, both a conversation between Telemachus and Penelope and the arrival of a stranger are frequently combined in the same scene. We are concerned with two of these scenes. Can other similar combinations give us any clues to the strange puzzles of this pair? What can other multiforms show us about the two in question?

Once again in connection with the beginning of Book 17 are we referred back to Book 1. In the first scene in Ithaca, the arrival of a stranger precedes rather than follows the conversation between Telemachus and Penelope, but both these elements are present. We are reminded by Telemachus' words to his mother when she complains about the bard's song that the son's role now is to give orders to his mother; for Athena has visited him, and the days of his maturity are at hand. In Book 1 as in Book 17 he orders Penelope to go upstairs; in both cases she obeys without a word. There is no meeting of mother and son between that in Book 1 and that in Book 17, but in Book 4 we note that when the news of Telemachus' absence is reported to Penelope, she is comforted by Eurycleia and then bathes, changes, goes to her upper chamber, and prays, this time to Athena. Although she does not talk with Telemachus between Book 1 and Book 17, she does enter the great hall once in Book 16 to rebuke Antinous for the plot to kill her son. Eurymachus swears falsely that no harm will come to Telemachus from the suitors; thereupon Penelope, without further word, returns to her chamber to weep for Odysseus — the same words being used here as in the passage in Book 1.

A pattern emerges, then, in which we see Penelope enter the scene to rebuke someone and to be herself in turn rebuked or ignored and, especially by her son, sent back to her room. For this reason we do not question Telemachus' sending her back to bathe and pray in Book 17; the sense of Penelope's theme is thus being carried out. This is what happened to her both times when she has appeared before. And it is in part what happens when we see her again in Book 18 after the match between Irus and Odysseus, when she comes into the hall and rebukes Telemachus for allowing a stranger to be badly treated. Telemachus corrects her; matters have turned out well for the stranger in this match. When Penelope enters again in Book 19, Telemachus has gone to bed, but by a sort of attraction there is rebuking in the scene that follows; the maid Melantho rebukes Odysseus and is rebuked in her turn by both Odysseus and Penelope. The pattern is kept with different actors. Whatever the logic of the situation, the sense of the patterns prepares us to accept Telemachus' rebuke of his mother's silence in Book 23. This has ever been the general tenor of their exchanges of words and, indeed, of most of the entrances of Penelope.

Such comparison with other appearances of a theme may show us in this case why we accept without much question the postponing of Telemachus' report to Penelope, and it is possible that the habit of a pattern may have caused such an illogical situation in the narrative. But it is not enough here, because Homer has himself given a reason, although late, for the postponement, namely that the suitors were present and their presence deterred Telemachus. Perhaps Homer thought that it was clear that hostile people were on the scene when Telemachus was greeted by Penelope. It is more likely that Telemachus' story had to be saved until Theoclymenus was present. The preserving of smaller habitual patterns has helped to gloss over or to make palatable to the hearer a breaking, or at least mingling of larger patterns. Theoclymenus is a nuisance, a disturbing influence, yet Homer insists on him.

When Athena at the beginning of Book 15 appears to Telemachus in Sparta, urging him to return home, she makes no mention of this hitchhiker, but she advises Telemachus to leave his ship before it reaches the city and to spend a night at Eumaeus' hut, sending the swineherd ahead to tell Penelope that he has returned safe and sound. This is not what happens. It is clear by now, I believe, that we are dealing with a song that is a conflation, an oral conflation, I maintain, of a number of versions of the return song. Formula analysis of a passage is useful in establishing the orality of a text, in textual criticism, and in poetic evaluation. The study of thematic repetitions, as we have just seen, also helps to establish orality; to confirm textual readings; in limited ways to explain structural patterns; to provide the aura around the theme which corresponds to that around a formula. As units of composition, formula and theme are as indispensable to the scholar as they are to the singer. Yet we have, I think, demonstrated that there is a class of problems that can be answered only by reference to a multiple-text study like that in the appendix — in other words, by awareness of the multiplicity of versions in and around songs belonging to an oral tradition.

The singer begins in Book 17 to follow a pattern of the return of Telemachus that is correct for a Telemachus (or anyone else) returning home with a report, provided there is no Theoclymenus who should be either with him or at someone else's house. Similarly, in Book 23 the singer is following a pattern that is perfectly all right if there were no Telemachus in the hall with Odysseus when Penelope entered. Other factors are involved in both these cases, but part of the difficulty is that the patterns are suitable for simple not for complex situations; for straight-line versions rather than for mixed versions.

But, if I am not mistaken, it is not merely that two themes have been juxtaposed, or that one was started and then interrupted by another. It seems that themes have been telescoped together in a distinctive way. Telemachus' report is postponed; what takes its place is a different thematic complex beginning with the arrival of the stranger and his entertainment. The stranger has news of Odysseus also, and this fact links the two themes, the theme of Telemachus' report and that of Theoclymenus. The two reports are juxtaposed, that of Telemachus which is the tale of Menelaus; that of Theoclymenus, which is the prophecy of a seer. This is one way of looking at the telescoping, but it does not provide a motive strong enough for such radical countering of logic as Telemachus' lack of response to his mother's first question. Suppose, however, that the Theoclymenus episode were really the arrival of Odysseus disguised as Theoclymenus, with Penelope wishing to ask him about Odysseus. We have a hint of something of this sort with Mentes in Book 1, when it is suggested that if he had only stayed he might have given information about Odysseus. The Yugoslav parallels would support such a supposition very strongly.[26] But this version simply cannot stand with one in which an Odysseus is already on his way to town or about to leave for town with Eumaeus. What are telescoped together, then, are not a report of Telemachus and a prophecy, but a report of Telemachus and a deceptive story by Odysseus. There seems to be evidence, in other words, of a version in which Telemachus met his father at Pylos and returned with him, and another version in which he met Odysseus at Eumaeus' hut. They have been put together in oral tradition as we have it in this song of Homer's. The result is duplication often with one element in the duplication being vestigial or partial, and hence an apparent postponement and suspense, or an inconsistency.

Duplication or repetition is a characteristic of the portion of the song we are now analyzing. For example, there are repeated buffetings and insulting of Odysseus. Blows begin when he is on the road to the palace with Eumaeus and they are joined by the goatherd Melanthius, who abuses Odysseus with words and then kicks him on the hip, after he has prophesied that "many a footstool from men's hands flying around his head his ribs shall rub, as he is knocked about the house" (17.231–232). This pattern is indeed found again in Book 17 when Antinous insults Odysseus as he begs food from him and the suitor hurls a footstool at him. Near the close of Book

18 the same theme occurs again. Eurymachus abuses Odysseus and hurls a footstool at him, missing him, but striking the right hand of the wine-pourer. And at line 284 of Book 20 the theme is introduced with the same words as the quarrel with Eurymachus: "Yet Athena allowed the haughty suitors not altogether yet to cease from biting scorn. She wished more pain to pierce the heart of Laertes' son, Odysseus." Ctesippus now taunts the hero and throws an ox-hoof at him. It misses him and strikes the wall. These actions all incur rebuke: Melanthius is rebuked by the swineherd, Antinous by the suitors, Eurymachus by Telemachus, and Ctesippus also by Telemachus. These incidents are multiforms of a single theme four times repeated, whose meaning, deeply bedded in the myth underlying the story, is that the resurrected god in disguise is rejected by the unworthy, who cannot recognize him. These episodes are actually testings.

The boxing match with Irus in Book 18 is a different kind of incident. It is a set contest between the representative or champion of the suitors and Odysseus, and its parallel is to be found in the trial of the bow! Odysseus in reality abandons his disguise in both scenes. For the boxing match Athena fills out his limbs and men wonder; Irus quakes and wants to run away. Here is a frustrated, a vestigial recognition scene brought about by accomplishing a feat of strength possible only to the returned hero. The match follows after the scene in which Penelope summons Eumaeus, asking him to bring the beggar to her so that she may question him about Odysseus; she has heard of his being struck by Antinous. Proceeding in the reverse order, we begin with (a) the abuse of Odysseus by Antinous, (b) rebuke by the suitors, (c) Penelope tries to meet Odysseus but is put off, and (d) vestigial recognition scene in the match with Irus. We can begin the pattern again with (a) the abuse by Eurymachus, (b) the rebuke by Telemachus, (c) Odysseus and Telemachus remove the armor from the hall, and (d) the recognition scene with Eurycleia. If we begin a third time, we have (a) the abuse by Ctesippus, (b) the rebuke by Telemachus, (c) Theoclymenus' prophecy of doom, the abuse of him, and his departure, and (d) the trial of the bow and recognition. This thrice-repeated general pattern is strengthened even more by the realization that in Book 17 (a) the abuse of Odysseus by Melanthius is followed by (b) the rebuke by Eumaeus, and (d) the recognition by the dog Argus! The third element in this pattern is variable, but the other three elements are clear: abuse, rebuke, "x," recognition.

Now the trial of the bow brings about the revelation of Odysseus to the farm hands and then to all else. The tale proceeds untroubled until line 58 of Book 23, when to our amazement (and that of Eurycleia as well) Penelope still has doubts. Thus what might have been the first recognition by Penelope, that of the trial of the bow, ceases to be a recognition and becomes only one link in a chain of evidence. When she descends to see her son, the suitors who are dead, and him who slew them — as she herself says — it is her first appearance since the setting of the trial by the bow. As she descends she even debates within her heart whether she should question Odysseus apart or whether she should rush to him as to her husband. We may wonder whether Homer is himself debating this question. At any rate, we find that a scene that begins to lead toward recognition is sidetracked into plans for safety following the slaying of the suitors, plans concocted by Odysseus and Telemachus while Penelope, as it were, "stands by."

Loosely associated with these plans is a bath taken by Odysseus. This bath has caused Homerists much trouble;[27] for Penelope simply, it seems, waits for Odysseus' return, their recognition scene being suddenly postponed again in a most brutal way. It is the second time at least (the first being the refusal of Odysseus to go to Penelope's chamber) that poorly motivated postponement has occurred. The bath belongs in the tale of the return — it surely has ritual significance. Even on the most realistic grounds it should be required after the grime and blood of the slaughter. Eurycleia urged a change of clothes on Odysseus earlier, right after the slaughter, at the end of Book 22, which Odysseus refused, thus putting off the doffing of his disguise until the scene with Penelope. This earlier reference makes one suspect that the placing here by Homer may be deliberate. He indicated that he had a choice — as he does fairly frequently. The bath cannot be delayed any longer; it must come before Odysseus and Penelope begin to speak in earnest about the signs which they alone understand.

It seems to me that the singer was about to embark on the final recognition scene between husband and wife — Penelope will know him when he emerges from the bath without disguise, whether the bath was taken before she came on the stage or while she waited — when he was once again turned from it by Telemachus material. Yet the ingredients of the "second" recognition by Penelope (the trial by the bow being the first) stay in place, namely, there is conversation about the state of his clothes, he bathes, he emerges in bright glory. This recognition also then has become another link in the chain of evidence, and the final recognition now follows immediately. Although it would seem that Penelope has not moved from her chair in the hall, one might argue that she now "appears" again on the stage of the singer's and hearer's attention. And this will be her final appearance in the song.

Just as the accumulating of disguises emphasizes by duplication the force of the testing of recognition, so the threefold recognition by Penelope, the last following the ritual cleansing and loss of the traces of death, leaves no doubt of the importance of this element in the story. Logical inconsistency there may be, but there is no mythic ambiguity. The conflation in oral tradition has resulted in increased power of the myth.

In terms of mythic meanings the coming of age of Telemachus is emphasized by his journey and its success, by the presence of a god on his side, ultimately by his ability to draw the bow of Odysseus, if it were not that he was restrained by his father. We tend to forget that Penelope tells us that Odysseus had instructed her to wait until Telemachus' beard grew before she remarried. The dramatic piling up of evidence of Telemachus' change to manhood stresses the fact that the time for remarriage has come. It is the last moment for Odysseus' return. In the myth of death and resurrection the darkest hour of devastation is at hand, and the return of the dying god, still in the weeds of the other world of deformity but potent with new life, is imminent.

*   *   *

The inner logic of the tale of Odysseus makes it impossible that the story could be stopped at line 296 of Book 23. I do not believe in interpolators any more than I believe in ghosts, even less, but had Homer not continued beyond that point, someone would have had to or the narrative would have remained unfinished.

The first section of this "continuation" really contains no difficulty, and Page[28] seems to me to be entirely correct when he says that were it not for the Alexandrians this passage would not have come under question. Such résumés are perfectly normal in oral poetry, and numerous examples can be found.[29]

The second scene of the continuation (23.344–the end; 24.205–411), the recognition of the returned hero by his parent, in the case of the *Odyssey*, his father, is a well-established element in the general story of return. Whatever the reason may be, the hero has one surviving parent at home; the other is dead. In the Yugoslav variants outlined in Appendix III, it is invariably the mother who is alive, and only once (Parry 1939) is the father even mentioned in the early part of the story, only to be quite forgotten later. The mother usually dies after the recognition takes place and is duly buried by her son. It is not surprising that the Yugoslav songs have chosen the mother rather than the father to be the surviving parent, since she plays a much larger role in Yugoslav poetry than does the father. For some reason the return of the hero is associated with the death of one of the characters in his immediate circle upon recognition. (In the case of the *Odyssey* it is the dog Argus who dies when he recognizes his master; in the Yugoslav songs it is the mother!) Recognition by a parent is a necessary element in the story and a regularly recurring part of the theme of recognitions.

It is not the recognition itself, then, which causes trouble in the *Odyssey*, but its *position* in the poem. That its place after the recognition by Penelope is not governed by rational or sentimental reasons is clear. Eumaeus told Odysseus straightway about his father's situation. They are already outside of town, and nothing would seem easier than for Odysseus to relieve his father's distress by going at once to him. This might have involved an earlier recognition by Eumaeus, but there seems to be no earthly reason why this would have done any harm, since Eumaeus has been proved loyal. Obviously the oral poet is not motivated by such considerations of reasoning. This approach is clearly not productive.

The order of recognitions in the Yugoslav songs in our chart gives support to the placing of the recognition by the parent after that by the wife. In the ten songs in which the parent is mentioned, only once does the recognition by the mother occur before that by the wife, although in one case it is ambiguous. In six of these instances the mother recognizes her son immediately after the wife. There seems then to be reason to believe that the singer of the *Odyssey* was following a common practice in the order of recognitions in respect to that of wife, parent. In these songs, of course, the mother is in the same physical place, in the same house with the wife, but in the classical Christian Yugoslav song of *The Captivity of Janković Stojan*,[30] the mother is out in the vineyard, and the hero goes to her after the recognition by the wife and the settlement with the suitor. In the *Odyssey*, once Odysseus has gone to town, the recognition with Laertes can take place only after affairs have been settled in the city.

The objection that the structure of the scene of recognition itself is faulty because it is so long drawn out has no basis in the logic of oral epic. The lengthy deceptive story may seem merciless to us, but it is so integral a part of the recognition scene, particularly of one so elaborately told as this, that it would have been illogical to omit it. Anyone versed in recognition scenes would scarcely think to question it. In the Yugoslav material (see Appendix III) the deceptive tale told to the mother is even more merciless, for she hears that her son is dead and buried and that the man before her was an eye-witness of that death and the instrument of the burial. She has not even hope. The son leaves her and reveals himself to others before he gives any alleviation of his mother's grief. Whatever the reason may be for the deceptive story in return songs, it is so much part of the thematic complex, that we should not label as faulty any recognition scene in which it occurs. It is natural and right in that context.

In spite of all this, there is something wrong with this scene from the point of view of oral epic. Equally as important as the deceptive story is the element of disguise. Indeed the deceptive story makes no sense without the disguise. Salih Ugljanin felt so strongly about this that he stopped in the middle of his song and sang it over again from the point at which he had told of his hero donning the armor of a guard whom he had killed. When Odysseus left his palace he put on his own splendid armor! The only kind of recognition scene which could have been used after this (unless Laertes was blind, which he was not) was the variety in which the hero comes up and says, "Here I am, your son is back." But the elaborate recognition by scar and trees depends on disguise and is associated with deceptive story.

That the recognition by Laertes belongs earlier, before Odysseus has changed his disguise, even before he went into town, is indicated in the beginning of the scene. When he accosts his father, Odysseus pretends that he has just arrived in the island and inquires if he is really in Ithaca and if the old man knows anything about a friend of his named Odysseus. Although there is logically no objection to these questions as they are and where they stand, they would certainly be as well situated earlier in the song, soon after Odysseus' arrival in Ithaca, even better placed indeed. It seems most likely, therefore, that a multiform of the recognition theme designed for one place has been transferred to a position normally taken by another multiform of the theme. Thus an inconsistency has arisen. We have observed this kind of shift in the Yugoslav songs and know it to be not uncommon in oral epic.

Homer does his best as always to gloss this over. Odysseus tells Telemachus, "But I will put my father to the proof, and try if he will recognize and know me by the sight, or if he will fail to know me who have been absent long" (24.216–218). He also disposes of his weapons (but not his armor) before he goes to meet his father. He is hesitant whether to go straight to his father and tell him directly of his return to Ithaca. These bits make me strongly suspect that Homer was aware of the difficulty, but that the traditional recognition scene with Laertes could not be eschewed.

We have seen that Homer probably had authority for the position of the recognition by the parent following that of recognition by the wife. This undoubtedly facilitated the shift. But there was also authority for meeting and even recognition by parent and son earlier in the song. At least one of the Yugoslav songs shows the order of mother, wife, rather than the reverse. In Volume I, No. 4, the mother is among the first to recognize her son, and her death and burial occur before the recognition by the wife. It will be noted, moreover, that in these songs, whatever the order of the recognitions, the mother is among the very first whom the son meets on his return and to whom he tells the deceptive story. Recognition comes only after an interval. There is, then, good authority for the earlier position of this theme, at least for the encounter and the deceptive story; but also for the recognition itself.

If we have information to show us that the scene is really out of place (provided one can use this term in discussing oral epic), we ought to have some basis also for hazarding an opinion as to where the scene would have been "in place." There are, I think, three points at which it might well have occurred, in two of which at least Homer himself indicates that he was about to embark upon a scene with Laertes but gave it up. We can learn much about the structure of the *Odyssey* as oral epic by examining these three passages.

The first is toward the end of Book 15, after line 389. In Book 14 Odysseus was received by Eumaeus; he told his deceptive tale, tested Eumaeus, and found him both good and loyal. As Book 14 closes, we could expect either a recognition of Odysseus by Eumaeus or the meeting of Odysseus with another person whom he tests with the deceptive story. Both patterns we can find in our Yugoslav material. Instead of either of these, however, we are directed to Sparta with Athena and Telemachus. The pattern is interrupted by the return to the Telemachus thread in the poem. The return to this thread here may have been made easier by the fact that one of our expectations is of another meeting and deceptive story. In Book 15, line 301, while Telemachus is on his voyage home, we are back with Odysseus in Eumaeus' hut. Odysseus turns the conversation to affairs in the palace in town and asks about his father and mother. Eumaeus tells him about them. Here, at line 389, I think, we are ready for the expedition with Eumaeus to Laertes' farm for the recognition with the father. But the flow is interrupted again by Eumaeus' tale of his own life, which lasts late into the night. This tale, if I read the signs correctly, should be part of a recognition scene between Eumaeus and Odysseus. We saw that the stage had already been set for this recognition before the interlude with Telemachus in Sparta. We have examples in the Yugoslav material in which the recounting of how someone came to know the hero or his family is part of a recognition theme leading to the question, "By what means would you recognize him if he were to appear?" [31] Eumaeus' tale, then, may be a fragment of a recognition scene that is never completed, but is attracted to this position because such a scene is expected here. Moreover, it is also the kind of tale that Odysseus might tell as a deceptive story, another part, as we know, of the recognition complex. From this point of view it might be said to take the place of the deceptive story to Laertes, which could have come at this point. Surely at the end of Eumaeus' story (line 495) we might have gone on to the Laertes recognition scene on the following day.

But once again the Telemachus thread interrupts, and instead of the recognition scene with Laertes we have one with Telemachus. The pattern is kept, but Telemachus has taken Laertes' place and the singer has again postponed the recognition with the parent! In other words, by this point, Eumaeus' recognition has been twice postponed and so has the recognition with Laertes. In each case the interruption has been caused by the Telemachus part of the story: at the end of Book 14 and at 15.495 for Eumaeus; at 15.389 and 495 for Laertes. The first interruption may contain a vestigial recognition scene (or at least the deceptive story part of it, including disguise) between Telemachus and Theoclymenus-Odysseus; the second interruption is a full-fledged recognition. By these maneuvers the first recognition remains that between Odysseus and his son.

What an amazing feat of construction. How cleverly indeed have the two threads been woven together! Telemachus and Odysseus have met and recognition has taken place. Homer and the singers of ancient Greece (for we have no proof that Homer did this himself, but must realize the probability that this was the way he heard the story) have accomplished the masterly interweaving of plots by following the lead of the elementary forces in the story itself!

The last opportunity for the recognition by Eumaeus and by Laertes before the whole party goes to town comes in Book 16 at line 298, after the recognition by Telemachus. At this point the singer shows his awareness of the possibility and excludes it once and for all. Odysseus instructs Telemachus not to tell Laertes, nor the swineherd, nor anyone else until they have sounded them out, although he suggests that they might make trial of some of the men. Telemachus objects even to this. At line 456, just before Eumaeus' return from town, Athena transforms Odysseus into a beggar again, and the singer comments: "for fear the swineherd looking in his face might know, and go and tell the tale to steadfast Penelope, not holding fast the secret in his heart" (16.457–459). At this point Homer is clearly and consciously following a pattern that will have the recognitions by the swineherd and the father later in the song.

There are two matters worthy of notice in connection with this final opportunity for Laertes' recognition of his son. At the time when Telemachus arrives and sends Eumaeus to town to tell his mother that he is safely back (thus, incidentally, duplicating the messenger sent from the ship to tell Penelope the news), Eumaeus suggests that he stop by the farm on his way and inform Laertes of his grandson's safety. Telemachus hinders him from this and states that the best news to tell the old man and anyone else would be that his father has returned. Laertes is certainly on the singer's mind.

The second valuable clue is in Odysseus' suggestion that they sound out some of the men, the suggestion voted down by Telemachus. By rejecting the recognition of Laertes the singer has also rejected the possible assistance of certain minor characters scarcely noticed in reading the poem, namely the old man Dolius and his sons, who are actually the last people to recognize Odysseus. It may be pure speculation, but it is possible that Eumaeus is a duplication of the group of Laertes, Dolius, et al., or that in some songs of the tradition we would find him either completely absent or a member of that group. By having him as a separate figure, the singer is forced later to associate the neatherd with him. There are real signs of the traditional, oral combining and recombining of configurations in this part of the *Odyssey* as elsewhere. Certainly if any scene in the poem is a part of it, that scene is the recognition of Laertes. We have no less an authority than Homer himself, as well as Greek tradition, and the whole tradition of the Return since Homer's day.

Having investigated the question of where the scene might have been, there being doubt that as constituted it is in its "proper" place, we must now consider why it is where it is. Actually, it has been put at one of the most significant places in the story. After the recognition by the wife and the essential remarriage and the settlement of affairs with the suitors, as represented at least by their slaying, Odysseus, or the returned hero, must depart from home. Teiresias has told Odysseus this in the Underworld, and Odysseus has just told Penelope that this is his fate. The *Telegony* takes Odysseus, after the burial of the suitors by their kinsmen, first to inspect his herds in Elis, then to Thesprotis, and after each of these journeys back again to Ithaca, where he is finally killed by Telegonus. We are told that when Odysseus returned from Elis he performed the "sacrifices ordered by Teiresias," action which does not gibe very well with what we know of Teiresias' instructions from the *Odyssey* (although all we learn about what happened in Elis is that he was entertained by Polyxenus and received a mixing bowl as a gift, and that the story of Trophonius and Agamedes and Augeas followed).[32] But that is in the *Telegony*. It helps to show that Greek epic tradition relates that Odysseus did continue his travels. They are, however, ignored by Dictys.

At this point in the Yugoslav songs the hero returns to his former captor. The recognition scene, which involves a *departure* from home and a *return* to the country, has been placed where a departure and return occur in the Yugoslav material, and where a departure is found in the *Telegony*. *The Captivity of Janković Stojan* tells of a departure to the vineyard where the hero had first met his mother, although there is no return to captor. In this song a substitution has taken place; return to vineyard is substituted for return to captor. The essence of departure and return is kept. In the *Telegony* the journey to Thesprotis, at least, seems also to be a return. The deceptive story told to Eumaeus (Book 14) and to Penelope (Book 19) tells of Odysseus in that land. Visiting the herds in Elis may be parallel to the visit to Laertes' farm.

But the references to herds in Elis, to Proxenus, and to the story of Trophonius seem to be of special interest. A glance at the article on Proxenus (3) and (4) in Pauly-Wissowa[33] is sufficient to assure one that all these elements are in some way connected with the lower world and with chthonic cult. Thesprotis too in Epirus is distinguished by the river Acheron, a well-known entrance to the Underworld, and the gateway to Dodona. The *Telegony* provides evidence, therefore, that Odysseus not only went on further travels but that those further travels were somehow connected with the other world from which he had just come. Everything in oral tradition points to the conclusion that at this moment in the story of

Odysseus' return there should be departure from Penelope and another visit to that strange world from which the hero had been rescued or released. The journey out to the country to Laertes' farm for the recognition with the hero's parent suits the requirement of departure from Penelope and, perhaps, a mild idea of return in the fact that he had come into town from the country.

The singer is, to be sure, not satisfied with this substitute. As soon as Odysseus and Telemachus have set out from town, the singer lets them go their way, and the story continues without them in that strange puzzle that is the Second Nekyia (Book 24.1–204). In some form or other a journey to the other world belongs, and is in fact required, here, as we have seen above. The pull of the significant pattern is strong. Whatever problems the present form of the Underworld journey in the last book of the *Odyssey* poses for us (and they are many and not to be ignored), however abrupt its introduction here, and the return to the Laertes scene when this passage is completed, the forces that hold together a song in oral tradition demand that some such journey occur at this moment in the tale. If there is any passage that could be termed "out of place" in the ending of the *Odyssey* it is not the Second Nekyia.

The first difficulty brought forth in the passage itself is that Hermes Psychopompos is not found elsewhere in Homer and is hence unhomeric, in fact not at home in Greek epic. We cannot take this too seriously, I think. Actually we have two songs. Anyone acquainted with traditional material can realize how infinitesimal a part of any tradition are two texts, no matter how long and how rich. True, souls go to the Underworld fairly frequently in the Homeric poems and Hermes might have been introduced to conduct them, but he is not. It seems to me that there is something special about this particular departure of souls on their journey to Hades that requires someone as companion if not guide for them, something special that does not occur elsewhere in Homeric song.

The journeyer in this case should have been Odysseus; for there is some reason to think that he was supposed to bring these suitors back as ransom or sacrifice or for purification. The Yugoslav patterns at this point in the story help us in suggesting this possibility (see Appendix III). In them the hero is released for ransom and he always returns with it to his captor. In some cases the ransom is the head of his wife's suitor, in at least one case it is his son, often it is one or more other heroes or their horses or weapons, which are but substitutes for them. Yet Odysseus, unlike the Yugoslav heroes, cannot make this journey. For one thing, he is busy elsewhere. But the feeling is strong that there must be someone at their head, and Hermes is a good choice. Was it not he who brought the message from Zeus to Calypso releasing him from the other world? Was not Hermes involved in some way with his coming back into the world of reality?

It is also objected that the geography of the journey is peculiar and unlike that of other Homeric journeys, or references to such, to the lower world, with the exception, at least, of Ocean Stream. I submit that the geography here is especially fitting for Odysseus. At least it takes the suitors off in the direction of Thesprotis, whence Odysseus pretended he had come and whither the *Telegony* says he later went. For Hermes guides the suitors from Ithaca across the Ocean, past Leucas to the Gates of the Sun, which is to say to the entrance to the lower world. With all that has been written about Leucas,[34] I cannot understand Page's rhetorical question: "Who ever heard, before or since, of a Rock Leucas, or White Rock, near the entrance to Hades across the river Oceanus?"[35] The river Oceanus is where you want it to be, it seems to me, and if you are in Ithaca, or anywhere else in Greece, it is not far away, unless you want it to be, of course.[36] The Island or promontory of Leucas, noted for its white rock from which human sacrifice was made for purification or to appease Apollo, as any traveler knows, is across a narrow strait from Corcyra, not far north of Ithaca. The White Rock is a clue not merely geographically but also ideologically to this journey; it indicates, I believe, the nature of the slaughter of the suitors, as sacrifice or purification for Odysseus. As for its being near the entrance to Hades, one needs only to look again at the map to see that it is not far south of Thesprotis and the river Acheron; indeed, for anyone going there from Ithaca, it is right on the road. This is, in short, another version of the journey of Odysseus to Thesprotis, exactly what one might expect to find just at this point.

It would be wrong to leave any discussion of the Second Nekyia without referring to the likelihood that both its position and its content — and perhaps its very existence — are due to the parallel with the Agamemnon type of return story, which we have noted as being often on Homer's mind in the dictating of the *Odyssey*. We know from the *Nostoi* that there was a descent to the land of Hades[37] and we have assumed that it was made by one of the heroes in his wanderings before returning home. Is it possible that the journey to the Underworld in the *Nostoi* occurred at the end and that the traveler was Agamemnon after his murder, or since we do not know whether Orestes' vengeance was included in the *Nostoi,* might the traveler have been Aegisthus himself? If the parallel is still operating here, then not only the Second Nekyia but also the final reconciliation at the close of the *Odyssey* is not merely the tying together of loose threads but as necessary a conclusion of the feud as either the murder of Aegisthus by Orestes or the final placating of the Furies. Viewed from this light these final sections of the *Odyssey* are inevitable because of the influence of the related pattern of the Orestes story.

On the level of myth the existence of these two parallel Returns, both in the same song, but also in the same tradition, must give us pause. They are contradictory. One of them would seem to be the return from the other world to set aright devastation at home, to bring new life, to be ever repeated, the myth of death and resurrection, the other a myth of return to death, of tragedy and annihilation, demanding righteous vengeance, the inexorability of original sin, as exemplified in the curse on the House of Atreus. Yet the coupling of two such contradictory patterns, the one concerned with life and the other with death, should not amaze us. They are complementary, not contradictory.

CHAPTER NINE

THE ILIAD

The essential pattern of the *Iliad* is the same as that of the *Odyssey;* they are both the story of an absence that causes havoc to the beloved of the absentee and of his return to set matters aright.[1] Both tales involve the loss of someone near and dear to the hero (Patroclus and Odysseus' companions); both contain the element of disguise (the armor in the *Iliad*);[2] in both is the return associated with contests or games and followed by re-marriage (Achilles with Briseis, Odysseus with Penelope), and, finally, in both a long period of time is supposed to elapse, or to have elapsed.

The story of the Trojan War is a simple one of bride-stealing and rescue. It belongs primarily to Menelaus, Paris, and Helen, and might have re-mained uncomplicated even if the struggle did call forth the armada of Achaeans and a host of Trojan allies. But bride-stealing in epic was mythic before it became heroic and historical. The rape of Persephone in all its forms as a fertility myth underlies all epic tales of this sort, and until the historical is completely triumphant over the mythic, all such tales are likely to be drawn into the pattern of the myth.

I believe that it was the element of the length of the Trojan War, itself apparently an historical fact, which drew unto its story the bride-stealing theme. Once thus sanctified, the war became the setting for tales of absence and return, the mythic death and resurrection, associated with fertility myth and ritual. The story of Odysseus is one form of these tales; that of Achilles is another. In the former the length of time causes no difficulty (even though it is doubled by the addition of another form of the story, a form involving wanderings), because the lapse of time coincides with the absence from home. In the *Iliad* the length of the war is not conceived of as coincident with the absence of Achilles from battle. The reason for this is that the death of the substitute for Achilles, Patroclus, is stressed in the *Iliad,* whereas it is only vestigial in the *Odyssey;* Anticleia's role in the narrative is unimportant, yet her counterparts in the Yugoslav tradition are kept even to this day (see Appendix III).

The story pattern of the god who dies, wanders for a period of time in the other world, and then returns, requires the element of length of time because this element has seasonal significance. It is kept and stressed in heroic tales that follow this pattern, such as the *Odyssey*. But the death of the substitute is final unless he is considered to be wandering in the lower world in need of rescue, in which case we enter into another complex of themes of search and rescue, the complex in which the Telemachus part of the *Odyssey* belongs. In these cases, however, the substitute is not really a substitute but a form of the god himself. The substitute is a ritual figure, a sacrifice, and his story is terminated by his death. With this ritual figure the element of length of time has no meaning; his absence is forever. Even when the human substitute is really killed or really dies (rather than simply being lost or wandering) and is sought and found in the lower world by a loved one, he cannot be brought back. And if he returns, as significantly enough Patroclus does,[3] it can be only as a ghost or in a dream.

The emphasis on the death of the substitute, Patroclus, in the *Iliad*, in the framework of a story of absence and return, has deprived that story of the element of length of absence. Yet the element is kept as vestigial. It belongs to the story of the war, and hence events are told that we should expect to find at the beginning of the war and not in its tenth year; it belongs with the story of Achilles' absence, the duration of which, together with the duration of the war, has been telescoped into a much shorter period of time. In the Dictys version, in which the death of Patroclus occurs long before Achilles' withdrawal, point is made of two truces, one of two months' and the other of six months' duration, between the withdrawal of Achilles and his return to battle.[4] In the *Iliad*, the story of the substitute's death has been placed at the point of return, and so the entire tale of the war thus far is concentrated between Achilles' withdrawal and return.

Thus in Book II when Agamemnon makes trial of the army we are in the last year of the war, but when the army reassembles and we enter into the Catalogues, a theme properly belonging to the beginning of the war, but yet not out of place here either, we find ourselves in a series of events that are logical only or chiefly in the beginning, but questionable after nine years of fighting. Helen's pointing out the Greek leaders to Priam is scarcely sensible if the Greeks have been battling before his eyes for nine years. The single combat between Paris and Menelaus in which Menelaus claims the victory and nearly ends the war is surely better placed somewhere nearer its beginning. Zeus' plan as just announced is not working out very well, but this is because the events immediately following its announcement really belong earlier.

It is true that we might explain the presence of these incidents merely by saying that Homer went off the track in the reassembly theme and inadvertently went back to the beginning of the war. We might argue that in his desire to lengthen the story he has included everything he knew of the war up to this point. Such an argument and such an explanation would be consistent with oral composition. The trial of the troops and the reassembly are bound together by association of themes. The assembly and the single combat are also bound together by association. The singer has unwittingly, or wittingly, modulated backward. All this is true. But I believe that there is a more significant reason for the return to the beginning. This material belongs with the story and is fitting. It is not mere background, not a scenic and artistic backdrop for the staging of the tale of Achilles. It has meaning in the larger tale of the war and in the tale of Achilles' absence, the kind of essential meaning that makes epic song effective and draws multiforms together into a concentrate.

The events leading up to the wrath of Achilles in Book I follow a pattern similar to that of the poem itself. The daughter of Chryses is captured and given to Agamemnon; her father seeks her release, offering ransom; Agamemnon refuses the offer and sends Chryses away. Chryses prays to Apollo; the plague is sent; Agamemnon returns the girl to her father. Interlocking with the last theme, the pattern begins again in another form: Agamemnon's concubine is taken from him with the consent of the Achaeans and under the protection of Achilles; Agamemnon asks them to replace her with another as his due; they refuse, and, following his prerogative, he takes Achilles' concubine. With the appeasing of Agamemnon the first repetition of the pattern seems to be broken, but in reality the refusal of the Achaeans leads to the quarrel between Agamemnon and Achilles (parallel to the plague, in the pattern). Thus, whereas from one point of view the taking of Briseis satisfies Agamemnon's anger (parallel to the return of Chryseis), from another point of view the acknowledgment of error by Agamemnon and the embassy mark, or should mark, the end of trouble, corresponding also to the last scene of the pattern, the return of Chryseis.

The difference of the working out of the basic pattern in these two cases is caused by the fact that in the first instance Apollo is a god who must be appeased when wronged or hurt, but in the second instance Agamemnon, divine king though he be, cannot really demand restitution when hurt, especially when that hurt is the result of an offense against the god. The story pattern fits the actions of a god, but when a mortal replaces the god, the pattern itself seems to condemn him on the grounds of *hybris*. The only possible outcome is either death or capitulation.

The taking of Briseis starts the pattern again for the third time. The wrath of Chryses-Apollo caused the wrath of Agamemnon, which caused the wrath of Achilles-Thetis-Zeus, the main tale of the *Iliad*. The third pattern is like the first, but since Achilles is mortal, though the son of a goddess, and not, like Chryses, the representative of a god, the pattern of his story has affinities to that of Agamemnon's wrath. Achilles acts both as god and as mortal. When Achilles' pleas that Briseis not be taken from him prove vain in spite of his threats to sail back home, Achilles, like Chryses, goes to the shore and prays. This is obviously parallel to the Chryses pattern. But Achilles has also, like Agamemnon, taken things into his own hands by his action of withdrawal from the fighting. The plan of Zeus to give victory to the Trojans and defeat to the Achaeans corresponds to the plague sent by Apollo in the Chryses pattern. The withdrawal of Achilles has the same effect in the Agamemnon pattern. Thus the defeat for the Greeks fits into the same place in the three patterns of the story; (a) in Agamemnon's wrath, (b) in Achilles' wrath as god, and (c) in Achilles' wrath as mortal.[5]

There are three devastations and three returns because Achilles' actions follow three patterns. The complexity of the *Iliad* and some of its apparent inconsistencies come from the working out of all three patterns in this one song. The hurt caused by the taking of Briseis would have been satisfied by the embassy, but by then two other patterns were operative; it would have been satisfied by a possible return of Briseis in Book XVI, a vestige of which we see in Achilles' conversation with Patroclus when Achilles shows an almost-willingness, and allows Patroclus to enter in his stead as a compromise. But another pattern is still left in operation, the most powerful pattern in the *Iliad,* the pattern which began with the withdrawal of Achilles. This pattern is the tragedy of Achilles, but the art and irony, the *hybris* of Achilles, arise from the fact that all three patterns are interlocked in the song.

The embassy should have been the final scene, parallel to the return of Chryseis to her father and to Apollo, in all three patterns. When Athena restrained Achilles from drawing his sword, in Book I, during the quarrel with Agamemnon, she intimated that this would be so. She told him: "Some day three times over such shining gifts shall be given you by reason of this outrage"[6] (I. 213–214). Yet this is not the case. In terms of story patterns, there are two possible explanations of Achilles' refusal to accept the terms of the embassy. In order to understand them we must note that the element that would have been omitted by Achilles' acceptance is the death of Patroclus. It is possible that in the Chryses pattern the return of Chryseis implied her sacrifice to Apollo. This would mean that before the final appeasement there must be sacrifice of a human life. Although we know that Apollo did not disdain such sacrifices (at the Leucadian rock maidens were sacrificed to Apollo),[7] this solution does mean reading something into the *Iliad* that is not there.

On the other hand, the refusal of the embassy is parallel to Agamemnon's refusal of the ransom of Chryses (still within the Chryses pattern, before the Agamemnon pattern begins). The difference is that whereas up to this point we have seen Achilles playing Chryses to Agamemnon, now we find him playing Agamemnon to Chryses. In other words, he was the bereaved seeking restitution, the god seeking retribution, but now he is the mortal refusing to accept just return. And by slipping into the role of Agamemnon he brings further disaster upon the Achaeans and on himself, thus prolonging the story until the final reconciliation with Agamemnon and the return of Briseis to Achilles. This suggestion of a move from one pattern to another is one possible solution, made even probable by the thematic correspondences (a) of Achilles-Chryses praying to the god and (b) of Achilles-Agamemnon refusing an embassy offering ransom. However, although this might suffice to renew the fighting and to take us back to war (the plague), it would not be sufficient, I believe, to lead to the death of Patroclus, without recourse to the idea of the sacrifice of the maiden Chryseis. Of course, from Agamemnon's point of view, Chryseis was sacrificed.

There may be truth in all of this, but if so, I think it is subsidiary to and supporting the other possibility: that by his withdrawal from the fighting Achilles has brought another powerful pattern into play, that of death and return. The story pattern of the wrath, the one that we have been considering, leads to the troubles of the Achaeans, even to the duplication of those troubles before and after the embassy. But it does not in itself seem to include the death of Patroclus. This appears to belong to another pattern into which the story of the wrath has modulated.

That the pattern of the wrath is really a pattern of bride-stealing and rescue is clear in the case of Chryses and Agamemnon quarreling over Chryseis, because Agamemnon has stolen Chryseis and Chryses seeks to rescue her. But it is equally true of Agamemnon and Achilles quarreling over Briseis; for Agamemnon steals her from Achilles, who wishes to rescue her. We are reminded that the Trojan War is also a tale of bride-stealing and rescue. The pattern of the wrath, however, would not by itself lead to the killing of Hector. It should lead after the reconciliation with Agamemnon to the victory of the Achaeans with Achilles at their head. The killing of Hector is part of the feud begun by the death of Patroclus, another feud which is ended by the reconciliation with Priam. Feuding patterns have a tendency to recur.[8] Achilles' return to battle should mean the end of the Trojan War according to the pattern of the story of wrath. But the wrath is introductory. The withdrawal of Achilles is the key; for by it we modulate from the wrath pattern to a pattern of death and return, which in turn evokes the complex of death by substitute. And that death, Patroclus', leads into another feud, between Hector and Achilles.

Captivity and rescue tales, of course, are closely allied to stories of captivity and return, as we have seen in previous chapters. They are sometimes combined, as we have also seen in the *Odyssey* and in the Yugoslav charts in Appendix IV. The relationship between them is close because of the captivity theme itself. But the coincidences are even greater when the captivity is of long duration and is pictured as causing devastation at home. In the wrath patterns at the beginning of the *Iliad* the duration is not specified as long, but rather presented as short. Hereby we have seen a difficulty arising in the poem, a difficulty involving the apparent return to the beginning of the war. But the second element, devastation at home, links them clearly with the captivity-return pattern.

Agamemnon plays the part of captor in the first two cases in the *Iliad*, first as the captor of Chryseis, who is rescued by Chryses, and then of Briseis, who is "rescued" by Achilles. But by the time of the embassy his role has changed; we find him offering ransom as would either a rescuer or a captive. Achilles, when he prays to Thetis, is the rescuer (note again the parallel with Chryses), but by the time of the embassy he refuses ransom, and here he acts as captor. This is because we have modulated via the withdrawal to another, closely related, story pattern.

The idea of withdrawal is, of course, inherent in the idea of captivity. But there is another sense of withdrawal, that of return home, withdrawal from the war, which appears in the first book of the *Iliad*. Chryses wishes the Greeks victory and a happy return homeward.[9] Achilles, at the beginning of the assembly of the Achaeans, suggests that they will have to return home if both war and pestilence ravage them.[10] At the beginning of the quarrel Achilles threatens to depart for Phthia if his prize is taken from him; for this is not his war. Agamemnon tells him to go ahead home.[11] The subject does not come up again until Book II, and then in a controversial and important incident, when Agamemnon makes trial of his men.[12] We must consider this incident with some care. For one thing, it has been said that it does not follow logically from what precedes it, the baneful dream. Secondly, it is here that we learn for the first time that we are in the ninth year of the war. Until now we might very well have been at the beginning of the war. Thirdly, it is the start of the modulation back to events at the beginning of the war. In short, there seems to be something seriously wrong here. Except for the intervention of Athena in Book I and her speech,[13] which would seem to indicate that the death of Patroclus was not in all singings of the wrath of Achilles, this is the first real difficulty in the *Iliad*. Her intervention is also inconsistent with the statement by Thetis later,[14] that all the gods are on vacation in Ethiopia, whence they return twelve days later for the *Iliad*'s first scene on Olympus.

The sequence in which the testing of the troops occurs is as follows: after twelve days the gods return to Olympus and Thetis plots with Zeus; Zeus sends the deceptive dream; Agamemnon tests the troops. Restated in terms of essential ideas, this gives us return after long absence, deceptive story; testing (the number twelve is significant as twelve months, although sometimes we find it as days and sometimes as years also; cf. the nine days of the plague and the nine years of the war).[15] We recognize this sequence as belonging to the return story. True, the characters are different and the shift from the gods to Agamemnon is puzzling. But the sequence that Homer is following is a well-established one. In the inner logic of oral song the testing of the troops belongs with what precedes it, namely, deceptive story and return. The idea of return has haunted Book I, as we have seen.

The shift to Agamemnon, which has come about by his repetition of the deceptive story of the baneful dream, has occasioned Homer's reference to a long period of time, and for him the nine years of the war properly provide that reference. By it, we have moved from an event, the withdrawal of Achilles, which belongs at the beginning of a period of troubles, to the culmination of a period of troubles and to return home. The modulation back to the beginning of the war is accomplished, as we have noted, by the assembling of the troops, leading to the catalogues. The return of the gods from their twelve-day vacation started a sequence in which the testing was in place, but in the larger sequence of the story beginning with the withdrawal of Achilles, a sequence in which return and all its associated ideas have played a part, the testing was out of place and premature, as was the return itself.

In the books which follow (II–VII) the war begins, and the Achaeans, perhaps contrary to our expectations, are almost victorious. At the end of Book VII and the beginning of Book VIII we reach a complex of themes that throws us back again to the end of Book I and the beginning of Book II and to the story of Achilles, who has been almost forgotten in the intervening episodes.

Book I ended with the feasting of the gods and their going to sleep. Book VII ends with the feasting of the Achaeans after the building of the wall, and their going to sleep. At the beginning of Book II we find Zeus wakeful, plotting the destruction of the Achaeans; at the end of Book VII Zeus plots their destruction all night long. The results of his scheming are different in each case. In Book II the result is the baneful dream; in Book VIII the result is an assembly of the gods at dawn, when Zeus tells them to refrain from fighting. After this he repairs to Ida and watches the battle resumed, until at midday he balances the scales and things go worse for the Achaeans. Hera and Athena band together to stop the carnage, but Zeus intervenes and recalls them. He tells them that nothing they can do will change the fate which has been decreed:

> "For Hektor the huge will not sooner be stayed from his fighting
> until there stirs by the ships the swift-footed son of Peleus
> on that day when they shall fight by the sterns of the beached ships
> in the narrow place of necessity over fallen Patroklos." (VIII. 473–476)

This is the first we hear about the death of Patroclus. This plan is different from the earlier one in Book II. But the general sequence here is the same as that in the earlier passage: feasting, sleep, a sleepless, plotting Zeus, and action proceeding from his plot.

What follows has also a parallel in Book II, and is germane to our previous considerations. Night falls and the Trojans keep watch after a speech by Hector. Meanwhile, Agamemnon, at the beginning of Book IX, summons an assembly, as in Book II. Now he suggests to the Achaeans, and not in a testing mood, that they return home. The similarity to events in Book II is striking. The interchange following this suggestion is reminiscent of what follows the threat of Achilles during the quarrel to return home to Phthia. It is now Diomedes, who in words like those of Agamemnon, says that Agamemnon, indeed all the rest of the Achaeans, may return home, but he will stay and fight until Troy is taken. Nestor intervenes here, as he did in Book I, and suggests a meeting of the council. At that meeting he urges Agamemnon to appease Achilles, and the embassy is the result.

Agamemnon's suggestion for returning is fully in place in Book IX, whereas, although we can trace the singer's thinking in Book II, I believe, it is there out of place. The words are the same in both books:

> "Zeus son of Kronos has caught me badly in bitter futility.
> He is hard: who before this time promised me and consented
> that I might sack strong-walled Ilion and sail homeward.
> Now he has devised a vile deception and bids me go back
> to Argos in dishonour having lost many of my people.
> Such is the way it will be pleasing to Zeus who is too strong,
> who before now has broken the crests of many cities
> and will break them again, since his power is beyond all others.
> Come then, do as I say, let us all be won over; let us
> run away with our ships to the beloved land of our fathers
> since no longer now shall we capture Troy of the wide ways." [16] (IX. 18–28)

The Chryses pattern, we saw, instructed us that the return of Briseis should mean the end of the wrath. Athena promised Achilles, when she restrained his hand, that he would receive threefold payment for the rape of Briseis. This promise, too, would lead us to believe that Achilles would accept the return of the girl with additional gifts as appeasement for his wrath. But the words of Zeus shortly before have notified us that this embassy is doomed to failure because Patroclus first must die. The Chryses pattern is completed formally, but we have been occupied with another pattern (that of death and return) since the withdrawal of Achilles. Now for the first time we can state this with assurance. Zeus has told us so himself. Achilles' anger was godlike (cf. Apollo) and its effects were godlike (cf. the plague). Achilles the bereaved, the hurt, has been satisfied. The return of Briseis was all that was asked for in the Chryses pattern. The new pattern demands human sacrifice. And so Achilles, prolonging his withdrawal in the role of his own captor, refuses the inadequate ransom, and thus insists on Patroclus' death. So far, then, in the new pattern we have an absence that causes devastation and requires human sacrifice for return. The quarrel of Agamemnon is of no import after the embassy. The devastation of the Achaeans, however, is of significance after the embassy, and must continue until Patroclus' death. Now all hinges upon that.

But the action of the *Iliad,* almost in consternation, as it were, that the embassy has not turned out as envisaged from the beginning of the song, comes to a stop at the end of Book IX, and takes a rest before continuing. Book X, the Doloneia, could be omitted without anyone being the wiser; many feel that the *Iliad* would be better without it. Yet it is there and we have no evidence that justifies our eliminating it, since it does not contradict anything in the song. I am not sure that we can find a satisfactory answer at the present time to the question of why the Doloneia is included in the *Iliad,* but we can indicate its relationship in respect to thematic patterns with other parts of the song. And this knowledge may lead us in the direction of possible solutions. Book X opens with the scene of all the Achaeans asleep by the ships except for Agamemnon, who is worried about the fate of his forces. And associated with his worry is a simile of a storm.[17] With this opening we are thrown back to the beginning of the previous book (IX) which discovers the Achaeans in panic, their panic emphasized by another storm simile;[18] here, too, Agamemnon is singled out as wandering about among his captains. In fact, we are reminded of a still earlier scene, the opening of Book II, where we find all the gods and men asleep except for Zeus, who hits upon the plan of the baneful dream, which he sends to the sleeping Agamemnon in the form of Nestor. There is a kinship in the opening of these three books, a kinship made closer by the fact that each of these books presents particular problems in the structure of the *Iliad*.

After the opening, the pattern in each case continues with the calling of an assembly, although the technique employed is not the same in all three books. In Book II Agamemnon orders the heralds to summon an assembly, while he holds a council of kings by Nestor's ship. In Book IX Agamemnon orders the heralds to summon every man by name, and he himself assists. There is no meeting of the council of kings, but the assembly gathers immediately. In Book X the pace is much more leisurely, Agamemnon's worries are described, and then Menelaus'; the latter goes to seek his brother and they exchange ideas about a plan; then Agamemnon seeks out Nestor. Menelaus has alerted Odysseus and Diomedes, and soon we find that a council of the kings has been summoned. These are all multiforms of a favorite theme, that of the assembly.

It seems that either Book IX or Book X could follow immediately upon the action of Book VIII. This would perhaps point to the fact that they are in some sense duplications, or that one is an intruder. As a matter of fact, Books IX and X are possibly interchangeable; at any rate their order could be reversed. It may be that we are dealing with two versions of the story, which have been amalgamated, one in which there was a *successful* embassy to Achilles, thus having a different ending to the tale; the other without an embassy but with a Doloneia leading into the Patroclus episode. I am inclined to feel that the mixing of a story of Achilles without a Patroclus substitute and one with Patroclus has again caused difficulty in the structure of the *Iliad*. But whatever the answer may be, we shall undoubtedly reach it by way of a careful analysis of the repetition of thematic patterns.

*   *   *

The story of Patroclus really begins in Book XI, but it is interrupted at the very beginning of Book XII and does not reappear until the middle of Book XV, briefly, and at the beginning of XVI, where it is fully resumed. After this there seem to be no further interruptions.

It might be said that there is some vestige of a return after the embassy; for it is in Book XI that Achilles shows interest in the fate of the Achaeans and sends Patroclus to find out what is going on. Patroclus' entrance on the field of battle, first as a messenger, and then in the stead of Achilles into the battle itself, is Achilles' return by proxy. In fact, Patroclus' mission to spy out the situation for Achilles is strangely like the mission of Diomedes and Odysseus in the Doloneia.

Patroclus' entrance into the battle parallels that of Achilles, for whom he is a double. He enters in disguise in Achilles' armor (not quite complete, for the spear is lacking) and with Achilles' horses. The disguise is soon forgotten, to be sure, but it is there, and it is operative at the point of his victory over Sarpedon. Glaucus' words to Hector seem first to ignore it.[19] Zeus takes from Sarpedon his protection, as Apollo does from Hector. Even as Achilles was almost overcome by the river, so Patroclus was almost overcome by Apollo, at the wall of Troy. Disguise, recognition, a struggle with an opponent (supernatural) who almost overcomes him, link Patroclus' fighting with that of Achilles. Only their ultimate fates in the battle are different, although Patroclus' death in Achilles' armor and in his stead is also Achilles' death by proxy. The laments for Patroclus by the Greeks in general, by his friend Achilles, and by Briseis, as well as his funeral games, all form part of the complex. They are reminiscent, and significantly so, of the deceptive story in the Yugoslav return songs, where the returned hero falsely says that he is dead and that his friend buried him, and where this announcement is followed by the laments of wife and friends, sister, and so on. The funeral games themselves parallel the wedding games in the Yugoslav songs. Patroclus' death is the false death of the hero. And it is followed by the hero's own return.

We would not be inclined to see any similarity between the withdrawal of Achilles and the absence of Odysseus, between the devastation caused by that withdrawal and the destructiveness of the suitors, certainly not between the death of Patroclus and that of Anticleia, nor between the role of Thetis-Zeus and that of Athena-Zeus, were it not for the character of Achilles' return to the fighting.[20] Achilles' return is portentous. If he has been "disguised" as Patroclus before, he now appears as himself to the Trojans, unarmed, but glorified by Athena.

> But Achilleus, the beloved of Zeus, rose up, and Athene
> swept about his powerful shoulders the fluttering aegis;
> and she, the divine among goddesses, about his head circled
> a golden cloud, and kindled from it a flame far-shining . . .
> so from the head of Achilleus the blaze shot into the bright air.
> He went from the wall and stood by the ditch, nor mixed with the other
> Achaians, since he followed the close command of his mother.
> There he stood, and shouted, and from her place Pallas Athene
> gave cry, and drove an endless terror upon the Trojans. . . .
> The charioteers were dumbfounded as they saw the unwearied dangerous
> fire that played above the head of great-hearted Peleion
> blazing, and kindled by the goddess grey-eyed Athene.
> Three times across the ditch brilliant Achilleus gave his great cry,
> and three times the Trojans and their renowned companions were routed.
> There at that time twelve of the best men among them perished
> upon their own chariots and spears.[21] (XVIII. 203–206, 214–218, 225–231)

This is a mystical and magic passage, and we realize here that Achilles is more than a human hero, that he is a symbolic figure. It seems to me important that Achilles cannot wear his own armor nor is his new armor ready — though in the divine economy, I suspect, it might have been possible, had it been fitting for Achilles to be seen in it at this point.

> Then in answer to her spoke Achilleus of the swift feet:
> "How shall I go into the fighting? They have my armour.
> And my beloved mother told me I must not be armoured,
> not before with my own eyes I see her come back to me.
> She promised she would bring magnificent arms from Hephaistos.
> Nor do I know of another whose glorious armour I could wear
> unless it were the great shield of Telamonian Aias.
> But he himself wears it, I think, and goes in the foremost
> of the spear-fight over the body of fallen Patroklos."
>   Then in turn swift wind-footed Iris spoke to him:
> "Yes, we also know well how they hold your glorious armour.
> But go to the ditch, and show yourself as you are to the Trojans." (XVIII. 187–198)

He must be recognized and for that reason he must be recognizable. The similarity to the appearance of Odysseus, beautiful and transformed by Athena before his son Telemachus, is, I think, not forced.[22] There is something mystical and otherworldly in both these returns and recognitions.

The ashen spear of Achilles, too, has its counterpart in the bow of Odysseus. It is noteworthy that this spear is not carried by Patroclus, for only Achilles can wield it. It is an heirloom, like the bow. It, not the armor of Hephaestus, is the distinguishing mark of Achilles.

Achilles' fight with the river, however, corresponds to the near death of Odysseus in the sea before his landing at Phaeacia, when he is saved by the intervention of Ino.[23] A struggle which almost ends in disaster for the hero is regularly found in connection with return songs; hence, the fight with the river is thoroughly at home in this tale of Achilles. In the Yugoslav material there is a parallel in certain songs in the battle with the last of the sentinels on the mountains before the hero reaches home.[24] Beowulf's battle with Grendel's mother belongs in the same category with the fight with the river, as does the battle between Charles and Baligant in the *Roland*.[25] An excellent parallel can be found in Jacob's striving with the angel in *Genesis*, chapter 32, a portion of the Scriptures rich in latent folklore meanings with duplication of incident. There is evidence in older traditions that it was not an angel with whom Jacob struggled but a river spirit whom he had to overcome before the river could be passed.[26]

By the killing of Patroclus a feud has started in this heroic society, and according to its rules Hector must in turn be killed, Hector or one of his kin. The element that makes the situation somewhat different in the *Iliad* is that Patroclus has been killed by decree of Zeus or of fate. The gods have here been the aggressors. Patroclus is a sacrifice. It is Apollo who has killed Patroclus, and now one of Apollo's men, Hector, must pay.

This is no ordinary feud, indeed. The parallel with the return complex has been fruitful and helpful in understanding some of the developments in this part of the *Iliad,* but it is not enough. For the closest parallel to Patroclus we must turn to the epic of Gilgamesh. It seems more and more likely that the Near Eastern epics of ancient times were known to the Greeks of Homer's day or that they had some effect upon Greek epic before his day. In the epic, Gilgamesh and his friend Enkidu have broken the taboos of the gods. The gods decide that Enkidu shall perish and not Gilgamesh. And Gilgamesh, when told of this decision by Enkidu, to whom it has been revealed in a dream says: "Me they would Clear at the expense of my brother!"[27] Here as in the *Iliad* it is the decree of the gods that the friend be killed for the hero. Gilgamesh, like Achilles, is part divine, "two thirds of him is god, [one third of him is human]."[28] Enkidu's death is followed by the lament of Gilgamesh over his friend. Thus far is the parallel between Achilles and Gilgamesh clear. But here the correspondence seems to end; for now Gilgamesh departs over the steppe, and sets out for the island of the blest to visit Utnapishtim to learn the secret of eternal life. Only in the peaceful ending of the two poems, the reconciliation of Gilgamesh with his failure to learn that secret and with his loss of the plant of eternal youth, and the reconciliation of Achilles with Priam, is there a similarity of spirit.

CHAPTER TEN

SOME NOTES ON MEDIEVAL EPIC[1]

It is perfectly understandable that the oral theory, as it is called, is known best to Classicists, who have been trying to look at Homer from its point of view since the days of Milman Parry. Thanks to Professor Francis P. Magoun, Jr., and to his students, the theory has also attracted the attention of scholars in Old English, and its applicability is now being warmly discussed in the learned journals.[2] Most recently it has been applied as well to some of the Middle English Romances.[3] Here too discussion promises to be heated and healthy, possibly also fruitful. Some application of the theory to the *chansons de gestes* has been started by Professor Jean Rychner[4] at Neuchatel, and it is hoped that others will follow along the same path. But, to the best of my knowledge, none of the other medieval epics has been subjected to analysis and scrutiny according to the principles of composition of oral narrative poetry. It is beyond the scope of this chapter to do more than to indicate, as I have tried to do with the Homeric poems, some lines of investigation, and to suggest, often I fear only tentatively, some possible results. Anything more must remain for a separate volume.

The formulaic character of the Old English *Beowulf* has been proved beyond any doubt by a series of analyses beginning with my own in 1949 (see Chart VIII), which Professor Magoun improved and elaborated in 1953,[5] and which Professor Creed has carried to its ultimate detailed conclusion.[6] The documentation is complete, thorough, and accurate. This exhaustive analysis is in itself sufficient to prove that *Beowulf* was composed orally. Thematic study has also been begun for *Beowulf*,[7] but the concept of theme which Professor Magoun and others have been using differs to some extent from that presented in this book, although I feel that there is no basic conflict but rather a difference of emphasis. I should prefer to designate as motifs what they call themes and to reserve the term theme for a structural unit that has a semantic essence but can never be divorced from its form, even if its form be constantly variable and multiform. It is not difficult to see that even from this point of view there are themes in *Beowulf*: repeated assemblies with speeches, repetition of journeying from

CHART VIII [8]

Beowulf maþelode,   bearn Ecgþeowes:
‾‾‾‾‾‾‾‾‾‾‾‾‾‾‾‾‾‾‾‾‾1
‾‾‾‾‾‾‾‾‾‾‾‾2   ‾‾‾‾‾‾‾‾‾‾‾‾3
"Geþenc nu, se maera   maga Healfdenes,
‒ ‒ ‒ ‒ ‒ ‾‾‾‾‾‾‾‾‾‾‾‾‾4
‒ ‒ ‒ ‒ ‒‾‾‾‾5   ‾‾‾‾‾‾6

1475   snottra fengel,   nu ic eom siðes fus,[7]
‾‾‾‾‾‾‾‾8   ‒ ‒ ‒ ‒ ‒ ‒ ‒ ‒ _9
goldwine gumena,   hwaet wit geo spraecon,[10]
‾‾‾‾‾‾‾‾‾‾11   ‾‾‾‾‾‾ ‒ ‒ ‾‾‾‾12
gif ic aet þearfe   þinre scolde
‒ ‒ ‒ ‒ ‒ ‒ ‒ ‒ ‒ ‒ _13
‾‾‾ ‾‾‾‾‾‾14   ‒‒ ‾‾‾15
aldre linnan,   þaet ðu me a waere[16]
‾‾‾‾‾‾‾17   ‒ ‒ ‒ ‒ ‒ ‾‾‾‾18
forðgewitenum   on faeder staele.[19]
‒ ‒ ‒ ‒ ‒ _20   ‾‾‾‾ ‒ _21

1480   Wes þu mundbora   minum magoþegnum,[22]
‾‾‾ ‒ ‒ ‒ ‒ _23   ‾‾‾‾ ‾‾‾‾‾24
hondgesellum,   gif mec hild nime;[25]
‒ ‒ ‒ ‒ ‒ _26   ‾‾‾‾‾‾‾‾27
swylce þu ða madmas,   þe þu me sealdest,[28]
‒ ‒ ‒ ‒ ‾‾‾‾‾29   ‒ ‒ ‒ ‒ ‒ ‒ _30
Hroðgar leofa,   Higelace onsend.[31]
‒ ‒ ‒ ‒ ‒ _32   ‒ ‒ ‒ ‒ ‒ ‒ _33
Maeg þonne on þaem golde ongitan   Geata dryhten[34]
35   ‾‾‾‾‾‾‾‾36

1485   geseon sunu Hraedles,   þonne he on þaet sinc starað,[37]
‒ ‒ ‒ ‒ ‒ ‒ ‒ _38   ‒ ‒ ‒ ‒ ‒ ‒ ‒ ‒ ‒ ‒ ‒ _39
þaet ic gumcystum   godne funde
‒ ‒ ‒ ‒ ‒ ‒ ‒ ‒ ‒ ‒ ‒ _40
‾‾‾‾‾‾ ‒ ‒ ‒ ‒ ‾41   ‾‾‾ ‾‾‾42
beaga bryttan,   breac þonne moste.[43]
‾‾‾‾‾‾44   ‒ ‒ ‒ ‒ ‒ ‒ ‒ ‒ _45

one place to another, and on the larger canvas the repeated multiform scenes of the slaying of monsters.

Thus the arrival of Beowulf in the land of Hrothgar (lines 223b ff.) and the arrival of the hero back in the land of the Geats (lines 1912b ff.) are multiforms of the same theme, both distinguished by the watchman, yet different in their detailed elaboration. One can see the same theme (a) in the assembly in Heorot, when Hrothgar welcomes Beowulf and there is the wrangling between Unferth and the newly arrived stranger, wrangling in which an old story is told, followed by laughter and the entrance of the queen (lines 405ff.) and (b) the feasting after the fight with Grendel (lines 1063ff.) with its ancient tale of Finn and the appearance of the queen following the minstrel's song.

There are two larger problems in connection with *Beowulf* which the method of comparative study may help in solving. One is the question of the structure of *Beowulf*, its "unity"; the other whether *Beowulf* might be a "transitional" text. What has already been said in Chapter Six above concerning the second of these problems can be brought to bear here. Analysis of *Beowulf* indicates oral composition. The corpus of Anglo-Saxon heroic poetry is so small that it is scarcely possible for us to know its tradition well enough to assert that *Beowulf* breaks away from that tradition of formula and theme. It seems to be more logical to assume that a text so analyzed belongs to the category of oral dictated texts unless one has sufficient evidence from the tradition itself on which to base a judgment that it is "transitional." It might be foolhardy to generalize to the extent of including the Anglo-Saxon religious poetry, for example, the *Christ, Genesis, Andreas,* etc., in the category of heroic poems, or rather as traditional heroic poems. It must be said, however, that the evidence of Caedman's dream[9] and of the song of the bard in *Beowulf* —

He who could tell of men's beginning from olden times spoke of how the Almighty wrought the world, the earth bright in its beauty which the water encompasses; the Victorious One established the brightness of sun and moon for a light to dwellers in the land, and adorned the face of the earth with branches and leaves. He also created life of all kinds which move and live[10] —

would seem to indicate the possibility that Christian religious narrative had been accepted' into the tradition. Perhaps it would be wiser to say that the pagan myths had given place to or had been reinterpreted in terms of the Judaeo-Christian myth.

In regard to the unity of *Beowulf,* to the question as to whether we are dealing here with one, two, or three poems, it seems to me that in the absence of manuscript evidence to the contrary we must accept the singleness of our poem. More specifically we should recognize that it represents one dictated performance by a single singer, undoubtedly over more than one day of dictating and writing. It might very well be that the story of Beowulf's fight with the dragon was sometimes separately sung; it is conceivable, though I must confess not probable, that the incident of Beowulf's undersea adventure with Grendel's dam was also a subject that was sung separately. But from Chapter Five above on the subject of "what is a song" it should be clear that the fact that these parts *might* or *could* be sung separately would not militate against *Beowulf* as a single song.

A glance at Parry 6580 from Murat Čustović of Gacko in Appendix III will show how easy it is for the singer to continue to narrate about a hero or about action leading out of incidents that would perhaps in normal performance close a song. In other words, in dictating, a singer would very possibly continue narrating, let us say, about Beowulf, about a third encounter with a monster and about the hero's death, thus perhaps adding one song to another. One does not need a written tradition, as the Yugoslav example shows, in order to produce such a phenomenon. But I believe that when the singer does add material it is because of an association that often goes deeper than association of one rescue with another, or of one monster-fight with another. On these grounds, I believe that the dragon episode in *Beowulf* may have a deeper significance and be more integrally related to the hero and to his previous adventures than can be explained by any biographical or chronological tendency.

The hero, Beowulf, is marked as one of those with whom are associated story patterns of wandering into another world, there to encounter and overcome the king and queen of that world and to return victorious. He is a mythic figure of death and resurrection. Achilles and Odysseus, as we have seen, belong in this same category. Beowulf shows some detailed relationship with the Achilles-Patroclus pattern as well. A case might be made for Aescere as a Patroclus, that is, the close friend who is killed before the encounter of the hero with the enemy. Indeed, unless one interprets his death in this manner, he is at a loss to understand it; for Beowulf is apparently present at the time of Aescere's slaughter and does nothing about it. We have said in the previous chapter that mythic heroes of this type can die by substitution or symbolically, or by undergoing an "almost-death." It would probably be accurate to say that Beowulf, like Achilles, has undergone death twice, even three times, in the poem before the dragon episode. First his journey itself into the land of Hrothgar is an expedition into the other world; he dies by substitution in the person of Aescere; and he undergoes an "almost-death," similar to Achilles' fight with the river, in his struggle with Grendel's dam.

Yet tradition tells of the deaths of such heroes. The *Iliad* does not contain the tale of Achilles' death, but it occurs elsewhere in the Cycle,[11] and the same can be said for the death of Odysseus, which is foretold in the *Odyssey* and occurs in the *Telegony* (otherwise than as foretold). The classic and most sophisticated example of death of the savior hero, aside from the Christian myth itself, comes from Akkadia and Sumeria of more than four thousand years ago in the epic of Gilgamesh. Here is our earliest example in epic of death by substitution; Enkidu dies for Gilgamesh. Gilgamesh like Achilles struggles with the horror of his own mortality and is reconciled to it. We do not know of his death, but we do know that he died. When gods became demigods, the possibility of a dying god who is not resurrected came into being in the framework of the myth of death and resurrection. In other words, when a mortal took over the story of the dying god, it was inevitable that eventually in tradition his death without resurrection would have to be recorded.

But his death would, by the very association with the god and with his mythic significance, take on the attributes of a sacrifice, of a ritual, a solemn ceremony. It was as a scapegoat, as a symbol for others, that his mythic, multiform deaths had taken place. It is not surprising that his definite end should have the same character. There is nothing new in the interpretation of Beowulf's fight with the dragon as a fight with death itself, overcome by

the human sacrifice of life's champion.[12] Such an interpretation is sup-
ported by the epic myths that gave rise to the narrative stuff of the poem
Beowulf. But the Christian tradition could tolerate but one resurrection;
symbolically Beowulf in tradition, a tradition that had lost the sense of the
symbol, could survive both Grendel and Grendel's dam but he must
eventually die without resurrection in this world. That death could be, and
should fittingly be, one in which the hero is his own substitute.

La Chanson de Roland

In the case of *Beowulf* we are dealing with only a single manuscript, but
when we turn to the *Chanson de Roland* and to *Digenis Akritas* we come
upon a richer manuscript tradition.[13] No lengthy analysis has been made of
the formula structure in the *Chanson,* although Rychner's work[14] leads in
this direction. However, an examination of a passage, chosen at random,
illustrates the extent to which formulas are used in the *Chanson.* Only the
Oxford manuscript of the song has been employed as material for the
analysis of ten lines in Chart IX.[15]

CHART IX

Li quens Rollant par mi le champ chevalchet,
————————1 ————————————2
Tient Durendal, ki ben trenchet e taillet,
————————3   4
Des Sarrazins lur fait mult grant damage.
————————5————————————6
Ki lui veïst l'un geter mort su l'altre,
————————7 _ _ _ _ _ _ _ _ _8
Li sanc tuz clers gesir par cele place!
————————9   10
Sanglant en ad e l'osberc e la brace,
_ _ _ _ _ _11_ _ _ _   12
Sun bon cheval le col e les espalles.
————————13 _ _ _   14
E Oliver de ferir ne se target,
————15   _ _ _ _ _16
Li .XII. per n'en deivent aveir blasme,
————17 ————————————18
E li Franceis i fierent e si caplent.
————————19 _ _ _ _ _ _ _ _20

It seems clear from the chart that the *Chanson* is formulaic beyond any
question. The first part of the line is obviously much more hospitable to
formulas than the second part. This is undoubtedly because of the assonance
at the end of each line. Nevertheless, at least half of the lines are formulaic
in their second part, and there are parts of formulas even in most of the
other lines.

From Chart IX and its notes we can readily discern formula systems such as the following, which shows how useful *tient, trait,* or *prent* in first position in the line is with a three-syllable noun-object extending to the line break:

$$
\left.\begin{array}{c}
(\text{trait}) \\
\text{tient} \\
(\text{prent})
\end{array}\right\}
\left\{\begin{array}{l}
\text{Durendal} \\
\text{Halteclere} \\
\text{Tencendur} \\
\text{ses chevels} \\
\text{ses crignels} \\
\text{sun espiet} \\
\text{sun escut} \\
\text{l'olifan}
\end{array}\right.
$$

Such analyses seem to indicate that the *Chanson* as we have it in the Oxford manuscript is an oral composition.

When one approaches the problem of the relationship between several manuscripts of the same song (e.g. of the *Digenis Akritas* or of the *Chanson de Roland*), the knowledge that we are dealing with oral compositions, coupled with an understanding of how such songs are collected, is helpful. We have seen from the Yugoslav examples that variation, sometimes not great, sometimes quite considerable, is the rule in oral composition. When there is exact line-for-line, formula-for-formula correspondence between manuscripts, we can be sure that we are dealing with a written tradition involving copied manuscripts or with some circumstance of collecting in which a fixed text has been memorized.

If one were to disregard all other elements and parts of the manuscripts and to judge only from this single passage, one would conclude after perusing Chart X that the Italianized Venice IV is either copied directly from the Oxford manuscript or is a copy of a copy. In line 3 "des Sarrazins" has been interpreted as "de qui de Spagna" by Venice IV, and the tenth line of Oxford has been omitted; line 10 in Venice IV is the eleventh line in the Oxford manuscript. The second half of line 11 of Venice IV does not correspond, nor does line 12. In spite of these differences it would seem that this passage has been either memorized and turned into Italianate French or copied from manuscript.

On the other hand, a comparison of the same *laisse* in the Chateauroux manuscript with the Oxford (Chart XI) seems to show a relationship which might be that of oral texts of the same song. The first line is quite different; the second agrees in the very common first half-line formula, "tint Durendart"; the third line is the same, but it is a common line; lines four through eight in Chateauroux are quite different; but line 9 of Chateauroux is the same as line 8 of Oxford; and line 10 of Chateauroux corresponds in its first half to line 9 of Oxford, although this is a very common formula ("li

CHART X [16]

Oxford	Venice IV
Li quens Rollant par mi le champ cheval-chet,	Li cont Rollant parmé la camp çivalçe,
Tient Durendal, ki ben trenchet e taillet,	Tent Durindarda, che ben trença et ben taile,
Des Sarrazins lur fait mult grant damage.	De qui de Spagna el fa si gran dalmaçe.
Ki lui veïst l'un geter mort su l'altre,	Chi l'un veest çeter mort sor l'autre,
Li sanc tuz clers gesir par cele place!	Lo sang tut cler en saie for et desglaçe!
Sanglant en ad e l'osberc e la brace,	Sanglent n'est son uberg et son elme,
Sun bon cheval le col e les espalles.	Son bon cival el col et l'espalle.
E Oliver de ferir ne se target,	E Oliver del ferir no se tarde,
Li .XII. per n'en deivent aveir blasme,	Li doç ber no de ma aver blasme.
E li Franceis i fierent e si caplent.	
Moerent paien e alquanz en i pasment.	Morunt païn alquant si s'en spasme.
Dist l'arcevesque: "Ben ait nostre bar-nage!"	
"Munjoie!" escriet, ço est l'enseigne Carle.	Dist l'arcivesque: "Nostra çent se salve! Or plaxesse a Deo, de tel n'aves asa Çarle!"

CHART XI [17]

Oxford	Chateauroux
Li quens Rollant par mi le champ cheval-chet,	Rollanz fu proz et de mult fier coraje:
Tient Durendal, ki ben trenchet e taillet,	Tint Durendart par mot ruste bataille;
Des Sarrazins lur fait mult grant damage.	De Saraçins a fait mot grant doumage;
Ki lui veïst l'un geter mort su l'altre,	Cel jor mostra si ben son vasalage.
Li sanc tuz clers gesir par cele place!	Qi l'atendit ne fist mie qe saje:
Sanglant en ad e l'osberc e la brace,	La teste i pert, ne demande autre gaje;
Sun bon cheval le col e les espalles.	Sanc et cervelle fait voler en l'erbaje,
	Tot a son cors sanglant et son visage.
E Oliver de ferir ne se target,	Et Oliver de ferir ne se targe;
Li .XII. per n'en deivent aveir blasme,	Li .XII. per, qi sunt de haut parage,
E li Franceis i fierent e si caplent.	Ferent et caplent desor la gent sauvage:
Moerent paien e alquanz en i pasment.	Murent paien a duel et a hontage.
Dist l'arcevesque: "Ben ait nostre bar-nage!"	Dist l'arcivesqe: "Nostre gent est mot sage! Bien se defendent a cest estrot pasage. Car pleüst Deu, qi fist oisel volage, Chi fust li rois cui avons fait domage!"
"Munjoie!" escriet, ço est l'enseigne Carle.	

.XII. per"). Chateauroux line 11 begins with the last half of Oxford line 10, but finishes differently; the first half of line 12 and the first half of line 13 in Chateauroux correspond to the beginnings of lines 11 and 12 respectively in Oxford, but the rest of the *laisse* is quite different. And we might note that the words of the archbishop in Venice IV correspond in part to his words in Chateauroux. At the end of the *laisse,* Venice IV (as elsewhere in fact) has

CHART XII [18]

Chateauroux	Cambridge
Rollanz fu proz et de mult fier coraje:	Roullant fut preux et de fier courage,
Tint Durendart par mot ruste bataille;	Tint Durandal par son riche barnage,
De Saraçins a fait mot grant doumage;	De Sarrasins y fait moult grant domage.
Cel jor mostra si ben son vasalage.	Le jour y monstre si bien son vasselage,
Qi l'afendit ne fist mie qe saje:	Cil qui l'atent y fait moult grant folage,
La teste i pert, ne demande autre gaje;	La teste prent, il ne quiert aultre gage,
Sanc et cervelle fait voler en l'erbaje,	Sang et cervele fait voler par l'erbage,
Tot a son cors sanglant et son visage.	
Et Oliver de ferir ne se targe;	Et Oliver de ferir ne targe;
Li .XII. per, qi sunt de haut parage,	Li .XII. pairs qui sont de haut parage,
	Ne ly Franceys ja n'y aront hontage!
Ferent et caplent desor la gent sauvage:	Dist l'arcevesque: "Nostre gent est mult sage!
Murent paien a duel et a hontage.	Fierent et chaplent sur celle gent sauvage:
Dist l'arcivesqe: "Nostre gent est mot sage!	Meurent paiens a deul et a hontage.
Bien se defendent a cest estrot pasage.	Bien se desfendent a ceul estroit passage;
Car pleüst Deu, qi fist oisel volage,	Car pleüst Dieu, qui fist oysel sauvage,
Chi fust li rois cui avons fait domage!"	Que fust cy ly rois a qui avon fait homage!"

been influenced by the Chateauroux type of manuscript, in spite of its closeness to Oxford. This is still a kind of relationship that is within a written manuscript tradition.

In Chart XII, which places the same passage from the Chateauroux manuscript side by side with the corresponding passage from the Cambridge manuscript, we can see that the relationship between these two, *on the basis of this passage,* is that between copies. This is apparent although there is some confusion in the order of lines toward the end of the passage, and although one line has been omitted in Cambridge that is in Chateauroux, while there is one line in Cambridge that is not in Chateauroux.

It is easy to divide these four manuscripts then into two groups. We believe that the Oxford–Venice IV group (that is Venice IV insofar as it follows Oxford, namely to line 3865 at least) is oral as shown by our analyses. The relationship between Oxford and Chateauroux looks like that between two oral versions and may be such, but one must note that Oxford is assonantal and Chateauroux is rhymed. And although the "author" or scribe of Chateauroux is not always consistent, he seems to have changed the lines that do not end properly for his rhyme scheme, which is "-age." So he changes line 1, but neglects to change line 2 (an oversight that Cambridge remedies), keeps line 3, because it already has his rhyme, but changes lines 4–7, because they do not have it, and so forth.

Strangely enough he also changes line 12, in spite of the fact that it ends with "barnage"! We had best agree with the majority that the relationship between Oxford and Chateauroux is a written one, a conscious literary changing of one manuscript (or manuscript group) characterized by assonance in order to produce a rhymed text. But I should like to suggest that the whole question of these *remaniements* should be reviewed again in light of oral composition. For the present we begin with an oral Oxford manuscript, from which the others named have been derived.

*　　*　　*

In our remarks on *Beowulf* above we have noted that the dragon episode may very well be organic in Beowulf tradition and that the singer, if joining together separate songs, was doing so in accordance with the subconscious forces of attraction that are operative in oral tradition. It is significant that many of our medieval texts are divisible into at least two and sometimes three parts. It is so with *Beowulf, Chanson de Roland,* the old Spanish *Cid,* the *Nibelungenlied,* and *Digenis Akritas.* Criticism has tried to defend their unity on artistic or logical grounds, but it has seldom if ever attempted to see these poems as traditional units with their parts belonging together by a kind of mythic necessity or by thematic attraction.

One can see, I believe, a traditional force at work (together with other forces) in the addition of the Baligant episode at the end of the *Chanson de Roland.* Indeed, we can trace parallelisms of mythic meaning between *Beowulf* and the *Chanson.* Let us take as a point of departure the scene in which Baligant has nearly overcome Charlemagne in single combat. Charlemagne's prayer finally gives him the strength at the last desperate moment by miracle to kill Baligant. The parallel is clear. Beowulf in the mere is lying on his back, with Grendel's dam astride his chest and ready to dispatch him. He is saved by catching sight of a fragment of a giant's sword lying nearby with which he kills the monster. We have already noted in Chapter Nine parallels in the *Iliad* and in the *Odyssey,* of Achilles nearly overcome by the river, Skamander, but saved by Hephaestus, and of Odysseus about to drown when rescued by Ino. The scene is in the other world and the hero is locked in mortal combat with the king of death. For the myth to be effective, he must overcome death and return.

If we pursue the parallel between Charlemagne (and his representative Roland) and Beowulf, we find a few striking details. But first we must admit the possibility that Roland is a substitute for Charlemagne, that he plays a role not unlike that of Patroclus. If we agree that Roland and Charlemagne are the same, then we see Roland, like Beowulf, wounding his adversary (Marsila in the *Chanson,* Grendel in *Beowulf*), and wounding him essentially in the same way in both poems. Beowulf tears Grendel's arm from its socket, and then the monster escapes to his lair. Roland cuts off Marsila's arm in single combat, after which Marsila escapes and returns to

Saragossa. They both seek solace from a female, Grendel from his dam, Marsila from his wife, and they both die as a result of the wounds. Their deaths lead directly to ravages by new characters: by Grendel's dam and by Marsila's overlord, Baligant. The structure of incident is amazingly similar in both these songs. Whatever the mythic meaning may be, there is a strong force of association which brings a second encounter with an enemy into the story when the pattern of the first encounter is mutilation, escape, and death elsewhere.

The Baligant episode is as necessary to the story of the *Chanson* as is that of Grendel's dam to *Beowulf*. It may be sufficient to explain this in terms of a feud but it would probably be more accurate to say that some mythic significance has yielded to a sociological explanation of similar intensity. Charlemagne, in the details of his final battle with Baligant, has taken over mythic material, and we should not be surprised that the parallel with Achilles is strong. This is true in spite of the great difference of age between the two heroes, Charlemagne, the old man with the long, white, flowing beard, and the twenty-year-old impetuous Achilles. Although the listeners' attention is occupied mostly with Roland, it is Charlemagne to whom the song belongs.

Digenis Akritas[19]

Digenis Akritas seems to have been a historical person of the eighth century of our era. The epic about his ancestry, birth, marriage, adventures, and death survives in five Greek metrical manuscripts, a Russian prose version dated by Grégoire in the twelfth century, and a late Greek prose version.[20] I shall be concerned primarily with the five Greek metrical versions, all of which are in the vernacular showing more or less archaizing of language and in the political fifteen-syllable meter. Only one of these is dated, O (Oxford), which belongs to 1670 and is the latest manuscript. For the others I follow Grégoire's dating:[21] the earliest is G (Grottaferrata) in the fourteenth century; the other three, A (Athens, formerly Andros), T (Trebizond), and E (Escorialensis), are sixteenth century. E and T are acephalic, and E is in very poor condition, with some lacunae. A and T are divided into ten books; O and G into eight books. E has no book division. The story as told in these manuscripts is essentially the same in all of them, but there is, nevertheless, considerable divergence in the telling. I shall not attempt to prove that any of these manuscripts is an oral text. They have been through the hands of learned men, or at least educated men who knew how to read and write. But I shall suggest tentatively that one of these manuscripts, E, is very close to being an oral text, and that the others have enough oral characteristics to show that there is an oral text behind them and that some signs of oral technique of composition have survived in them in spite of their literary, written, and learned character.

It is by now a truism that no two performances of an oral epic are ever textually exactly alike. Not only is such textual divergence typical and fundamental in oral style, but also, as we have said earlier, if two texts are nearly word-for-word exact, they cannot be oral narrative versions but one must have been either memorized or actually copied from the other or from the same original. Let us look at the same passage in the five Greek metrical manuscripts. I reproduce them here from Krumbacher's article, written in 1904, at the time he announced in Munich the discovery of the Escorialensis.[22]

E 298–301

ἀνέγνωσαν τὰ γράμματα καὶ οὕτως ἐδηλῶναν·
καὶ ὡς ἤκουσεν τὰ γράμματα, ἐθλίβην ἡ ψυχή του,
ἐκαύθηκαν τὰ σπλάγχνα του, ἐχάθην ἡ καρδιά του,
ἤκουσεν διὰ τὴν μάνναν του . . .

G 2. 105–106

ὡς δὲ εἶδεν ὁ ἀμηρᾶς τὴν γραφὴν τῆς μητρός του,
ἐσπλαγχνίσθη κατὰ πολὺ ὡς υἱὸς τὴν μητέρα,

T 235–236

καὶ ὡς ἤκουσε τὰ γράμματα, ἐθλίβη ἡ ψυχή του,
καὶ ἡ καρδία του τιτρώσκεται, ἠλέησε τὴν μητέρα,

O 655–658

τότε του δίνουν τὴν γραφή, ἀνοίγει καὶ διαβάζει
καὶ τότες ἀφ' τὴν πίκρα του βαρειὰ ἀναστενάζει,
γιατ' ἐπικράθηκεν πολλὰ τὸ πῶς του καταρᾶται
ἡ μάνα . . .

A 685–686

καὶ ὡς ἤκουσε τὰ γράμματα, ἐθλίβη ἡ ψυχή του,
καὶ τὴν καρδίαν τιτρώσκεται, ἠλέησε τὴν μητέρα,

Even from Krumbacher's brief sampling one could see that the Trebizond and Athens manuscripts are almost word-for-word the same. We might justly conclude that these are copies of the same original; and I do not believe that anyone would quarrel with us. We should also say that Oxford is far from the other four, but that Athens, Escorialensis, and Grottaferrata are somewhat alike.

A better idea of their similarity can be obtained from a comparison of somewhat longer passages from the three manuscripts. I have chosen the beginning of the Escorialensis manuscript, which is acephalic.

E 1–17

" Κρότοι καὶ κτύποι καὶ ἀπειλαὶ μὴ σὲ καταπτοήσουν,
μὴ φοβηθῇς τὸν θάνατον παρὰ μητρὸς κατάραν·
μητρὸς κατάραν φύλαττε καὶ μὴ πληγὰς καὶ πόνους.
Μέλη καὶ μέλη ἂν σὲ ποιήσουσιν, βλέπε ἐντροπὴν μὴ ποιήσῃς
5 ἂν κατεβοῦμεν.
    Τοὺς πέντε ἃς μᾶς φονεύσουσιν καὶ τότε ἃς τὴν ἐπάρουν·
μόνον προθύμως ἔξελθε εἰς τοῦ Ἀμηρᾶ τὴν τόλμην·
τὰ δυό σου χέρια φύλαττε καὶ ὁ Θεὸς νὰ μᾶς βοηθήσῃ.''
Καὶ ὁ Ἀμηρᾶς ἐκαβαλλίκευσεν, εἰς αὐτὸν ὑπαγαίνει·
10 φαρὶν ἐκαβαλλίκευσεν φιτυλὸν καὶ ἀστερᾶτον·
ὀμπρὸς εἰς τὸ μετῶπιν τοῦ χρυσὸν ἀστέραν εἶχεν,
τὰ τέσσαρά του ὀνύχια ἀργυροτζάπωτα ἦσαν,
καλιγοκάρφια ὁλάργυρα ἦτον καλιγωμένον,
ἡ οὐρά του σμυρνωμένη μὲ τὸ μαργαριτάριν.
15 Πρασινορρόδινος ἀετὸς εἰς τὴν σέλλαν ἐξ ὀπίσω
καὶ ἠσκιάζει τὰς κουτάλας του ἐκ τοῦ ἡλίου τὰς ἀκτῖνας·
κοντάριν ἐμαλάκιζε βένετον χρυσωμένον.

A 324–345

" καὶ κρότοι, κτύποι, ἀπειλαὶ μὴν σὲ καταπτοήσουν,
325 μὴν φοβηθῇς τὸν θάνατον, παρὰ μητρὸς κατάραν.
Μητρὸς κατάραν φύλαγε, κομμάτια κατακόπτου,
καὶ ὅταν ἀποθάνετε ἐσεῖς οἱ πέντε ὅλοι,
τότες ἃς τὴν πάρουσιν ἐκεῖνοι πάντες, ὅλοι·
μόνον προθύμως ἔξελθε στοῦ Ἀμηρᾶ τὴν τόλμαν,
330 μὲ τὴν βοήθειαν τοῦ Θεοῦ, τοῦ μόνου δυναμένου,
ἔχω τὸ θάρρος εἰς αὐτὸν τὴν ἀδελφὴν νὰ πάρῃς.''
Αὐτὸς δ' ἀκούσας τῆς μητρὸς τοὺς λόγους παραυτίκα
τὸν μαῦρον ἐπιλάλησε στὸν Ἀμηρᾶν ἐπῆγεν,
καὶ μετ' αὐτὸν οἱ ἀδελφοὶ ἐφθάσασι κατόπιν,
335 ἄλογα ἐκαβαλλικεύσασιν ἀρματωμένα οὗτοι.
Καὶ ὡς εἶδεν ὁ Ἀμηρᾶς τὸν νέον Κωνσταντῖνον,
τῆς κόρης τὸν αὐτάδελφον, ποὺ 'ρχετον πρὸς ἐκεῖνον,
φαρὶν ἐκαβαλλίκευεν φιτυλόν, ἀστερᾶτον,
ἔμπροσθεν εἰς τὸ μέτωπον χρυσὸν ἀστέρα εἶχε,
340 τὰ τέσσαρά του νύχια ἀργυροτζάποτ' ἦσαν,
καλλιγοκάρφια ἀργυρᾶ ἦταν καλλιγωμένον,
πρασινορρόδινος ἀετὸς στὴν σέλλαν ἦτον πίσω,
ζωγραφισμένος ἦτονε μὲ καθαρὸν χρυσάφι,
τὰ ἅρματά του λάμπασιν ἡλιακὰς ἀκτῖνας
345 καὶ τὸ κοντάρι, ἤστραπτεν, σὰν Βενετιᾶς χρυσάφι.

G 1. 134–164

"Μὴ ὅλως, λέγων, ἀδελφέ, φωναὶ καταπτοήσουν,
135 μικρόν τι δειλιάσωσι, πληγαί σε ἐκφοβήσουν·
κἂν γυμνὸν ἴδῃς τὸ σπαθὶν, φυγεῖν οὕτω μὴ δώσῃς,
κἂν ἄλλο τι δεινότερον εἰς τροπὴν μὴ ἐκφύγῃς·
νεότητος μὴ φεῖσαι σὺ παρὰ μητρὸς κατάραν,
ἧς εὐχαῖς στηριζόμενος τὸν ἐχθρὸν καταβάλεις·

140 οὐ γὰρ παρόψεται Θεὸς δούλους ἡμᾶς γενέσθαι·
      ἄπιθι, τέκνον, εὔθυμον, μὴ δειλιάσῃς ὅλως.''
      Καί, στάντες πρὸς ἀνατολάς, Θεὸν ἐπεκαλοῦντο·
      "Μὴ συγχωρήσῃς δέσποτα, δούλους ἡμᾶς γενέσθαι.''
      Καί, ἀσπασάμενοι αὐτόν, προέπεμψαν εἰπόντες·
145 " Ἡ τῶν γονέων μας εὐχὴ γένηται βοηθός σου!''
      Ὁ δὲ ἐφ' ἵππου ἐπιβὰς μαύρου, γενναιοτάτου,
      σπαθὶν διαζωσάμενος, λαμβάνει τὸ κοντάριν,
      ἐβάσταξε καὶ τὸ ραβδὶν εἰς τὸ ραβδοβαστάκιν·
      τὸ δὲ σημεῖον τοῦ σταυροῦ φραξάμενος παντόθεν,
150 τὸν ἵππον ἐπελάλησεν, εἰς τὸν κάμπον ἐξῆλθε·
      ἔπαιξε πρῶτον τὸ σπαθίν, εἶθ' οὕτως τὸ κοντάριν.
      Καί τινες τῶν Σαρακηνῶν ὠνείδιζον τὸν νέον·
      "'Ἴδε ποῖον ἐξέβαλον πρὸς τὸ μονομαχῆσαι
      τὸν τρόπαια ποιήσαντα μεγάλα εἰς Συρίαν!''
155 Εἷς δέ τις τῶν Σαρακηνῶν Ἀκρίτης Διλεβίτης
      γαληνὰ πρὸς τὸν Ἀμηρᾶν τοιόνδε λόγον ἔφη·
      " Ὁρᾷς τὸ καταπτέρνισμα ἐπιδέξιον ὅπως,
      σπαθίου τὴν ὑποδοχήν, γύρισμα κονταρίου;
      Ταῦτα πάντα ἐμφαίνουσι πεῖραν τε καὶ ἀνδρείαν·
160 ὅρα λοιπὸν μὴ ἀμελῶς τὸ παιδίον προσκρούσῃς.''
      Ἐξέβη καὶ ὁ Ἀμηρᾶς εἰς φάραν καβαλλάρης
      θρασύτατος ὑπῆρχε γὰρ καὶ φοβερὸς τῇ θέᾳ,
      τὰ ἄρματα ἀπέστιλβον ἡλιακὰς ἀκτῖνας·
      κοντάριν ἐμαλάκιζε βένετον, χρυσωμένον.

TRANSLATIONS

E 1–17

"Let clanging and crashing and threats not affright you!
Fear neither death nor anything except your mother's curse!
Beware your mother's curse, but pay no heed to blows and pain!
If they tear you to pieces, see that you shame us not,
5 If we should go down!
Let them kill the five of us, and then let them take her!
Only go forth boldly to meet the might of the Emir!
Guard your two hands, and may God help us all!"
And the Emir mounted and set out against him.
10 He mounted his piebald, star-marked steed.
In the midst of his forehead he had a golden star,
His four hoofs were silver adorned,
The nails in his shoes were of silver,
His tail was stiff with pearls.
15 Green and red was the eagle that perched behind the saddle
And shaded his shoulders from the rays of the sun.
The lance he wielded was of blue and gold.

A 324–345

"Let clanging and crashing and threats not affright you!
325 Fear neither death nor anything except your mother's curse!
Beware your mother's curse, and do your utmost!
And when all five of you die,
Then let them all take her!
Only go forth boldly to meet the might of the Emir,

330   With the help of God, who alone has power!
      I have faith in Him that you will find your sister."
      When he had heard his mother's words, straightway
      He urged on the black horse and set out against the Emir,
      And after him his brothers brought up the rear,
335   Mounted on their fully caparisoned steeds.
      And when the Emir saw the young Constantine,
      The twin brother of the girl, proceeding against him,
      He mounted his piebald, star-marked steed.
      In the midst of his forehead he had a golden star,
340   His four hoofs were silver adorned,
      The nails in his shoes were of silver.
      Green and red was the eagle that perched behind the saddle,
      Painted it was with pure gold.
      His weapons shone like the rays of the sun,
345   And his lance gleamed like Venetian gold.

      G 134–164

      Saying, "No wise, brother, let the shouts affright you
135   Nor ever shrink, nor let the blows appal you;
      If you see the sword naked, give not way,
      Or anything more terrible, never fly;
      Heed not your youth, only your mother's curse,
      Whose prayers supporting you, you shall prevail.
140   God shall not suffer us ever to be slaves.
      Go child, be of good heart, fear not at all."
      And standing towards the east they called on God:
      "O Lord, never allow us to be slaves."
      Having embraced they sent him forth, saying,
145   "So may our parent's prayer become your helper."
      He mounting on a black, a noble horse,
      Having girt on his sword, took up the lance;
      He carried his mace in the mace-holder,
      Fenced himself all sides with the sign of the cross,
150   Impelled his horse and rode into the plain,
      Played first the sword and then likewise the lance.
      Some of the Saracens reviled the youth:
      "Look what a champion is put out to fight
      Him who great triumphs made in Syria."
155   But one of them a Dilemite borderer
      Spoke softly to the Emir a word like this:
      "You see him spurring, and how cleverly,
      His sword's parry, the turning of his lance.
      All this exhibits skill as well as courage;
160   See then you meet the child not carelessly."
      Forth came the Emir riding upon a horse,
      Most bold he was and terrible to view,
      His arms were glittering with sunny rays;
      The lance he wielded was of blue and gold.

                        (Mavrogordato translation, pp. 11–12)

It is not easy to understand these three as copies from the same original.
Could they be closely related oral versions?

The textual differences between E, A-T, and G in many passages *look* like the textual differences between oral versions of an oral poem. Let us apply the formula test to these *Digenis Akritas* texts.

The passage in Chart XIII is from the Athens manuscript and shows that on the basis of its nearly five thousand lines there is a fair number of formulas in the sampling, although the result is not so impressive as in *Beowulf* or in *Roland*.

CHART XIII

A 628–637[24]

'Η μήτηρ δὲ[1] τοῦ 'Αμηρᾶ,/ἡ τοῦ 'Ακρίτου μάμμη,[2]

ὡς εἰς ἀλήθειαν ἔμαθε[3] τὰ κατ'αὐτῆς υἱοῦ τε,[4]

ἀπὸ Συρίας ἔστειλεν/[5] τὰ γράμματα τοιαῦτα,[6]

θρήνων μεστὰ ὑπάρχοντα[7] ὀνειδισμῶν καὶ πόνων,[8]

τῆς δὲ τοιαύτης τε γραφῆς[9] ἦσαν οἱ στίχοι οὗτοι.[10]

" Ὦ τέκνον μου, ποθεινότατον,[11] μητρὸς παρηγορία,[12]

πῶς ἐχωρίσθης ἀπ' ἐμοῦ[13] κ'ἐπῆγες εἰς τὰ ξένα;[14]

'Ετύφλωσας τοὺς ὀφθαλμούς,[15] ἔσβεσας καὶ τὸ φῶς μου,[16]

πῶς ἀπαρνήθης συγγενεῖς,[17] πίστιν καὶ τὴν πατρίδα,[18]

καὶ ἐγενόμην ὄνειδος[19] εἰς ὅλην τὴν Συρίαν;"[20]

An analysis of parts of Grottaferrata shows some tendencies toward formulization but the vocabulary differs. From the Grottaferrata manuscript we find the following formulas, for example:

(1) ὦ τέκνον ποθεινότατον

ὦ τέκνον ποθεινότατον, πῶς μητρὸς ἐπελάθους	2.53
Ὦ τέκνον ποθεινότατον, ὦ ψυχὴ καὶ καρδία,	4.81
Ὦ τέκνα ποθεινότατα, οἰκτείρατε μητέρα	1.70

(2) ὦ τέκνον μου γλυκύτατον

Ὦ τέκνον μου γλυκύτατον, οἰκτείρησον μητέρα·	2.89
Ὦ τέκνον μου γλυκύτατον, φῶς τῶν ἐμῶν ὀμμάτων,	3.132
Ναί, τέκνον μου γλυκύτατον, ὁ πατὴρ ἀπεκρίθη,	4.291
ὦ παιδίον γλυκύτατον, καβαλλάρην ἐμπρός μου·	2.290
Ὦ ἄνερ μου γλυκύτατε, αὐθέντα καὶ προστάτα,	2.120

(3) ὁ ᾿Αμηρᾶς εἰς φάραν καβαλλάρης

᾿Εξέβη καὶ ὁ ᾿Αμηρᾶς εἰς φάραν καβαλλάρης	1.161
καὶ ὕστερον ὁ ᾿Αμηρᾶς εἰς φάραν καβαλλάρης.	2.294

(4) εἰς τὸ καβαλλικεύειν

τὸ δὲ παιδίον εὔθιον εἰς τὸ καβαλλικεύειν·	4.242
διελάλησαν ἅπασιν εἰς τὸ καβαλλικεῦσαι.	4.597

(5) ἐν τῷ ἰδίῳ ἵππῳ

Ταῦτα εἰπὼν εἰσπήδησεν ἐν τῷ ἰδίῳ ἵππῳ	4.663
καὶ ὑποδέχεται αὐτὴν ἐν τῷ ἰδίῳ ἵππῳ,	4.782
῾Ως γὰρ ταύτην ἀνήγαγον ἐν τῷ ἰδίῳ ἵππῳ,	5.237
ὡς πρὸς ἐμὲ κατήρχετο σὺν τῷ ἰδίῳ ἵππῳ.	6.258
῾Η δὲ εὐθὺς ἐπέβηκεν ἐφ᾿ ἵππῳ τῷ ἰδίῳ,	6.530

But generally speaking one does not find formulas so readily in Grottaferrata as in Athens. If one proceeds by the method of taking a common word and listing all lines in which it is used in the manuscript, one seems to find fewer repetitions of phrase and consequently greater variety of phrasing in Grottaferrata than in Athens.

But the really significant test is not whether one can find formulas or repeated phrases in a manuscript, but rather how frequent they are in any

CHART XIV [25]

Καί, τὸ σπαθὶν δραξάμενος, κινᾷ πρὸς τὸ θηρίον·
————————————1—————————2
ὅταν δὲ ἐπλησίασεν, ἀποπηδᾷ ὁ λέων,
——————————3   4
καὶ χαρζανίσας τὴν οὐρὰν ἔδερε τὰς πλευράς του,
                5   6
μεγάλα βρυχησάμενος εἰς τὸν νέον ἐξῆλθε.
                7———————8
Τὸ δὲ παιδίον τὸ σπαθὶν εἰς ὕψος ἀνατείνας
———————————9—————————10
κρούει τον κατὰ κεφαλῆς πλήρης εἰς τὴν μεσίαν,
——————————11——————————12
καὶ διεσχίσθη ἡ κεφαλὴ ἄχρι τῶν ὤμων κάτω.
                13   14

given passage. Chart XIV is a sample of a passage of Grottaferrata (4.180–186) analyzed for formulas, using only the Grottaferrata manuscript itself for material. This can be compared with the preceding chart for the Athens manuscript. A look at this passage and at the notes verifies our feeling that although there are formulas in the manuscript, they are not all-pervasive as in a true oral text.

The Escorialensis, in spite of its roughness and brevity, presents us with a number of formulas. Here are some typical formulas from Escorialensis:

(1) τοιοῦτον λόγον λέγει

καὶ μετὰ τοῦ δακτύλου του τοιοῦτον λόγον λέγει·	54
Καὶ τότε ὁ Φιλοπαπποῦς τοιοῦτον λόγον λέγει.	677
Καὶ τότε καὶ ὁ στρατηγὸς τοιοῦτον λόγον λέγει·	987
ἀντάμα οἱ πέντε ἐστενάξασιν, τοιοῦτον λόγον εἶπαν·	188
Καὶ τότε πάλιν ὁ 'Αμηρᾶς τοῦτον τὸν λόγον λέγει·	18
γλυκέα τὸν ἐφίλει καὶ τέτοιον λόγον λέγει·	534

(2) τὸ φῶς τῶν ἀπελάτων

Ὁ θαυμαστὸς βασίλειος, τὸ φῶς τῶν ἀπελάτων,	622
Πότε νὰ δοῦν τὰ μάτια μου τὸ φῶς τῶν ἀπελάτων	636
νὰ γομωστοῦν τὰ ὀμμάτιά μου τὸ φῶς τῶν ἀπελάτων;	637

(3) φαρὶν ἐκαβαλλίκευσεν

φαρὶν ἐκαβαλλίκευσεν φιτυλὸν καὶ ἀστερᾶτον·	10
φαρὶν ἐκαβαλλίκευε, πολλὰ ἦτον ὡραῖον,	1486
Γοργὸν ἐκαβαλλίκευσαν ἄλλοι τριακόσιοι ἀγοῦροι,	944
γοργὸν ἐκαβαλλίκευσαν θεῖος καὶ ὁ πατήρ του	1031

(4) εὐθὺς ἐκαβαλλίκευσαν

Εὐθὺς ἐκαβαλλίκευσαν εἰς τὸν κάμπον κατεβαίνουν·	32
Καὶ εὐθὺς ἐκαβαλλίκευσεν εἰς τὸν οἶκον ἀποβγαίνουν,	482
εὐθὺς ἐκαβαλλίκευσα καὶ ἐπῆγα εἰς τὸ κοράσιον·	1578
χθὲς ἐκαβαλλικεύσαμεν ὁμάδι καὶ οἱ πέντε	425

(5) πηδᾷ, καβαλλικεύει

Καὶ τότε ὁ νεώτερος πηδᾷ, καβαλλικεύει,	1009
Καὶ ὡς εἶδεν τοῦτο ὁ Κίνναμος πηδᾷ, καβαλλικεύει,	1274
Γοργὸν πάλιν σηκώνεται, πηδᾷ, καβαλλικεύει,	1281
Καὶ τότε καὶ ὁ Φιλοπαπποῦς πηδᾷ, καβαλλικεύει,	1357
Καὶ πάραυτα ὁ 'Αμηρᾶς πηδᾷ καβαλλικεύγει,	566
καὶ μὲ τὸν λαόν του καὶ μὲ τοὺς ἀγούρους του πηδᾷ καβαλλικεύγει	567
καὶ ὅσοι οὐδὲν τὸν ἐγνώριζαν, πηδοῦν καβαλλικεύουν.	927

(6) πηδᾷ καὶ ἐκαβαλλίκευσεν

πηδᾷ καὶ ἐκαβαλλίκευσεν καὶ ἐπῆρεν τὸ σπαθίν του	831
πηδᾷ κ' ἐκαβαλλίκευσε καὶ παίρνει καὶ κοντάριν	1555
Πηδῶ καὶ ἐκαβαλλίκευσα τὴν θαυμαστὴν τὴν φάραν,	1440

(7) Καὶ αὐτὸς ἐκαβαλλίκευσεν

Καὶ αὐτὸς ἐκαβαλλίκευσεν ὁ Διγενὴς 'Ακρίτης,	752
Καὶ αὐτὸς ἐκαβαλλίκευσεν, εἰς αὐτὸν καταβαίνει	938
Καὶ ὁ λαὸς ἐκαβαλλίκευσεν μετὰ πολυχρονίων·	1060
Καὶ ὁ 'Αμηρᾶς ἐκαβαλλίκευσεν, εἰς αὐτὸν ὑπαγαίνει·	9
Καὶ οἱ πέντε ἐκαβαλλίκευσαν, εἰς τὸν 'Αμηρᾶν ὑπάγουν·	58
Οἱ πέντε ἐκαβαλλίκευσαν καὶ ὑπὰν εἰς τὸ Χαλκοπέτριν,	332

(8) Γοργὸν ἐπῆρα τὸ ραβδὶν

Γοργὸν ἐπῆρα τὸ ραβδὶν καὶ προσυπήντησά τους,	1173
γοργὸν ἐπῆρεν τὸ ραβδὶν καὶ προσυπήντησέν τους·	974
γοργὸν ἐπῆρα τὸ σπαθὶν καὶ προσυπήντησά του·	1133

One can note from these formulas the following systems built around
the verb for mounting or riding a horse; with the kind of horse as the
direct object:

$$\left.\begin{array}{l} \varphi\acute{\alpha}\rho\iota\nu \\ \gamma o\rho\gamma\acute{o}\nu \end{array}\right\} \quad \grave{\epsilon}\kappa\alpha\beta\alpha\lambda\lambda\acute{\iota}\kappa\epsilon\upsilon\sigma\epsilon\nu \ (-\sigma\alpha\nu)$$

with an adverb preceding the verb:

$$\left.\begin{array}{l} \epsilon\mathit{\dot{\upsilon}}\theta\acute{\upsilon}s \\ \chi\theta\acute{\epsilon}s \end{array}\right\} \quad \grave{\epsilon}\kappa\alpha\beta\alpha\lambda\lambda\acute{\iota}\kappa\epsilon\upsilon\sigma\alpha\nu \ (-\sigma\alpha\mu\epsilon\nu)$$

or with a preceding subject:

$$\left.\begin{array}{l} \varkappa\alpha\grave{\iota} \ \acute{o} \ '\!A\mu\eta\rho\tilde{\alpha}s \\ \varkappa\alpha\grave{\iota} \ o\acute{\iota} \ \pi\acute{\epsilon}\nu\tau\epsilon \\ o\acute{\iota} \ \pi\acute{\epsilon}\nu\tau\epsilon \\ \varkappa\alpha\grave{\iota} \ \alpha\mathit{\dot{\upsilon}}\tau\acute{o}s \\ \varkappa\alpha\grave{\iota} \ \acute{o} \ \lambda\alpha\acute{o}s \end{array}\right\} \quad \grave{\epsilon}\kappa\alpha\beta\alpha\lambda\lambda\acute{\iota}\kappa\epsilon\upsilon\sigma\epsilon\nu \ (-\sigma\alpha\nu)$$

For comparison with the passages analyzed for formulas from the Athens
and Grottaferrata manuscripts, the passage from Escorialensis (lines 1274–
1280) similarly analyzed will be useful (Chart XV). It is worth stressing
that Athens has 4778 lines, Grottaferrata 3709, and Escorialensis only 1867
lines. The analyses in each case are based only on material from the
manuscript from which the passage is taken. Because of the frequency of
formulas in the evidence presented here, in spite of the limited amount of
material for analysis, and because of the irregularity of the lines in the
manuscript itself, I might tentatively suggest for consideration by the
specialists that Escorialensis may be an oral manuscript unskillfully written
down from dictation. It is instructive to compare the irregular lines in
Escorialensis with the recited texts in Parry and Lord, Volume II (for
example, No. 11).

CHART XV [26]

$$K\alpha\grave{\iota} \ \grave{\omega}s \ \epsilon\mathit{\tilde{\iota}}\delta\epsilon\nu \ \tau o\tilde{\upsilon}\tau o \ \acute{o} \ K\acute{\iota}\nu\nu\alpha\mu os \ \pi\eta\delta\tilde{\alpha}, \ \varkappa\alpha\beta\alpha\lambda\lambda\iota\varkappa\epsilon\acute{\upsilon}\epsilon\iota,$$

$$\varkappa\alpha\grave{\iota} \ \grave{\epsilon}\pi\acute{\alpha}\nu\omega \ \mu o\upsilon \ \grave{\epsilon}\pi\iota\lambda\acute{\alpha}\lambda\eta\sigma\epsilon\nu \ \mathit{\tilde{\iota}}\nu\alpha \ \rho\alpha\beta\delta\acute{\epsilon}\alpha\nu \ \mu o\tilde{\upsilon} \ \delta\acute{\omega}\sigma\eta.$$

$$K\alpha\lambda\grave{\eta}\nu \ \rho\alpha\beta\delta\acute{\epsilon}\alpha\nu \ \acute{\epsilon}\delta\omega\varkappa\alpha \ \tau\grave{\eta}\nu \ \varphi\acute{\alpha}\rho\alpha\nu \ \epsilon\mathit{\dot{\iota}}s \ \tau\grave{o} \ \varkappa\epsilon\varphi\acute{\alpha}\lambda\iota\nu,$$

$$\varkappa\alpha\grave{\iota} \ \mu\grave{\epsilon} \ \tau\grave{o}\nu \ \varkappa\alpha\beta\alpha\lambda\lambda\acute{\alpha}\rho\eta\nu \ \tau\eta s \ \acute{\epsilon}\pi\epsilon\sigma\epsilon\nu \ \acute{\epsilon}\mu\pi\rho o\sigma\theta\acute{\epsilon}\nu \ \mu o\upsilon,$$

$$\varkappa\alpha\grave{\iota} \ \grave{\epsilon}\gamma\grave{\omega} \ \pi\acute{\alpha}\lambda\iota\nu \ \tau\grave{o}\nu \ \acute{\epsilon}\lambda\epsilon\gamma\alpha, \ \grave{\alpha}s \ \sigma\eta\varkappa\omega\theta\tilde{\eta}, \ \mu\grave{\eta} \ \varkappa\epsilon\mathit{\tilde{\iota}}\tau\alpha\iota.$$

$$`` \ '\!E\gamma\epsilon\acute{\iota}\rho o\upsilon \ \grave{\alpha}\pi' \ \alpha\mathit{\dot{\upsilon}}\tau o\upsilon, \ K\acute{\iota}\nu\nu\alpha\mu\epsilon, \ \varkappa o\iota\tau\acute{o}\mu\epsilon\nu o\nu \ o\mathit{\dot{\upsilon}} \ \varkappa\rho\tilde{\omega} \ \sigma o\upsilon$$

$$\acute{\alpha}\mu\epsilon \ \pi\epsilon\rho\iota\sigma\omega\rho\epsilon\acute{\upsilon}\tau\eta\tau\iota, \ \varkappa\alpha\grave{\iota} \ \pi\acute{\alpha}\lambda\iota\nu \ \grave{\alpha}\nu \ \theta\acute{\epsilon}\lambda\eta s \ \acute{\epsilon}\lambda\alpha.``$$

Turning next to the test of enjambement, one sees necessary enjambement
frequently in the Oxford manuscript of the *Digenis Akritas,* which dates

from 1670 and is in rhymed couplets. Both the rhyme and the enjambement point here to a "literary" text:

O 269–282

'Ως εἶδαν οἱ Σαρακηνοὶ ὅτι 'πῶς ἐνικήθη
ὁ 'Αμηρᾶς καὶ εἰς τῆς γῆς τὸ χῶμα ἐτυλίχθη,
τρέχουν καί τον ἀρπάζουσιν νὰ μήν τον θανατώσῃ
ὁ Κωνσταντῖνος κ'εἰς τῆς γῆς τὸ χῶμα τόνε χώσῃ,
καὶ καθὼς τον ἀρπάξασιν τοῦ λέσιν· " μὴ θελήσῃς
πλει', ἀφέντη, μὲ τὸν Κωνσταντῆ νὰ 'βγῆς νὰ πολεμήσῃς,
275 μόνο ἀγάπην ἂν 'μπορῇς κάμε μ'αὐτὸν γιὰ νά 'χῃς
ἀνάπαψιν καὶ ἀφοβιὰ εἰς ὅποιον τόπο λάχῃς."
"Ὅμως 'σὰν ἐσυνέφερεν ὁ 'Αμηρᾶς 'φοβήθη
μήπως καὶ ἀφ' τὸν Κωνσταντῆ 'πάγῃ μέσα 's τὰ βύθη
τοῦ "Αδου καὶ ἐτρόμαξεν καὶ γιὰ τοῦτο καθίζει
280 εἰς τ ἄλογο καὶ 'γλήγορα 's τὸ στράτευμα γυρίζει·
καὶ φεύγοντας ἐγύρισεν πάλι καὶ φοβερίζει
τὸν Κωνσταντῖνον, κ'ἤρχισεν μὲ λόγια νὰ ὑβρίζῃ.

TRANSLATION

When the Saracens saw how the Emir
270 Was being overcome and covered in the mound of earth,
They ran and took him, in order that him might not slay
Constantine and put him into the mound of earth;
So straightway they took up his body. "Do not wish
More, my lord, to go and do battle with Constantine.
275 Only be reconciled with him, if you can, that you may have
Rest and freedom from fear whatever may befall."
When the Emir recovered his senses, he feared lest
He might be despatched by Constantine to the midst of the depths
Of Hades, and he trembled and for this reason sat
280 Upon his horse and quickly returned to the army.
And he turned back the fleeing and he affrighted
Constantine, and began to taunt him with words.

On the other hand the following example from the Athens manuscript, dated by Grégoire in the sixteenth century, shows the kind of unperiodic enjambement we have seen in the Slavic examples earlier:

A 2030–2042

2030 'Ως τὸν εἶδεν ὁ Διγενὴς τὴν κόρην τότε 'λάλει·
"Βλέπεις, καλή μου, Σαρακηνόν, ποὺ μᾶς καταδιώκει,
ἄρτι, κυρία, πρόσεξε πῶς θέλω νὰ τὸν κάμω."
'Εσήκωσε τὴν λιγυρὴν στὴν γῆν τὴν ἀποθέτει,
2035 αὐτὸς ἐκαβαλλίκευσεν ἐπῆρε τὸ κοντάρι,
καὶ πρὸς ἐκεῖνον ἔτρεξεν καὶ προσυπήντησέν τον,
καὶ πρῶτον τὸν ἐλάλησε· "Σαρακηνέ μου δέχου."
Καὶ τὸ κοντάριν ἔσυρε ὀμπρὸς στὴν κεφαλήν του,
εὐθὺς ἀπεθανάτωσε κεῖνον καὶ τ'ἀλογόν του,
καὶ πάλιν μεταστράφηκεν ὄπισθεν εἰς τὴν κόρην.
2040 Καὶ ἄλλοι τριακόσιοι ἀγοῦροι τὸν 'φθάνουν
καβαλλαραῖοι καὶ πεζοὶ ἦλθασι πρὸς ἐκεῖνον,
ἔκραζον δέ, ἐφώναζον καὶ ταραχὰς ἐποίουν.

TRANSLATION

2030 When Digenis saw him, he spoke to the girl:
"My dear, you see the Saracen pursuing us;
Pay heed now, my lady, to how I shall deal with him."
He raised the sweet maid and put her upon the ground,
While he himself mounted and took up his spear,
2035 And he set out to meet him and confronted him,
And first he addressed him: "Saracen, receive my blow!"
And he hurled his spear at his head.
Straightway he killed him and his horse,
And he went back again to the girl.
2040 And another thirty youths came up,
Riding and on foot they came toward him,
And they cried out and shouted and made a great din.

In respect to enjambement, therefore, the Athens manuscript might be oral, but this feature, unlike formulaic structure, is far from being sufficiently decisive for us to call this manuscript oral. All we can say is that it is not the same kind of "literary" style as that of the Oxford manuscript or of Virgil. Indeed, the Oxford manuscript is the only *Digenis Akritas* manuscript that' has a predominance of necessary enjambement. All the other manuscripts exhibit the unperiodic, adding, style of oral poetry. This feature as we have said before, is symptomatic, however, rather than decisive because it persists into written poetry.

The variations in thematic mixture among the manuscripts of *Digenis Akritas* are but further proof that somehow or other we are dealing with oral tradition. Perhaps the most characteristic result of thematic mixture is the narrative inconsistency. Two themes that do not go together are for one reason or another placed together in the same poem. The following examples are from the Grottaferrata manuscript. In the story of the Emir, the brothers search for their sister in the heap of slain maidens and conclude that she has been killed. Their hearts filled with vengeance, they return to the Emir's tent. But their words to him are simply:

Give us, Emir, our sister, or else kill us.
Not one of us without her will turn home,
But all be murdered for our sister's sake.[27]

Only in an oral poem could such an inconsistency be found. I submit that no literary poet would commit so obvious an error. Another example is found when the Emir receives the letter from his mother, asking him to return to Syria.[28] The Emir goes to his wife, and she agrees to go with him. But a few lines later, after the theme of the brothers' dream has intervened, the singer has already forgotten the agreement of the wife, and the Emir departs alone, giving his wife a ring. This certainly looks like oral construction. Examples could be multiplied, but these are sufficient to indicate that here too on the level of thematic structure our manuscripts of *Digenis Akritas* exhibit some of the characteristics of oral poetry.

And why should they not? Grégoire, Entwhistle,[29] and others have all indicated that *Digenis Akritas* was formed from oral ballads. If this is true, it should not be surprising to find oral characteristics in the epic. I think, however, that there is reason to hold another view, namely that the epic of *Digenis Akritas* was from its inception a single, unified oral epic, and that the so-called Akritic ballads are not survivals of elements that went into the making of the *Digenis Akritas* but should perhaps be thought of as existing side by side with it.

It is customary to think of *Digenis Akritas* as a double romance, and to suppose that the tale of the Emir, Digenis Akritas' father, was a separate story and that the tale of Digenis Akritas became attached to it in a very natural way, making the exploits and marriage of the son follow chronologically the marriage of the father. I should like to suggest that there is something more than this which connects these two parts of the epic. The key, I think, is to be found in the character of Digenis Akritas. His youthful precocity, his learning, his hunting of wild beasts, his encounter with the dragon, his saving of maidens, and even his death mark him as a particular kind of hero. The pattern of his life and adventures can be found in many other epics, from the ancient Babylonian Gilgamesh, in which some of his characteristics belong to the hero Enkidu and some to Gilgamesh, to the Serbocroatian epics of Zmaj Ognjeni Vuk and the Russian Vseslav Epic.[30]

There is always something special about the birth of these heroes that explains the particular role and mission which they are to fulfill in their lives. In almost every case they are the offspring of man and god or of man and animal. Gilgamesh, as we have seen, is two-thirds god and one-third man, Enkidu is divinely created, Volx Vseslav'evič's mother is human, but his father was a snake. Only in the Serbocroatian tale are both parents human. But even here the birth of the wondrous hero is greeted by cosmic disturbances as in the Russian tale. There is a hint of such disturbances at the creation of Enkidu.[31] The legend of Alexander of Macedon[32] belongs in the same category. The birth of these heroes explains their character; for they are the result of the union of two disparate elements. I might even be so bold as to suggest that the name Digenis indicates even more than the fact that his mother was Christian and his father Moslem. But be that as it may, the tale of Digenis' birth and of his antecedents is an integral part of the epic. The astrological prologue of Book I of the Athens manuscript, with its emphasis on the maiden and her destiny fits this idea. Much has been blurred by the processes of oral tradition; the significance of the connection has vanished, but the connection itself has remained in the fact of the so-called double romance.

In the story of Digenis himself, Grégoire, with the help of the Russian version, has indicated the importance of the Philopappas episode in connection with the abduction of Eudokia.[33] And Entwhistle has brilliantly indicated in the last article that he wrote, published posthumously in the *Oxford Slavonic Papers*,[34] that there must be a connection between the abduction and the death of Digenis. Unfortunately one must disagree with Entwhistle, one of the most learned and astute of ballad scholars, in his conclusion that *Digenis* was composed from separate ballads. It is ironic that he himself has furnished material for the opposite theory.

If one cannot reconstruct an original text, and if one cannot reconstruct with any degree of exactness the myriad thematic complexes which the poem has shown in the past, one can, I believe, reconstruct a basic form, a more or less stable core of the story. No matter how fluid the song content may be, there is always this stable core of narrative or of meaning that distinguishes one song from another. In the case of *Digenis Akritas*, it is the age-old tale of the demigod who lives a wonder-working life among men, who champions and saves, but who has within him a mortal element which leads inevitably to his death. The tale of Digenis must begin with the story of the marriage of his mother and father; it must as inevitably end with the hero's death. Indeed, I would suggest that this epic has tenaciously survived, even when misunderstood, because of the basic grandeur of its myth.

But the epic of Digenis in time went through the many sea-changes inherent in oral composition and recomposition. I do not think that we should conceive of these as Grégoire does as redactions of an original text or as *remaniements*. How then are we to envisage the composition of the several manuscripts which we possess? I think we may justly hazard the opinion that the Escorialensis manuscript is directly from oral tradition; and at the other end of the spectrum, that the Oxford manuscript is a literary reworking from some previous manuscript of the song, presumably one like the Grottaferrata, which is also divided into eight books. Certainly behind the other two manuscripts, Grottaferrata and Athens, is an oral form of the story, as we have indicated above. It might be that this oral form was written down and formed a canonized text for singers who were like the rhapsodes of ancient Greece (as opposed to its ἀοιδοί) or like the *narodni guslari* of Yugoslavia. It would not be inconsistent with the facts, I believe, to suppose then that (1) Escorialensis is a rhapsode version of this canonized text, written down either by or from the rhapsode and (2) Grottaferrata and Athens are rhapsode versions that have been retold once more by a man whose repertory of tales included as well the current romances of chivalry, and who has attempted to relate the story of Digenis as a romance. Yet, these romances may also be from oral tradition, and the wedding here of epic and romance is a most natural one. In other words one can see here that epic and romance are not really separate genres, but actually the same genre of oral narrative poetry. In a chivalric and religious age the older heroic epic naturally assumes the coloring of its age, and the oral style allows for change, for multiplication of incident, and for general expansion.

Only when these versions exist on paper can we speak of the learned editor who has divided the tale into books, eight or ten as the case may be, and provided these books with introductions as in the Athens manuscript. Our texts have been touched up to look like Homeric epic as it existed in Alexandrian manuscripts and later editions. To this editor would certainly be due the references in the text to Homer and the "shield of Achilles" type of description of Digenis' palace. Yet even the little introductions and the "learned" references are done in a style almost indistinguishable from the rest, by analogy with the patterns and rhythms of oral poetry; for vestiges of this method of composition survive for a long time into the age of writing.

H. J. Chaytor has told the fascinating story of medieval man's laborious reading aloud of manuscripts, making them out letter for letter and word for word.[35] And when man wrote in his vernacular, his thought processes, his method of composing vernacular poetry by theme and formula changed but slowly. Much of the outward mechanics of the oral style, as we have seen, persisted in written poetry, and thus the boundary between the two became and remained blurred to all but the initiate. One should not, however, mistake ambivalence for transition. We know now that the author (and I use the word advisedly) of the "transitional" has already crossed the border from oral to written. It may not be possible in the case of many of our medieval texts to know with certainty whether we are dealing with an oral or a written product, but we may reach a high degree of *probability* in our research; especially if we realize the certainty that it is either the one or the other.

In Conclusion

Yet after all that has been said about *oral* composition as a technique of line and song construction, it seems that the term of greater significance is *traditional*. Oral tells us "how," but traditional tells us "what," and even more, "of what kind" and "of what force." When we know how a song is built, we know that its building blocks *must* be of great age. For it is of the *necessary* nature of tradition that it seek and maintain stability, that it preserve itself. And this tenacity springs neither from perverseness, nor from an abstract principle of absolute art, but from a desperately compelling conviction that what the tradition is preserving is the very means of attaining life and happiness. The traditional oral epic singer is not an artist; he is a seer. The patterns of thought that he has inherited came into being to serve not *art* but religion in its most basic sense. His balances, his antitheses, his similes and metaphors, his repetitions, and his sometimes seemingly willful playing with words, with morphology, and with phonology were not intended to be devices and conventions of Parnassus, but were techniques for emphasis of the potent symbol. Art appropriated the forms of oral narrative. But it is from the dynamic, life principle in myth, the wonder-working tale, that art derived its force. Yet it turned its back on the traditional significance to contemplate the forms as if they were pure form, and from that contemplation to create new meanings.

The nontraditional literary artist, sensing the force of the traditional material whence his art was derived, but no longer comprehending it, no longer finding acceptable the methods of the traditional, sought to compensate for this lack by intricacies of construction created for their own sake. The old patterns were not only thus given new meanings, but a kind of complexity, which could be attained only through writing, was also cultivated as an end in itself. When we look at oral poetry and observe in it something that looks like these new forms and complexities, we may be deluded. Enamored of the meretricious virtues of art, we may fail to understand the real meaning of a traditional poem. That meaning cannot be brought to light by elaborate schematization, unless that schematization be based on the elements of oral tradition, on the still dynamic multiform patterns in the depths of primitive myth.

APPENDIX I

Comparison of Texts of "Bećiragić Meho" by Two Different Singers
Parry 12468 and 12471

Invocation. Mumin Vlahovljak 1–16, Avdo Međedović 1–30
1. *The scene of the assembly: description of assembly*

Mumin (17–36)

Thirty men of the Border were drinking wine at the gate of Udbina. Mustajbey of the Lika was at their head with seven standard-bearers; Mujo of Kladuša was at his right with four standard-bearers; at his left was Durutagić Ahmo with four standard-bearers. In their midst was Child Halil serving drinks to the aghas.

Avdo (31–137)

Praise of Bosnia in the time of Sulejman the Magnificent (31–51). Thirty-six aghas were sitting and talking in the stone loggia in Kanidža. Mustajbey was at their head with seven standard-bearers; at his right was Hrnja Mujo with four standard-bearers; at his left Durut Ahmetagha with four standard-bearers. A brief description of each is given as he is named. Next to Mujo was the Ajan of Kanidža, then Kozlić Hurem, Arap Mehmedagha, the Dizdar of Kanidža, and Ramo of Glamoč. In their midst Child Halil was serving drinks. He is described. The aghas put aside their wine glasses and began to drink brandy and then to boast; their boasts are listed. The aghas were all rich and all were merry.

2. Description of Bećiragić Meho

Mumin (37–47)

The poor orphan Meho was at the foot of the assembly, near the door. He wore only cotton pants and shirt, but he had a fine sash and two beautiful golden pistols. Nobody in the assembly offered him coffee or tobacco or a glass. He gazed sadly at the company.

Avdo (138–171)

Near the door of the tavern sat a sad young man. He did not wear breastplate or helmet with plumes, but only cotton trousers and a silk shirt; over his fine sash was an arms belt in which were two golden pistols. They are described. He hung his head and gazed at the aghas. Nobody spoke to him nor offered him a glass. His heart was wilted like a rose in the hands of a rude bachelor.

3. *Arrival of the messenger*

Mumin (48–76)

When the aghas had drunk their fill, there was a creaking of the door of the tavern and a messenger arrived, gave greetings, which were accepted, and then asked if he had arrived at Udbina. Halil told the Latin that he had. Then the Latin asked for Mustajbey, and Halil pointed him out. The messenger did obeisance to Mustajbey and then stood before him to speak.

Avdo (172–272)

The beys looked out over the plain and saw a cloud from which a rider emerged on a black horse, carrying a letter on a branch. He was a Latin. The beys pondered in fear as to what the message might be. Mustajbey called his standard-bearers Desnić and Memić to go down to meet the messenger. The messenger approached them, gave greetings which were accepted, dismounted, and entered the loggia and greeted the aghas and beys. He asked them if he had arrived at Unđurovina and Kanidža. Mustajbey said that he had. The messenger noted that Mustajbey was the most honored man in the assembly and asked his name and rank. Mustajbey told his name and listed the places over which he ruled. The messenger did obeisance before Mustajbey and then stood before him to speak. (Avdo has made some changes in action here — up to this point, except for the change of Udbina to Kanidža, the differences have been descriptive ornamentation. The changes in action, however, are not essential to the story. Avdo simply uses a technique of his own for the arrival of messengers.)

4. *Delivery of the letter*

Mumin (77–130)

The messenger asked for Bećiragić Meho. The letter was for him. Mustajbey looked at Meho, was ashamed, and told the Hungarian that Meho was not there, but asked him to give the letter to him and he would give it to Meho. The messenger refused, saying that he would first lose his head rather than give the letter to anyone else; for he had vowed not to do so. He would rather return with the letter. Meho then spoke, chiding Mustajbey for not acknowledging him. The messenger went to Meho and put the letter in his hands, but he thought in his heart as he did so of how unfortunate Anđelija, the daughter of the Ban of Janok, was in such a hero.

Avdo (273–422)

The messenger praised Mustajbey's fame, and then asked him, after stressing that he was a stranger and after paying compliments to the assembled aghas and beys, if Bećiragić Meho was there, and, if not, where his house was. Mustajbey was overproud and ashamed of a poor youth without family and property. He told the messenger that Meho was not there, and asked him to give him the letter. He would then deliver it to Meho and bring back an answer. The messenger said that he had received the letter as a trust and would die before giving it to anyone except Meho. Meho then went to Mustajbey and upbraided him for his feeling of shame: Mustajbey has riches and power now; but everything comes in time; time builds towers and time destroys them. Meho said he had once been of the best family, but time and destiny had deprived him of all. The Latin looked at Meho, liked him not, but approached him, thinking in his heart how unfortunate was Ana, the daughter of the Ban of Janok. She could not have found a worse man in all Bosnia. Her hand had been sought by the best of the Christian nobles, and she had chosen this Meho! But he gave the letter to Meho.

5. Payment and departure of the messenger

Mumin (131–176)

Meho was embarrassed because he had no gift for the messenger. Finally he remembered the pistols and gave them to the Latin. The Latin thought to himself that he had carried letters for twelve years to the greatest nobles but never had anyone done this before. Meho had given him everything he had. The Latin returned the pistols, saying that such pistols were for such a hero as Meho. Anđelija had promised to pay him well if he found Meho and delivered the letter. With these words the messenger departed.

Avdo (423–558)

Meho took the letter, broke the seal on it, and read it. Mustajbey asked him whence the letter came. Meho put the letter in his bosom and blushed; for he had no money even to shave or to buy tobacco, to say nothing of enough to give a gift to the Latin from far away. Great was Meho's woe; it was as if the sky had fallen on him, in the midst of so many nobles (who are briefly listed). The Latin told him that he was from far away and asked for a gift for the return journey, to shoe his horse and have a drink. Meho's cheeks flamed and water poured from his forehead when the Latin thus accosted him and he saw what he might expect from Mustajbey. His hand went to his sash and he took out his two golden pistols and gave them to the Latin with thanks for having brought the letter and for having been faithful to his word. Meho added that if anyone should ask the Latin, he should not be ashamed. Meho said that he had once been a landholder and that he was of good family, but he had been in captivity in Germany and today he remained without anything except God and his health. The pistols, he said, were worth a thousand ducats. He could sell them for drink and to shoe his horse. Meho said he had no money and was really a stranger without fatherland. He went about the beys and aghas, he said, until their hearts inclined them to give him shelter. After this speech the Latin thought in his heart that he had been carrying letters for twelve years, letters of all kinds, and even to kings, indeed even to Maximilian in Vienna, but not even he had given him such a gift. Usually he got a ducat or ten, two more often than four, and when he got ten, that was a real event. Meho had given him everything he had. He could not leave such a hero without his pistols, he thought. He returned them to Meho, saying that he was merely testing Meho. His mistress had given him money for the journey, telling him that he should bring back a reply from Meho if Meho were still alive. She said that she would give him as much money again when he returned. Meho replied that the messenger should give greetings to Ana explaining that great woes had fallen upon him, but that all would turn out well. The messenger left the room and mounted his horse. He said farewell and departed with Meho's *bon voyage*.

6. *The letter, Meho's request, Mustajbey's answer*

Mumin (177–238)

Meho opened the letter and read it. Anđa inquired if he was well and remarked that she thought he would never forget her. She had done him great service. She had turned away many suitors and written Meho several letters to which there were no replies. Now her father would marry her to Đuro of Radane. She asked Meho to come to Janok that they might see one another and be together once more.

Meho approached Mustajbey and requested from him clothing, armor, and weapons, for a trip to Janok. He promised to pay him back; he promised he would return.

Mustajbey cursed Meho (the bey was in his cups) saying that he had already given three horses and three sets of clothes to Meho, and had not received them back. Meho had given them to someone else. He had no horse or money to give Meho. Let Meho not even seek permission for leave.

Avdo (559–702)

Meho read the letter and hung his head. Mustajbey asked why he was sad, and Meho told him that the letter was from his betrothed in Janok who had saved his life when he was in prison there. She had fallen in love with him and asked that he take her with him to the Krajina, if he ever returned. She had had many suitors, kings, bans, generals, and captains, but had remained unwed. She was an only child and very beautiful (she is described, lines 594–606). She would turn Mustajbey's head. Meho himself wondered that she had fallen in love with him. Now her father had given her to Đuro of Radane, and the wedding guests were expected in the middle of the following month. She has written to him (and now he quotes the letter) that she has done him great service, including the learning of Turkish and the Moslem faith. She asked him to take her with him, but he went back and has surely found other women at home and forgotten Anđa. She will not forget him until they light candles for her. Meho, she writes, must come to her at least to say goodbye (end of letter). Meho then in the same speech asked Mustajbey to give him clothes for the sake of his son Bećir. He would not ask for weapons, since he had two good pistols, but he would ask for weapons for fighting from horseback, for a horse, that he might go to Janok to see Anđa.

Mustajbey became very angry and cursed Meho. He had no horses to lend and no clothes. He had already lent him the same three times. He didn't even ride the horses or load them, but gave them to someone else. The same with the clothing and with weapons. Meho had better forget Anđa. She wouldn't

have any king; how would she marry him? He would only bring dishonor to
them all.

7. Meho's reply — the tale-within-a-tale

Mumin (239–1262)

Meho upbraided Mustajbey for his attitude. Did Mustajbey not remember
when a decree had came from the sultan ordering him to capture Nikola Vodogazović of Janok, dead or alive, or else to forfeit his own life? In vain Mustajbey
offered great possessions to the champion who would come forward, but none
came. Then he went to Kanidža; the nobles there noticed his unhappiness and
asked him the cause. He told them and offered in addition the hand of his
daughter Zlata and half the inheritance of his son Bećir. Again none came,
and Mustajbey was about to kill himself when Meho stayed his hand and agreed
to go, without any reward.

Meho's preparations are told fully (360–423). He went to Janok to the tavern
of Jela, who warned him that Nikola and his captains and sirdars were in the
tavern. He entered, destroyed all except Nikola, whom he took captive. His
horse leapt over the walls of Janok, evaded his pursuers, and from Ramo's Well
on Kunar Meho rode on Nikola's shoulders to Mustajbey's tower in Ribnik.

Mustajbey sought someone who would lead Nikola in bonds to the vizier
in Budim. Meho volunteered. In Budim he was well received, but at night he
went down to the stable to see his horse, and on the way back, he opened a
door and found the vizier and his nobles entertaining Nikola, and he heard
them plotting the destruction of the Turks of the Krajina. Nikola was wearing
Meho's clothes and weapons. They attacked Meho and bound him. The vizier
gave him to Nikola to take back to Janok. Nikola mounted on his shoulders.
At the end of the first day Meho was put in the dungeon at Osat; of the second
at Grabić; and of the third at Janok.

At night, Anđa, the daughter of the Ban of Janok, went to the dungeon and
brought him a bed, blankets, food and drink. This went on for a year before
someone learned of it and informed the ban. He did not want to hurt his one
and only child, so he wrote to the emperor in Vienna, asking what to do with
Meho. The emperor replied that he should send Meho to Vienna so that the
nobles of Vienna might see what beasts are captured in the mountains. That
night Anđa told Meho about the letter (with details) and took away the bed
and bedding and put Meho in chains again. The next day Meho was taken
from prison and bound and sent under guard to Vienna, where all the nobles
were gathered at the gate beside the Danube and on the bridge over the river.
When Meho came to the bridge he jumped high into the air and came down
on the bridge so hard that it quaked and all the nobles were frightened. The
empress scolded the emperor, and the emperor sent Meho to the seacoast to
serve in the galleys for over four years.

His condition was so bad that he finally sent a petition to the emperor to
kill him, but the emperor had him sent back again to prison in Janok, where
Anđa brought the bed and food again and took care of him for a year. Again
this was discovered and the ban wrote again to Vienna for instructions. The

emperor this time ordered him to execute Meho. Anđa told Meho of his impending execution. She said farewell, took the bed, put the chains back on Meho, and departed. The next morning Meho was taken to the courtyard and seated while four executioners danced about him. At six o'clock they were to cut off his head. A prize was offered to the first who succeeded. Just as six o'clock struck an unknown rider came into the courtyard, a Hungarian. His eyelashes covered his eyes. He declared that he was a postman from Vienna and that he carried orders from the emperor not to kill Mehmed. He drew his sword and killed those in the courtyard and released Meho, taking him up on his horse. The horse jumped over the gates and they fled across the plains and mountains until they came home. "If you do not believe this, Mustajbey, ask my uncle Durutagić Ahmo."

Avdo (703–3895)

Avdo's story is essentially the same as the above, but with much more description. Avdo makes much of the fact that Meho did not go to Janok in disguise but in the clothes of a Turkish border warrior. When he arrived in Budim, Meho was asked by the vizier about this very detail, and this led to Meho's telling the vizier the whole story again about his capture of Nikola Vodogazović. Meho's leap, which frightened all, including the empress, was on dry land, and the bridge was not mentioned. There is no doubt about the identity of the man who finally rescued Meho from execution. After the unknown had taken Meho on his horse, he told Meho who he was, even his uncle Durutagić Ahmo in disguise. There are some changes of name, especially that of the girl, who is Anica and Ana, rather than Anđelija and Anđa.

8. Offers of assistance

Mumin (1263–1320)

Mustajbey turned to Ahmo, who spoke in tears to Meho. "Why ask these things of Mustajbey? Here is a string of coral. Go to your aunt in our tower at Orlovce, and let her prepare my horse and my weapons for you. She will give you money as well. I shall find another horse and follow you to Janok." When Halil heard this, he dropped his glass and offered Meho his watch, telling him to go to his sister Hajkuna in Kladuša. She would give him his horse (a famous strawberry roan), weapons and money and the clothes that he wore only once in the year. Then Mustajbey's son Bećir said that he would borrow his father's horse and give it to Meho and follow him to Janok. Meho accepted Halil's watch and departed for Kladuša.

Avdo (3896–3977)

Mustajbey hung his head and knew not what to do. Ahmet spoke to Meho telling him it was useless to ask Mustajbey. "Beys do not look upon poor people." He offered him a golden kerchief to take to his aunt, who would give him his horse. Ahmet would find another. Only this time, Meho must disguise the horse and himself. His aunt would give him a disguise and money. He must dress well, that Ana be not ashamed to have turned away so many suitors for a poor

Turk. Meho kissed his uncle's hand and wept. Halil then embraced Meho. He told him that Hrnjičić's (Halil's) horses were ready for him. "Go to Kladuša and treat Hajkuna as a sister. Give her this kerchief and tell her that Halil sent you. She will give you clothes and money and prepare you as she does me." Meho embraced Halil and departed from the tavern for Kladuša.

(The next two themes are reversed in the two versions.)

9. The preparations

Mumin (1321–1426)

Hajkuna saw Meho coming and went to meet him at the gate. He gave her the watch, and she asked him why Halil had sent him to her. He asked her for the horse, weapons, clothes and money. She led him to her room, brought out the clothes, which are described, and he dressed. While he dressed, she prepared the horse and led him to the courtyard. She gave Meho the money; he mounted, and she said farewell to him. He went through Udbina, and the aghas watched him.

Avdo (4030–4310)

Meho, in the meantime, went to Kladuša to the court of Hrnjica and knocked on the gate. Hajkuna was in the harem, embroidering by the window and singing. When she heard the knock, she opened the window and asked who it was, stating that her brothers were in the tavern in Udbina. Meho asked her to come down, and told her who he was and that Halil had sent him to her. She came down, and after greetings were exchanged, Meho told her his story and asked for the horse, etc. She took him to Halil's room and showed him the clothes, telling him to take what he wished, while she went down to prepare the horse. Meho dressed himself in the disguise of a Viennese standard-bearer. The details are given. In the courtyard he found Hajkuna and the horse. The horse's trappings are described. She (Mujo's wife) had also prepared provisions, which she put in his saddlebags. She gave Meho the reins and he mounted from the mounting block. The two women said farewell. When he left, the two women remarked to one another that it was a disgrace that such a hero was left to go alone to die in Janok. Meho passed through Udbina, and the aghas stood at the window and watched him pass.

10. Young Bećir and Mustajbey

Mumin (1427–1524)

When Bećir saw what had happened, he approached his father, Mustajbey, and told him that he wished he were not his son; it were better had he not been born. What good were his father's riches to him? It had been easy for his father to gain such honors, as long as there were heroes like Meho. Bećir disinherited himself from his father. Then he asked him to give permission for him to take his horse and to gather the men of the Border to follow after Meho. Mustajbey was drunk. He told Bećir to do what he wished. Bećir went to the tower and fired the cannon for three days, as Mustajbey continued to drink. When the men of the Border heard, they thought that the emperor had attacked and they all gathered at Grbava. When they heard what was wrong, they were ready to go with Bećir.

Avdo (3978–4029)

Meho departed and Bećir said to his father that he was ashamed of what had been done to such a hero as Meho. Would he had not been born! Were he his father, he would have his horse prepared and would summon the army and go to Janok and do battle. The girl would not go without a fight. He should not let the hero go alone. With him went the honor of all the Turks. Mustajbey then told his son that if he felt so strongly about it, he could take his horse and his seven standard-bearers. There was the Lika, there the cannon. "Do what you wish; I shall not hinder you."

11. Meho and Jela in Janok

Mumin (1525–1693)

When Meho arrived at Janok, the plain was filled with tents and tables with drinks, but no one was there. No one noticed or spoke to Meho as he entered town and went down the main street to Jela's tavern. Jela came out to meet him (she is described). Greetings were exchanged. She took his horse to the stable and led him to a secluded room. They sat down to drink. She asked why no word had come from him all these years. He told her that he was a wanderer, and why he had come to Janok. He asked about the tents and was told they were for Anđa's wedding guests. (The story here is told as if Meho had come to Janok without any knowledge of Anđa's impending wedding.) She will be married to Đuro from across the sea, and all seven kings will be present. They have gone down to the shore to meet the bridegroom and his company. Just a short time after this, the guests returned to the tents, and more guests from nearby towns arrived. That evening Meho asked Jela if she could find a way of bringing him together with Anđa.

Avdo (4311–4705)

Meho's journey to Janok is described, the mountains crossed, the conversations with his horse are related, etc. (4311–4392). No mention is made of the tents on the plain of Janok, but nobody noticed him as he crossed it, because he was in disguise. He entered the town, and as he went along, the shop girls talked with one another about him and his horse. Meho pretended not to hear. He went to Jela's tavern. Jela was outside playing the tambura and singing a song about Mehmed and weeping. He approached and asked her why she was weeping. He had come, he had not deceived Ana. She embraced him, gave his horse to servants and took Meho to a secluded room. She asked him why he had not come before, and he told her about having to borrow the horse, etc. She told him about Đuro of Radane. He asked if Ana had any idea of his coming. No, she wept all the time. Meho began to drink heavily. She asked him if he had brought anyone with him, and he replied that things would happen as God wills. When evening came he asked Jela to arrange a meeting with Ana.

12. Meho and Anđelija (Anica)

Mumin (1694–1888)

Jela put on her cloak, took a lantern and went along the streets to Anđa's dwelling. Lights were burning, and she knocked. Anđa was taking her clothes from chests and weeping, saying that she had not gathered them for Hungarians but for Turks. Would that Meho would come that she might say farewell to him! She cursed him for leaving her and said she was a Turk; she recalled his promises when he was in prison. Jela asked what she would give for news of Meho. Anđa took off her necklace and gave it to Jela. If she could arrange a meeting for them she would gild her arms to the elbows, and would give her her freedom. Jela said that Meho was in her tavern, and Anđa put on a cloak immediately and went with Jela. In the tavern she and Meho sat long and drank and talked. Anđa told him of her suitors and how she was now being given by force to Đuro. She asked him to see her once again on the morrow as she leaves in the coach; he should accompany her to the parting of the roads, hers leading to the sea and his to the mountains. He said that he would be at the gate as she passes and she must raise the curtain of the coach, so that they may look upon one another again. Finally she took her cloak and departed from the tavern. Meho did not sleep the rest of the night, but drank until dawn.

Avdo (4706–5041)

Jela prepared herself and went along the street to the harem of Anica. At the door she heard Ana weeping and taking out her gifts. She mourned over her gifts which she had thought were for the heroes of Unđurovina, for the Turks. She had thought that she herself was intended for Meho, and she cursed her days. Jela entered and begged Ana not to part thus in tears. Ana again bewailed her lot, and then Jela asked what she would give for news of Meho. For one look at Meho she would give an eye — is there anything more precious than eyes? Jela asked for only a ducat: Mehmed is in her tavern. The Turks are not liars, but keep their word. The viziers have taken all his wealth. Halil has lent him the wherewithal for the journey. Jela told her to wait until nightfall. At nightfall she put on her cloak and took a lantern, and went to the tavern. When she took off her cloak her beauty shone (she is described). The lovers embraced and conversed, she wept and he comforted her. He told her that she would not go to the enemy without a fight. He asked her in what vehicle she would depart on the morrow. She told him in a coach and described the retinue which would accompany her. She told him he could do nothing; for the forces of the enemy were too great. She said that she would order Pletikosa Radovan, who would be in charge of the beasts of burden carrying her clothes, to drive them off the road so that the Latins would never have them. Meho should take his stand at the right of the gate and when she passes, he should call to her to lift the curtain, so that they might see one another. She begged him then to take his sword and cut off her head. Then she left the tavern. Meho drank until dawn.

13. *Meho accompanies Anđa to the crossroads*

Mumin (1889–1985)

At dawn the heralds summoned the wedding guests to prepare to depart. Meho prepared his horse, mounted, and offered to pay Jela. She refused, but he gave her a gift of money, and then departed down through the market place, until he came to the city gate. Then came the coach. When it was opposite Meho, Anđa lifted the curtain. She was dressed in mourning and weeping. She said to Meho in Turkish that he should see her bridegroom. Meho looked at Đuro, who was terrible to look upon. Meho followed along beside the coach, talking to Anđa in Turkish. They came to the crossroads, and Meho was troubled and knew not what to do.

Avdo (5042–5748)

In the morning the heralds summoned the wedding guests' hosts, who went out to meet the arriving wedding guests from Radane. After supper there were festivities. After midnight the heralds announced that they should prepare to depart with the girl in the coach. Meho asked Jela to prepare his horse. Jela bewailed his fate, but Meho urged her to do his bidding. She prepared the horse and told him not to desert his master.

(At this point, line 5187, which comes after a pause,
Avdo reverts to the Turks in Udbina.)

Meanwhile the aghas were talking in Udbina and telling Mustajbey that when the sultan sent him to them, he had been well received and had been obeyed, but now he has gone too far: no one is greater than God. The Koran teaches that the high should humble themselves and help the poor. They were wrong in letting Meho go alone. Tale upbraided Mujo for inaction and told him to raise Kladuša: he will raise Orašac. He will go to Glamoč to borrow Ramo's horse for Halil so that he too may go with them. They can leave their forces on Mount Zvezda and go together alone to Janok to see what is going on there. Mujo took a last drink and stumbled out. Tale sent his standard-bearer to raise Udbina and other places; Arnautović urged Kunić Hasanagha to raise his forces, and Kunić urged Arnautović to gather others, to whom would be added the forces of Mustajbey and young Bećir. In Kladuša Mujo gave orders for gathering his men, told his wife to get his clothes ready and his sister Hajkuna to prepare his white horse. Thus they gathered to meet at the rendezvous on Mount Zvezda to help the orphaned Meho.

(Now we go back to Janok with Meho, line 5541.)

Jela brought Meho's horse and he mounted. He offered her pay. She refused, but he gave her a gift. Anica summoned her servant Radovan and gave him orders about the beasts carrying her dowry. He was to drive them across Zvezda to the Turkish border. If all went well, she would give him great rewards. He promised to obey. He went forth before the wedding guests with the burdens and in the middle of the plain turned and drove them to Kanidža as he had been ordered.

Meho rode to the city gate. The coach and retinue approached. The bridegroom is described. Ana saw Meho and spoke to him in Turkish. She urged him to kill her. Meho paid no attention, but rode forward to the crossroads in great trouble as to what he should do.

14. *The final battle*

Mumin (1986–2294, the end)

Meho looked up and saw two white horses and two monks on them reading books and talking to one another. One said that it seemed to him for reading the books that there would be a battle at Janok that day. Meho looked closely; one was Tale and the other Mujo Hrnjica. Meho shouted, drew his sword, and attacked Đuro, cut him in half in the middle, and took Anđa from the coach. The battle started. There appeared Bojičić Alija with three hundred men; then Osman Arnautović with three hundred; Gojenović Ibro with one hundred and twenty-four; Ćelić Osmanbey with twelve hundred; Mustajbey's standard-bearers, Đulo and Ćerim, followed by Begović Bećir. Meho's uncle, Durutagić Ahmo, had gone with Bećir to the sea coast and captured the ships of the wedding guests. At last the wedding guests began to flee to the coast and those who had accompanied them to flee back to the city. Some of the Turks followed each group, but Ahmo's army was waiting at the coast. When the wedding guests had been destroyed, the army with Ahmo went to aid the army before Janok. Janok was taken and plundered. They took three hundred and sixty captives. The booty was divided among the Turks, special portions being given to the families of those who had been killed in the battle, or wounded.

Now the army became wedding guests for Bećiragić Meho and Anđa. As such they returned to Meho's tower in Kanidža. Hasan Pasha Tiro met them and entertained them in Kanidža as if Meho were his own son.

"I heard this song in Taslidža in my inn from the Turk Huso Ćoravi. I have not heard from that day to this such a singer. There he is and there is his song. If it is worthy, then I too am pleased."

Avdo (5749–6313, the end)

There Meho saw two monks riding and reading. One said to the other: "Is what is happening in Janok according to God's will?" The other replied that injustice was being done. Meho looked more closely and saw that these were Tale and Mujo. Meho sang a little song saying that one land and two masters make it hard for the serfs; so also one maiden and two bridegrooms among the wedding guests. The guests who heard did not understand. Meho cut Đuro in two and the fight began. Tale fired his rifle as a signal to the Turks to attack. Meho went up to the coach and was surrounded, but Tale and Mujo aided him.

Young Bećir and Halil were near the edge of the plain of Janok with their standard-bearers, Memić and Desnić, and their men. Bećir had sent Durutagić

Ahmo and Velagić Selim with their company to the coast to prevent the wedding guests from embarking. Zuko of Stijena and Arnaut Osman with their men had been assigned by Tale to close in behind the wedding guests as they emerged from Janok and see that no one else came from the city. The rifles of the following fired: Arnaut Osman, Bojičić Alija, Tanković Osman, Kunić Hasanagha, Zorića Šaban, Šarac Mahmutagha, Velagić, the ajans of Vrljika and Pločane. The hosts mingled, and the shouts and fighting are described. They fought for three days and three nights. Tale left the plain and went to the coast on the fourth day to see how things were with Bećir by the ships. With his rested troops he had cut down the wedding guests who had sought to flee to the coast. Then he visited the troops with Zuko of Stijena near Janok. The gates were surrounded by corpses, the Turkish banner waved. He returned to the plain. Meho was there by the coach guarding Anica. The Turks began to assemble their ranks. Bećir and the remnant of his forces came from the coast. Tale went across the plain to meet Mujo. With Mujo were Kurtagić Nušin, Kunić Hasanagha, Arnaut Osman, Vlahinjić Alija, Alemkadunić of Čekrk. Half the army had been killed, and there were many wounded. Tale turned back and in the middle of the plain he found Belaj the standard-bearer, the hodža, and Šaćir with captives and booty. The Turks buried their dead and cared for their wounded. Then they opened the gates of Janok and took plunder. Then they set out for home.

On Mount Zvezda they met Radovan with the burdens. The Turks rejoiced for Meho and for the riches he had gained. They rested the night there, and the next day they proceeded to Kanidža. When Hasan Pasha Tiro heard of their coming, he made preparations to receive them. The next day Meho and Anica were married. May they have many children. The following day there was a horse race. Finally the wedding guests dispersed.

APPENDIX II

Comparison of Four Versions of "Marko and Nina"
by Petar Vidić

Parry 6

Marko is drinking wine with his mother, his wife, and his sister (1–4).

He tells them that they may look for the sun and the moon, but never again for him. His mother asks him where he is going, and he tells her that he is going into the sultan's army for seven years (5–15).

When Marko joins the army, he greets the sultan, who takes away his sword and his horse. Marko is to serve for seven years and then his sword and horse will be returned to him (16–24).

Marko receives a letter from his mother saying that his tower has been captured by Nina, his mother trodden upon, and his wife taken captive (25–30).

He goes to the sultan and asks for his horse and sword, his blood-brother

Parry 804

Marko arises early in his stone tower and drinks raki. With him are his mother, his wife, and his sister Anđelija (1–7).

He tells his mother that he has caused much sorrow and done many heroic deeds, and that yesterday a letter came from the sultan calling him to the army. He is to bring his horse and his sword, and stay for a period of a year and fifteen days (8–20).

He tells her that when Nina of Koštun hears that Marko has gone, he will come to Prilip, capture his tower, steal his treasure and his wife, and tread upon his mother. If that happens, she is to write him a letter and send it by falcon. Then the sultan will send him against Nina (21–38).

Marko prepares himself and says farewell to his mother, repeating the instructions just given. He departs (39–51).

Marko goes to the army (52).

When Nina hears that Marko has gone, he comes with his brothers to Prilip, burns Marko's tower, treads on his mother, and takes his wife and sister captive (53–63).

Marko's mother writes him a letter, and sends it by his falcon (64–71).

When the falcon arrives he seeks out Marko and delivers the letter (72–77).

Marko reads the letter and flies into a rage. He writes a petition to the sultan,

Parry 805

Parry 846

Marko arises early in his tower in Prilip and drinks raki. With him are his mother, his wife, and his sister Anđelija (1–6).

Marko arises early in his stone tower. With him are his mother and his wife (1–5).

Marko says that a letter arrived the day before from the sultan calling him to serve in the army for nine years (7–10).

A messenger arrives with a letter for Marko. He reads it and is silent. His mother asks him where the letter is from and why it makes him sad. Marko says the letter is from the sultan calling him to serve in the army for nine years and to bring his horse and sword (6–30).

He tells his mother that if Nina of Koštun should come and capture his tower, take away his wife and sister, and tread on his mother, she should write him a letter and send it to him by his falcon (11–22).

If Nina of Koštun hears, he will come to Prilip, tread on Marko's mother, and take away his wife and sister Anđelija. If that happens, his mother is to send him a letter by his falcon, who will be able to find him in the army. His mother agrees to do this (31–54).

Marko prepares to depart. He tells his wife to look for the sun and moon, but never again for him. He goes to Carigrad (55–65).

When Marko joins the army he greets the sultan, who takes his horse and sword. Marko serves the sultan for nine years (66–77).

Nina and his three brothers capture Marko's tower, take his wife and sister, and tread on his mother (23–30).

Nina and his four brothers hear (in the ninth year) that Marko is in the army, and they go to Prilip. They capture Marko's tower, take away his wife and sister, and tread on his mother (78–96).

Marko's mother writes a letter telling him what has happened, and sends it by his falcon (31–46).

Marko's mother writes a letter telling him what has happened, and sends it by his falcon (97–122).

The falcon seeks out Marko and delivers the letter (47–51).

The falcon seeks out Marko and delivers the letter (123–127).

Marko reads and is angry. He writes to the sultan, who gives him back his

Marko reads and is angry. He shows the letter to the sultan, who gives him

Parry 6

Aliagha, and 12 warriors, that he may attack Nina. His request is granted. Marko dresses himself and his men in monks' clothing, but they keep their weapons under their robes (31–48).

They depart and travel until they are near Koštun (49–51).

At the spring Zloglav they meet twelve women washing clothes, among them Marko's wife. She does not recognize him, but she recognizes his horse and weeps. She asks the monk where he got Šarac, and Marko tells her that Marko is dead, and that in return for burying him, he had given him the horse. The monk has come to Nina with his companions to marry him to Marko's wife. He tells her to take word to Nina that he will be there that evening. This she does, telling Nina the whole story about Marko and the monks (52–88).

Marko and his companions arrive and are welcomed by Nina. Marko's wife serves them wine. Marko asks permission to dance a little and it is granted (89–103).

Parry 804

telling him the story. He asks permission from Delibaša Ibro to present it to the sultan. The permission is granted, the sultan reads the petition and tells Marko to choose 12 warriors, with Ibro at their head, to take his sword and his horse, and to bring back Nina's head. Marko chooses his men and horses (78–113).

They depart, Marko urging them to ride hard to the city of Prilip (114–120).

When they come to a spring, they sit down to rest and drink. Marko tells his companions that it will not be easy to take Koštun, but there is a church nearby where he will ask for some monks' robes for himself and them. They go to the church, and Marko makes his request. The monk refuses. Marko kills him and his 12 neophytes, and he and his companions put on their disguises. Thence they proceed to Koštun (121–179).

When they arrive, Marko rides into the courtyard. Marko's wife is at the window, and she asks him where he got her master's horse. He tells her that Marko died nine years ago and that he had given him the horse in return for burying him. He says that he has heard that Nina has taken Marko's wife and sister, and he has come to marry them. He is admitted (180–212).

Nina entertains them with raki, wine, and meat, and asks Marko to drink to the soul of Marko and the health of Nina. Marko says he will drink a little and then dance. He will perform the

Parry 805

Parry 846

horse and sword, and his choice of 12 warriors. The sultan says to bring back Nina's head (52–71).

back his horse and sword, and his choice of 12 warriors with Delibaša Ibro at their head. The sultan says to bring back Nina's head. Marko chooses his men (128–154).

They depart (72–75).

They depart (155–159).

On the mountain they stop to drink. Marko says they will go to a church and ask for monks' clothes, and they do. The monks refuse, and Marko kills them, and he and his companions disguise themselves in monks' clothes. They proceed to Koštun (76–110).

On the mountain they stop to drink. Marko says they will go to a church and ask for monks' clothes. The monks refuse, and Marko kills them, and he and his companions disguise themselves in monks' clothes. They proceed to Koštun (160–194).

When they arrive at a spring near Koštun where Marko's wife and sister are washing clothes, his wife recognizes Šarac, and asks where the monk got Marko's horse. Marko says that he died nine years ago. He has heard that Nina will marry and he has come for that. He sent his wife to tell Nina. Marko tells his men to stay outside. Nina asks where Marko got the horse, and he says Marko gave it to him for burying him. Marko goes into the tower (111–155).

When they arrive at a spring near Koštun where Marko's wife and sister are washing clothes, his wife recognizes Šarac, and asks where the monk got Marko's horse. Marko says that he died nine years ago, and gave him the horse for burying him. He sends his wife to tell Nina that the monk has come to marry the two. He leaves his men outside and rides into the courtyard. Nina asks where he got the horse, and Marko tells him. He also tells him that he has come to marry him. They enter the tower (195–241).

Nina entertains Marko with wine, and Marko asks permission to dance a little for the soul of Marko and the health of Nina. The permission is granted (156–165).

Nina entertains Marko with wine and meat and Marko asks permission to dance and sing a little for the soul of Marko and the health of Nina. The permission is granted (242–256).

Parry 6

Parry 804

marriage in church the next day. Nina says to sing as much as he wants (213–228).

Marko dances and the tower shakes. Nina says that others have danced, but the tower has never shaken. Marko says that others have danced, but never Kraljević Marko. He swings his sword and cuts off Nina's head, and kills some of the servants (104–119).

Marko dances and sings to the soul of Marko and the health of Nina. Nina asks where he got such strength; all Koštun is shaking. Then Marko cries out: "For the soul of Nina, and the health of Kraljević Marko!" He swings his sword and kills Nina (229–247).

Marko sets fire to the tower. Nina's brothers flee, and Marko pursues them. He kills Jasenko at Rudine, which was afterwards called Jasena; he kills Šćepan at Rudman, which was afterwards called Šćepan's Cross; he kills Radoje at Ravno, which was afterwards called Radimlja (120–133).

Nina's brothers flee and Marko and his companions pursue them. They kill Šćepan at Šćepan's Cross, Jasenko at Jasena, Radoje at Radimlja, and Mina at Mejdan Pusti. (The version is confused here.) They set up a monument, and then gather up the heads (248–273).

Nina's retainers meet Marko, Aliagha, and the 12 warriors in the ravines, and Aliagha and the warriors are killed. Marko erects a monument to them. Then he catches the last brother and cuts off his head. Here too he erects a monument (134–149).

Marko returns and takes his wife away to Prilip (150–154).

They return to Koštun. Marko and Ibro set fire to the tower (274–279).

Parry 805

Parry 846

Marko dances, and Nina says he shakes the tower. Marko asks permission to sing, and it is granted. Marko shouts: "For the soul of Nina!", swings his sword and cuts off Nina's head (166–177).

Marko dances, and Koštun shakes. Nina says that to judge by his strength this must be Marko. Marko dances and sings for the soul of Nina and the health of Marko. His sword swings and he kills Nina (257–271).

Nina's three brothers flee and Marko and his men pursue them. He kills Šćepan at Šćepan's Cross, Jasenko at Jasena, and Radoje at Radimlja. He erects a monument at each place. He gathers their heads. He himself has lost only one man (178–191).

Nina's brothers flee and Marko and his men pursue them. They kill Šćepan at Šćepan's Cross, Jasenko at Jasena, and Radoje at Radimlja. They erect monuments at each place (272–285).

Marko returns with his wife, his sister, and his men to Prilip (192–200).

They return to Koštun. Marko gathers the heads in a bag, and returns to Prilip, having set fire to Koštun. Ibro is missing (286–310).

In Prilip Marko shows Nina's head to his mother, and tells her that he will trouble her no more. Marko eats and drinks (201–212).

They go to Marko's tower and eat and drink and rest (311–317).

Marko goes to the sultan. He gives him the heads and reports that Ibro has been killed. The sultan rewards him and sends him back to Prilip, with greetings to his mother, and the offer of assistance whenever Marko needs help. Marko returns to Prilip (213–234).

Marko takes the heads to the sultan, who sends him home to Prilip with the offer of assistance whenever he needs it. Marko returns to Prilip (318–324).

APPENDIX III

Return Songs

A. Parry 6818, by Alibeg Begović in Bijelo Polje
B. Parry 12417, by Šaćir Dupljak in Bijelo Polje
C. Parry 6229, by Avdo Avdić in Gacko
D. Parry 6580, by Murat Čustović in Gacko
E. Parry 1905, by Franje Vuković in Bihać
F. Parry 1939, by Murat Žunić in Bihać

a. Parry 6812, by Husein Dupljak in Bijelo Polje
b. Parry 12384, by Šećo Kolić in Bijelo Polje
c. Parry 12408, by Mustafa Čelebić in Bijelo Polje
d. Parry 12465, by Avdo Međedović in Bijelo Polje
e. Parry 1280a, by Jašar Krvavac in Gacko
f. Parry 1920, by Murat Žunić in Bihać

The telegraphic style of this and of the following appendix is used not merely to save space, but also in order to bring closer together the corresponding parts of the several texts and thus to facilitate the comparison of themes.

Introductory Theme One: Capture of the Hero

D

Place is Zadar. Three prisoners are shouting: Alagić Alija, Zorbac Mustafagha, and Čejanović Meho. Alagić tells his story: father dead, mother reared him for twelve years, and he became Četnik. At sixteen he had won his horse and arms; at eighteen the sultan sent him a sword; at twenty-four mother urged him to marry Zlata of Bey Kumalić. On wedding night a bloody hero arrived; the Vlahs had attacked Lika. Wife urged him to go. He was captured by Matić Kapetan seven years ago. Feels sorry for unloved Zlata. Zorbac tells his story: he has no family except for a band of thirty Četniks. Attacked by Matić Kapetan with army bound for Border, who captured him and gave him to Ban of Janok seven years ago. Feels sorry for families of thirty Četniks. Meho tells his story: father died when he was four. At fifteen he raided, gathering money.

f

Song opens with marriage of Bosnić Osmanbey of Glasinac. Wedding guests go to Taslidža for Zlata. Girl won't ride horse and is brought back in golden litter with golden apple on top. On way back, race is declared from apple tree to king's house. Youth rides by litter and girl urges him to enter race. He is standard-bearer of Osman. She gives him permission to enter race. Standard-bearer wins. Brings news of arrival of girl to Bey. In midst of festivities messenger arrives from sultan and delivers firman. Sultan at war with four kings. Turks besieged in Hotin. Sultan calls Bey to army as commander. Bey agrees to go. Wedding ceremony held. After a time in marriage chamber, Bey looks out window and sees youths hurling stones and jumping, among them standard-bearer. Bey comes down and all run away except standard-bearer, who asks Bey where he is going. Bey says to imperial army. Tells standard-bearer to get ready. Wife (bride) complains. Bey gives her money for seven years. Tells her to wait that time and even an eighth, but in ninth to marry again. Bey departs. Bey goes to vizier in Sarajevo. Vizier gathers Bosnian army. Ban leads army to Mt. Pokoja, where he meets sultan's messengers to say sultan has gone to Hotin with rest of army. Bey proceeds and joins sultan. Sultan gives him command. He has one success after another against enemy, but finally is betrayed by pashas and viziers into hands of king of Moscow, in whose prison he languishes for twelve years. His men, including standard-bearer were killed in final encounter when viziers withdrew their armies. In nineteenth year of absence the king of Moscow has son born and declares festival to which he invites the king of Lehovo, who asks if Osman is still in prison. They go to see Osman. Lehovo buys Osman from king of Moscow, takes him to Lehovo, feeds and houses him comfortably.

Introductory Theme Two: Capture of Radovan

A

Place is Zadar. Cannon rejoicing, but no conversation or speech. Radovan goes directly to prison. No jailer mentioned. Prison described. Radovan walks around and sings a little about prison.

B

Serfs gather with thorns before castle; list complaints: Radovan captures maidens, kills youths. King sends serfs away, promises help. Writes letter to priest Milovan, Radovan's godfather, to betray Radovan. Priest writes Radovan, inviting him to christening of son. Sends letter with messenger, letter delivered, messenger tipped. Radovan reads letter, slaps thigh. Mother asks why. Radovan explains. Mother urges him to go, Radovan hesitant, does not trust priest. Mother prevails. Radovan dresses, arms, prepares horse. Goes to priest at border. Radovan and priest drink. Next morning priest seeks special wine, which he drugs. Radovan sleeps, is bound, put in coach, taken to Janok. Cannon rejoicing at capture of Radovan. They beat Radovan into consciousness. He curses priest. No conversation. Radovan is taken directly to prison. Prison is described.

C

Place is Zadar. Ban lists complaints against Radovan: killed brother, captured sister and married her to gypsy. Radovan says he has lived full life, but threatens that Mujo will come and take vengeance. Ban afraid but calls jailer, gives orders, and says he will take his bones, make them into powder, and shoot from cannon. Prison is described.

D

Meho's story is interrupted by arrival of jailer with new prisoner. Alagić asks who he is — Uskok Radovan.

E

Uskok Radovan sets out to seek blood brother, Šarac Mehmedagha. Radovan is in disguise. Lost in fog. Comes to well of Mitrović Ilija. Ilija sends soldiers to capture him. After fight they take him to Ilija. Ilija asks why he has come. Radovan tells of Šarac lost twelve years and of how he was lost in fog and captured. Ilija sends him to Gavran Kapetan. Gavran sends him to Zadar. Ban puts him in jail.

F

Radovan takes horse to well by tower of Smiljanić Sirdar. Sirdar sends men to capture him. Fight. Horse killed, Radovan captured. Sirdar asks him to leave Mustajbey and come over to their side. Radovan refuses. Sirdar takes him to Ban of Zadar, who offers same terms. Radovan refuses, is put in jail.

Introductory Theme Three: Conversation between Radovan and Hero

A

On rock in middle is a prisoner with long hair. Greetings. Prisoner asks Radovan who he is. Recognitions. Prisoner is Arnaut Osman. Has been there eleven years. No other prisoner mentioned. Osman asks about: Border, houses, buljukbaše, kafana, han. Asks if Turks remember him. Asks about: house, mother, wife. Radovan answers about: Border, houses, buljukbaše, kafana, han; Turks do remember him, but have heard of his death seven years ago. Otherwise Radovan would have sought him. Tells of: house, mother, horse, sword, wife to marry dizdar in fifteen days. Osman shouts and kicks door.

B

Radovan sees old prisoner on a stump. Greetings. Chains described. Novljanin Alija had hoped Radovan would rescue him. Alija asks about: his house, horse, dogs, tambura, mother, wife. Radovan answers about: house, horse, tambura, dogs, weapons, mother. Alija asks about: kafana and if Turks remember him. Radovan answers about: kafana and that Turks remember, but heard of his death a year ago. His wife about to remarry soon, in ten or twelve days — to Šarac Mahmutagha. Alija shouts day and night.

C

Radovan sees hero in dry corner. Recognitions, Ograščić Alija. Alija says he had hoped Radovan would rescue him. Has been there twelve years without seeing sun or moon or anybody. No other prisoner is mentioned. Alija asks about: Border, tavern, if Turks remember him, about house, mother, sister, wife, son Hadžija. Radovan answers about: tavern, Turks remember him, tower in ruins, mother begs, sister unmarried, wife to marry Halil, son is cowherd.

D

Alagić Alija asks Radovan about: Border, tavern, aghas, mother, wife. Radovan answers: mother conquered, tower ruined, wife about to marry Halil. Alija shouts.

E

Thirty prisoners. Greetings. One is sitting on stone, playing šargija and singing. At end of song, goes to Radovan and greets him. Recognize immediately. Šarac asks when Radovan left Lika. Radovan says week ago. Recounts story of capture, including conversation with Ilija. Šarac asks about: house, horse, servant Bilaver, mother, wife, pistols, tambura. Radovan answers about: house, horse, Bilaver, mother, pistols, sword, and tambura. All well except mother cries. Wife will marry Halil in week. Radovan advises him to shout three days and four nights.

F

Radovan finds Šarac Mehmedagha of Gospić with thirty prisoners. Šarac is described. They recognize each other immediately. Radovan tells Šarac he was in Lika three days ago. Šarac asks about: *father,* mother, wife, twin sons. Answer: mother dead, father, Osmanagha, blind, twins play in grandfather's lap. Wife to marry Halil and leave sons and father-in-law.

Theme One: Shouting in Prison

a

Prisoner shouts for twelve years. Knows neither summer nor winter. Prison and prisoner described. Banica goes to ban. Place is Zadar. She asks either release or execute prisoner or she will take twin sons and throw them into sea and then flee home to Malta. Ban goes to prison and asks prisoner why he is shouting. Prisoner is Kovčić Muratbey. Prisoner says he dreamed a dream that wife remarried, mother dead, house ruined.

A

Ban hears, calls jailers to ask cause. Osman says cause is wife's remarriage. Asks ban to ransom on oath to kill dizdar and bring head to ban. Jailers give message. Osman is brought to ban. Ban asks cause; Osman answers. (No banica)

b

Thirty prisoners are shouting in Božur. One does not shout. He tells others they are new prisoners, but he has been there twelve years. He has heard that his wife will marry again, Uzun Ahmedagha of Cetinje, fifteen days hence. Uzun had captured Anđa, daughter of Ban of Kaltuk, but girl will not become Moslem. Uzun will hold horse race with her as prize, at prisoner's home in Havala. Ban of Božur hears this story and comes to jail, asks prisoners why they shout. They complain of conditions in prison. Ban asks single prisoner about story he just heard.

c

Place is Zadar. Prisoner shouts three days, four nights. Disturbs ban, banica, and twin sons. Banica sends ban to prison grating to ask what is wrong. Ban goes. Prisoner is Kovčić Muratbey. Bey has recently received letter. Retells story of own wedding — was interrupted on wedding night as he was lifting bride's veil. Bride sent him with others on raid in which he was captured. If he wouldn't go, she would. Horse had returned home after bey's capture. Letter from mother, saying Šarac Mahmutagha is about to marry wife against her will in fifteen days. She has sent letter to her brother, Alagić Alija, to stop Šarac, but he is afraid of vizier.

B

Queen is disturbed by Alija's shouting. On third morning goes to king, complains: release or kill him, or she will take two cradles, throw into sea, kill self. Children cry. King sends jailer. Alija brought into courtyard, given wine. King asks cause of shouting. Alija says it is wife's remarriage.

d

Prisoner shouts in Zadar for twelve days and twelve nights. Frightens banica and children, twins, son and daughter. Ban scolds her for leaving harem, first time in twelve years of marriage. She tells him why. She describes prison. It is eight years since he captured Kara Omeragha. Either release or kill him. Require three oaths of a Turk for ransom, or she will go home and leave children. Ban tells her he will not release Omer but will execute him. There has been no trouble since he has been in prison. He calls jailer Rade and with him goes to prison. Omer is described. Ban asks him why he shouts. Omer says he had been married only three years when captured by ban. Feels sorry for wife and mother. After first year letter from mother told of birth of son. Three years later another letter told name of son, Kara Mujo. Another letter told when they sent him to school. After four years another letter told of smallpox. Another letter told that boy had smallpox but recovered. He now writes from school to mother asking about father. Two years later another letter tells that wife wants to marry and leave son, but only suitor is Šarac Mahmutagha. Omer had replied to mother to write when wedding guests would come. This letter had just arrived.

e

Place is Janok. Prisoner shouts three days, three nights, disturbs banica and two sons. She goes to ban. Release or kill him, or she will go home to General Jovan. Ban calls jailer to bring Turks from jail. Have been there twelve years, Alagić Alija and with him Velagić Selim. Prisoners are described. Ban asks why they shout. Alija is not worried about Border or house, wife, mother, or two sons, but tired of jail. Ban says Alija cannot be pardoned, too many crimes: killed ban's two brothers and father. Will take his bones, etc. Ban offers to bargain with Selim.

C

Alija shouts three days and three nights. Banica is disturbed, their two sons frightened. On fourth morning wife goes to ban. Takes quilt from head, complains: kill or ransom him. Threatens to throw two sons and self into sea. Ban promises. Sends wife back to room. Watches from window. Jailer goes to prison, releases Alija, takes him across courtyard to ban. Ban inquires cause of shouting. Alija says prison is cause.

D

Banica Jerinja is disturbed by Alija's shouting and goes to ban. She says children are crying and asks that prisoner be released or killed. Otherwise she will throw children from the tower and jump into the sea. Ban sends jailer to bring Alagić. Ban asks Alija why he shouts; Alija tells of things at home.

E

Shouting annoys ban, banica, baby. Ban sends jailer to find out what is wrong. Šarac asks jailer to ask ban to let him come to see him. Offers horse and sword to jailer, who reports that ban allows Šarac to come. Šarac is described. He explains situation at home.

F

Šarac shouts for jailer, asks him to go to ban and request release on oath in order to settle affairs at home. Offers jailer his horse. Jailer goes to ban and tells him the news Radovan had given Šarac. Asks for release. Ban refuses, but banica and jailer intervene. Ban goes to jail.

Theme Two: Bargaining for Release

a

Prisoner asks to be released for ransom or to be killed. Ban asks for horse, one thousand ducats, sword. Bey gives oath and is released.

A

Ban asks what oath Osman will give to return to jail and bring dizdar's head. Osman gives three oaths of a Turk and Albanian "besa."

b

Ban says he will release prisoner and will give him horse, if he will enter race and bring Anđa to him unloved. Prisoner agrees and is released.

c

Bey asks ban to release him, promising that he will return. Ban refuses. Banica intervenes. She requires oath of a Turk. Ban refuses again, but she wins. Ban goes to prison. He requires oaths of a Turk, horse, sword. Bey agrees to bring these and to return to prison. He is released.

B

Alija asks to be released in order to kill suitor. He promises suitor's head. King refuses. Queen intervenes and asks Alija for oaths to return to prison. Alija gives three oaths of a Turk.

d

Omer asks ban to release him on oaths for ransom or to kill him. Ban will not accept ransom, but will release him on oaths to return to prison. Omer gives oaths and is released.

e

Ban requires oaths of a Turk, horse, sword. Selim agrees to bring these and to return to prison, and he is released.

C

Ban asks for one thousand ducats, horse, saddle, pistols, sister, and son Tadija. Alija allows all but sister. Ban asks for Tadija instead. Alija agrees.

D

Ban bargains. Asks for wife (error), one thousand ducats, horse, sword. Alija agrees and is released.

E

Ban refuses release, but banica intervenes. Ban will release if Šarac will return and bring one hundred ducats. Šarac agrees.

f

Lehovo explains to Osman that he had been captured by Osman's father at Kosovo and had been treated by father as he treated Osman. King releases Osman without ransom as Osman's father had released him. Lehovo asks Osman whether he will go straight to Bosnia or to Stambol, warning him he will be killed in Stambol. Osman says he will go to Stambol first.

F

Šarac asks for release. Ban will not ask ransom, but Šarac promises to return to jail. Thirty prisoners guarantee his return with their lives. Ban agrees. Radovan asks for release, but refuses to leave Mustajbey. Ban says he will execute him in week.

Theme Three: Preparation for Journey Home

a

Chains are taken off and tattoo put on Murat's chest to indicate he is prisoner. Ban gives money to have his hair cut. (No mention that hair is actually cut.)

A

Ban calls servants to wash Osman, cut hair, and bring new clothes, but Osman refuses. Will close eyes, take staff and pouch to beg. Ban offers horse and arms, but Osman refuses, since own horse and arms are home. Wants only passport, which he receives with one hundred ducats.

b

Prisoner is given food, drink, rest for week, clothes, armor, and horse (his own, twelve years in stable). As the prisoner departs, the ban asks his name. It is Poro of Havala.

c

Bey is cleaned up; hair and nails are cut. Puts on beggar's clothes. Takes staff.

B

King calls servants to shave Alija, cut hair and nails, but Alija refuses. Asks for passport, money, and staff. Leaves.

d

Chains are taken off, but ring is left around neck. Ban changes mind and has ring removed. Omer is described. Ban asks if he wants to be cleaned up. Omer doesn't care, but banica insists. They also give him old clothes (neither good nor bad). Omer is taken to tavern to drink and eat. Given money. Departs.

e

Ban gives money to Selim. Alija asks Selim to tell mother not to expect him. Alija returns to prison.

C

Ban brings servants to wash Alija, cut hair and nails, but Alija refuses, since it will be easier to beg ransom. He does ask for staff, and agrees to return in forty days.

D

Alija is cleaned up. They give him something to eat and drink. He rests, and departs.

E

Servants wash Šarac, shave, cut nails. Jailer puts ring around neck of prisoner. Ban gives him money. Šarac thanks ban and banica. Jailer gives staff.

f

Lehovo gives him money, puts him on ship for Stambol.

F

Šarac takes staff.

Theme Four: Journey Home

a

Murat goes to Udbina to the tower of Mujo.

A

Ban watches Osman depart. Osman goes to tavern to drink, then across plain. Passes three hundred sentinels on way to tavern on border. Tavern maid, Ruža, is his blood sister, but does not recognize him. He drinks heavily. Ruža asks who he is, but he is angry and does not answer. He proceeds home.

b

Poro departs. At border, horse is frightened. Poro sees golden bird on branch. Bird asks him to wrap it in handkerchief, and put it in his belt to give to his bride to put under her belt on night of marriage to Uzun. Poro takes bird as directed and proceeds home.

c

Bey goes over mountains (named) to Udbina. Wedding guests are on plain.

B   missing

d

Omer travels day and night across mountains (named). Sees towers of home and his own repaired house.

e

Selim crosses mountains to border. Sees in distance one tower in good repair and one tower in ruins, with cuckoo. Meets shepherd and asks whose towers those are. The good one is Alija's, the ruined one is Selim's. Cuckoo lamenting is Selim's mother; the sheep are Alija's. Tells of marriage of Selim's wife to Vrsić Ibrahim. Selim goes down mountain.

C

By city gate Alija has begged one thousand ducats. In midst of plain Alija rests and wishes for horse. Travels all night.

D

Alija crosses mountains (named) from which he sees tower and horses. Descends to Ribnik and tower.

E

Travels over mountains (named), rests, finally sees tower and approaches spring near Udbina.

f

Osmanbey arrives at Stambol at dawn. Hears muezzin and weeps. His sorry state described. Old man appears. Asks who he is. Osman tells him. Also reminds him that it was he (old man) who had brought him letter from Sultan years ago. Tells Osman to be careful and takes him to his own home. That night tells him to flee and not to come to Stambol until a firman arrives with half of the golden seal on it. Mehmed Efendi (old man) will try to clear him with sultan. Osman goes to Bosnia.

F

Šarac crosses plain and mountains to Buhovica. Rests and looks toward tower in Gospić. Hears drums and trumpets of wedding guests. Goes to tower and tent of Mujo.

Theme Five: From Arrival in Home Country to Arrival in Own House

a

Mujo does not recognize Murat, who gives deceptive story about Murat's death. He receives gifts. Wedding guests arrive and Mujo explains whose they are (Murat's wife and Šarac.) Murat goes to his own tower.

A   missing

b   missing

c

Šarac says he and wedding guests will give alms if bey will tell him of Murat.

Murat tells deceptive story of death. Gifts given for health of wife, who is praised by Šarac.

B

In Kladuša Alija finds Mujo, Halil, and thirty aghas in green bower. Tells deceptive story of Alija's death. They give gifts and tell of coming wedding. Guests arrive.

d   missing

e

Selim spreads cloak beside the road. Mujo, Halil, and other guests, including Tale, give gifts. (No deceptive story.) Selim goes to Alija's tower and tells Alija's mother, sister, and two sons, where he is, but promises to rescue him. They recognize him by his voice.

C

Next day Alija meets Mustajbey, Mujo, and wedding guests of son Hađo returning from Kaniđa with bride. Alija spreads out coat to beg. Bey asks who he is. Alija says Bunić Mujo. Bey asks about Alija and Alija says he died in prison, etc. Bey gives alms and asks Alija not to tell wedding guests about Alija's death because of son's wedding. Hađo would go to Zadar and ask ban why he killed father. Alija tells same story to Mujo and other guests. Son approaches, singing about father, asks who Alija is. Alija answers Bunić Mujo. Where is Alija? Alija tells story of death. Son gives alms and declares that when he has delivered bride he will go to Zadar. Twelve đevers pass and ask for Alija. Bride also asks and is given deceptive story. All give alms. Tale is last. Alija goes by short cut to Uzdvorje. Sees repaired tower. Courtyard gate opens.

D   missing

E

Evening; Šarac stops to pray. Thirty maidens come from Udbina for water. He hides in grass. After maidens have taken water, they dance. Šarac approaches. They ask who he is. Says he is son of Omeragha of Mostar, released for ransom to visit dying mother. Deceptive story about Šarac. Gifts. Girls tell about coming wedding. Guests have arrived. Girls return to Udbina. After prayer Šarac returns to Udbina.

f

When Osman arrives at road to Tasliđa, whence they had brought his bride twenty years ago, he meets wedding guests with old man, Usuf Alajbey, Osman's uncle. Osman gives deceptive story. He is Parmaksuz Alagha of Kladuša and had gone with Osman's army years ago. Deceptive story of death of Osman. Wedding guests are those of Mehmedbey, Osman's son, born after Osman's departure. Usuf points out youth to father. The standard-bearer for wedding guests is Selim, son of Osman the standard-bearer. Osman asks permission to go with them so that he may get clothes. Usuf tells nephew to give horse to Osman. Meho objects, saying he had promised not to give horse to anyone but father. Uncle insists. Osman asks for pistols to shoot when he brings news of arrival of wedding guests. Horse recognizes master. Uncle amazed at horse's actions. Osman asks son if grandmother alive. Yes, but blind from weeping. Mother alive, still waiting for Osman. Osman rides to tower and shoots pistols.

F

Šarac goes to tower of Mujo. Gives deceptive story, saying he is Bećiragić Meho of Skradin, and that Šarac is dead. Mujo sighs. Games, race; Šarac enters with Halil, and wins. Halil wants to fight but is stopped by Mujo.

Theme Six: Arrival Home and Recognitions

a

Šarac Mahmutagha is given deceptive story about Murat. Gives gift. Also guests give gifts. Murat goes to wife and maids and tells deceptive story. Wife cries. Gives gifts for soul of Murat. Murat takes šargija and sings. He doesn't wonder at Ban of Zadar for releasing him, nor at Mujo — only Tale had said the prisoner looked like Murat — doesn't wonder at mother, but wife didn't recognize him nor any Turk. Goes to room and gets weapons, then to horse, who recognizes him. He mounts, jumps over wall, shouts at Šarac. Šarac flees, but Murat kills him and scatters guests. Murat goes to tower to mother, who is mourning son. Recognition. Mother tells him not to harm wife, dies. Murat drives out maids, buries mother.

A

Osman knocks at gate and tells mother he has news of Osman. Mother doesn't recognize him. Osman tells deceptive story of death and burial. Mother gives alms in name of son. Osman calls wife to door. Tells same story. She gives alms for health of dizdar not Osman. Osman goes to tavern. Drinks. Keeper asks who he is and says he had neighbor Osman who drank like that. Osman takes keeper to upper story and shows passport. Wedding guests arrive. Osman, drunk in tavern, sees them. Festivities at house. Osman arrives, drinks. Dances on staff and one leg. Dizdar throws him money. He sings; wedding guests are amazed at voice of old beggar. Goes to horse in stable. Horse recognizes him. Goes to tower, sees mother weeping in one room, wife with maids in another, the dizdar drinking in another. Gets sword. On way back tells mother that Osman will return tonight. Kills dizdar, announces himself to maids and wife. Takes wife to stable and ties her up. Goes to mother and tells her truth. Next morning announces his arrival to wedding guests from tower, scolds them, and they depart.

b

Poro comes upon wedding guests. Calls mother to come to rose garden. Deceptive story of Poro's death: has sent Poro to accompany bride. Poro asks for tambura. Mother takes him to son's room, which has not been opened. Mother will not listen, but leaves. Wife hears (song not given). She recognizes him and goes to his room. They embrace. Poro tells her what to do with bird. He will accompany her. He takes horse and joins wedding guests, enters race for Anđa, wins girl, gives her to mother. Wedding guests leave with bride and Poro. At Cetinje, bride is taken to marriage chamber. Uzun hears bird and thinks Mejruša is pregnant. Calls judge for annulment — let her take child and seek a husband from door to door. Poro hears from window. Bride asks for Uzun's horse, which is refused and then given. Poro enters and asks for Mejra in marriage and horse. Judge marries them. Mejra takes out bird and shows it to Uzun and announces Poro has returned. Uzun kills himself. Poro takes Mejra home and tells mother he is son. Mother embraces and dies. Burial.

c

Murat climbs stairs in tower. Mother exclaims to wife that tower has not shaken so since Murat was captured. Wife weeps. Murat knocks and asks entrance to beg. Wife asks mother's permission, granted. Deceptive story of death. Mother gives cloak of Murat to Murat for soul of son. Wife gives money. Goes to wedding chamber, where he had been only one night. Takes tambura, sings. (Song not given.) Horse hears, hounds hear, recognize. Wife runs to him, also mother. Embrace. Murat dresses, takes arms and horse, goes to tent of Šarac. Šarac flees, Murat overtakes and kills him. Tale arrives, also Alagić Alija, Murat's uncle. Aghas sit down and drink.

B

Alija goes to tower, meets two sentinels, tells deceptive story. They weep. Goes to blind mother, tells deceptive story, gifts. Asks mother about: Alija's horse, hounds, sword, tambura, pistols, cloak. Mother explains that wife is leaving her one third of possessions, all clothes and arms, but is taking horse. Alija goes to wife's room, tells deceptive story, wife and maids give gifts to health of new groom. Alija goes to horse and hounds, who recognize him, then to wedding guests and Šarac, who give gifts for health of Šarac. Alija returns to mother, gets Alija's sword and tambura. At courtyard gate sings: doesn't wonder at mother, but at wife. Alija goes to stable and mounts horse, attacks and kills Šarac, drives away maids and kills wife. Declares himself to mother, who dies.

d

At gate Omer asks for alms. Mother doesn't recognize him. Says no one home but herself and child, nine years old. Who is he? Omer doesn't give name, but says he has been imprisoned ten years. Mother takes him in. He tells deceptive story that he is Uskok Mališan of Ada. Had been in prison with Omer and had read all her cards. Omer is dead. He is seeking ransom. Mother gives food and tells of wedding in week. He goes to horse. Recognition. Wife hears him tell horse that he is glad he hadn't forgotten him, since his wife had. She laments. Omer kills wife. Mother comes and scolds him for what he has done. He tells her who he is. Recognition. Mother faints; Omer revives her. Tells her not to tell his son. Omer changes and goes to Mahmud in Predvorac. Šarac's friends see Omer from distance and say it looks like Omer. Šarac recognizes him and horse. Tries to shut gate but friends won't let him. Omer from gate challenges him to combat. Omer kills Šarac and returns to Udbina.

e

Selim goes to his own tower. Goes to horse and servant Ibrahim, who is weeping. Ibro recognizes him by his voice, horse recognizes him. Selim asks

Ibro not to tell. Goes to mother, who gives gift for soul of Selim. Finds sister embroidering and weeping. Gift. Wife is with maids. Gift for soul of Selim. Returns to mother, sups, sleeps. At midnight takes tambura and sings. Wonders at Vrsić taking away wife. Mother hears, recognizes him, asks no harm be done to wife. Selim suggests they give sister to Vrsić. This is done next morning. Guests depart. Selim is shaved, hair and nails cut.

C

In yard three kolos are being danced. Wife comes from tower, meets prisoner, asks name. Deceptive story of death and burial of Alija. Wife gives alms, tells of son's wedding, cries. She has no champion. Alija agrees and while wife prepares his horse, he goes to barber, who recognizes him. Alija asks him not to tell. Barber gives him clothes. Goes to horse, who recognizes master. Goes to meet wedding guests. Contest. Alija races horse back to tower. Outraces Mujo. Alija goes to garden and fountain and hides in rose arbor. Wedding guests arrive, festivities. Son takes bride to chamber. Alija sits on chair by fountain and drinks wine from son's cup. Slave girl Kumrija comes to fountain. Says if Hađo saw him, he would kill him, since no one may sit in that chair except him. Alija asks her how she would recognize Alija. Has mark on right arm. Would recognize him when she washed and clothed him. Alija shows mark and asks her to unlock his room, and while he gets tambura and sings, she should tell son, wife, and wedding guests of his arrival. He sings; doesn't wonder at son, but at wife. Wife, Mustajbey, Mujo, and son go to room. "Why didn't you tell us?"

D

They are throwing stones. Alija joins game, wins. Jumping contest. Alija wins. In tower goes to mother, who tells of coming marriage. Alija takes tambura and sings. Wife runs to mother, who listens and weeps, and asks Alija who he is and whence he comes. Deceptive story of death. Alija has come to gather ransom. Gift from mother, gift from wife to health of Halil. Goes to wedding guests. Gifts. Alija takes tambura in tower and sings. Wife weeps, goes to mother, swears it is Alija. Looks at him and recognizes him. Asks him to roll up sleeve. Sees mark and screams. Mother comes. Embraces son. Halil hears news, gets on horse, and flees.

E

In courtyard Šarac finds guests. Goes to stable; servant Bilaver is with horse. Šarac asks permission to touch horse. Servant warns him. Šarac embraces horse. Horse nibbles at Šarac's neck. Bilaver recognizes master. Šarac warns him not to tell. Goes to tower, finds aghas, joins them. Deceptive story, gifts. Goes to mother. Deceptive story about Šarac, gift. Goes to own room and gets pistols. Goes to wife. Deceptive story about Šarac. Wife weeps, gifts. Šarac returns pistols to room, goes to aghas and drinks. Mujo asks if he would like to join game and win money for ransom. Race with Halil; Šarac wins. Halil's fight stopped by Mujo. Šarac goes to room for tambura and sings. Doesn't wonder at horse, but at mother. Mother comes to room, embraces him, and faints. Wife and aghas come. They embrace.

f

Wife sees him and goes to mother. Someone like Osman is in courtyard. Mother scolds. Guests arrive. Osman goes to room. Takes šargija and sings. Doesn't wonder at wife nor son, nor mother, but at uncle. Wife hears. Goes to mother, who listens and they with uncle and son go to Osman. They clean him up. Son is wed. Double rejoicing. Next morning Osman makes coffee and wakes youngsters.

F

Šarac goes to stable and horse. Groom Milovan recognizes him. Šarac tells him not to tell. Sends Milo to get pistols, to kill wife. Šarac goes to wife, deceptive story. Wife cries. Šarac asks why she is leaving tower. She says his father is giving her away. She gives gifts for soul of Šarac, not for health of Halil. He shouts to maids to leave and declares who he is. They go to tell Mujo.

Theme Seven: Return to Enemy

a

Murat prepares himself and horse and goes to Zadar. Ban comes to meet him. Murat challenges him to duel, if he is displeased at Murat's keeping of his oath. Ban laughs and they embrace.

A

Osman is cleaned up, dressed, and takes dizdar's head. He gives wife to mother, who kills her. Osman mounts, departs. At border he stops and drinks with Ruža, tavern maid, who now recognizes him. Sentinels send news to Zadar that he is coming. Osman arrives and delivers head to ban.

b

After a week, Poro returns to enemy country. Takes girl to Božur.

c

Murat prepares horse and sword and returns to Zadar. Ana, daughter of ban, watches him arrive. Murat gives horse and sword to ban and is put into prison.

B

On the third morning Alija arms himself, takes horse, money, spear, and head of Šarac, and goes straight to Janok. In the courtyard he dismounts and calls to king that he has money and head. Guard sees Alija and horse.

d

Omer puts horse back in stable and sword and arms back on peg. Puts on Dalmatian clothes. Takes staff and tells mother he is returning to ban. Asks her to rear son Mujo to avenge father. Don't tell him truth about mother, but say she went mad. Mother faints. He leaves, goes to Zadar.

e

Selim prepares himself and horse. Promises Alija's mother he will rescue him.

Then Selim goes to Janok. Ban sees him coming. He is well received for a week. On ninth day, ban suggests Selim teach son Marijan how to ride horse. Selim does and escapes with son. Exchange of letters reveals demand of Selim for Alija, horse, clothes, and weapons of Bey Jakirlić, and a bootful of money.

C

Alija tells son terms of ransom. Son says he will return with father and settle with ban. Next morning guests depart. Father and son go to Zadar.

D

Alija takes money, horse, and sword. Journeys (trip described) to Janok. Leaps over moat, scorning drawbridge. Delivers ransom.

E

Mujo sends guests home, but he remains. Šarac and Mujo disguise themselves and return to Zadar, Mujo goes to tavern with instructions from Šarac as to what to do. Šarac goes to ban.

f

Several letters arrive from Stambol asking Osman to go to the sultan, but only the seventh has half of golden seal. Osman goes then to Stambol with Bey Ljubović and Bey Ristočić.

F

Mujo makes up with Šarac, saying he really was not after wife, but wanted to know where Šarac was. Tells Halil to take guests back to Kladuša. Mujo and Šarac go to Mustajbey and explain Rade's situation to him. He will help. Šarac goes to Zadar and returns to prison. Mustajbey collects army. Tale takes picked troop with Đulić and Vrsić as standard-bearers. Go to coastland. Send forward Ćelebić Hasan as scout in disguise. Hasan sees procession on way to monastery with girls and money; sees Rade bound and other Turks in disguise at various places. At monastery sees more Turks in disguise. Rade recognizes his horse, which Hasan is riding, and asks Hasan where he got it. He says he killed Hasan and got horse. Rade weeps. Then they release Rade and there is battle. Girls flee into church and they take ban into church and close doors. Big battle. They hand over ban to Mustajbey and go back to mountains.

Theme Eight: Settlement

a

They sit down on grass. Ban returns sword and horse, but keeps money.

A

Ban offers to free Osman if he promises never to attack Zadar. Osman agrees if ban will release Radovan. Ban finally is persuaded by all. Radovan is brought before him, but Radovan refuses to become a shepherd. Osman offers him tower and land, but he still refuses. Radovan is returned to prison. Banica goes to him at midnight and finally persuades him, giving him money, asking him not to send Osman back to prison. Next day agreement is reached. Ban writes Mustajbey to come to border to receive back Osman and Radovan.

b

Poro will not give over girl until ban releases thirty prisoners and gives them clothes, arms, horses, and money.

c

Ana goes to Murat in prison, offers release if he will take her to Udbina and marry her. He says he has a wife, but Ana says she will be her servant. She opens prison, takes him to her room, gives him clothes, and drinks. They mount, but Murat goes back, kills ban and takes head. As they leave, he shouts alarm. They are pursued, but escape to Udbina. Rejoicing in Udbina. Wife receives Ana well. Ana becomes Turk and is married to Murat.

B

King offers to release and to return arms and horse if Alija will swear not to attack Janok again. Alija will not leave Radovan in prison. Is about to go to prison again when king says if Alija will stand guarantor for Radovan, he will release them both. Alija agrees. They are released and return home.

d

Ban is about to despair of Omer's return when he arrives. Omer will not tell ban what really happened, but pretends it was joke about wife marrying again. They drink and then Omer is put in chains and returned to prison.

Three years later when Mujo was sixteen and ready for marriage, Omer dreamed dream of smoke which settled on Udbina and his tower. Lightning struck walls, and from them son rode out onto plain. Omer shouts. Banica goes to ban. Ban goes to Omer, who tells him of dream, and asks for release. Ban refuses, interprets dream as Mujo's wedding. Ban returns and for four days and nights Omer sings. Ban and banica amazed. Ban and two generals see cloud of dust on plain, from which a wounded youth emerges on horse. It is Jovo of Kozar, wounded in battle with Turks. Jovo reports. Leader of army was youth with pock marks, who sends ban greeting, saying he cannot come to Zadar now because he is about to marry the sister of the captain of Gradašac, but in about a week he will come to ransom father. His name is Kara Mujo the Little. Jovo dies. Ban sends to prison to tell Omer that banica asked that he be released. Omer says to tell ban he is happy in prison, has good dreams now. Ban sends banica to him; she persuades him. They give him wonderful clothes, arms, horse. Send him to son's wedding. Omer and banica become blood brother and blood sister. He agrees to keep son from attacking Zadar. Omer goes home.

e

Ban has Alija cleaned up and goes to meet Turks at border. After exchange, Tale attacks Hungarians. Alija captures ban, who is turned over to Mustajbey and executed. All go home.

C

Alija gives ban money, son, horse. Ban returns money and releases Alija to go home, but keeps son and horse. Son tells father in Turkish that he will reach home before him. Hađo (son) tells horse in Turkish not to let anyone touch him. Ban is asked by son Tadija for horse as gift, but Tadija can't get near him. Ban asks Hađo to teach son to ride horse. He does and escapes with him. Banica won't let soldiers fire on fleeing pair. Hađo arrives before father. Letters are exchanged. Hađo will release Tadija for Radovan and whatever ransom Radovan sets. Radovan requires money for Alija to repair house, release of thirty prisoners, with good clothes, arms, and horses, etc. Banica forces ban to agree when Radovan says he will have Tadija sent to Tartary. Hađo dresses Tadija as Turk and gives him horse. Exchange is brought about.

D

Ban returns all to him. Offers to build tower for him if he will go to Kladuša and bring him Halil's head. Alija agrees. Rests for week. Asks release of thirty prisoners. Granted. They are given equipment. All return to Alija's tower in Ribnik. All the Border hears of this and gathers at Ribnik, including Mustajbey, Dizdar, Dizdarević Meho, Mujo, Halil, Little Omer, Tale, et al. Rejoicing for week.

E

Next morning Mujo takes golden apple, meets nurse with ban's son Marko. Mujo captures child and flees. Pursuit, but soldiers cannot shoot because of child. Ban sends letter to Mujo. Mujo demands the thirty prisoners and horses. Ban gets twelve barbers to clean up prisoners, dresses them in new clothes, gives them horses. Sends them to Border, where ban's men get child. All return home.

f

Osman gives sultan letter of traitors. Sultan would give him gifts. Osman asks only permit to kill anyone he wants in Stambol. Kills three hundred in three months. Sultan gives him powers of judgment in war. Osman goes home.

F

Exchange of prisoners. Return ban to Zadar and Šarac to Turks. The thirty prisoners are released with horses, guns, clothes. All go home.

Theme Nine: Sequel

a

On return journey, Murat meets Osmanbey with sister of Todor, whom he has captured and is bringing to ban. (Text is corrupt for few lines.) Murat offers to give horse for girl to return to father. Osman says that since his spear had not struck Murat, he will give girl to him for one thousand ducats to take to Zadar. Murat returns to Zadar with girl. Guards meet him, capture, and take to ban. Murat explains situation; girl confirms it and tells of her capture while milking sheep. Ban returns to Murat the thousand ducats given for girl.

They say farewell. Murat returns home to wife. A year later, Murat perishes at unknown place on mountains and wife bears son Ibrahim.

D

Mustajbey tells son, Uzejir, that it is seven years since Zlatija and Bećirbey were captured, now in Aršan. He will gather Border for rescue. Men of Border gather at his tower. Mustajbey asks Dizdar to count army, and they depart over the mountains (described). At Višnica, Mustajbey seeks messenger to ask Ban of Janok to provide food for them. Dizdarević Meho goes. He greets the sentinels in Italian. Tells ban if he does not provision them, they will attack. Granted. After food, Turks attack city. Capture ban, open prison, release thirty prisoners, with Kavrajić Alija, who has been there seven years. Meho finds Duždević Jela and takes her. She, Ana, and Kružković Mara, have opened the gates. Battle. Panđa Mehmedagha brings children to Mustajbey, who has set himself up in palace in Janok. The Turks gather after battle at Višnica. Tale has captured Ban of Janok and gives him to Mustajbey. Mujo has captured Smiljanić, and Meho has captured Mrkonjić. Mustajbey says he will release ban for ransom: two barrels of treasure, horse, sword, cloak. Asks for volunteer to go to Janok to bring these. Halil volunteers. Banica recognizes Halil because he has been in service of ban for seven years. She gives him ransom. He sees Ana. Asks her to go with him. She agrees. They bring ransom and provisions to army. Ban is released. Army returns to tower of Kavrajić Alija in Ribnik.

APPENDIX IV

Return-Rescue Songs

A. Parry 1921 and 1940, by Murat Žunić in Bihać
B. Parry 6431, by Mujo Velić in Bihać
C. Parry 897, by Hajdar Habul in Gacko
D. Parry 923, by Suljo Tunović in Gacko
E. Parry 275a, by Hajdar Ðozo of Bare

Theme One: Shouting in Prison

A

Place is Zadar. Prisoner, Zaim Alajbey of Glasinac, is shouting. Had gone to window in morning, asked sun if it was shining on Glasinac, his mother, and his wife, or was his house in ruins, his mother dead, and his wife returned to her family? Ban hears and goes to jail. Zaim does not rise to meet him. When asked, explains his faith will not allow. Has been there seven years. Asks either to be released for ransom or to be killed.

B

Place is Zadar. Thirty prisoners are shouting, especially Bunić Mujo. Dizdarević Meho tells him to be quiet. He has been in prison twelve years and has not cried. Mujo says he would cry if he had wife and child at home. Meho says he has house, mother, little sister eight years old, serfs, horse. His sister ready to marry, but he still won't cry. Ban hears conversation, goes to jail. All prisoners rise to greet him except Meho. Ban asks prisoners why they are shouting. They say they are homesick and ask to be released. Meho says nothing.

C

Place is Janok. Two prisoners, Buničević Mujo, Dizdarević Meho. Mujo tells Dizdarević how he went raiding on border, captured daughter of Ban of Janok. (Blank record) Ban asks Meho why he did not rise to greet him. Meho describes prison. Has been there three years. Ban says he will execute him. Meho says he has nothing to be sorry about.

D

(Beginning missing) Bunić Alibey and Ðulić Nuhan are brought before the ban. Ban asks Bunić why he is shouting. Bunić has been there twelve years. Asks either to be released or to be killed.

E

Two prisoners in Požun, Alijić Alija and Velagić Ibrahim. They talk of how they were captured, what they are most sorry about. Alija tells how he had just brought home a bride when his sister announced they were being attacked. Alija joined in defense, was captured, but horse went home. Has been in prison seven years. Is most sorry about bride. Shouts three days. Disturbs banica and two sons. Banica goes to ban, complains. If he will not release prisoner or execute him, she will go home and leave children. Ban goes to jail. Alija asks to be released or to be killed. Ban refuses, asks what is wrong: Alija describes prison.

Theme Two: Bargaining for Terms

A

Ban says that Zaim has tried to capture his daughter Ruža and has been taken prisoner, but he will release him for one hundred ducats, horse, clothes given him by sultan, hostage, and bird that he had given to sultan. Zaim would agree to all except last two, which are with sultan. Ban will not release. Zaim warns him to look out for Ruža. Ban says he will gather his bones and throw them into sea.

B

Ban says he will release all thirty except Meho. In a week he will roast him alive, wrap his ashes in paper and send them to Mustajbey.

C

Ban asks Mujo if he will give one thousand ducats. Mujo agrees and is released.

D

Ban requires one thousand ducats, his best suit of clothes, sword that sultan had given him, horse, and sister. Bunić would give all but sister. Ban puts him back into lower dungeon, but releases Đulić without ransom.

E

Ban requires fifty serfs, seed, oxen, mills for cloth, mills for grain, one thousand ducats, horse with trappings, and wife. Alija refuses to give wife. Ban will execute Alija and take bones, etc.

Theme Three: Message Home

A

Zaim writes letter. Has paper in pocket. Writes in blood with little finger to mother to sell everything; writes to wife to take horse and remarry.

B

Meho asks Mujo to go to his house and tell his mother to sell their goods, including horse; his sister to marry a mighty hero to avenge her brother even in ninth year; then go to Kozličić Nura (bride), tell her to marry again. Tell mother to go to Mustajbey, scold him for not rescuing him. Mazul Alibey will be there; scold him. When Mazul had been in prison in Malta for twelve years, Mustajbey had sent men to find him. They had disappeared. Mazul's mother had come to Meho asking him to find son. He went to seacoast, searched for year, went to Ćorfez, asked ship captain about Mazul. Captain said he was in Malta. Meho got money from Mazul's mother for passage. While she was getting money, he went to visit his own mother and sister. After week, went to Vrljika. Mazul's mother gave him money. He went to captain, who took him to Malta. Meho came upon woman with three-year-old son. Meho gave boy golden apple. Mother invited him to their tavern in tower of King of Malta. She was queen. Meho was disguised as general. King, queen, child came. Child ran to Meho. Queen asked him if he would cut child's hair. Meho said he was son of King of Ćorfez, in service of emperor in Vienna for seven years. He had come in search of a wife. They told him there were many girls at church. They would help him find one. Next morning they went to church. He stayed in Malta a month looking for Mazul. Again he found sea captain, who told him that king would go to sea with army for a month. He should abduct child. Captain would give them passage. Meho abducted child. Wrote king for exchange of prisoners, which was carried out (full treatment). When Mazulbey left King of Malta, he repented having killed king's two brothers. Mazul's mother reimbursed Mazul for money spent and gave gifts.

C

Meho asks Mujo to take message to blood brother Tanković Osman, not to expect him again. Then to go to his mother, tell her of execution. Tell sister to marry. Then go to Lika to scold Mustajbey for not rescuing Meho, Mujo, and Halil.

D

Bunić gives message to Đulić. Tell mother not to wait for son, but to sell goods. Wife to marry again and take horse. Sister to marry a mighty hero.

E

Alija asks ban by life of two sons to allow him to send letter home. Alija dictates, ban writes. Alija tells mother where he is in prison and of coming execution. Advises her to divide his things among friends (list given), sell horse and give money to bride and send her home, build mosque for him with school.

Theme Four: Journey of Messenger

A

Zaim finds messenger, who comes to grating of prison and agrees to take letter. Mother will reward him. Messenger goes home, puts on walking clothes, goes to Glasinac to tower of Zaim.

B

After Meho's story, Mujo leaves prison, is given money and pass by ban. With stick in hand, goes to Mount Velibit, to tower of Tanković Osman.

C

Mujo goes to barber; gets shave and manicure. Then to tavern; eats and drinks. Says good-by to friends and crosses mountains.

D

Đulić departs. When he comes to a place above Bunić, he looks at town and recognizes Bunić's tower. He proceeds to it.

E

Alija finds messenger, who goes to tower.

Theme Five: Arrival of Message

A

Message delivered to mother and wife of Zaim. Wife puts on men's clothes, prepares horse, rides to Stambol. Puts up at han and tells keeper she is Osmanpasha of Travnik and seeks school of Sultan Sulejman, where she has blood brother, Mehmedbey of Bosnia. Keeper, Omer, goes to school, gets Meho. Wife asks how she can see sultan. They prepare petition. Sometime later Meho and schoolmaster, Talib, take her to sultan with directions how to proceed in audience. She reveals identity to sultan, tells story, gives him Zaim's letter. Sultan sends her home, says he will seek Zaim. Instructs Ahmedpasha to raise army and to go to Bosnia to Mustajbey, to bring back Ban of Janok dead or alive or lose his own head. (In Parry 1940 the message is given in full.)

B

Mujo delivers message to Tanković Osman, Meho's mother and sister, and betrothed, and to Mustajbey, Mujo, Halil, and Mazulalibey. He tells women that he and the other heroes will rescue Meho. He recounts again to Mazul much of the long story given before. They all agree to gather forces and go to Zadar. They gather them. Mustajbey prepares to lead them.

C

Mujo gives messages to Tanković Osman, Meho's mother and sister, and finally to Mustajbey, Mujo and Halil, who decide to go to Meho's execution. Mustajbey gathers the Border. While they are waiting for men to arrive, Mujo's brother Ibro joins him. Last to arrive is Tale. Bunitević Mujo is lacking a horse; Mustajbey sends Đulić to get Meho's horse. Meho's sister promises to marry him if he will put Meho on the horse.

D

In courtyard Đulić sees woman grooming horse. He knocks. Woman goes into house to get rifle, but opens when she hears it is Đulić, who tells her message from Alija. Wife refuses to marry again, but will care for mother. Mustajbey arrives. Đulić scolds wife for having him as lover, but is told he is really courting Alija's sister. Đulić goes to bey and arranges marriage. Guests arrive and bring bride to bey. In marriage chamber girl reminds Mustajbey of promise of rescuing brother before marriage consummation. He leaves that night. He sets out for Zadar, where he is recognized, captured, and put in prison. When word of this reaches Alija's sister, she gives orders to have Alija's horse prepared. She dresses as a man and sets out for Zadar.

E

Wife reads letter to mother and sends servant Huso to tavern to give letter to Mustajbey, who says he cannot save Alija. Požun is too strong a citadel. Huso reports to wife. She then sends him to their father with the letter. He refuses to help, and even curses and threatens. Huso reports. She tells him to disguise the horse. She disguises herself, says farewell to mother, mounts, departs. Mustajbey and aghas watch. She and horse are frightened on Mount Jadika. Journey described. At first guardpost she is questioned for passport. She says she is from Vienna, sister's son of Ban of Požun, sent to attend execution. Guard gives her pass for the other twenty-nine posts. She arrives at city gate.

Theme Six: Rescue

A

Wife goes to Glasinac, but en route decides not to stop. Continues to Cetina to tower of Mahmutagha. Mahmut sees her, has her called in. He asks if she is Bey Ljubović. She does not lie, but says she is his sister and wife of Zaim. She tells him her story. He tries to dissuade her, saying sultan will be angry and he will send his men to rescue Zaim. She persists and asks for disguise. She dresses and mounts. Mahmut gives route. At Zadar's gate she sees boy crying, cursing ban, and mentioning Mustajbey. He explains his name is Vojvodić Nikola. Was servant of ban. Ban gave daughter Ruža to Mate of Ćorfez. Nikola wanted to dance at wedding then in progress, but ban drove him away. Wants to complain to Mustajbey. Wife says if he will take her to ban, she will plead his cause. She pretends to be from Vienna and tells ban she will report him to emperor. Ban asks her to join dance and instructs daughter to take her to her room. Ruža does. Ruža reports to father that wife instructs him to settle well with Nikola. Ruža explains to wife that she is being married to an old man she doesn't like, but she is in love with prisoner, Zaim. Ban had discovered she was visiting him and had taken keys from her. Wife instructs Ruža to tell father to take Zaim and give him food and drink, because emperor had not ordained such treatment of prisoners. She will take Zaim to Vienna. At night Ruža tries to buy Zaim from wife and to take both of them from Zadar. Ruža gets Zaim, who is puzzled by wife. Wife goes to ban, who is asleep, kills him. Puts his head under her cloak, so daughter will not see. When she returns, Ruža and Zaim have fled, but she joins them in courtyard. Next morning banica discovers headless husband and calls son. No pursuit. As Zaim and others are crossing plain, Nikola joins them. On mountain they meet sons of Mahmutagha and later the army from Stambol with Mustajbey. Mustajbey asks Zaim who freed him, but he does not know. Wife declares her identity and gives sword to Zaim. She gives head to pasha. They all return home. Zaim remarries wife and also marries Ruža, who becomes Moslem. Zaim builds tower and gives land to Nikola. All get praise and gifts from sultan. (In Parry 1940 told more fully. Ban gave daughter to Captain Peter.)

B

At Rudina, Maljković Stipan, Mazul, and others, including Uskok Radovan, volunteer to go in disguise to Zadar. Radovan suggests they tell the sentinel at gate they are from Vienna, to find out from ban if he needs help against the Turks. On the way, guns of Zadar boom. They ask an old man watching sheep why. He tells them of coming execution and that many soldiers will be present. At gate Radovan's ruse is successful. They are welcomed by ban. Next day, prisoners are brought out for execution. Meho recognizes friends in disguise. Two others are condemned with Meho, according to priest's books; remaining twenty-eight prisoners are to be set free. Meho tells ban his actions against Christian garrisons. Ban strikes him and battle is started by Maljković Stipan, who kills ban. While fight in courtyard is going on, Mustajbey enters and tries to stop it, but just then the armies outside begin to pursue his army. There is a big battle. Turks are victorious. They go back to Zadar for prisoners, whom they outfit with clothes, arms, and horses, captured in Zadar, and with money. All return home.

C

Forces set out. When they draw near, heroes volunteer for rescue, including Buničević Mujo, Ibro, Halil, Ðulić, and others. When Meho appears by church, he sings about Halil. Buničević Mujo and brother appear before ban just as Meho weeps and explains to ban that he hears neighing of his horse. Ban kills horse from under Ibro and asks Mujo if he has brought ransom. Mujo says he has not, rides up and releases Meho. Fight begins. Turks rescue Meho and capture ban.

D

Sister goes to tavern of Pava for night. She is seen out walking by ban's daughter, who falls in love with her and sends for her. Pava takes her to castle. Sister declares identity, asks help. Girl suggests stealing ban's son, whom she will give to her. This is done. Banica misses child. Scolds ban, who has Alija brought before him. Tells him to send letter to sister asking what she wants in return for child. She asks for Alija. Ban brings Alija out of jail, cleans him up and feeds him. Alija demands money, clothes, Mustajbey, Ana, and golden table. Alija returns with booty. Child is brought to border and returned to ban.

E

Wife goes to tavern, hears cannon. Keeper tells of pending execution; suggests Ana, ban's daughter, could find wife for him in kolo of girls. Wife goes to courtyard to watch kolo. When Ana sees wife, she runs into house, calls slave Kumrija to bring wife in. Finally wife reveals her identity to Ana and tells her purpose. Ana will help if wife will take her to Turkey. She is in love with Ibro of Rudin. Wife agrees. Wife is instructed to wait for procession to church, to cut Alija's bonds, put him on horse, and come to her coach, where she will have clothes for her. Alija will then rescue them both. In procession prisoner is described. He recognizes his horse, but not the rider. Before execution, Alija sings of coming battle. Wife releases him, puts him on horse, goes to coach. Turks under Tale and Mustajbey attack. Tale is described. Turks are victorious. All return home.

APPENDIX V

Example of Father - Son Transmission

Another example of transmission of a song from father to son also comes from Kolašin in Montenegro, and, as in Chapter Five, the texts were recorded years after the teaching and learning had been accomplished. The father is Mirko Danilović, 60 years old at the time of recording in 1935, and illiterate; the son is Rade Danilović, 28 years old at that time and literate. The song, "Mitrović Stojan and the Vizier of Travnik," Mirko tells us he learned from his grandfather. (Mirko, Parry 6796; Rade, Parry 6777). In this case the song of the son is longer than that of the father; 500 lines, as compared to 342 lines. We have a third version of this song from another singer of the same general district, i.e. Montenegro in and around Kolašin, and we can use this version as a rough control (Parry 6717). It was sung by Stanko Pižurica, 65 years old, and illiterate, the best of our Montenegrin singers. His song is much longer than the other two, 757 lines.

The first theme is a kind of assembly theme in which there are, however, only two speakers. Thirty rebels are drinking. Young Stojan Mitrović is serving the wine, and when he pours it for his father, he fills the glass only half full and pours it on the green grass. The father asks the reason for this censure, and the young man explains that on his wedding night, or the day after it, his father had taken him away from home to join the rebels. That was twelve years ago, and now Stojan longs to see his wife and other members of the family. His father says that he can go in a few days, when Easter Sunday comes. (Mirko, lines 1–35, speaks only of the wife whom Stojan had left, and says nothing of other members of the family; Rade, lines 1–43, and Stanko, lines 34–129, both mention the mother, two brothers, and two sisters, in addition to the wife.

The length of Stanko's version comes from expansion: the father asks his son if he is angry because he is lacking money, clothes, a horse, and other accoutrements, and the son answers that he is not angry because of this, nor that, since these could be corrected easily, but he is angry that . . . And we are reminded of the similar theme in "Smailagić Meho." Stanko also expands the young man's answer by having him say that his wife may marry again, that if he met his mother on the street he would not recognize her, if he met his brothers on the mountains he might kill them both, if he met his sisters, he might capture them both and sell them to Turkey. This text is of considerable interest in itself, but for our present purposes it is useful in keeping us from claiming, at this point in the song, that Rade has himself invented the place of the other members of Stojan's family in the tale. Either Mirko's text in this theme is not typical, or Rade picked up these details from elsewhere.

The second theme contains the preparations of Stojan for the journey to Sarajevo and his father's instructions to him as to what he is to do and what not to do. Mirko's description of the preparations is brief (lines 44–59); Stojan puts on fine armor, is given a huge Bulgarian cloak by his father, which is even small for the son, and he saddles his horse in Turkish fashion. Rade's description is somewhat longer (lines 49–78), but he covers the same main points. There are a few added details: Stojan washes before dressing; his father twists his sash for him in Turkish fashion; he looks like a Bulgarian from Sofia. In this part of the theme it is clear that Mirko was the teacher of Rade; for their texts are rather close. Our control text begins with the preparing of the horse, lines 137–150, and then proceeds to a very lengthy description of the dressing and arming of Stojan, lines 152–221.

Stojan, now disguised, must be instructed by his father in a series of recognitions and taboos. In Mirko's text Stojan is to twist his sash in Turkish fashion when he arrives in Sarajevo, and to ride his horse like a Turk. Before the church he must dismount and tell his horse in Greek not to let anyone touch him. At the church door he will find his mother lamenting her son; he should give her fifty ducats and tell her to buy a covering and a shirt. By the altar in the church he will find two priests; they are his brothers and he should give them twenty ducats. Outside the church he will find a kolo dance of young wives, among whom the most striking will be his wife; he should give her whatever he wishes. Stojan departs singing, and his father goes back lamenting (lines 61–102). We see now that the mother and brothers are present in Mirko's song, but the sisters are still absent.

Rade's text (lines 82–145) adds something to Mirko's, and it also changes the order of events slightly. Stojan will first go into the church and see his two brothers, to whom he will give thirty ducats each; next he will meet his mother at the door when he leaves the church. In front of the church he will find a kolo dance of maidens in which will be his two sisters, to whom he will give twenty ducats each. After this comes the kolo in which his wife will be found. At each encounter he is warned by his father not to pay any attention or say anything to the other people, lest "a serpent sting him" and the Turks recognize him. His father's last admonition is not to drink from a cask of wine that he will find. In other respects Rade's version is like his father's. Rade stresses the taboos, whereas his father had stressed what Stojan *should* do.

Stanko's text (lines 226–300) is not much longer than Rade's here. Stanko says nothing about speaking to the horse in Greek or in any language. After the liturgy Stojan is to stay in the church and to give a gift of unspecified amount to his two brothers. Next comes the mother outside the church; then the sisters, not in a kolo dance but walking among the other people outside the church. He will recognize them because they look like him. On the other side of the church he will find his wife walking. She is distinguished by her beauty; and here, as in the other versions, she is also distinguished by the fact that she is wearing three necklaces. Stojan is warned not to show himself to be recognized by any of these people, lest "a serpent sting him." After these meetings and gift-givings Stojan is to go to the tavern in front of the church and there to drink wine and rakija, after which he is to mount his horse and return to the mountains. These last instructions, of course, differ markedly from Rade's text.

Stojan goes to Sarajevo, encounters the members of his family, and finally breaks the taboo about drinking wine. It might also be said that he breaks the taboo about speaking to his kin, if the texts mean that there should be a taboo (they are not clear on this point). In Mirko's text, Stojan forgets to speak to his horse in Greek (or, at least, Mirko forgets to tell us about it!), as he had been instructed to do. (Rade is specific here.) Stojan gives his mother the money and tells her that he has seen Stojan recently and that her son has sent her the money. She asks him to wait, because he looks much like Stojan, but he goes inside. He then gives money to his brothers, and when they see him they drop the books from their hands and weep. When asked by the deacons why they did this, the brothers say they have seen the wounds of God and weep. Stojan finds the dance and grasps one of his wife's necklaces. She shouts that if he knew whose wife she was he would not dare even to look at her. He asks her who her husband is, and she replies, stating that he had disappeared twelve years ago. Stojan tells her that her husband died long ago and asks her to accept him. She assures him that she would rather have Stojan dead than him alive. At this Stojan gives her a gift of money; she looks closely at him, weeps, and covers her face with her handkerchief. Stojan then finds the wine and drinks it. The theme ends at line 193 in Mirko's text.

As before, Rade has expanded on his father's telling, or more properly, the text which we have from him is more elaborate than that from his father. He does have Stojan speak to his horse in Greek! The order of encounters is somewhat different, as it was in the instructions. First come the two brothers, to whom he gives money, telling them that it is a gift from Stojan, whom he has seen recently. It is the Turks not the deacons who ask them for an explanation of their dropping the books and weeping. Rade's song, it can be seen, provides clearer motivation than does Mirko's for the actions reported. After the brothers comes the mother, and Rade's handling of this meeting is much like Mirko's. Then Rade tells of the encounter with the sisters, which is missing in Mirko's text. Stojan gives them a gift and tells them it is from Stojan; they weep but hide their tears in handkerchiefs. In the meeting with his wife, Stojan breaks his wife's three necklaces and spills the beads on the ground. Otherwise Rade's text is much like his father's here also, as in the final episode with the drinking of the wine.

By now it is abundantly clear, I think, that we are dealing with a return story strangely like the *Odyssey* in its basic framework. Rade's story seems simply to be better told than Mirko's; perhaps in the days when Rade learned it from his father the old man sang it more fully. Yet it would not be amiss for us to check his telling against our control in Stanko's text. His handling of this series of meetings is not so long as that of Rade, although the order is the same as his. He pours money onto the holy altar for the brothers, telling them it has been sent them from Stojan, and then he turns his back and leaves; there is no dropping of books or weeping here. The meeting with the mother is much the same as in the other texts. As for the sisters, although no kolo dance was spoken of in the instructions, Stojan finds them in a kolo; he gives them the money, saying it is from Stojan. They weep, and he departs. There is even greater difference in the scene with the wife. Stojan finds her again in a kolo dance, which was not mentioned in the instructions, and she is described as wearing the three necklaces; but the necklaces are not grasped by Stojan, as in the other two texts.

Stojan, in Stanko's song, enters the kolo and steps on his wife's foot. She pushes him away saying that if he knew who she was, he would not even dare to look at her, to say nothing of stepping on her foot. He gives her a hundred ducats saying that they are from Stojan with greetings. That is all. Stojan then goes to the tavern, drinks, gives money to the tavern keeper as a gift from Stojan to buy drinks for all the people at the fair. He departs to the plain.

The Brunhilde of the Balkans makes her appearance in the section of our song that tells of Stojan's capture by the Turks. Mirko and Rade call her "the powerful maiden" (*devletka đevojka*), but Stanko specifies her as "the Arab maiden" (*Harapka đevojka*). All three texts relate how Stojan comes upon the Turks playing heroic games, that he joins them in hurling stones and jumping and that he bests them. In their anger they bring forth "the powerful maiden," and she competes with Stojan and wins. He then takes off his disguise of the Bulgarian cloak, standing forth in shining gold as a mountain rebel. Thus unencumbered he out-throws and out-jumps the Amazon.

At this point two other characters are introduced, both of whom recognize Stojan, but the first is not believed by the Turks, and only when the second identifies him, do they act and capture him, finally turning him over to the vizier in Travnik, since they themselves do not know what to do with him. Mirko and Rade agree as to who these two people are. One is the smith Jovo (*kujundžija Jovo*) and the other is a woman called *bula bumbulova*, "nightingale woman." The smith says that he recognizes Stojan because he had stolen the breastplate he wears from his smithy. The woman says she recognizes him because he had stolen from her shop the shirt of gold that he wears. Mirko and Rade differ only in the order of appearance of these two: in Mirko's tale the woman appears first, in Rade's the smith.

Stanko's text, our "control," doubles the male characters in this recognition scene, and in a way it also doubles the female personae. When she is bested by Stojan, the "Arab maiden" says that since Stojan had gone to the rebels twelve years ago, nobody has been able to overcome her, and it looks to her that Stojan has returned. At this moment young Ibrahim (occupation unspecified) arrives and recognizes Stojan because he is wearing a green coat that he had taken from Ibrahim's back. The Turks pay no attention to this. Then the woman Bungurova (*sic*) comes and recognizes him by the silk shirt he is wearing, which he had taken from her back. She is not believed, but finally the smith Ramo recognizes Stojan because he is wearing the golden breastplate, taken from his back; his name is on it.

This theme, stopping at Stojan's capture and binding, ends in Mirko at line 249; in Rade at line 374; in Stanko at line 553. In considering what has happened in transmission from Mirko to Rade, the significant point is that the order of appearance of these two characters is the only change. We have now seen a number of instances of change in the order of events in transmission. This seems to be a characteristic phenomenon.

The final large theme of the song relates Stojan's escape from the sentence of execution imposed upon him by the vizier in Travnik. All three texts tell how the vizier asks him what he has done, how Stojan replies that he captured the vizier's father and mother and sold them into slavery, and that he captured the vizier's wife and made love to her for three years and returned her to the vizier for ransom. The vizier sentences Stojan to death, but Stojan by a ruse persuades the executioners to release his arms. He then fights his way to freedom and returns to the mountains. Rade's telling of this is somewhat longer than his father's (lines 375–500 in Rade; 250–342 in Mirko) and he differs in the following: Mirko states that Stojan sold the vizier's mother for thirty fuses, Rade for thirty pouches of tobacco. In both songs, the vizier's wife intervenes for Stojan, but Mirko has her order that Stojan's arms be freed so that they may take his shirt of gold before killing him, whereas Rade has her order that he be taken into the courtyard so as not to befoul the castle with his blood. In the courtyard Stojan then tells the executioners to take off his shirt of gold for themselves before they kill him, because the blood will spoil the gold. In both cases the executioners release his arms. In Mirko's text Stojan kills the three executioners and then the vizier himself, together with a few men around him. In Rade's Stojan kills the two executioners; the guards oppose him but he kills them. In both texts he escapes to Mount Romanija to find his whole family mourning for him. In Mirko's text their wailing is turned to singing when he arrives. In Rade's, when Stojan arrives he sings a song about a falcon that had broken its wings but had gotten them again: "Now, Mount Romanija, rejoice, here is your gray falcon, your falcon, Dmitrović Stojan!" This song is a link with other return tales, especially with the song of the Captivity of Janković Stojan; for it is by a song about a bird that the hero brings about recognition of the long-absent but returned hero.

The control text, as before, is much longer than the songs of the Danilovići (lines 554–757). There are some differences from their texts, and some points in which Stanko is closer to Rade than to Mirko. When the Turks of Sarajevo are debating what to do with Stojan, a certain Zuko the standard-bearer appears and tells them that the vizier in Travnik is seeking Stojan and offering rewards. So the men of Sarajevo in reality sell the hero to the vizier. In Stojan's tale to the vizier, which is longer than his story in the other texts, the order is mother, father, and wife, rather than father, mother, and wife. As a kind of refrain, one finds that Stojan's opening lines to the vizier are the same in all texts, *Dorijane, travnički vezire,/Dorijane i od dorijana!* ("You big chestnut horse, Vizier of Travnik, Big chestnut horse and son of a big chestnut horse!")

In his first raid Stojan had killed three hundred, taken much money and thirty captives, including the vizier's mother, whom he had taken to the mountains and fattened like a sow and then sold to merchants for thirty pouches of cut tobacco, which his thirty rebels smoked. The second raid was like the first, except that it was the father who was captured and fattened, and he was sold for thirty pair of sandals, which the thirty rebels wore out. In the third raid he killed five hundred, took a hundred ducats and sixty captives, among them the vizier's wife, whom he kept for six months and then sent back.

The vizier's wife does not intervene on Stojan's behalf in Stanko's story, but Stojan is taken into the streets by three executioners to be killed. Stojan himself persuades them to take off his golden clothing before they kill him. They release his arms, and he kills them, and then returns to the vizier and his wife. When the vizier sees him, he pardons everything he has done and offers him money and even his wife, but Stojan cuts off his head, kills his two sons, and plunders his castle. Nothing further is said of the vizier's wife. When Stojan reaches the mountains, he tells his story to his father and the rebels. Nothing is said of his family.

APPENDIX VI

The Song of Milman Parry

*

*

Bože mili, na svemu ti fala!
Što ću pjevať istina je prava.

U hiljadu devetoj stotini
I trideset i trećoj godini,
5   Poletijo soko tica siva
Od lijepe zemlje Amerike.
On preleće zemlje i gradove,
Dok on dođe do morske obale.
Tu ga čeka od čelika lađa,
10   Pa u lađu soko uletijo,
I junačka odmorijo krila.
Lađa mu se zove Saturnija,
I brza je kao gcrska vila.
To ne bijo soko tica siva,
15   Već Profesor Milman Parry slavni!

Naša će ga pričať istorija,
I spominjať u mnoga vremena.
To je čovjek dobrih osobina,
A kiti ga mudrost i vrlina,
20   Dobra srca a pogleda blaga.
A naša mu istorija draga.
Pjesme naše on je zavolijo,

I zbog njih se amo uputijo,

U junačku našu otadžbinu.
25   Put ga vodi preko oceana.
Brod ga nosi Saturnija slavna,

Napravljena od čelika ljuta.
Ne može joj ništa sprečiť puta,
Već po moru razgoni valove,

30   Kao soko tice golubove.
Okean je hitro preletijo,
Do jadranskog mora doletijo.

Dear God, praise to Thee for all!
What I shall sing is the straight truth.

In one thousand, nine hundred
And thirty three,
5   A gray falcon flew
From the beautiful land of America.
He flew over lands and cities,
Until he came to the shore of the sea.
There a steel ship awaited him,
10   And the falcon flew onto the ship,
And rested his heroic wings.
The name of the ship is Saturnia,
And it is as swift as a mountain vila.
That was not a gray falcon,
15   But Professor Milman Parry the glorious!

Our history will speak of him,
And remember him for many ages.
He is a man of good qualities,
Wisdom and uprightness adorn him,
20   Of good heart and mild glance.
And our history is dear to him.
He has become enamored of our songs,
And because of them he has set out hither,
To our heroic fatherland.
25   His path leads him across the ocean.
The ship carries him, the Saturnia the glorious,
Constructed of fierce steel.
Nothing can bar its path,
But over the sea it drives away the waves,
30   As a falcon drives away doves.
Swiftly he flew over the ocean,
He flew to the Adriatic sea.

Malo pođe, našem Splitu dođe,	A little while passed and he came to Split,
I tu se je malo odmorijo.	And here he rested a little.
35 Pa otale dalje polazijo,	35 Then from there he went further,
Dubrovniku zdravo dolazijo.	And came safely to Dubrovnik.
Saturnija tu se ustavila,	There the Saturnia stopped,
I svoja je sidra utvrdila.	And hauled in its sails.
Milman Parry s pristaništa pođe,	Milman Parry departed from the wharf,
40 Pa u hotel Imperial dođe.	40 And came to Hotel Imperial.
Tu je sjeo pa se odmorijo,	There he sat down and rested,
I ladna se vina napoijo,	And drank his fill of cool wine,
I tu nađe sebi pratioca,	And there he found a companion for himself,
Hercegovca bistroga mladića,	A keen Hercegovinian youth,
45 Po imenu Nika Vujnovića.	45 By name Nikola Vujnović.
Sjutri danak jesu polazili	On the following day they departed
Po junačkoj našoj domovini,	Throughout our heroic homeland,
Da guslare naše ispitaju,	To seek out our guslars,
Jer ga srpske gusle zanimaju.	For the Serbian gusle interests him.
50 Pro Hrvatske jesu polazili,	50 Across Croatia they travelled,
I njezine ljepote vidili.	And they saw her beauties.
Tu mu pjesme pjevaše guslari,	There guslars sang songs for him,
Što činiše vitezovi stari.	Of what the knights of old had done.
Iz Hrvatske tad se uputijo	From Croatia he then set out
55 Kroz lijepu našu Slavoniju,	55 Across our beautiful Slavonia,
Dok on dođe u zemlju Srbiju,	Until he came to the land of Serbia,
U Beograd našu prestolnicu,	To Belgrade our capital,
Od uvijek našu perjanicu,	Since time immemorial our crest.
I tu kupi pjesme od junaka,	And there he gathered songs of heroes,
60 Što činiše jade od Turaka.	60 Of what sorrows they had given the Turks.
Kad tu mnogo pjesama kupijo,	When he had gathered many songs there,
Otole se zdravo uputijo	Thence he set out safely
Kroz junačku našu Šumadiju,	Across our heroic Šumadija,
Što proslavi srpsku istoriju,	Which makes famous Serbian history,
65 I u Bosnu profesor došao,	65 And the professor came to Bosnia,
I tu mnogo pjesama skupijo.	And there he gathered many songs.
Od sve Bosne u najlepšem gradu,	In the most beautiful city of all Bosnia,
Gizdavome šeher Sarajevu,	The lovely city of Sarajevo,
Profesor se bješe ustavijo,	The professor stopped,
70 I divno se junak odmorijo.	70 And wondrously the hero rested.
Kad je divnu Bosnu ostavijo,	When he left wondrous Bosnia,
Uputi se u Herceogvinu,	He set out for Hercegovina,
U junačku našu pokrajinu.	For our heroic borderland.
Do Mostara grada dolazijo,	He came to the city of Mostar,
75 I tu se je malo odmorijo.	75 And there he rested a little.
Odmori se u hotel Vilsonu.	He rested in Hotel Wilson.

Onda reče pratiocu svomu:	Then he said to his companion:
"Tu je lepo, tu ćemo sjediti,	"It is beautiful here, here shall we sit,
I ladna se vina napojiti."	And drink our fill of cool wine."
80 Tu je jedan danak predanijo,	80 There he spent one day,
A sjutri dan rano uranijo,	But the next day he arose early,
I Mostara grada ostavijo,	And he left the city of Mostar,
Jer do Stoca 'oće putovati,	Because he wanted to travel to Stolac,
I nekoje pjesme napisati.	And to write down some songs.
85 U Stocu su danak predanili,	85 In Stolac they spent a day,
I dosta su pjesama skupili.	And many songs they gathered.
Pa otale Milman Parry pođe,	Then thence Milman Parry departed,
Pa u divno Nevesinje dođe.	And came to wondrous Nevesinje.
Kada dođe Nevesinju ravnu,	When he came to level Nevesinje,
90 Koje ima istoriju slavnu,	90 Which has a glorious history,
Od junačkih svojijeh sinova,	Of its heroic sons,
A našije' slavnih pradedova,	And of our glorious forebears,
Tu pregleda varoš Nevesinje,	There he looked over the town of Nevesinje,
I tu ga je očaralo milje.	And there it enchanted him.
95 Tu pregleda divne okoline,	95 There he looked over the wondrous surroundings,
Gleda polje a gleda planine.	He looked at the plain, and gazed at the mountains.
Tu najviše sastavi pjesama	There he gathered most songs
Od guslara Voj'čić Milovana.	From the guslar Milovan Vojičić.
Tu je bijo tri bijela dana.	He was there for three white days.
100 Kad četvrti danak osvanuo,	100 When the fourth day dawned,
Uranijo Milman profesore,	Professor Milman arose early,
Prije dana i bijele zore.	Before daylight and white dawn.
Na noge je lagane skočijo,	He leaped to his light feet,
Nevesinje grada ostavijo,	Left the city of Nevesinje,
105 Gacku ravnu pravo odlazijo,	105 Went straight to level Gacko,
Jer tu mnogo imade pjesama,	For there are many songs there,
A i dosta srpskije' guslara.	And plenty of Serbian singers.
Tu je sjeo, pa se odmorijo,	There he sat and rested,
I pjesama dosta nakupijo.	And gathered plenty of songs.
110 Onda Gacko grada ostavijo,	110 Then he left the city of Gacko,
U Bileću tad se uputijo.	And then set out for Bileća.
Tu on sjede nekoliko dana,	There he stayed for several days,
I sasluša priče od junaka.	And he listened to the tales of heroes.
Kad profesor iz Bileće pođe,	When the professor departed from Bileća,
115 Pravo zdravo u Trebinje dođe,	115 He went sound and straight to Trebinje,
I trebinjske ljepote vidijo,	And he saw the beauties of Trebinje,
I Trebinje ostavijo grada.	And he left the city of Trebinje.
Dubrovniku uputi se sada.	Now he set out for Dubrovnik.
Vozom pođe, u Dubrovnik dođe.	He went by train and came to Dubrovnik.
120 Divnog grada na moru razgleda,	120 He surveyed the lovely city by the sea,

I njegove starine pregleda.
Zanima ga, milo mu vidjeti,

Jer će ovu zemlju ostaviti.
Kad je naše krajeve vidijo,
125 Ljepoti se nji'noj začudijo,
On se divi, i vrlo mu žao,

Što još dalje ne ostade amo.
Kad iz grada Dubrovnika pođe,
On na divno ˌpristanište dođe,
130 Đe pristaju lađe i đemije,
Koje nose pro mora delije.
Kad tu dođe Milman Profesore,
Divno naše pregledava more,
Jadran plavi naša slava stara,

135 Đe naš mornar divni sanak sanja.

Našeg mora razgleda krasote,
Rijetke (su) ovake ljepote.
Onda našu zemlju ostavijo,
I putovat' dalje naumijo.
140 Kad profesor putovati htjede,

On u lađu Saturniju sjede.

Saturnija poleće pro mora,
Kao soko pro zelenih gora.
Profesora tamo čeka dika,
145 Domovina dična Amerika.
Zbogom pošo Milman Profesore!
Zdravo sinje prebrodijo more,

I u svoju došo domovinu!
Pošten bijo i ko te rodijo!

Spjevao

Milovan Vojičić
Nevesinje, dne 20 septembra
1933 god.

And looked over its antiquities.
He was interested, pleased he was to see it,
For he will leave this land.
When he had seen our country,
125 And had wondered at its beauty,
He was amazed, and he was very sorry,
That he was not staying longer here.
When he left the city of Dubrovnik,
He came to the wondrous quay,
130 Where stop the ships and galleys,
That carry champions across the sea.
When Professor Milman came there,
He surveyed our wondrous sea.
The blue Adriatic is our ancient glory,
135 Where our sailor dreams a wondrous dream.
He looked at the beauties of our sea.
Rare are such beauties as these.
Then he left our land,
And thought to travel further.
140 When the professor was about to depart,
He took his place in the ship Saturnia.
The Saturnia flew across the sea,
As a falcon across the green hills.
There his pride awaits the professor.
145 The beloved homeland America.
Farewell, Professor Milman!
Safely may you cross the deep blue sea,
And come to your homeland!
Honor also to him who begot you!

Composed by

Milovan Vojičić
Nevesinje, on the twentieth day of
September 1933

❧ NOTES

NOTES

CHAPTER ONE

Introduction

1. In 1935, when Parry returned from Yugoslavia, he began a book entitled "The Singer of Tales." This was to contain the results of his study of the problems of oral form. He had written only a few pages before his death. These pages have been published in my article, "Homer, Parry, and Huso," *AJA*, 52:34–44 (Jan.-March 1948).

2. The Milman Parry Collection is now housed in the Harvard University Library. It contains over 3500 twelve-inch aluminum phonograph discs recorded in various parts of Yugoslavia in 1934 and 1935. There are both epic and lyric songs in the collection as well as recorded conversations with the singers about their lives and their art. There are over 12,500 texts in the collection, some of which are on the phonograph records; the remainder are songs taken down by dictation. Fuller accounts of the Parry Collection may be found in "Homer, Parry, and Huso," *AJA*, 52:34–44, in *Serbo-Croatian Folk Songs*, by Béla Bartók and Albert B. Lord (New York, 1951), and in the introduction to Volume I of *Serbocroatian Heroic Songs*, by Milman Parry and Albert B. Lord (Cambridge, Mass., and Belgrade, 1954), which is the first volume of translations of Parry Collection texts to appear. Volume II containing Serbocroatian texts translated in Volume I has also been published. Volumes III and IV of the series, which it is expected will contain over twenty volumes, are in preparation.

3. *L'Epithète traditionnelle dans Homère* (Paris, 1928).

4. See his "Studies in the Epic Technique of Oral Verse-Making. I: Homer and Homeric Style," *HSCP*, 41:73–147 (1930), and "II: The Homeric Language as the Language of an Oral Poetry," *HSCP*, 43:1–50 (1932).

5. See Note 1 above.

6. "Studies in the Epic Technique of Oral Verse-Making. I: Homer and Homeric Style," *HSCP*, 41:80.

7. I emphasize the creative or dynamic role of the individual performer throughout this book in order to counteract the impression in some quarters that the oral poet is *merely* a transmitter; that all originality is closed to him. Perhaps the words "create" and "originality" are too strong; they may lead to misunderstanding. Yet I believe that the evidence of the actual texts, both as studied from the Parry Collection, and as reported in studies by other scholars who have worked with an abundance of texts and variants, indicates that at the moment of performance the singer, or narrator, produces something unique. The degree of uniqueness varies with the particular circumstances and with the individual performer, provided, of course, that one is dealing with a true oral poet and not with a mere reciter to begin with. It would, however, be a mistake to equate the creative process and function of the oral poet with those of the literary poet, as I attempt to show later in the book. A somewhat different point of view is presented in an important paper, published in 1929, "Die Folklore als eine besondere Form des Schaffens," *Donum Natalicium Schrijnen* (Nijmegen-Utrecht, 1929), pp. 900–913, by P. Bogatyrev and R. Jakobson. They apply very interestingly on a theoretical level Saussure's distinction between *langue* and *parole* to folklore. It might be worth suggesting that we have in the case of oral epic performance something that is

neither *langue* nor *parole*, but some third form; as Lévi-Strauss has intimated in the case of myths (see his paper, "The Structural Study of Myth," *Journal of American Folklore*, 68(1955):430. Or again with Lévi-Strauss we might question whether we have something that is both *langue* and *parole* at the same time under different aspects, thus making a third form of communication, or of relationship, peculiar to oral verbal art.

8. See Marcel Jousse, *Etudes de psychologie linguistique. Le style orale rythmique et mnémotechnique chez les verbo-moteurs* (Paris, 1925).

9. It should be clear from this and from what follows that sacred texts which must be preserved word for word, if there be such, could not be *oral* in any except the most literal sense. Bogatyrev and Jakobson (p. 912) mention the Vedic hymns and say: "Dort, wo die Rolle der Gemeinschaft allein in der Aufbewahrung eines zu einem unantastbaren Kanon erhobenen dichterischen Werkes besteht, gibt es keine schöpferische Zensur, keine Improvisation, kein kollektives Schaffen mehr."

10. Or perhaps in some cases because what was in writing belonged to the ecclesiastical and not to the popular milieu. See, in the case of Russia, Jakobson's "Commentary" to the English translation of A. N. Afanas'ev, *Russian Fairy Tales* (New York, 1945), pp. 632 ff.

11. Flavius Josephus, *Contra Apionem*, i, 2.

12. François Hédelin, Abbé d'Aubignac, *Conjectures académiques ou Dissertation sur l'Iliade* (Paris, 1715).

13. See Joshua Whatmough, *Poetic, Scientific, and Other Forms of Discourse* (Berkeley and Los Angeles, 1956), p. 86.

14. See F. M. Combellack, "Contemporary Unitarians and Homeric Originality," *AJP*, 71:337–364 (1950).

15. Parry and Lord, I, 3.

16. The recent book of Cedric Whitman, *Homer and the Heroic Tradition* (Cambridge, Mass., 1958), and the work of several years ago of Rhys Carpenter, *Folk Tale, Fiction, and Saga in the Homeric Epics* (Berkeley and Los Angeles, 1946) are important exceptions.

CHAPTER TWO

Singers: Performance and Training

1. See Note 7, Chapter One. The wisest accounts of singing and of field work are to be found in the writings of Matija Murko, a true pioneer. See especially his posthumously published *Tragom srpsko-hrvatske narodne epike*, vols. I and II (Zagreb, 1951), and his earlier works listed therein. All of these are important, but the following should be emphasized as reports of actual trips and of recording: "Bericht über eine Bereisung von Nordwest Bosnien und der angrenzenden Gebiete von Kroatian und Dalmatien behufs Erforschung der Volksepik der bosnischen Mohammedaner," *Sitzungsberichte der kaiserlichen Akademie der Wissenschaften in Wien*, phil.-hist. Klasse, 173:1–52; "Bericht über phonographische Aufnahmen epischer, meist mohammedanischen Volkslieder im nordwestlichen Bosnien im Sommer 1912," *Mitteilung der Phonogramm-Archivs-Kommission der kaiserlichen Akademie in Wien*, No. XXX, *Anzeiger* der phil.-hist. Klasse 8:58–75 (1913); "Bericht über eine Reise zum Studium der Volksepik in Bosnien und Hercegowina im Jahre 1913," *Sitzungsberichte der kaiserlichen Akademie der Wissenschaften in Wien*, phil.-hist. Klasse, 176:1–50; "Bericht über phonographische Aufnahmen epischer Volkslieder in mittleren

Bosnien und in der Hercegowina im Sommer 1913," *Mitteilung der Phonogramm-Archivs-Kommission,* XXXVII, *Sitzungsberichte der kaiserlichen Akademie der Wissenschaften in Wien,* phil.-hist. Klasse, 179:1–23; and *La poésie populaire épique en Yougoslavie au début du XXe siècle* (Paris, 1929).

Worthy of note also are the accounts of singers in the Matica Hrvatska's *Hrvatske Narodne Pjesme,* III (Zagreb, 1898), xi–lvi, written by the editor of Volumes III and IV, Luka Marjanović. One must also mention the work of Gerhard Gesemann, whose most lasting contribution to South Slavic scholarship still remains his edition of *Erlangenski rukopis starih srpskohrvatskih narodnih pesama* (Sr. Karlovci, 1925). See his "Nova istraživanja narodnih epskih pesama," in *Naša narodna poezija,* ed. Milivoje V. Knežević (Subotica, 1928), pp. 7–13; "Nova istraživanja o narodnom epu u vardarskoj banovini," *Glasnik skopskog naučnog društva,* 11:191–198 (1932); and "Volksliedaufnahmen in Südslavien durch die Deutsche Akademie," *Stimmen aus dem Südosten,* 3/4:1–6 (1937/38). An evaluation of the singer Vučić in M. Murko, *Tragom srpsko-hrvatske narodne epike,* I, 16–17, 379–380, is not without interest.

2. Parry, like Murko, found the Moslem tradition very interesting. It was conducive of the kind of long songs that were useful for Homeric research, and he spent much time in collecting from Moslem singers. Alois Schmaus in his *Studije o krajinskoj epici* (Zagreb, 1952), pp. 103–109, reviews the collections and works dealing with the Moslem epic, to which his own book is devoted. He too knew and wrote about Salih Ugljanin in Novi Pazar. See especially his "Nekoliko podataka o epskom pevanju i pesmama kod Arbanasa (Arnauta) u Staroj Srbiji," *Prilozi proučavanju narodne poezije,* 1:107–112 (1934), and "Beleške iz Sandžaka," *ibid.,* 5:274–280(1938) and 6:117–125(1939).

3. See Marcel Jousse, *Etudes de psychologie linguistique. Le style orale rythmique et mnémotechnique chez les verbo-moteurs.*

4. For a similar situation among the Kara-kirghiz singers, see W. Radloff, *Proben der Volkslitteratur des Nördlichen Türkischen Stämme* (St. Petersburg, 1885), V, xviii–xix. For other descriptions of the practice in central Asia, see V. M. Žirmunskij and H. T. Zarifov, *Uzbekskij narodnyj geroičeskij epos* (Moscow, 1947). See also V. M. Žirmunskij, "Nekotorye itogi izučenija geroičeskogo eposa narodov srednej Azii," *Voprosy izučenija eposa narodov SSSR* (Moscow, 1958), pp. 24–65; and Thomas G. Winner, *The Oral Art and Literature of the Kazakhs of Russian Central Asia* (Durham, 1958), especially chapter three.

5. The singer does not actually mean this. The subject of exact re-singing is discussed fully in Chapters Four and Five.

6. See Martin P. Nilsson, *Homer and Mycenae* (London, 1933), p. 202: "We may put it thus that not the poems but the poetical art is learnt."

7. Linguistics, of course, offers such a technical vocabulary, but a proper understanding of it is limited to a very few specialists. Moreover, I believe, it is fair to say that this vocabulary is still in formation.

CHAPTER THREE

The Formula

1. M. Parry, "Studies in the Epic Technique of Oral Verse-Making. I: Homer and Homeric Style," *HSCP,* 41:80 (1930).

2. C. M. Bowra, *Heroic Poetry* (London, 1952), p. 222.

3. Bowra still clings to this idea; *ibid.*, p. 231. See also *Tradition and Design in the Iliad* (Oxford, 1930), pp. 87 ff.

4. A study of Serbocroatian metrics should begin with Luka Zima, "Nacrt naše metrike narodne obzirom na stihove drugih naroda, a osobito Slovena," *Rad jugoslavenske akademije znanosti i umjetnosti*, 48:170–221 (1879) and 49:1–64 (1879), and the monumental work of Tomislav Maretić, "Metrika narodnih naših pjesama," *Rad*, 168:1–112 (1907) and 170:76–200 (1907), and *Metrika muslimanske narodne epike* (Zagreb, 1936). Svetozar Matić's "Principi umetničke versifikacije srpske," *Godišnjica Nikole Čupića*, 39:119–162 (1930) and 40:51–72 (1931) sums up all previous work; it is reviewed, together with other works on South Slavic poetry, by Roman Jakobson, *Slavische Rundschau* 4:275–279 (1932). André Vaillant, "Les chants épiques des Slaves du sud," *Extraits des Cours et Conférences, 30 janvier, 15 février, et 15 mars 1932* (Paris, 1932) devotes considerable space to metrics. It too is interestingly reviewed by R. Jakobson in *Byzantinoslavica* 4:194–202 (1932). See also R. Jakobson, "The Kernel of Comparative Slavic Literature," *Harvard Slavic Studies*, 1:26 ff. (1953) and "Studies in Comparative Slavic Metrics," *Oxford Slavonic Papers*, 3:21–66 (1952), which is reviewed at considerable length by Kiril Taranovski in *Prilozi za književnost, jezik, istoriju i folklor*, 12:350–360 (1954). Taranovski's own article, "O jednosložnim rečima u srpskom stihu," *Naš jezik*, 2:26–41 (1950) is of interest also, as is the book of Franz Saran, *Zur Metrik des epischen Verses der Serben* (Leipzig, 1934), which was published posthumously. Radovan Košutić's *O tonskoj metrici u novoj srpskoj poeziji* (Belgrade, 1941) was also reviewed at great length by K. Taranovski, "O tonskoj metrici prof. Košutića," *Južnoslovenski filolog*, 18:173–196 (1949–50). Finally Taranovski's book on Russian metrics, *Ruski dvodelni ritmovi* (Belgrade, 1953) is not lacking in interest here as the latest work of importance in Slavic metrics.

5. M. Parry, *L'Epithète traditionnelle dans Homère*, pp. 11–15, *et passim*.

6. See R. Jakobson, "Über den Versbau der serbokroatischen Volksepen," *Archives néerlandaises de phonétique expérimentale*, 8/9:135–144 (1933).

7. See R. Jakobson, "Studies in Comparative Slavic Metrics," *Oxford Slavonic Papers*, 3:27 (1952), where this phenomenon is explained by the "tendency to avoid closed syllables at the end of the line." See also Matija Murko, "Nouvelles observations sur l'état actuel de la poésie épique en Yougoslavie," *Revue des Etudes Slaves*, 13:31 ff. (1933).

8. R. Jakobson in his "Studies in Comparative Slavic Metrics," *Oxford Slavonic Papers*, 3:24 ff. (1952) has listed as the first metrical constant of the Serbocroatian epic decasyllable, "Isosyllabism: each line contains ten syllables." This is certainly an almost invariable norm. A check of the singing of Stanko Pižurica, the best of the Montenegrin Christian singers with whom Parry worked in Kolašin and from whom we have an abundance of material tends to uphold these findings that among such singers in Montenegro, the classical terrain (as it is often thought of) for South Slavic epic, the ten-syllable line is practically invariable in regard to the number of its syllables. Apart from mistakes made in rapid composition, the perfectly normal slips of the tongue, there are a number of regular abnormalities, so regular, indeed, that they have affected formula construction. A detailed study of this is out of place in this book, but the following may be noted. In Parry and Lord, II, the textual notes indicate all metrically abnormal lines. A sampling of the first three songs of Ugljanin sung for the records shows 42 eleven-syllable lines: 12 of these clearly begin with a dactyl — *e.g.* Vazda je Mujo četom četovao (II, No. 1:793), Ala ne boj se, pile sokolovo (No. 1:863), Pa ću je, care, tebe pokloniti (No. 2:826), Ibrahim paša četvrti je bio (No. 2:1152), Lasno je sići ka Zadaru gradu (No. 4:1748) — and 7 more are ambivalent, in that they might be considered to begin with an extra-metrical syllable; 13 have a dactyl in the second foot — *e.g.* Proj se vraga i bijela Bagdata (No. 1:46, No. 2:46), Viknu redom sve paše

i vezire (No. 2:810), Ja ću bana i do tri đenerala (No. 4:1470); 8 have a dactyl in the third foot, that is after the break — e.g. Da se Bosna pominje do vijeka (No. 1:224), A sultanu koljko ga žao bilo (No. 2:1170), Stara majka sto i kusur godina (No. 4:307), Kako sam se grdna obradovala (No. 4:732), Šta je bilo banu i kapetanim' (No. 4:1556); and one strange case has a dactyl in the fourth foot. It is to be noted that a number of these instances bring together two vowels without elision.

In Bihać in northern Bosnia, Moslem singers accompany the songs on the plucked *tambura*. Ćamil Kulenović in Parry Text 1950 sang 55 eleven-syllable lines in the first 500 lines, most of which begin with a dactyl. Here are examples from this and another text of Ćamil's: Ban ga otočki i ban šibenički (Parry 1951:11), Kako bi tude sva četiri bana (1951:18), Tako mi boga i zakona moga (1951:27), Ja sam ga jednom bijo ufatijo (1951:28), Lipu ga Zlatu timar tefterdara (Parry 1950:243), Jedno ga grlo četiri đerdana (1950:249), Dorat mu svezan kod gradske kapije (1950:152), Kolki sam godić u svilenu pasu, Tolki je Turčin u bijelu vratu (1950:148–149). Maretić pointed out this phenomenon in 1936 as a characteristic of Moslem epic, it being especially common in Volumes III and IV of the Matica Hrvatska Collection. See T. Maretić, *Metrika muslimanske narodne epike* (Zagreb, 1936), pp. 218–220. It *may* be that in northern Bosnia this initial dactyl is somehow related to the instrumental accompaniment of the tambura used by Moslem singers. In the Novi Pazar district this seems not to be true. It *may* be that the Moslems there, many of them of Albanian descent, are less respectful of the *deseterac*, and it is perhaps worth noting that the tambura (Albanian *çifteli*) is used in some parts of the north of Albania for epic. From my experience there in 1937, however, the tambura is used chiefly among the Christians for the shorter local and historical songs, purely Albanian and octosyllabic mostly. For remarks on the use of the decasyllable by Albanians in Albania in Albanian see Stavro Skendi, "The South Slavic Decasyllable in Albanian Oral Epic Poetry," *Word*, 9:339–348 (1953). This whole subject is worthy of more careful study.

9. Unfortunately, most printed collections are not very useful for this kind of study, because the texts have been subjected to strict editing out of abnormalities and little music exactly annotated is available. On the whole all of the admirable work that has been done has been on the basis of comparatively little recorded material; one would probably be shocked to know just how few recorded lines of epic verse have been used. No large body of songs on phonograph records was available for study before the Parry Collection was made.

10. *Učinijo* is actually pronounced and printed in Parry and Lord, *Serbocroatian Heroic Songs*, in the passage quoted, as *ućinijo*, with ć instead of the normal č. It is thus that the singer sang the word, reflecting his own dialect. Here and in other instances henceforward I have normalized the spelling in such cases. The exact pronunciation can be found in the published volumes.

11. I see no reason to place the noun-epithet formulas in a separate class from all the other formulas, as Bowra does (*Heroic Poetry*, p. 222). They are not the only formulas that do not advance the narrative.

12. For other examples see Matija Murko, "Nouvelles observations sur l'état actuel de la poésie épique en Yougoslavie," *Revue des Etudes Slaves*, 13:43 (1933), and *La poésie populaire épique en Yougoslavie au début du XXe siècle* (Paris, 1929), p. 24.

13. M. Parry, "Studies in the Epic Technique of Oral Verse-Making. I: Homer and Homeric Style," *HSCP*, 41:118–121.

14. The supporting evidence is collected in my unpublished thesis in the Archives of Harvard University.

15. A check of the other lines in the chart would yield approximately the same results.

16. Bowra, *Heroic Poetry*, pp. 234 ff. Parry, *L'Epithète*, pp. 218 ff.

17. See A. B. Lord, "Homer and Huso III: Enjambement in Greek and South-slavic Heroic Song," *TAPhA*, 79:113–124 (1948), from which these figures are taken. See also M. Parry, "The Distinctive Character of Enjambement in Homeric Verse," *TAPhA*, 60:200–220 (1929). I follow the definition of enjambement given by Parry, *ibid.*, pp. 203–204: "Broadly there are three ways in which the sense at the end of one verse can stand to that at the beginning of another. First, the verse end can fall at the end of a sentence and the new verse begin a new sentence. In this case there is no enjambement. Second, the verse can end with a word group in such a way that the sentence, at the verse end, already gives a complete thought, although it goes on in the next verse, adding free ideas by new word groups. To this type of enjambement we may apply Denis' term *unperiodic*. Third, the verse end can fall at the end of a word group where there is not yet a whole thought, or it can fall in the middle of a word group; in both of these cases enjambement is *necessary*. . . . To know where there is no enjambement we must gauge the sentence. The varying punctuation of our texts, usually troublesome, will not do. I define the sentence as any independent clause or group of clauses introduced by a coordinate conjunction or by asyndeton; and by way of showing that this definition is fitting I would point out that the rhetoricians paid little heed to the sentence as we understand it: for them the unit of style was the clause, and the only group of clauses of which Aristotle speaks is the period." The statement of Jakobson, following perhaps a more widely known definition of enjambement, that there is no enjambement in Serbocroatian epic, is correct, although rare exceptions can be found.

18. For a fuller study of this passage, see A. B. Lord, "The Role of Sound Patterns in Serbocroatian Epic," in *For Roman Jakobson* (The Hague, 1956), pp. 301–305.

19. Bowra (*Heroic Poetry*, pp. 222ff.) puts all such repetitions together under the name of formula, distinguishing in formula only the noun-adjective combinations. This, it seems to me, is too cavalier a treatment. There are significant differences between the several groups.

20. V. Bogišić, *Narodne pjesme iz starijih, najviše primorskih zapisa* (Belgrade, 1878), No. 6, p. 18. In the songs of Salih Ugljanin, I have noted only one reference to a tavern maid (Ruža); this is in Parry 653 (Synopsis VI in I, p. 213) "Halil Hrnjičić Rescues the Daughter of the Vizier of Travnik." A more interesting instance is in Zogić's "Bojičić Alija Rescues Alibey's Children" (I, No. 24, pp. 255ff.). Another case in point is in Alija Fjuljanin's "Halil Hrnjičić and Miloš the Highwayman" (I, No. 31, pp. 309ff.).

21. T. B. L. Webster, *From Mycenae to Homer* (London, 1958), p. 94.

CHAPTER FOUR

The Theme

1. See my "Composition by Theme in Homer and Southslavic Epos," *TAPhA*, 82:71–80 (1951). The most interesting work on themes, other than indexing, with which I am acquainted has been done not in the field of epic but in the related fields of folktale and myth. In folktale see V. Propp, "Morphology of the Folktale," Part III of *International Journal of American Linguistics*, vol. 24, No. 4, October, 1958 (Bloomington, Indiana, 1958). In myth the work of Claude Lévi-Strauss, "The Structural Study of Myth," *Journal of American Folklore*, 68:428–444 is very significant. Professor

Propp has also published an excellent handbook of Russian epic: *Russkij geroičeskij epos* (Leningrad, 1955).

2. The following quotations from R. M. Volkov, "K probleme varianta v izučenii bylin," *Russkij fol'klor*, 2:98–128 (1957) are pertinent: "A study of the variants of the given introduction in the hands of both narrators likewise shows convincingly that the verbal formula of the feast is stable, but not unchangeable: the narrator preserves it in essence, but does not strive to remember it in detail, freely varying its verbal form in agreement with his own thought" (p. 104); and "The analysis of the introduction, 'the feast,' in A. M. Krjukova's telling does not allow one to agree with the statement of Hilferding that the 'loci communes' are unchangeable, that every narrator 'chooses for himself from a mass of ready typical pictures a more or less sizeable stock, depending upon his memory, and, having fixed them, he constantly uses this stock in all his *byliny*.' It is impossible to agree with this assertion that the narrator knows the typical places (loci communes) by heart and sings them completely the same, no matter how many times he has repeated the *bylina*" (p. 105). Translations mine.

3. This text is defective because the recording at this point is not clear.

4. V. Bogišić, *Narodne pjesme iz starijih, najviše primorskih zapisa* (Belgrade, 1878), p. 20.

5. The song is "Bećiragić Meho." Mumin's song is Parry 12468; Avdo's is Parry 12470, and Lord 202.

6. Hivzo himself describes the process in Parry 12474. Avdo's song is Parry 6840. Both will be published in Volume IV, with translations in Volume III. See also Lord 35, Avdo's version of this song in 1950.

7. Friedrich S. Krauss, *Smailagić Meho* (Dubrovnik, 1886). A German translation of Šemić's song can be found in C. Gröber, *Mehmeds Brautfahrt. Ein Volksepik der süslavischen Muhammedaner* (Vienna, 1890).

8. Parry 6841 and 12375.

9. The song covers two text numbers in the Parry Collection: 12389 and 12441. See also Lord 33, Avdo's version of this song in 1950.

10. Other similar examples can be found in Makić's song, Parry 683 (Parry and Lord II, No. 28) lines 104, 841–842, 854–855, 876–877, 914–915, 926–928.

11. *Digenes Akrites,* edited with an introduction, translation, and commentary by John Mavrogordato (Oxford, 1956), lines 1199–1208.

12. Passages from the *Iliad* are quoted in the translation by Richmond Lattimore (Chicago, 1951).

13. In the Novi Pazar material on the letter writing theme set out above we have already noted individual differences among the singers in their handling of that theme. I am delighted to find corroboration of this principle in P. D. Ukhov's article "Tipičeskie mesta (loci communes) kak sredstvo pasportizacii bylin," *Russkij fol'klor* 2:129–154 (1957): "Inasmuch as the typical formulas of one narrator differ from the typical formulas of all other narrators, and inasmuch as the typical formulas are peculiar to him and are employed in all *byliny* narrated by him, this regularity can be used as a key for determining authorship ('narratorship') of those texts of *byliny* the author (narrator) of which is not known; if the typical formulas of one product agree with the typical formulas of another, then their attribution to a single author (narrator) is indisputable" (p. 137). See also his article "Iz nabljudenij nad stilem sbornika Kirši Danilova," *Russkij fol'klor,* 1:97–115 (1956), where this method has been applied. Translation mine.

14. See below, pp. 117–118.

15. In this respect I conceive of the theme and of the song in about the same way that Jung and Kerenyi conceive of the archetype of the myth. See C. G. Jung and

C. Kerenyi, *Introduction to a Science of Mythology, The Myth of the Divine Child and the Mysteries of Eleusis* (London, 1951), pp. 104ff. The patterns of which I speak later in this chapter and in the next are only working schemes, not absolutes. Lévi-Strauss says at one point concerning myth in "The Structural Study of Myth," *Journal of American Folklore*, 68:432 (1955): "To put it in even more linguistic terms, it is as though a phoneme were always made up of all its variants."

16. It is, of course, true that written literature is filled with inconsistencies and it is also true that we often see in oral texts inconsistencies which are only apparent, because we apply realistic criteria to traditional material. Even in the case which follows it might be argued in that way. Yet the traditional artist is not illogical and there is a limit of ingenuous ignorance that we can assign to him.

17. Pp. 112–113.

CHAPTER FIVE

Songs and the Song

1. See Gerhard Gesemann, "Kompositionsschema und heroisch-epische Stilisierung" in his *Studien zur südslavischen Volksepik* (Reichenberg, 1926), pp. 65–96. Of interest also in connection with song structure is A. Schmaus, *Studije o krajinskoj epici* (Zagreb, 1953), *passim*.

2. Cf. Makić's statements in Parry and Lord, *Serbocroatian Heroic Songs*, I, 266-267: N: What's the song which you sang just now? S: That's the song about when the two pashas spent the winter [the first line of the song]. N: Where? S: At Temišvar. N: All right. If anyone were to say to you: "Sing me such and such a song." What would he say to you? Or, if you were to say to someone: "I sang such and such a song," meaning the one you sang just now? What is it called? What name shall we put on it? . . . all right, "two pashas spent the winter," but — S: In Sement. "Sing me the song about Temišvar." That's it, the song of Temišvar . . . that's what people say to me . . . N: What happened at Temišvar? S: What happened? You've already heard what happened. When the pashas spent the winter and all seven kings surrounded them. N: I know, but there are many songs about Temišvar. . . . Have you ever heard that there are more songs about Temišvar than just that one? S: I haven't heard any songs about Temišvar except this one. N: Well, I've heard that there are other songs about Temišvar. S: Well, what isn't there in the world? Every singer has his own songs. N: Then what shall we put that song down as? What's its name? S: Its name is "At Muhač."

3. As an example of a song that has not been perfected by much singing and is close in frequency of performance, if not in time, to its first singing, see Salih Ugljanin's song of the Greek War (Parry and Lord, I and II, No. 10).

The only actual text I know of made up in our presence in 1934 is a song, coaxed out of Salih Ugljanin, about Parry and Nikola and the collecting. It is in Parry Text 655, records 965–966. Actually the songs made up about collectors are not very good examples because collectors and collecting are not inspiring nor proper subjects of epic! I give the conversation which preceded Salih's song:

Nikola: Would you be able to make up a song about how we came here and found you to sing songs for us? Salih: Oho! Then I would be able. N: You would? In Bosnian? S: In Bosnian. Parry: Right away? S: Right away. N: Now? S: Now, while you are here. Since you have come now, right? N: Yes. S: I wouldn't be able to do it in that time. I wouldn't, by God! N: Would you be able, beginning now, sitting here, to tell it straight off, as in a song? S: Well, I don't know. Let me see now.

I don't know what. . . . N: No, no, but how we came here and how we found you. S: Since you came here. N: Yes. Parry: How you have worked for us. How you dictated songs. S: Ha! Parry: How Nikola wrote them. S: Yes, Yes. N: Could you do that? S: I could. Now, this one which I told you, I could tell it to you. N: Again you have not understood me! S: I can't do anything. N: Could you make up a song? S: Ha! N: How you recited to me and I wrote the songs. Could you create a song about that? How we gave you fifty dinars a day and sometimes sixty, and cigarettes and tea and other things, and. . . ? S: By Allah, that I could. And in Bosnian? N: Yes. How will it be? Come on, begin so that we may see. S: What's the name of the boss? N: Milman. S: Milman? N: Yes. S: And you're Nikola? N: Yes. S: As for the other let him. . . . (Lord is referred to here in the next room at the recording machine.) N: What? What did you say? S: We won't· include him, you know, but only you two. Parry: All right, as you like. N: Come on, Salja, let's hear it! S: Let me see, on what day did we begin? Parry: But nicely, you know! As if to the gusle. S: Yes, by Allah! N: We began to work here on Monday, and today is Saturday. S: Yes, indeed, and we worked all day until it was night. N: Yes. S: Every day until· it was night we worked. N: Yes. S: And so we shall sing a song. I'll speak more loudly, right now.

Od kratkoga vakta i zemana,	Since a short time ago,
Ima puno, tamo šes' da.. taman šes' dana,	All of six da.. exactly six days,
Pa od dana ponedijonika,	Well, since Monday,
Kako ođe smo na skupnicu.	We have been gathered here.
5 Ja i Nikola pesme iskazali,	5 Nikola and I have recited songs,
Ja kazao, Nikola pisao,	I dictated and Nikola wrote,
Od ob jutra do do noći ravne.	From morning until level night.
Sve smo redom pesme ispisalji,	We have written out all songs one after another,
I mene su pošteno platilji.	And they paid me honorably.
10 I ja sam svaki dan dolazijo,	10 And I came every day,
Sve od jutra do večere ravno,	Ever from morning until evening straight,
I sve po jednu smo pesmu ispje.. is-pisalji,	And ever a song each day we sa.. wrote,
I aćik smo je dokazalji,	And frankly we declared,
Od koga smo pesmu taku ćulji,	From whom we heard such and such a song,
15 I svakome ime upisalji,	15 And we wrote the name of each,
I Nikola redom upisao,	And Nikola recorded them one after another,
I u grohot smo se osmijali,	And we laughed heartily,
I ćajeve poćesto smo pilji,	And rather frequently we drank tea,
A cigara preko hesapa gorjeli.	And we burned cigarettes beyond counting.
20 Tako je bilo za šes' dana ravno.	20 So it was for six days straight.
Danas šesti što smo uradilji.	Today is the sixth we have been working.
Nekoljiko ćuda poprićalji.	We have related several wonders.
Veljiki smo smijeh otvorilji.	We have started great laughter.
Nekoljiko jada poprićalji,	We have related several sad tales,
25 Što su stari pričalji iftijari,	25 What the aged elders have related,
To smo danas mi ponovilji.	That we have repeated today.

N: Go on, keep on talking! P: Is there any more? S: There isn't. N: There isn't any more, is that it? S: Yes. For six days, I counted out the days for you, that we drank tea and wrote.

For a song about Parry or in his honor, written by Milovan Vojičić and given to him, see Appendix VI.

4. The two songs are of about the same length, Nikola's version having 156 lines, and Salih's 142. The differences between them are: (1) Nikola has Marko suggest that they go to Golješ to steal the vile's horses: Salih mentions only that they are to look at them; (2) in requesting Relja to sing, Nikola has Marko say that he is sleepy and wants Relja to sing to keep him awake (lines 33–36): Salih omits; (3) Nikola has Relja reply to Marko that he is afraid to sing because of the wolves and bandits (lines 37–42): Salih omits; (4) on the other hand, Salih has expanded Marko's speech to Relja, in which he tells him not to be afraid, from Nikola's nine lines to fifteen, but the general contents are the same (N: lines 44–52, S: lines 33–47); (5) in Nikola's version Jevrosima offers her primacy to the vila who will pluck out Relja's eyes (lines 70–71): Salih omits; (6) Salih does not mention the name of the second vila (N: line 75); (7) Nikola has Anđelija say that she will bring to Jevrosima Relja's eyes (line 79): Salih omits; (8) Nikola's picture of Marko riding cross-legged on his horse and swearing like a drunkard (lines 86–87) is not repeated by Salih; (9) the effect of the whipping on the vila's flesh (lines 118–119) is omitted by Salih; (10) Nikola's detail of releasing the falcons to supervise the gathering of herbs by the vila (line 127) is omitted in Salih's version; (11) on the other hand, Salih has expanded Marko's speech to Relja in which he stops the beating and suggests the marriage (N: lines 137–141; S: 117–127); and (12) Salih has expanded the theme of the marriage itself from Nikola's six lines (151–156) to eleven (132–142).

5. For other examples see Kolašin texts, Parry 6771 and 489; 6780 and 6736, and Appendix V.

6. There are approximately 70 such experiments in the Parry Collection, most of them from the districts of Stolac (30) and Gacko (20). A number of instances (actually 8) will be found in vols. I and II in the material from Novi Pazar. From other regions there are a total of 12 experiments: 3 from Kolašin, 1 from Glamoč, 9 from Bihać, and 7 from Bijelo Polje. Including the Marko and Nina song in Appendix II, which we have analyzed (see Chart V), the experiment was applied 6 times to Petar Vidić. The song Marko and Nina was the only case in this group of Vidić's containing texts at an interval of a year, and using more than two texts; the other instances are of only two texts not separated by much time, only a few days. In each of these cases one text was sung for the records and the other dictated for Nikola Vujnović to write down; this fact must also be taken into consideration in comparing the texts.

7. As a final example of what may happen to a song over many years in the hands of a single singer, one may take Avdo Međedović's "Osmanbey Delibegović and Pavičević Luka" (Parry 12389; 12441). This second of the two longest songs in the collection is in one way even more remarkable than the "Wedding of Smailagić Meho." It was sung for the records in 1935 and not taken down from dictation. The text contains 13,331 lines and fills ninety-seven twelve-inch phonograph records. I have estimated that actual singing time was between sixteen and seventeen hours. The singer sang for three or four days, lost his voice, was given a ten-day vacation, and finished in another three or four days, the whole process taking about three weeks.

8. The Russian folklorist A. M. Astakhova has written: "A variant becomes interesting and significant not only as one of the indispensable links for the clarification of the bases of the plot, but also as a manifestation of the living creative energy of

the masses" (*Russkij bylinnyj epos na Severe,* Petrozavodsk, 1948, p. 5, quoted from R. M. Volkov, "K probleme varianta v izučenii bylin," *Russkij fol'klor,* 2:98 (1957).

CHAPTER SIX

Writing and Oral Tradition

1. For the Finnish traditional poetry see Domenico Comparetti, *The Traditional Poetry of the Finns* (London, 1898), especially pages 69ff., and Martti Haavio, *Väinämöinen, Eternal Sage* (Helsinki, 1952), translated from the Finnish by Helen Goldthwait-Väänänen.

2. Especially Nos. 5, 7–17. It may be that in the case of singers who use or have used both sung and "spoken" verse the performer at such times goes over from the one to the other. This was not the case with Salih Ugljanin, who, to the best of my knowledge, was never a reciter. It seems to me that the whole subject of "spoken verse" as reported in the article "O našim piesma͡ma," by Ioksim Nović, Otočanin, in *Ogledalo Srbsko,* I (1864) needs reviewing. There is a German translation of a considerable portion of this article in Vatroslav Jagić, "Die südslavische Volksepik vor Jahrhunderten," *Archiv für slavische Philologie* 4:233–238 (1880).

3. *Poema de mio Cid,* 5th edition, Clasicos castellanos (Madrid, 1946), with notes by Ramon Menendez Pidal.

4. The Greek texts of the various manuscripts can be found in the excellent *Basileios Digenes Akritas,* edited by Petros P. Kalonaros (Athens, 1941), vols. I and II. The Escorialensis is in vol. II. For a translation of this poem, from the Grottaferrata manuscript, see John Mavrogordato, *Digenes Akrites* (Oxford, 1956), in which the Greek appears opposite the English translation.

5. Bogoljub Petranović, *Srpske narodne pjesme iz Bosne i Hercegovine,* III (Belgrade, 1870), xiv–xv. Translation mine.

6. See my article "Homer's Originality: Oral Dictated Texts," in *TAPhA,* 84:124–134 (1953).

7. Led by C. M. Bowra. See his *Heroic Poetry* (London, 1952).

8. Especially the work of Francis P. Magoun, Jr. — "Oral-Formulaic Character of Anglo-Saxon Narrative Poetry," *Speculum,* 28:446–467 (1953), and later studies — and his students in Anglo-Saxon; most recently R. A. Waldron, "Oral-Formulaic Technique and Middle English Alliterative Poetry," *Speculum,* 32:792–804 (1957). This is very important and exciting work.

9. I thus return to the conviction of the first draft of this book in 1949, that in the last analysis a poem is either of the oral tradition or it is not. Only the man in the tradition can produce its style. I have labored over a number of different kinds of texts in the Parry Collection and elsewhere, published and unpublished; I have pondered and analyzed. It seems to me that there can be no compromise or middle ground, although there will be texts that may *look* transitional, cases in which we simply do not have enough information to tell.

10. Of particular interest are the songs written down by Milovan Vojičić in Nevesinje, Hercegovina, Parry Collection Nos. 24–36, 77–135, 215–273. Many of these were sent in notebooks to Parry at Harvard University during the winter of 1933–34.

11. Not only the quantity but also the provenance of the material is of importance for formula analysis. One must work with material of a single singer at a given time, and then outwards by concentric circles to his group, district, and so forth. Otherwise one uses material which is irrelevant to the song and singer under scrutiny.

12. See M. Parry, "The Distinctive Character of Enjambement in Homeric Verse," *TAPhA*, 60:200–220 (1929), and my article "Homer and Huso III: Enjambement in Greek and Southslavic Heroic Song," *TAPhA*, 79:113–124 (1948). Parry's definition of enjambement is given in full in note 17 to Chapter Three above.

13. Andrija Kačić-Miošić, *Razgovor ugodni naroda slovinskoga*, 1st edition, 1756; 2nd edition, much enlarged, 1759. I quote from the edition by Ivan Šarić (Zagreb, n.d.). I have not been able to find the following article which may be of interest here: Tomislav Maretić, "Der Bau des Zehnsilbers von Kačić" in *Glasnik srpske kraljevske akademije nauka*, 144:38.

14. Petar Petrović Njegoš, *Ogledalo srpsko* (Belgrade, 1951), edited by Radosav Bošković and Vido Latković, with notes by Latković.

15. Kačić, *op. cit.*, p. 22.

16. Njegoš, *op. cit.*, No. 31, p. 214. Taken by Njegoš from the 2nd edition of Sima Milutinović's collection, 1837, No. 168.

17. Maksim Šobajić, *Nevesinjski ustanak* (Nikšić, 1925), No. 1, p. 1.

18. Boško M. Šarović, *Prve jugoslavenske guslarske pjesme* (Sarajevo, 1931), "Spremanje rata i pogibija Ferdinanda 1914 godine."

19. Kačić and Njegoš have already been spoken of in notes 13 and 14 above. Ivan Mažuranić (1814–1890) is known especially as the writer of *Smrt Smailage Čengića* (The Death of Smailagha Čengić) an epic first published in 1846. Vuk Stefanović Karadžić (1787–1864), sometimes referred to simply as Vuk, is probably the best known of South Slavic literary figures. He was the first of the great collectors of folklore. Sima Milutinović-Sarajlija (1791–1847), a friend of Vuk, tutor of Njegoš, and a great individualist, wrote much, but is mentioned here especially as a collector of folk epic in his *Pjevanija Crnogorska i Hercegovačka*, 1st edition, 1833, 2nd edition, 1837.

20. A study by Vladimir Ćorović of Njegoš's ten-syllable line compared with the folk decasyllable can be found in *Misao*, 19:1371–1379 (1925). Frank Wollman's lengthy "Njegošův deseterec," *Slavia*, 9:737–791 (1930–1931) is more substantial.

21. *Gorski Vijenac*, lines 37–42.

22. "Četa," lines 119–132.

23. *Heroic Poetry*, p. 240.

24. See R. Jakobson, "Stihotvornye citaty v velikomoravskoj agiografii," *Slavistična revija*, 10:111–118 (1957).

25. Many lyrics can be found in the manuscript collection made by Nikša Ranjina which was begun in 1507. See Mihovil Kombol, *Poviest hrvatske književnosti do preporoda* (Zagreb, 1945), pp. 89ff.

26. Two such are inserted in Petar Hektorović's *Ribanje i ribarsko prigovaranje* (1st edition, 1568). The most recent edition is Zagreb, 1951, by Antun Barac. A song of Marko Kraljević and his brother Andrija is given at lines 523–591; and one about Radosav the Duke at lines 595–685. Juraj Baraković inserted another narrative ballad (about Majka Margarita) in his long poem *Vila Slovinska*, published in Venice in 1613.

27. For the texts see V. Bogišić, *Narodne pjesme iz starijih, najviše primorskih zapisa* (Belgrade, 1878), and Gerhard Gesemann, *Erlangenski rukopis starih srpsko-hrvatskih narodnih pesama* (Sr. Karlovci, 1925).

28. See note 13 above.

29. There is a recent book on this singer: M. Panić-Surep, *Filip Višnjić, Pesnik bune* (Belgrade, 1956). One should also note the criticism of him in Nović's article referred to in note 2 above. The step from these peculiar products to written *imitation* of oral epic is not great. For further information see M. Murko, "Nouvelles observations sur

l'état actuel de poésie épique en Yougoslavie," *Revue des Etudes slaves*, 13:43 ff. (1933).

30. Harvard University's Widener Library has an unusually large collection of these, thanks to Milman Parry.

31. Especially from Volumes III and IV of the Matica Hrvatska Collection, edited by Luka Marjanović, which contain Moslem songs: *Hrvatske narodne pjesme*, III (1898) and IV (1899). Kosta Hörmann collected his songs in 1888–1889 and the first editions of his two volumes were in those years. The second edition: *Narodne pjesme muslimana u Bosni i Hercegovini* (Sarajevo, 1933), I and II.

32. The best example of this in the Parry Collection experience is the phenomenal singer Avdo Međedović. See my article "Avdo Međedović, Guslar," *Journal of American Folklore* (1956), pp. 320–330.

33. Although there is, of course, an intimate relationship between the medieval epics and Romanticism.

CHAPTER SEVEN

Homer

1. For Parry's analyses see "Studies in the Epic Technique of Oral Verse-Making. I: Homer and Homeric Style," *HSCP*, 41:118ff. (1930).

2. Notes to Chart VII follow:

[1] Cf. μῆνιν ἀλευάμενος ἑκατηβόλου 'Απόλλωνος (E444, II711) and μῆνιν ἀπειπόντος μεγαθύμου Πηλείωνος (T75).

[2] Cf.

$$\mu\tilde{\eta}\nu\iota\nu \begin{cases} \mathring{\alpha}\lambda\epsilon\upsilon\acute{\alpha}\mu\epsilon\nu\text{os} & \text{(E444, II711)} \\ \mathring{\alpha}\pi\text{o}\epsilon\iota\pi\acute{\omega}\nu & \text{(T35)} \\ \mathring{\alpha}\pi\epsilon\iota\pi\acute{o}\nu\tau\text{os} & \text{(T75)} \end{cases}$$

$$\begin{matrix} \text{o}\tilde{\iota}\tau\text{o}\nu \ (\alpha350, \theta489) \\ \nu\acute{o}\sigma\tau\text{o}\nu \ (\alpha326) \end{matrix} \Big\} \quad \begin{matrix} \mathring{\alpha}\epsilon\acute{\iota}\delta\epsilon\iota\nu \ (\alpha350) & \mathring{\alpha}\epsilon\acute{\iota}\delta\epsilon\iota\text{s} \ (\theta489) \\ \mathring{\alpha}\epsilon\iota\delta\epsilon\nu \ (\alpha326) \end{matrix}$$

γιγνώσκω σε (E815)
σὺν σοί, δῖα (K290)
τῶν ἀμόθεν γε (α10)
ἄλλο τι δὴ σύ (ε173)
ἀργαλέον σε (ν312)
σὺν σοί, πότνα (ν391)
"Αρτεμι πότνα (υ61)
"Ηρη πρέσβα (E721,
Θ383, Ξ194, 243)

[3] A322, I166, II269, 653, Ω406, λ467, ω15.
[4] Cf. ὦ πόποι, ἦ δὴ μυρί' 'Οδυσσεὺς ἐσθλὰ ἔοργε (B272).
[5] E876, ρ287, 474.
[6] See note [4]. For ἄλγε' ἔθηκε see X422.
[7] Cf. πολλὰς δ'ἰφθίμους κεφαλὰς "Αϊδι προϊάψειν (Λ55).
[8] See note [7]
[9] Z487 (προϊάψει).
[10] Nonformulaic, but see note 12.
[11] Cf. ἡρώων τοῖσίν τε (E747 οἷσίν τε, Θ391, α101). For ἡρώων see I525,

E747, Θ391, α101, and ω88. For αὐτοὺς δέ cf. E747, Θ391, α101 (τοῖσίν τε), etc.

[12] Nonformulaic, but cf. καλλείψω, μή πώς μοι ἕλωρ ἄλλοισι γένηται (ν208).
[13] Nonformulaic.
[14] Cf. ἀντιβίοις ἐπέεσιν (Β378), and προβλῆτι σκοπέλῳ (Β396) and the related system:

$$
ἀνδράσι \begin{cases} πυγμαίοισι & (Γ6) \\ παυροτέροισι & (Β122) \\ δυσμενέεσσι & (E488, P158, T168) \\ γε θνητοῖσι & (K403, P77, Υ266) \end{cases}
$$

[15] λ297.
[16] Cf. αὐτὰρ ἐπεὶ τὰ ἕκαστα διαρρήδην ἐρίδαινον (H. Merc.313).
[17] For ἐξ οὗ δή see ξ379. For τὰ πρῶτα see Δ424, N679, P612, Ψ275, 523, 538, and cf. Z489, M420, α257, and θ268, and 553.
[18] See note [16].
[19] Cf. "Ατρεΐδη, κύδιστε, ἄναξ ἀνδρῶν, 'Αγάμεμνον (Β434, I96, 677, 697, K103, T146, and 199. Cf. also P12 'Ατρεΐδη, Μενέλαε, Διοτρεφές, ὄρχαμε λαῶν.
[20] Γ271, 361, I89, N610, T252, δ304.
[21] There are twenty-two instances listed by Parry, q.v.
[22] α7, Υ160. For instances of δῖος 'Αχιλλεύς see Parry, who lists fifty-three.
[23] For τίς τ' ἄρ in this position see Β761, and Γ226. For θεῶν in this position see Γ269, E442, Λ74, N55, 632, T96, Ξ201, 302, 342, O290, Σ107, Φ443, α338, γ147, δ364, η247, κ157, φ28.
[24] Cf. μένεϊ ξυνέηκε μάχεσθαι (H210).
[25] Υ66.
[26] Cf. Ζηνί τε καὶ Διὸς υἷι (X302).
[27] Cf. ὁ δ'ἤϊε νυκτὶ ἐοικώς (A47), παλαιῷ φωτὶ ἐοικώς (Ξ136)
        ὁ γὰρ πολὺ φέρτατός ἐστιν (A581, Β769 ἦεν)
   and ὁ γὰρ προγενέστερος ἦεν (Β555), etc.
[28] Cf. πάντῃ ἀνὰ στρατὸν εὐρὺν 'Αχαιῶν (A384),
        αἶψα μάλ' ἐς στρατὸν ἐλθέ (Δ70), and
        ἀνὰ στρατόν εἰσι (K66). For κακήν in this position, see the system:

$$
\begin{array}{ll} νύκτα φυλασσομένοισι & (K188) \\ ἤ τ' ἂν ὑπέκφυγε κῆρα & (Π687) \\ σχέτλιος, ὃς 'ρ' ἔριν ὦρσε & (γ161) \\ φύζαν ἐμοῖς ἑτάροισι & (ξ269, ρ438) \end{array}
$$

[29] Cf. ἀρετῶσι δὲ λαοί (τ114), δαινῦτό τε λαός (Ω665).
[30] Cf. οὕνεκ' ἐγὼ φίλον υἱὸν ὑπεξέφερον πολέμοιο (E377).
[31] See note [30]. "Ουνεκα is found in this position 13 times in the first 12 books: A111, 291, Β580, Γ403, 405, Δ477, E342, 377, Z334, H140, I159, 442, and Λ79.
[32] Nonformulaic.
[33] Β577, 614, I339, 516, 648, Π59, Λ130, 169, P71, etc.
[34] For ὁ γὰρ ἦλθε cf. ὁ δ'ἄρ' ἦλθε (H416), δέ οἱ ἦλθε (Β408, and Δ529), πρὸ γὰρ ἧκε (A195), etc. For θοὰς ἐπὶ νῆας 'Αχαιῶν cf. B8, 17, 168, Z52, K450, 514, Λ3, Ω564, etc. For ἐπὶ νῆας 'Αχαιῶν cf. H78, Θ98, K525, O116, P691, X417, 465, Ω118, 146, 195, etc. For ἦλθε θοὰς ἐπὶ νῆας 'Αχαιῶν cf. A371. For θοὰς ἐπὶ νῆας cf. Β263, Λ568, Π247, Ω1, etc.

[35] A372.

[36] Cf. λυσόμενος παρὰ σεῖο (Ω502). For the position of λυσόμενος cf. also ἀζόμενοι Διὸς υἱόν (A21).

[37] Ω502. For ἀπερείσι' ἄποινα cf. A372, 249, 427, I120, K380, Λ134, T138, Ω276, 502, 579.

[38] A373.

[39] Cf. the following system:

$$
\left.\begin{array}{ll}
τόξον & (\text{O}443) \\
ἔγχος & (\text{P}604) \\
κάπρον & (\text{T}251) \\
ὀξύν & (γ443) \\
οἶνον & (\text{o}148) \\
φᾶρος & (Θ221)
\end{array}\right\} \text{ἔχων ἐν χειρί}
$$

For ἔχων ἐν χερσίν cf. Ξ385 (χειρί), and for στέμματ' ἔχων cf. the following system:

$$
\left.\begin{array}{ll}
σκῆπτρον & (Σ557) \\
τεύχε' & (\text{H}137) \\
αἰγίδ' & (\text{O}361) \\
χεῖρας & (Σ33) \\
ἔλκος & (\text{T}52)
\end{array}\right\} \text{ἔχων}
$$

[40] A438, Π513, Ψ872 '(ἐκηβόλῳ 'Απόλλωνι).

[41] A374.

[42] Cf. χρυσέῳ ἐν δαπέδῳ (Δ2), and χρυσέῳ ἐν δέπαϊ (Ω285).

[43] Cf.

$$
\begin{array}{ll}
μάλα δὲ χρέω πάντας 'Αχαιούς & (\text{ I75 }) \\
κέκαστο δὲ πάντας 'Αχαιούς & (\text{ Ξ124}) \\
θάμβος δ' ἔχε πάντας 'Αχαιούς & (\text{ Ψ815}) \\
ἐφάμην ἥρωας 'Αχαιούς & (\text{M165}) \\
κτεῖναι δ'ἥρωας 'Αχαιούς & (\text{ N629}) \\
φοβέειν ἥρωας 'Αχαιούς & (\text{ O230})
\end{array}
$$

For πάντας 'Αχαιούς cf. A374, Γ68, 88, H49, Θ498, I75, Ξ124, Ψ815, γ137, 141, δ288, ω49, and 438.

3. See C. M. Bowra, *Heroic Poetry*, pp. 233ff.

4. "The Distinctive Character of Enjambement in Homeric Verse," *TAPhA*, 60:200–220 (1929). For the term "necessary enjambement" see note 17 to Chapter Three above.

5. "Homer and Huso III: Enjambement in Greek and Southslavic Heroic Song," *TAPhA*, 79:113–124 (1948).

6. See my "Composition by Theme in Homer and Southslavic Epos," *TAPhA*, 82:71–80 (1951).

7. There is an excellent treatment of the slowness of reading and writing in medieval times in *From Script to Print* (1945), by H. J. Chaytor, Master of St. Catherine's College, Cambridge. He writes:

"The medieval reader, with few exceptions, did not read as we do; he was in the stage of our muttering childhood learner; each word was for him a separate entity and at times a problem, which he whispered to himself when he had found the solution [p. 10] . . . the history of the progress from script to print is a history of the gradual substitution of visual for auditory methods of communicating and receiving ideas [p. 4]."

The task, yes, the very physical task, of writing down the *Iliad* and the *Odyssey* is a tremendous one.

8. "Minoan Writing," *AJA*, 58:77–129 (1954).

9. See note 3 to Chapter Five.

10. See especially H. T. Wade-Gery, *The Poet of the Iliad* (Cambridge, 1952).

11. *Hesiod, the Homeric Hymns, and Homerica*, edited by H. G. Evelyn-White, Loeb Classical Library (Cambridge and London, 1943), pp. 480ff.

12. *Homer and the Heroic Tradition*, pp. 79ff.

13. J. A. Notopoulos, "The Warrior as an Oral Poet: A Case History," *Classical Weekly*, 46:17–19 (1952).

14. See Robert H. Pfeiffer, *Introduction to the Old Testament* (New York, 1941; revised edition, 1948), pp. 282ff.

15. For these texts see James B. Pritchard, ed., *Ancient Near Eastern Texts Relating to the Old Testament* (Princeton, 1950).

16. S. N. Kramer, *Sumerian Mythology* (Philadelphia, 1944), pp. 13ff.

CHAPTER EIGHT

The *Odyssey*

1. See H. G. Evelyn-White, *Hesiod, The Homeric Hymns, and Homerica*. The best discussion of the Cyclic poets is still that in D. B. Monro, *Homer's Odyssey Books XIII to XXIV* (Oxford, 1901), pp. 340ff.

2. *Daretis Phrygii De Excidio Trojae Historia*, ed. F. Meister (Teubner, Leipzig, 1873). Dictys Cretensis' work, *Ephemeris de Historia Belli Trojani*, also edited by F. Meister (Teubner, Leipzig, 1872).

3. See J. B. Pritchard, ed., *Ancient Near Eastern Texts Relating to the Old Testament*, and S. N. Kramer, *Sumerian Mythology* (Philadelphia, 1944).

4. See, for example, the stimulating article by V. M. Žirmunskij, "Epičeskoe skazanie ob Alpamyše i 'Odisseja' Gomera," *Izvestija akademii nauk SSSR*, Otdelenie literatury i jazyka, 16:97–113 (1957). Under Professor Žirmunskij's editorship a handsome Russian translation of the Uzbek folk epic, *Alpamyš*, by Lev Pen'kovskij, was recently published: *Alpamyš, uzbekskij narodnyj epos* (Moscow, 1958). I am indebted to Professor Žirmunskij for copies of these works as well as for the little book on Homer, *Aedy*, by I. I. Tolstoj (Moscow, 1958).

5. Although it should be noted that Homer mentions the marriage of Menelaus' son, Megapenthes, in *Odyssey* 4.11.

6. *Odyssey* 12:70. For a list of early Greek epics, see the article on the epic cycle by William Francis Jackson Knight in the *Oxford Classical Dictionary*. Note also the article by C. M. Bowra on Greek epic poetry in the same dictionary, as well as Bowra's recent *Homer and His Forerunners*, Andrew Lang Lecture, Feb. 16, 1955 (Edinburgh, 1955).

7. In two others (Parry 6812 and 1939) sons are mentioned but they play no role. For another return with a son, see I, No. 32.

8. See Denys Page, *The Homeric Odyssey* (Oxford, 1955), pp. 83ff. and the excellent article on Theoclymenus in Pauly-Wissowa, Zweite Reihe X (1934), 1997–99.

9. See Parry and Lord, *Serbocroatian Heroic Songs*, I, No. 24.

10. See Parry and Lord, I, No. 24.

11. See Martti Haavio, *Väinämöinen, Eternal Sage*.

12. Passages from the *Odyssey*, unless indicated otherwise, are quoted in the translation of George Herbert Palmer, *The Odyssey of Homer* (Cambridge, Mass., 1912).

13. Dictys, VI, 6. See also Guido De Columnis, *Historia Destructionis Troiae,* Mediaeval Academy of America, Publication No. 26, edited by N. E. Griffin (Cambridge, Mass., 1936), pp. 261–262.

14. In Aeschylus' *Choephori,* Sophocles' *Electra,* and with less emphasis on Orestes' deceptive story in Euripides' *Electra.*

15. Quoted from the translation by E. V. Rieu (Penguin Books, 1951), p. 87.

16. See Evelyn-White, pp. 525–527.

17. See note 13 above.

18. Apollonius Rhodius, *Argonautica* 2:851ff.

19. Cedric H. Whitman, *Homer and the Homeric Tradition,* p. 288.

20. See Evelyn-White, p. 529.

21. *Ibid.* p. 527.

22. Guido De Columnis, pp. 258–259.

23. *Odyssey* 23:153ff. For a discussion of the awkwardness of this bath, see Denys Page, pp. 114ff.

24. See note 8 above.

25. The line δίσκοισιν τέρποντο καὶ αἰγανέῃσιν ἱέντες occurs only in these two passages, 4:626 and 17:168.

26. See Appendix III.

27. Denys Page, pp. 114ff.

28. *Ibid.* p. 116.

29. See, for example, Parry, 6431, from Mujo Velić of Bihać, given under Return-Rescue Songs in Appendix IV.

30. See V. S. Karadžić, *Srpske narodne pjesme,* vol. III, No. 25. For Parry Collection versions, see Parry and Lord, I, p. 340.

31. See, for example, Parry and Lord, I, No. 24.

32. See Evelyn-White, p. 531.

33. Pauly-Wissowa, XLV (1957), 1029–1032.

34. See the article on Leucas in Pauly-Wissowa, XXIV (1925), 2213–2257.

35. Denys Page, pp. 117–118.

36. See Pauly-Wissowa, XXXIV (1937), 2308–2361.

37. See Evelyn-White, p. 529.

CHAPTER NINE

The *Iliad*

1. This is, of course, basically no new idea. Émile Mireaux expressed it in his *Les poèmes homériques et l'histoire grecque* (Paris, 1948), and it follows from G. R. Levy's arguments in *The Sword from the Rock* (London, 1953).

2. Both the donning of Achilles' armor by Patroclus in Book XVI, which is a disguise for Patroclus, and also the new armor made for Achilles, which he puts on in Book XIX.

3. *Iliad* XXIII:65ff.

4. See Guido de Columnis, *Historia Destructionis Troiae,* ed. N. E. Griffin, who follows Dares and Dictys. Hector kills Patroclus in Book XV of Guido and Achilles withdraws from the fighting in Book XXV, having killed Hector in Book XXII.

5. For this technique of comparison of patterns see Claude Lévi-Strauss, "The Structural Study of Myth," *Journal of American Folklore,* 68:433 (1955).

6. Passages from the *Iliad* are quoted in the translation of Richmond Lattimore (Chicago, 1951).

7. See preceding chapter page 184 and Pauly-Wissowa, XXIV (1925), 2213–2257.

8. Evidence of this is abundant in the legend of Agamemnon and the vengeance taken by Orestes for his murder; in the many digressions in *Beowulf;* in the pattern of the *Nibelungenlied;* and even the whole corpus of Icelandic saga, which is a monument to a feuding society.

9. *Iliad* I:19.

10. *Iliad* I:59ff.

11. *Iliad* I:169ff.

12. *Iliad* II:114ff.

13. *Iliad* I:207ff.

14. *Iliad* I:423ff.

15. The numbers nine and twelve are also common in the Yugoslav return songs (see Appendix III), and in the songs of the taking of cities (cf. Parry and Lord, *Serbocroatian Heroic Songs,* I, No. 1). The number twenty found in these songs is probably an alliterative suggestion from the number twelve; *dvanaest* easily becomes *dvadeset.*

16. These lines correspond to *Iliad* II:111–118, 139–141.

17. *Iliad* X:5–10.

18. *Iliad* IX:4–8.

19. *Iliad* XVI:543.

20. *Iliad* XVIII:170ff.

21. The death of twelve men referred to at the end is prophetic of those who will be sacrificed at Patroclus' funeral.

22. *Odyssey* 16:170ff.

23. *Odyssey* 5:333ff.

24. Parry and Lord, I, No. 4.

25. See below Chapter Ten, page 206.

26. See the discussion of this passage in *The Abingdon Bible Commentary,* p. 240, and in R. H. Pfeiffer, *Introduction to the Old Testament,* p. 155.

27. J. B. Pritchard, ed., *Ancient Near Eastern Texts Relating to the Old Testament,* p. 86, lines 19–20.

28. *Ibid.* p. 73, Tablet I, (ii), line 1.

CHAPTER TEN

Some Notes on Medieval Epic

1. The material for this chapter is drawn in part from a lecture on medieval epic at the English Institute in New York in September 1956, and from a lecture at Dumbarton Oaks in the spring of 1955. For assistance with the Byzantine Greek material I am especially indebted to Dr. George C. Soulis of Dumbarton Oaks.

For the most recent discussion of comparative Slavic epic see V. M. Žirmunskij, "Epičeskoe tvorčestvo slavjanskih narodov i problemy sravnitel'nogo izučenija eposa," in the *IV. meždunarodnyj s'ezd slavistov, doklady* (Moscow, 1958); P. G. Bogatyrev, "Nekotorye zadači sravnitel'nogo izučenija eposa slavjanskih narodov," also in *IV meždunarodnyj s'ezd slavistov, doklady* (Moscow, 1958); and the various articles in *Osnovnye problemy eposa vostočnyh slavjan* (Moscow, 1958), published by the Institut mirovoj literatury of the Soviet Academy of Sciences in Moscow.

2. See Francis P. Magoun, Jr., "Oral-Formulaic Character of Anglo-Saxon Narrative

Poetry," *Speculum*, 28:446–467 (July 1953), and Adrien Bonjour, *"Beowulf* and the Beasts of Battle," *PMLA* 72:563–573 (September 1957).

3. Ronald A. Waldron, "Oral-Formulaic Technique and Middle English Alliterative Poetry," *Speculum*, 32:792–804 (October 1957).

4. Jean Rychner, *La Chanson de Geste, Essai sur l'Art Épique des Jongleurs* (Geneva and Lille, 1955).

5. See Magoun, *Speculum*, 28:446–467 (July 1953).

6. See the unpublished doctoral thesis of Professor Robert Creed of Brown University in the Harvard University archives. For an excellent example of the application of the oral theory to textual criticism, see Professor Creed's article *"Genesis* 1316" in *Modern Language Notes,* 73:321–325 (May 1958).

7. Stanley Greenfield, "The Formulaic Expression of the Theme of 'Exile' in Anglo-Saxon Poetry," *Speculum*, 30:200–206 (April 1955), and Francis P. Magoun, Jr., "The Theme of the Beasts of Battle in Anglo-Saxon Poetry," *Bulletin de la société néo-philologique de Helsinki*, LVI:81–90 (1955). Professor Creed is planning a full-scale investigation of the theme in *Beowulf.*

8. Notes to Chart VIII follow:

[1]   529, 631, 957, 1473, 1651, 1817, 1999 (Biowulf, Ecgðioes), 2425 (Biowulf). Rhythmic pattern is Pope D*2, 45 (p. 312). Syntactic pattern is subject (1), verb (2), appositive (3), patronymic (4). The figures in parentheses indicate the number of the measure in which the syntactic unit is included. Cf. 371 (Hroðgar m./helm Scyldinga), 1321, 456 (same), and also the variant pattern caused by alliteration 499 (Unferð m./Ecglafes bearn), 2862 (Wiglaf m./Weohstanes sunu), 3076 (Wiglaf m./Wihstanes sunu).

[2]   405 (on him byrne scan), 2510 (beotwordum spraec), 2724 (Biowulf m./he ofer benne spraec). For rhythmic pattern and syntactic pattern see note [1]. Cf. also 286 (Weard m./ðaer on wicge saet), 348 (Wulfgar m./þaet waes Wendla leod), 360 (Wulfgar m./to his winedrihtne), 925 (Hroðgar m./he to healle geong), 1215 (Wealhðeo m./heo fore þaem werede spraec), 1687 (Hroðgar m./hylt sceawode), 1840 (Hroðgar m./him on andsware).

[3]   2177 (swa bealdode). Rhythmic pattern is Pope D1, 1 (p. 358). For syntactic pattern see note [1]. Cf. 1550 (haefde ða forsiðod/sunu E.), 2367 (oferswam ða sioleða bigong/sunu E.), 2587 (þaet se maera/maga E.), 2398 (sliðra geslyhta/sunu Ecgðiowes). Cf. also 620 (Ymbeode þa/ides Helminga), 194 (þaet fram ham gefraegn/Higelaces þegn), etc. In the last instance note the reversal of noun and patronymic because of alliteration.

[4]   Syntactic pattern is imperative-adverb (1), demonstrative-adjective (2), vocative (3), patronymic (4). Cf. 2587 (þaet se maera/maga Ecgðeowes), 2011 (sona me se maera/mago Healfdenes).

[5]   Cf. 489 (site nu to symle/ond onsael meoto), 1782 (ga nu to setle/symbelwynne dreoh), and 2747 (bio nu on ofoste/þaet ic aerwelan) for the first measure; and 762 (mynte se maera/þaer he meahte swa), 675 (gespraec þa se goda/gylpworda sum), 2971 (ne meahte se snella/sunu Wonredes), and lines 2587 and 2011 given in note [4] for the second measure. Rhythmic pattern is Pope A3, 89 (p. 270). For syntactic pattern see note [4].

[6]   189 (swa ða maelceare), 2143 (maðma menigeo), 1867 (mago H./maþmas twelfe), and 2011 given in note [4]. Cf. also 1465 (huru ne gemunde/mago Ecglafes), and 2587 given in note [4]. Rhythmic pattern is Pope D2, 11 (p. 361). For syntactic pattern see notes [1] and [4].

[7]   Syntactic pattern is adjective (1), vocative (2), adverb-pronoun subject (3), genitive-adjective (4).

[8]   2156 (sume worde het). Cf. 1507 (hringa þengel/to hofe sinum), 1400 (wicg

wundenfeax./Wisa fengel), 2345 (oferhogode ða/hringa fengel). Rhythmic pattern is Pope B1, 4 (p. 336). For syntactic pattern see note [7].

[9] Cf. for the first measure 251 (aenlic ansyn./Nu ic eower sceal), 946 (bearngebyrdo./Nu ic, Beowulf, þec), and also 335 (heresceafta heap?/Ic eom Hroðgares), 407 (waes þu, Hroðgar hal!/Ic eom Higelaces), and 2527 (Metod manna gehwaes./Ic eom on mode from). For the second measure cf. 579 (siþes werig./Ða mec sae oþbaer), and 1794 (sona him seleþegn/siðes wergum). Rhythmic pattern is Pope A1, 1b (p. 247). For syntactic pattern see note [7].

[10] Pattern is vocative (1), genitive (2), relative-pronoun subject (3), pronoun indirect object-verb (4).

[11] 1171 (ond to Geatum spraec). Cf. 2419 (g. Geata./Him waes geomor sefa), 2584 (g. Geata;/guðbill geswac). Rhythmic pattern is Pope A2a, 34 (p. 258). For syntactic pattern see note [10], and cf. notes [3] and [6]. This is common pattern. Cf. also 120 (wonsceaft wera./Wiht unhaelo), 467 (hordburh haeleþa;/ða waes Heregar dead), etc.

[12] Cf. for first measure 1186 (hwaet wit to willan/ond to worðmyndum), and 1707 (freode, swa wit furðum spraecon). For the second measure cf. 2252 (gesawon seledream./Nah, hwa sweord wege), 3126 (Naes ða on hlytme,/hwa þaet hord strude), etc. Rhythmic pattern is Pope C1, 2 (p. 348). For syntactic pattern see note [10].

[13] This is a closely knit line syntactically and rhythmically, with no pause between the second and third measures. Note also the necessary enjambement at the end of the line. Syntactic pattern is conjunction-pronoun subject-preposition (1), noun-object (2), possessive pronoun (3), verb (4). Cf. 293 (swylce ic maguþegnas/mine hate). See also note [40].

[14] Cf. for the first measure 1822 (gif ic þonne on eorþan/owihte maeg), 2519 (waepen to wyrme,/gif ic wiste hu), and 1185 (uncran eaferan,/gif he þaet eal gemon), 2841 (gif he waeccende/weard onfunde), 1140 (gif he torngemot/þurhteon mihte), 944 (aefter gumcynnum,/gyf heo gyt lyfað). For the second measure cf. 1525 (ðeodne aet þearfe;/ðolode aer fela), 2709 (þegn aet ðearfe!/þaet ðam þeodne waes), and cf. also 1456 (þaet him on ðearfe lah/ðyle Hroðgares), 2694 (Ða ic aet þearfe (gefraegn)/þeodcyninges), 1797 (þegnes þearfe,/swylce þy dogore), and 2801 (leoda þearfe;/ne maeg ic her leng wesan). Rhythmic pattern is Pope A3, 68 (p. 265). For syntactic pattern see note [13].

[15] For the third measure cf. 2131 (þa se ðeoden mec/ðine life), 2095 (þaer ic, þeoden min,/þine leode), 1823 (þinre modlufan/maran tilian), 1673 (ond þegna gehwylc/þinra leoda), etc. For the fourth measure cf. 230 (se þe holmclifu/healdan scolde), 280 (gyf him edwenden/aefre scolde), 1034 (ongean gramum/gangan scolde), 1067 (aefter medobence/maenan scolde), etc. Out of 19 cases of "sculan" observed, all but 3 are in the fourth measure. For syntactic pattern see note [13]. See also notes [40] and [42].

[16] The syntactic pattern is object (1), infinitive (2), conjunction-pronoun subject-dative of reference (3) adverb-verb (4). Note that this line is connected to both the preceding and the following line by necessary enjambement.

[17] 2443 (aeðeling unwrecen/ealdres linnan). Cf. also 680 (aldre beneotan,/þeah ic eal maege), 1524 (aldre sceþðan,/ac seo ecg geswac), 2599 (ealdre burgan./Hiora in anum weoll), 2924 (þaette Ongenðio/ealdre besnyðede), 661 (gif þu þaet ellenweorc/aldre gedigest), 1469 (under yða gewin/aldre geneþan), 1655 (Ic þaet unsofte/ealdre gedigde), etc. Cf. also such formulas as 1002 (aldres orwena./ No þaet uðe byð), 1565 (aldres orwena,/yrringa sloh)´,1338 (ealdres scyldig,/ond nu oþer cwom), etc. For syntactic pattern see note [16].

[18] Cf. 313 (torht getaehte,/þaet hie him to mihton), 1833 (wordum ond

weorcum,/þaet ic þe wel herige), 203 (lythwon logon,/þeah he him leof waere), 2161 (hwatum Heorowearde,/þeah he him hold waere). For the fourth measure cf. also 881 (eam his nefan,/swa hie a waeron), 754 (forht on ferhðe;/no þy aer fram meahte), etc. Rhythmic pattern is Pope C1, 5 (p. 349). For syntactic pattern see note [16].

[19]   The syntactic pattern is participle (1 and 2), preposition-genitive (3), object of preposition (4). Note the necessary enjambement with the preceding line.

[20]   Cf. 1937 (handgewriþene;/hraþe seoþðan waes), 59 (Ðaem feower bearn/forðgerimed). Rhythmic pattern is Pope A1, 12b (p. 252). For syntactic pattern see note [19]. It is interesting to note the following from other Anglo-Saxon poems: Gu. 1107 (waeron feowere/forðgewitene), El. 1267 (nu sind geardagas/forðgewitenum), Met. 1052 waeron gefyru/forðgewitenum), El. 636 (is nu feala siðan/forðgewitenra).

[21]   Cf. 1950 (ofer fealone flod/be faeder lare), 21 (fromum feohgiftum/on faeder bearme), 1114 (Het þa Hildeburh/aet Hnaefes ade). Rhythmic pattern is Pope C1, 34 (p. 356). For syntactic pattern see note [19]. Cf. also Reb. 11 (on bearna staele), and Gen. 1113 (on leofes staele).

[22]   The syntactic pattern is imperative-pronoun subject (1), appositive (2), possessive pronoun (3), dative of reference (4).

[23]   For the first measure cf. 269 (leodgebyrgean;/wes þu us larena god), 407 (Waes þu, Hroðgar, hal!/Ic eom Higelaces), 386 (Beo ðu on ofeste,/hat in gan), 1226 (sincgestreona./Beo þu suna minum). Cf. also such lines as 2946 (Waes sio swatswaðu/Sweona ond Geata), and especially 2779 (þam þara maðma/mundbora waes), in which the order of the verb has been changed for the sake of the alliteration. For the second measure cf. 349 (waes his modsefa/manegum gecyðed), 373 (waes his ealdfaeder/Ecgðeo haten), 3046 haefde eorðscrafa/ende genyttod), etc. Rhythmic pattern is Pope C2, 22c (p. 295). Pope lists 118 examples of this rhythm. For instances of it in the second half line see Pope pages 352–53, where he cites 166 examples, and notes the frequency of the compound noun in the second or fourth measures. For the syntactic pattern see note [22].

[24]   Cf. the following examples in note [15] above: 2131, 2095, 1823, and 1673; and in note [13] above: 293, where "minum" occurs in this position in the line, but modifying a following noun. Cf. also 2804 (se scel to gemyndum/minum leodum), 2797 (þaes ðe ic moste/minum leodum), and for "magoþegn" in the second measure 2079 (maerum maguþegne/to muðbonan). For syntactic pattern see note [22].

[25]   The syntactic pattern is dative of reference (1 and 2), conjunction-pronoun object (3), noun subject-verb (4).

[26]   "Hondgesellum" is a *hapax legomenon* in *Beowulf*. Cf., however, the many instances in which the first half line is taken up by such a compound: 1495 (hilderince./Ða waes hwil daeges), 1511 (hildetuxum/heresyrcan braec), 1520 (hildebille,/hond sweng ne ofteah), 1526 (hondgemota,/helm oft gescaer), etc.

[27]   Cf. 452 (Onsend Higelace,/gif mec hild nime). Cf. also 447 (dreore fahne,/gif mec deað nimeð), 1491 (dom gewyrce,/oþðe mec deað nimeð). The rhythmic pattern is Pope C2, 22 (p. 353). For the syntactic pattern see note [25].

[28]   Syntactic pattern is adverb-pronoun subject-demonstrative (1), direct object (2), relative-pronoun subject (3) indirect object-verb (4). Note that this line is linked to the following by necessary enjambement.

[29]   Cf. 293 (swylce ic maguþegnas/mine hate), in which the first syllable of the noun takes the place of the demonstrative. For the first measure cf. 757 (swylce he on ealderdagum/aer gemette), 1156 (swylce hie aet Finnes ham/findan meahton), and 2869 (þeoden his þegnum,/swylce he þrydlicost), and 2767

Swylce he siomian geseah/segn eallgylden). For the second measure cf. 2490 (Ic him þa maðmas,/þe he me sealde), and cf. also 2788 (He ða mid þam maðmum/maerne þioden), 2779 (þam ðara maðma/mundbora waes), etc. Klaeber notes that "swylce" in this sense is used in all but one instance at the beginning of the half line (Glossary page 377 of the 1928 edition of *Beowulf*) The rhythmic pattern is Pope A3, 70b (p. 266). For the syntactic pattern see note [28].

[30] The rhythmic pattern is Pope C1, 2 (p. 348). Out of 74 instances he cites 22 with noun or pronoun plus verb in the fourth measure, including line 1482. Of these the following involve either the verb "sellan" or a pronoun before the verb: 72 (geongum ond ealdum,/swylc him God sealde), 1271 (gimfaeste gife,/þe him God sealde), 2182 (ginfaesten gife,/þe him God sealde), 2490 (Ic him þa maðmas,/þe he me sealde), 417 (þeoden Hroðgar,/þaet ic þe sohte), and 563 (manfordaedlan,/þaet hie me þegon). Cf. also 1751 (forgyteð ond forgymeð,/þaes þe him aer God sealde), etc. For syntactic pattern see note [28].

[31] The syntactic pattern is noun (vocative) (1), adjective (2), indirect object (3), verb (4). This line is linked with the preceding by necessary enjambement. "Onsend" has both its subject and its object in line 1482.

[32] Cf. 2745 (Wiglaf leofa,/nu se wyrm ligeð), 1216 (Bruc ðisses beages,/Beowulf leofa), 1758 (Bebeorh þe ðone bealoInð,/Beowulf leofa), and, with the reversing of noun and adjective for the sake of the alliteration, 1854 (licað leng swa wel,/leofa Beowulf), 1987 (Hu lomp eow on lade,/leofa Beowulf), 2663 (Leofa Biowulf,/laest eall tela). Cf. also 618 (leodum leofne;/he on lust geþeah), and its opposite, 3079 (Ne meahton we gelaeran/leofne þeoden), etc. The rhythmic pattern is Pope A2a, 28c (p. 256). For the syntactic pattern see note [31].

[33] Cf. 5 (monegum maegþum/meodosetla ofteah), 690 (snellic saerinc/selereste gebeah), 884 (sweordum gesaeged./Sigemunde gesprong), etc. Cf. also 452 (Onsend Higelace/gif mec hild nime), in which the shift in position is due to alliteration. The rhythmic pattern is Pope E, 7 (p. 370). For the syntactic pattern see note [31].

[34] Since the rhythmic pattern of the first half of this line is found here only, the line as a whole could not be considered as either formula or formulaic, although the second half of the line is a very common formula.

[35] The rhythmic pattern is Pope B2, 48 (p. 285). It is found only here in the first half of the line and once in the second half line, 1585 (reþe cempa,/to ðaes þe he on raeste geseah). See Pope, p. 345. This half line is nonformulaic.

[36] 1831 (Geata dryhten,/þeah ðe he geong sy), 2483 (Geata dryhtne/guð onsaege), 2560 (wið ðam gryregieste,/Geata dryhten), 2576 (Geata dryhten,/gryrefahne sloh), 2991 (geald þone guðraes/Geata dryhten), and the reverse 2402 (dryhten Geata/dracan sceawian), 2901 (dryhten Geata/deaðbedde faest). Cf. also 2419 (goldwine Geata./Him waes geomor sefa), and 2584 (goldwine Geata;/guðbill geswac), etc.

[37] Since the rhythmic patterns in both halves of the line are rare (see notes [38] and [39]), the line as a whole must be considered nonformulaic.

[38] The rhythmic pattern is Pope D1, 8 (p. 302). The syntactic pattern in both instances cited by Pope is the same, verb (1), substantive complex (2), although in 501 (onband beadurune — /waes him Beowulfes sið) the compound noun takes the place of the two nouns in 1485. For the second measure cf. 1847 (hild heorugrimme/Hreþles eaferan), 2191 (heaðorof cyning/Hreðles lafe), 2358 (Hreðles eafora/hiorodryncum sWealt), 2992 (Hreðles eafora,/þa he to ham becom) (it is interesting to note that in this instance the phrase is also preceded by "Geata dryhten" in the line before it), and 454 (hraegla selest;/þaet is

Hraedlan laf), which are all cases of the reverse order for the sake of alliteration. Cf. also 2025 (geong goldhroden,/gladum suna Frodan), and many other
formulas with "sunu" as a base: 524 (sunu Beanstanes/soðe gelaeste), 645
(sunu Healfdenes/secean wolde), 980 (Ða waes swigra secg,/sunu Ecglafes),
1009 (þaet to healle gang/Healfdenes sunu), etc. Cf. also other related rhythmic
patterns (D1), such as 758 (Gemunde þa se goda,/maeg Higelaces), etc. (See
Pope, p. 359)

[39] The rhythmic pattern is Pope C2, 30 (p. 355). This is the only case of this
pattern in *Beowulf*, but cf. also the related patterns, 996 (secga gehwylcum/
þara þe on swylc stara ð), 2864 (þaet, la, maeg secgan/se ðe wyle soð specan).
Cf. also 2796 (ecum Dryhtne,/þe ic her on starie), and 1603 (modes seoce/ond
on mere staredon).

[40] The syntactic pattern is conjunction-pronoun subject (1), dative (2), adjective
(accusative) (3), verb (4). Note the necessary enjambement with the following
line.

[41] Cf. 260 (We synt gumcynnes/Geata leode), 378 (þa ðe gifsceattas/Geata
fyredon), 556 (þaet ic aglaecan/orde geraehte), 571 (þaet ic saenaesses/geseon
mihte), and 894 (þaet he beahhordes/brucan moste). The rhythmic pattern is
Pope C1, 2c (p. 289). Pope notes the frequency with which compounds occur
in the second measure, and cites 58 such instances out of the 118 of this
pattern. For the syntactic pattern see note [40].

[42] Cf. 2789 (dryhten sinne/driorigne fand), 1810 (cwaeð, he þone guðwine/
godne tealde), 1969 (geongne guðcyning/godne gefrunon), 199 (godne gegyr-
wan;/cwaeð, he guðcyning), and for another instance of "funde" in the
second measure of the half line cf. 1415 (ofer harne stan/hleonian funde).
This rhythmic pattern (Pope A1, 1, page 325) is extremely common. Pope
notes 460 instances of it in the second half line, and 371 in the first (see note
[8]). For the syntactic pattern see note [40].

[43] The syntactic pattern is objective genitive (1), direct object (2), verb-conjunc-
tion (3), verb (4).

[44] 35 (on bearm scipes), 352 (swa þu bena eart). The rhythmic pattern is Pope
A1, 3a (p. 248). For the syntactic pattern see note [43].

[45] Cf. 1177 (beahsele beorhta;/bruc þenden þu mote), 894 (þaet he beahhordes/
brucan moste), 3100 (þenden he burhwelan/brucan moste), 2241 (brucan
moste./Beorh eallgearo), and for the position of "breac" cf. also 1216 (Bruc
ðisses beages,/Beowulf leofa), and 2162 (breostgewaedu./Bruc ealles well).
For the syntactic pattern see note [43].

9. Francis P. Magoun, Jr., "Bede's Story of Caedman: The Case History of an
Anglo-Saxon Oral Singer," *Speculum*, 30:49–63 (January 1955).

10. *Beowulf*, lines 90–98, R. K. Gordon translation.

11. In the *Aethiopis*. See H. G. Evelyn-White, *Hesiod, the Homeric Hymns, and
Homerica*, pp. 507–509.

12. See the most recent article on the symbolic interpretation of *Beowulf*: Peter F.
Fisher, "The Trials of the Epic Hero in *Beowulf*," *PMLA*, 73:171–183 (June 1958).

13. For an edition of the various manuscripts see Raoul Mortier, *Les textes de la
Chanson de Roland*, 10 vols. (Paris, 1940–44).

14. Rychner, *op. cit.*

15. Oxford manuscript, lines 1338–1347. Notes to Chart IX follow:

[1] Lines 194, 355, 663, 707, 751, 777, 792, 803, 1145, 1321, 1545, 1580, 1629, 1671,
1691, 1761, 1785, 1869, 1897, 2066, 2099, 2124, 2134, 2152, 2163, 2166, 2215,
2233, 2246, 2375, 2701.

[2] 3421. Cf. also 1098 par grant irur chevalchent; 2851 par grant vertut cheval-chent; and 3463 li amiralz chevalchet par le camp.

[3] 1583, 1870. Cf. 1550, 1953 tient Halteclere; 1324 trait Durendal; 3622 prent Tencendur; 2287 tient l'olifan; 2992, 3152 tient sun espiet; 3114 prent sun escut; 2596 trait ces chevels; 2906 trait ces crignels.

[4] Cf. 925 veez m'espee ki est e bone e lunge; 1276 ki est a flurs e ad or; 1354 ki est ad or e a flur.

[5] 1340. Cf. 1007, 1929 de Sarrazins; 1030, 1186 E Sarrazins; 202 de ses paiens; 588 de vos paiens; 177 des Francs de France.

[6] 3422. Cf. 3479 i ad mult gran damage; 1224 sin ad mult grant irur; 1987 en avrat grant damage; 2660 m'at fait guere mult grant.

[7] 1970. Cf. also 1680 ki puis veïst; 3483 ki dunc veïst; 1181 ki dunc oïst.

[8] Cf. 1971 un mort sur altre geter; 3878 vait ferir l'uns li altre.

[9] 1980, 3925.

[10] The only evidence I can find here is line 1694 . . . veez gesir par tere.

[11] Cf. 1056 sanglant en ert.

[12] Cf. 994 des osbercs sarazineis; 1227, 1575 e l'osberc li derumpt; 1647 e l'osberc jazerenc; 1721 jamais entre sa brace; 3939 Tierri entre sa brace; 3250 de elme ne d'osberc.

[13] 1610. Cf. 1266 sun bon espiet; 2032 sur sun cheval.

[14] Cf. 647 Guenelun par l'espalle; 1826 el col un caeignun; and 1109 e li colps e li caples; 2206 le doel e la pitet; 2276 sun cors e sun visage; 2902 ma force e ma baldur.

[15] 176, 576, 586, 903, 1351, 1990, 2216, 2963, 3186, 3690, 3755, 3776.

[16] Cf. 2805 puis escriet: "Baruns, ne vos targez!"; 1681 de lur espees e ferir e capler; 1415 li .XII. per ne s'en targent nient; 338 quant aler dei, n'i ai plus que targer; 1366 kar de ferir; 1198, 1226, 1584, 3424 vait le ferir; 1092 par ben ferir.

[17] 262, 325, 547, 560, 826, 937, 948, 965, 1415, 2792, 3187; des 1308; les 1513, 3756.

[18] 1718. Cf. 681 nel devez pas blasmer; 1063 pur mei seient blasmet; 1174 ne funt mie a blasmer.

[19] 1416, 1835, 3476.

[20] Cf. 3475 ben i fierent e caplent; 1416 i fierent cumunement; 1681 e ferir e capler.

16. Oxford, *laisse* 105, lines 1338–1350; Venice IV, *laisse* 101, lines 1256–1267.

17. Oxford, *laisse* 105, lines 1338–1350; Chateauroux, *laisse* 144, lines 2277–2292.

18. Chateauroux, *laisse* 144, lines 2277–2292; Cambridge, *laisse* 39, lines 577–592.

19. John Mavrogordato, *Digenes Akrites* (Oxford, 1956), is the only English translation.

20. For an edition of all the manuscripts see Petros P. Kalonaros, ed., *Basileios Digenis Akritas,* vols. I and II.

Important discussions of the Russian version are found in *Russian Epic Studies,* Memoirs of the American Folklore Society, vol. 42, edited by Roman Jakobson and E. J. Simmons (Philadelphia, 1949), and A. I. Stender-Petersen, "O tak nazyvaemom Devgenievom Dejanii," in *Scando-Slavica,* I (Copenhagen, 1954).

21. Henri Grégoire, *Digenis Akritas* (New York, 1942). See particularly the *stemma* on page 301.

22. K. Krumbacher, "Eine neue Handschrift des Digenis Akritas," *Sitzungsberichte der Koenigliche Bayerische Akademie der Wissenschaften,* 2:309–355 (1904).

23. Grottaferrata 1.155–160 are equal to Athens 356–361 and E 21–29.

24. Notes to Chart XIII follow:

[1]   294, 604; cf. 1274: καὶ ὁ λαὸς τοῦ ᾿Αμηρᾶ; 2483: πατρὸς αὐτῆς τοῦ ᾿Αμηρᾶ; 4303: Μητέρα δὲ τοῦ ᾿Αμηρᾶ.

[2]   Cf. 2280: ἡ μάννα τοῦ ᾿Ακρίτου; 4302: τὴν μάμμην τοῦ ᾿Ακρίτου; 2245: ἡ μήτηρ τοῦ ᾿Ακρίτου; 4304: πατὴρ ὁ τοῦ ᾿Ακρίτου; 3234: τοῦ Διγενοῦς τὸν λόγον.

[3]   Cf. 1002: ῾Η μήτηρ τοῦ δὲ ὡς ἔμαθεν. . . and 1885: ὁ πατήρ μου τὸ ἔμαθε.

[4]   There seems to be nothing very close.

[5]   Cf. 3970: ἀπὸ Συρίαν ἄπασαν; 2496: εἰς τὴν Συρίαν ἠθέλησα.

[6]   Cf. 2352: ἐπιστολὴν τοιαύτην.

[7]   4367.

[8]   Cf. 550: θλίψεών τε καὶ πόνων.

[9]   There seems to be nothing very close.

[10]   Cf. 2075: ἦσαν οἱ ἀδελφοί της; 3078: ἦτον ὁ λόγος οὗτος.

[11]   1.

[12]   Cf. 466: μικρὰν παρηγορίαν; 471: κόσμου παρηγορίαν; 2009: οἴμοι τέκνον γλυκύτατον, φῶς καὶ παρηγορία; 2925: αὐτοῦ παρηγορίας; 3281: ψυχῶν παρηγορίαι.

[13]   Cf. 718: οὐ χωρισθῆναι θέλω σοῦ; 465: πῶς νὰ σὲ ξεχωρίσωμεν ἐκ τῶν λοιπῶν σωμάτων, and 242: . . . ἀπ᾿ ἐμοῦ. . . and many other prepositions plus pronoun in the same position.

[14]   Cf. 2797: ἐπῆγα᾿ εἰς τοὺς γονέους; 2805: ἐπῆγα εἰς ἄλλον τόπον; 1672: ἐπῆγεν εἰς κυνήγιν; 979: κρυβέντες εἰς τὰ δάση; 1767: ἐξαίφνης εἰς τὰ νέφη; 1217, 1274: ἔφθασεν εἰς τὸ κάστρον; 2197; δοκοῦσα εἶναι ξένα.

[15]   There seems to be nothing very close, but cf. 4111: καλύψαι σου τοὺς ὀφθαλμούς.

[16]   Cf. 458: καὶ ἔσβεσας τὸ φῶς μας; 4260: ἡμαύρωσας τὸ φῶς μου; 4399: κ᾿ἐθάμπωσεν τὸ φῶς του.

[17 and 18]   Cf. 578: δι᾿ οὗ πίστιν ἠρνήσατο καὶ συγγενεῖς καὶ φίλους; 848: ὃς δι᾿ ἐμὲ ἠρνήσατο γένος τε καὶ πατρίδα; 1067: πίστιν πατρίδα ἠρνήσατο καὶ συγγενεῖς καὶ φίλους; 1352: τὰ πάντα γὰρ ἠρνήσατο πίστιν τε καὶ πατρίδα; 1006: ὁμοίος δὲ οἱ συγγενεῖς; 1012: εἰς μέρος μὲν οἱ συγγενεῖς; 1881: μετέπειτα οἱ συγγενεῖς; 731: οἰκεῖος καὶ πατρίδα; 2777: γονεῖς τε καὶ πατρίδα.

[19]   Cf. 3898: καὶ γέγονε περίφημος εἰς ἄπαντα τὸν κόσμον; 4286: καὶ φοβερὸς ἐγένετο εἰς ἄπαντα τὸν κόσμον; 4351: καὶ γέγονεν περίφημος εἰς ἄπαντα τὸν κόσμον; 3757: ἀνδρῶν γὰρ εἶναι ὄνειδος.

[20]   522. Cf. also 302: κ᾿ἐτράφη εἰς τὴν Συρίαν; 309: μέσα εἰς τὴν Συρίαν.

25. Notes to Chart XIV follow:

[1]   Cf. 1.147: σπαθὶν διαζωσάμενος; 4.1071: ποδὸς αὐτοῦ δραξάμενος; 6.216: σπαθὶν ἀράμενος αὐτοῦ; 6.252: καὶ τὸ σπαθὶν ἐπὶ τὴν γῆν.

[2]   Cf. 4.132: ἔφθασε τὸ θηρίον; 4.136: βαλὼν τὸ θηρίον.

[3]   3.111, 4.816 (ὅτε).

[4]   There seems to be nothing very close.

[5]   "   "   "   "   "   "   "

[6]   "   "   "   "   "   "   "

[7]   "   "   "   "   "   "   "

[8]   Cf. 1.150, 1.172: εἰς τὸν κάμπον ἐξῆλθε; 4.872: μετὰ λαοῦ ἐξῆλθε; 6.385: πρὸς Μαξιμοῦν ἀπῆλθε.

[9]   Cf. 4.135: τὸ δὲ παιδίον σύντομα; 4.242: τὸ δὲ παιδίον εὔθιον; 4.913: καὶ τοῦ Χοσρόου τὸ σπαθίν; 6.61: καὶ ἐξελκύσας τὸ σπαθίν; 1.193: πόρρωθεν ῥίπτει τὸ σπαθίν.

[10] Cf. 1.193, 1.200, 2.250, 4.684: χεῖρας εἰς ὕψος ἄρας; 6.74: εἰς ὕψος ὅλω τῷ θυμῷ τὸ σπαθὶν ἀνατείνας.
[11] Cf. 6.224: τῇ ῥάβδῳ κατὰ κεφαλῆς.
[12] 3.99.
[13] But cf. 6.653: καὶ μέχρι γῆς τὴν κεφαλήν.
[14] But cf. 6.259: μέσον τῶν δύο ὤμων.

26. Notes to Chart XV follow:

[1] 1539, 132: καὶ ὡς εἶδεν τούτους; 421: καὶ ὡς εἶδεν ὁ νεώτερος; 634: καὶ ὡς εἶδεν τὸν λέοντα; 789: καὶ ὡς τὸν εἶδεν; 1126: καὶ ὡς εἶδεν ὁ Φιλοπαπποῦς; 1359: καὶ ὡς τὸν εἶδεν ἡ Μαξιμοῦ.
[2] 566, 567, 1009, 1281, 1357; cf. 466: ἵνα καβαλλικεύσῃ.
[3] Cf. 1684: καὶ ἀπάνω κεῖται πιλωτόν; 430: καὶ οἱ πέντε ἐπιλαλήσαμεν; 1283, 1528: καὶ σύντομα ἐπιλάλησεν; 1262: καὶ τὴν καλήν μου ἐλάλησα.
[4] Cf. 768: ἵνα ῥαβδέα τοῦ δώσῃ; 1246: ἵνα ῥαβδέαν μὲ δώσῃ; 1270: ἵνα σπαθεὰν μὲ δώσῃ; 1283: καὶ κονταρέαν μὲ δώσῃ; 1540, 1557: τὴν κονταρέαν μὲ δώσῃ.
[5 and 6] Cf. 941: καὶ κονταρέαν τὸν ἔδωκεν ὀμπρὸς εἰς τὸ μπροστοκούρβιν; 1452: καὶ κονταρέαν μ'ἔδωκεν τὴν φάραν εἰς τὰ μηρία; 1558: Σπαθεὰν τῆς φάρας ἔδωκα, ἀπάνω εἰς τὰ κεφάλιν; 1727: καὶ ὡς ἔδωκα τὴν λέαιναν εἰς τὸ κεφάλιν; 975:... καὶ ἔδωκέν του ῥαβδέαν; 166: οὔτε φίλημαν μ'ἔδωκε.
[7] There seems to be nothing very close.
[8] 1251. Cf. 1690: καὶ στέκουν ἔμπροσθέν του; 1265: ἔμπροσθέν μου.
[9 and 10] 1286: καὶ ἐγὼ ταῦτα τὸν ἔλεγα, ἃς σηκωθῇ μὴ κεῖται; 1750: τοιοῦτον πάλιν λέγω σας; 1329:... πάλιν τὰ τοῖα λέγει.
[11] 1287. Cf. 1298: Ἐγείρου ἀπ' αὐτου; 189: Ἐγείρου ἡ Βεργόλικος.
[12] 1287. Cf. 417: κοιτόμενον εἰς τὴν κλίνην.
[13] There seems to be nothing very close.
[14] Cf. 1101:... καὶ ὅπου κελεύεις ἔλα; 1379: καὶ ἂν θέλῃς, κυρά.

27. *Digenis Akritas*, lines 259–261. Mavrogordato translation.

28. *Digenis Akritas*, lines 387ff.

29. See William J. Entwhistle, *European Balladry* (Oxford, 1939).

30. See Roman Jakobson and Gojko Ruzičić, "The Serbian Zmaj Ognjeni Vuk and the Russian Vseslav Epos," *Annuaire de l'Institut de Philologie et d'Histoire Orientales et Slaves*, X (Brussels, 1951), 343–355; and Roman Jakobson, "The Vseslav Epos," *Russian Epic Studies*, Memoirs of the American Folklore Society, vol. 42 (1949), pp. 56ff.

31. J. B. Pritchard, ed., *Ancient Near Eastern Texts Relating to the Old Testament*, pp. 75–76.

32. Francis P. Magoun, Jr., *The Gests of King Alexander of Macedon* (Cambridge, Mass., 1929), p. 150, lines 778ff.

33. Henri Grégoire, "Le Digénis Russe," *Russian Epic Studies*, Memoirs of the American Folklore Society, vol. 42 (1949), especially pp. 152ff.

34. William J. Entwhistle, "Bride-snatching and the 'Deeds of Digenis'," in *Oxford Slavonic Papers* (Oxford, 1953), IV, 1–12.

35. See Chapter Seven, note 7.

INDEX

CD for *The Singer of Tales*

Produced by Matthew Kay and Thomas Jenkins; designed and programmed by Ivan Audouin and Alexander Parker.

The accompanying CD contains music, transcriptions, and translations of the songs and conversations which represent the primary source material for Albert Lord's analysis. Also here are a selection of photos from Lord's Yugoslavian scrapbook, with his captions; and "Kino," a short film of a performance by Avdo Međedović, the best singer Parry and Lord encountered.

The 28 tracks in the main menu contain all the texts that are directly quoted in *The Singer of Tales*; songs that are paraphrased or otherwise abbreviated have been omitted. The passages and conversations recorded here are on pages 17, 18, 26–27, 39–42, 46, 55, 58–63, 69–70, 72–77, 82–83, 109–110, 126, and 286–288 of the text.

The music icon on Track 5 accesses Béla Bartók's musical transcriptions of the songs heard on this track. (Bartók worked at length on recordings from the Parry Collection during World War II. He wrote an article on the Collection that appeared in the *New York Times* on June 28, 1942. The entire article is available at <http://www.fas.harvard.edu/~mpc/bartok.html>http://www.fas.harvard.edu/~mpc/bartok.html</blockquote></x-html>.) On each track we list the singer, title, date, and page reference in *The Singer of Tales*. In addition, each song or conversation is identified by its catalogue number in the Milman Parry Collection of Oral Literature. These numbers are preceded by "PN" or "L": the former designates songs and conversations collected by Milman Parry and Albert Lord between 1933 and 1935; the latter, songs collected by Lord between 1950 and 1951. With respect to the earlier materials, the reader is directed to *The Index of the Milman Parry Collection, 1933–1935* (Kay 1995) for more information about the singers and the circumstances surrounding the recordings. In the conversations recorded on Tracks 1–4 and 27–28, "Nikola" refers to Nikola Vujnović, Parry and Lord's amanuensis and native informant.

The transcriptions and translations for the songs and conversations on the CD follow Lord's own transcriptions in *The Singer of Tales*. In those cases where the South Slavic text or English translation is not provided by Lord, we have consulted the published texts, where available (Parry 1953, Parry 1954, Parry 1980), as well as the unpublished transcriptions in the Milman Parry Collection. The line numbering for the songs follows that in *The Singer of Tales*. No attempt has been made to normalize spellings in the transcriptions. For example, we have left Nikola Vujnović's rendering of the perfect form "pilji" (Track 28, p. 4, l. 18), and others similar to it, and have not normalized it to *pili*.

In some instances our CD transcription is slightly different from that printed in *The Singer of Tales*. Several of the discrepancies are provided below:

Track 5, p. 3, l. 12: CD has "No na kući od zle domaćice" instead of "K'o na kući loše domaćice"

Track 18, l. 1: CD has "E urani Kraljevića Marko" instead of "A urani Kraljeviću Marko"

Track 22: CD has "siđe" (l. 6) instead of "side" and "sađe" (l. 12) instead of "sade"

Track 28, p. 3: CD has "N: But nicely you know. . . ." instead of "P: But nicely you know. . . ." These words were spoken by Nikola Vujnović, not Milman Parry.

Track 28, p. 3, l. 2: CD has "tama'" instead of "taman"

Track 28, p. 4, l. 11: CD has "ravne" instead of "ravno"

Track 28, p. 4, l. 15: CD has "upisat'" instead of "upisalji"

Track 28, p. 4, l. 23: CD has "smije'" instead of "smijeh"

Track 28, p. 4, l. 24: CD has "poprićat'" instead of "poprićalji"

Track 28, p. 4: CD has "S: Yes. I counted out six days for you. . . ." instead of "S: Yes. For six days, I counted out the days for you. . . ."

The title of the songs sung by Petar Vidić on Tracks 16–19 is actually "Marko Kraljević i Nina od Koštuna"; the CD follows *The Singer of Tales* (p. 71) in calling it "Marko Kraljević i Nina od Kostura." Finally, the transcription for Track 24, l. 14 is problematic. The present transcription follows Nikola Vujnović's version. Items enclosed in square brackets in the English translations indicate segments that do not appear in *The Singer of Tales*, but which are part of a given song or conversation. For example, in the "Razgovor" with Salih Ugljanin (Track 2), Milman Parry joins Nikola Vujnović in questioning the singer. Bracketed items in italics designate Lord's insertions in the original edition.

We have tried to preserve the archival quality of the recordings and for this reason have not attempted to eliminate the background noise that is noticeable on some of the tracks or otherwise "improve" the sound quality.

We would like to thank Professor D. E. Bynum, Casey Dué, and David Elmer for their help.

Matthew Kay

Audio tracks on this CD are accessible on any CD player; video portions require Windows/PC or PowerMac, in either case with 32 MB RAM, 600×480 video res.